THE REGIONAL ROOTS OF DEVELOPMENTAL POLITICS IN INDIA

T0317234

CONTEMPORARY INDIAN STUDIES

Published in association with the
AMERICAN INSTITUTE OF INDIAN STUDIES

Susan S. Wadley, Chair, Publications Committee/general editor

Books in this series are recipients of the
Edward Cameron Dimock, Jr. Prize in the Indian Humanities
and the
Joseph W. Elder Prize in the Indian Social Sciences
awarded by the American Institute of Indian Studies and
are published with the Institute's generous support.

THE REGIONAL
ROOTS of
DEVELOPMENTAL
POLITICS in INDIA

A Divided Leviathan

Aseema Sinha

Indiana University Press

Bloomington and Indianapolis

This book is a publication of

Indiana University Press
601 North Morton Street
Bloomington, IN 47404-3797 USA

http://iupress.indiana.edu

Telephone orders 800-842-6796
Fax orders 812-855-7931
Orders by e-mail iuporder@indiana.edu

The paper used in this publication meets the minimum requirements of
American National Standard for Information Sciences—Permanence of
Paper for Printed Library Materials, ANSI Z39.48-1984.

Manufactured in the United States of America

Library of Congress Cataloging-in-Publication Data

Sinha, Aseema, date
    The regional roots of developmental politics in India : a divided
leviathan / Aseema Sinha.
        p. cm. — (Contemporary Indian studies)
    Includes bibliographical references and index.
    ISBN 0-253-21681-8 (pbk. : alk. paper) — ISBN 0-253-34404-2
(cloth : alk. paper)
    1. Central-local government relations—India—Case studies.
2. India—Economic conditions—Regional disparities—Case studies.
3. Gujarat (India)—Politics and government. 4. Gujarat (India)—
Economic conditions. 5. West Bengal (India)—Politics and government.
6. West Bengal (India)—Economic conditions. 7. Tamil Nadu (India)—
Politics and government. 8. Tamil Nadu (India)—Economic conditions.
I. Title. II. Series.
    JS7011.S56 2004
    338.954—dc22
                                            2004013526

1 2 3 4 5   10 09 08 07 06 05

To the memory of my father and to my mother

Contents

Tables, Figures, and Maps

Tables

Figures

Maps

Preface and Acknowledgments

TODAY, STATES ARE vilified and criticized the world over. Market-based action, it is argued, must discipline the excesses of states. "Lessons" from the Indian experience are invoked to confirm this powerful worldview. The Indian model of development—during *both* its slow- and the recent high-growth periods—seems to confirm the conventional view that state failures are more crippling than market failures. This project seeks a way out of such dichotomous categories by challenging the dominant zeitgeist. The book argues that development is no longer a sole project of the nation-state or of globalized markets; subnational or infranational institutions mediate the process. Thus, the critics of the state have got it wrong because they failed to notice the nimble actions of subnational units—local governments in Russia and China, for example, and regional states in India—in shaping *both* dirigiste developmentalism as well as globalization. The search for developmental states has proceeded at the wrong level—the national level—while subnational developmental states and regional leaders continue to circumvent and modify the negative aspects of central regulation, while enhancing its positive characteristics. This argument displaces the analytical searchlight to subnational actors and institutions but also seeks to reevaluate national developmental trajectories in a different way. Nation-states must be understood in a disaggregated way, as a combined product of multiple actors and states. While provinces play a mediating role, they are also shaped by the larger context, whether it be global or national, in which they operate. This implies that the interaction and linkages across levels of analysis will yield a better and more complex theory of state than we currently have at our disposal.

These sets of arguments evolved over a long period of time and in interaction with numerous people. From conception to realization the production of this book has benefited in immeasurable ways from people and institutions around me. In 1985, while I was studying at the Lady Shri Ram College, I was required to write a book review. I chose Iqbal Narain, *State Politics in India*, 1976. I didn't know that understanding state politics in India would be what I would be doing almost fifteen years later! Faculty at Jawaharlal Nehru University stimulated my interest in a life of academics and gave me good social science training; for that, I will eternally remain grateful. The idea of this book first took shape in 1996 when I began thinking about my dissertation at Cornell University. There could have been no better place for its birth. Cornell University and my faculty mentors nursed the nascent idea and gave me the requisite training to carry it out. My greatest debt goes to Ronald Herring, who encouraged me to conduct comparisons of Indian states right from the beginning. His association with this project has been valuable; he knew when to push for chapters and, most of all, when not to interfere! He has gone through numerous drafts of the manuscript with patience and important insights. Richard Bensel's early interest in this project and his sustained involvement has been a constant source of imaginative ideas and comparative extensions. Mary Katzenstein has been with this project from the very beginning; her perceptive comments and her continuing ability to cast a fresh light on the project have been invaluable. Peter Katzenstein has been a tireless mentor and stimulating interlocutor and provided energetic input into my dissertation. He has been a careful and demanding reader, and I remain grateful for extremely prompt and helpful comments. Chris Way provided sharp and perceptive questions as well as generous encouragement. The game theoretical extensions of the project would not have been possible without his comments on the project. Hector Schamis served as the external examiner, and his input during the defense stage of the dissertation was extremely useful. Early comments from Sid Tarrow, S. Kaviraj, Mick Moore, Andy Rutten, and Walter Mebane were very helpful in the conceptualization stages.

I am more than grateful to my colleagues at the political science department at the University of Wisconsin–Madison for the collegial atmosphere and supportive environment in which the final manuscript has taken shape. I especially thank Mark Beissinger, Ed Friedman, and Melanie Manion for reading the full manuscript.

Most of all, I owe special thanks to John Echeverri-Gent for a sustained dialogue on various aspects of the manuscript over the years. His input has made it a much better book. Detailed comments from anonymous reviewers, from both the prize committee of the AIIS and Stanford University Press, were very valuable. Two discussants of my manuscript for the NETSAPPE (Network on South Asian Politics and Political Economy) workshop—Devash Kapur and Leela Fernandes—deserve special thanks for their very useful and constructive engagement. Their criticisms gave me a new perspective on key aspects of the manuscript. At the NETSAPPE workshop, comments from Patrick Heller, Lloyd Rudolph, Ashutosh Varshney, John Echeverri-Gent, Niraja Gopal-Jayal, Rob Jenkins, Andrew Wyatt, Karthik Muralidharan, Sridharan, Gurpreet Mahajan, Rahul Mukherjee, Supriya Roy Chowdhury, and Shail Mayaram were especially useful, although they made me go back to what I thought was the completed manuscript with new revisions!

A number of people have given comments on parts of the manuscript. I thank Amitava Dutt, Paul Hutchcroft, Andy Gould, Mariann Jelinck, Rob Jenkins, Subrata Mitra, Baldev Raj Nayar, Jaime Ros, Lloyd Rudolph, Matthew Rudolph, Susanne Rudolph, Lawrence Saez, Prakash Sarangi, Arun Swamy, David Stuligross, Aili Tripp, Kellee Tsai, George Tsebelis, Ashutosh Varshney, Douglass Verney, David Weimer, and Crawford Young. Gay Seidman's and Crawford Young's perceptive comments greatly improved the comparative chapter. Val Bunce's input was very crucial in revising that chapter. Conversations with Scott Mainwaring, Fran Hagopian, Richard Bensel, and Richard Snyder stimulated interesting comparative extensions.

In New Delhi, Chandra Mohan gave crucial advice and research help at many stages. Comments from Balveer Arora, Sanjaya Baru, Niraja Gopal-Jayal, and Sudha Pai were extremely useful during the research process. Rakesh Basant, Sebastian Morris, and Ravindra Dholakia in Ahmedabad offered crucial comments and advice when it was most needed. Professor Rakesh Basant and Mr. Mote of Arvind Mills provided invaluable advice and contacts and opened many doors for me. Kartikeya Sarabhai's help was important at a key stage of my research. In Calcutta, I must thank Amiya Bagchi, Debdas Bannerjee, Harihar Bhattacharyya, and Anjan Ghosh for many useful comments. Conversations with Shikha Mukherjee in Calcutta were stimulating and informative. In Chennai (Madras), the Madras Institute of Development Studies was my home and research base. There, Manabi Majumdar, M. S. S. Pandian, and Padmini Swaminathan provided valuable support and resources. Manabi's warmth made fieldwork in Chennai more bearable. And, conversations with Sanjay Subramanian were very stimulating. In addition, research assistance from Omar Khan, Simanti Lahiri, Xavier Marquez, Elizabeth Quade, and Yousun Chung proved very useful. Meenu Swaminathan, my sister, gave me very important help in photocopying crucial documents from Chennai.

In India, this book has taken me to New Delhi, Calcutta, Madras, Trivanadrum, Bombay, Ahmedabad, Baroda, Anand, Gandhinagar, Kalyani, and Burdwan. Funding from the American Institute of Indian Studies' dissertation fellowship was crucial for such extensive travel and research. I would also like to thank the Mellon Foundation for a graduate fellowship at Cornell University, some travel support from the Einaudi Center for International Studies at Cornell University, a Writing Fellowship from the Institute of World Politics, and a crucial fellowship at the Kellogg Institute, which greatly facilitated the final stages of the writing process. I owe special thanks to the members of the Kellogg Institute, University of Notre Dame, for providing a very congenial and lively environment for the revisions. I especially thank the NETSAPPE team for inviting me to present my book in front of a demanding set of readers in Bangalore. Various other institutions also provided a conducive context during the fieldwork stages. The Center for Studies in Social Sciences, Calcutta, provided affiliation. I employed the resources of the Indian Institute of Management both at Calcutta and Ahmedabad.

Rebecca Tolen and Jane Lyle of Indiana University Press shepherded the manuscript through the production process, while Carol Kennedy provided copyediting help. Sue Wadley and the AIIS prize committee performed a valuable service by instituting a prize for which generations of junior scholars would remain grateful. I also thank Muriel Bell for her encouragement and positive response.

The long years of research would have been impossible without the understanding of my mother and my late father, who allowed me to be very different from what they were. I must also thank my friends who have kept me sane through this process: Subrata, Madhulikha, Debyani, Lawrence, Karen, Srini, Rina, and Rahul. Sarah Mckibben, Heidi, Christina, and Gardner were wonderful friends and close confidants. I thank Sarah and Heidi for being such wonderful friends and also for their editing help. Anindya's encouragement and tough-minded yet supportive comments were indispensable to this project from the start to the finish. He has contributed immeasurably to this project and my work; I cannot thank him enough for years of companionship and much else. With such help, all remaining errors can be safely attributed to my obstinate traits!

A Note on Terminology

THE WORD *state* has multiple usages in this book: state, regional states, and the central state. Throughout I use "state" with a small *s* to refer to the general concept of the state. This denotes the architecture of bureaucratic institutions and is used to distinguish from "government" or "regime." In the existing literature on Indian federalism, Indian provinces are also called states, but in this book I use the term "provinces" or "regional states" when I intend to refer to subnational states. Most scholarship on India uses "State" with a capital *S* to denote provincial states; thus, in verbatim quotes from other sources provinces are sometimes referred to as "States" in this book. The federal government in India is referred to interchangeably as the "central state" or "Center" or "Union government," consistent with the usage in the literature on India.

The word *regional* can be used to refer to transnational units such as south Asia or infranational units such as western India; in this book, I use the term "regional" to denote subnational or substate units analogous to political boundaries of provinces. Where it is used to qualify "state," it refers to provinces, to distinguish that use from the larger concept of the Indian "nation-state" and from the general notion of the "state."

Abbreviations

ACM	Antoni Carlos Magalhaes
ADMK	Ann Dravida Munnetra Kazhagam
AGP	Asom Gana Parishad
AIADMK	All-India Anna Dravida Munnetra Kazhagam
AICC	All India Congress Committee
AP	Andhra Pradesh
ASI	Annual Survey of India
BJP	Bharatiya Janata Party
BCCI	Bengal Chamber of Commerce and Industry
BT	*Business Today*
CEC	Central Election Committee (of the Congress Party)
CEMIG	Electrical Centers of Minas Gerais (an electricity company of the regional government of Minas Gerais)
CEO	chief economic officers—to denote the heads of private firms
CG	central government
CII	Confederation of Indian Industry
CIL	Conversion of Industrial License
CM	Chief Minister
CMIE	Center for Monitoring the Indian Economy
Congress (I)	Congress Party of India (Indira)
Congress (O)	Congress Party of India (Organization)
CPI	Communist Party of India
CPI(M) or CPM	Communist Party of India (Marxist)
CPSU	Communist Party of the Soviet Union
CWC	Central Working Committee
DGTD	Director General of Technical Development

DK	Dravidar Kazhagam (Party of the Dravidians)
DMK	Dravida Munnetra Kazhagam (Party for the Progress of Dravida)
EDP	Entrepreneurship Development Program
EPW	*Economic and Political Weekly*
FDI	foreign direct investment
FERA	Foreign Exchange Regulation Act
FICCI	Federation of Indian Chambers of Commerce and Industries
FSU	Former Soviet Union
GCCI	Gujarat Chamber of Commerce and Industry
GDP	Gross Domestic Product
GHCL	Gujarat Heavy Chemical Corporation
GIDC	Gujarat Industrial Development Corporation
GIIC	Gujarat Industrial Investment Corporation
GITCO	Gujarat Industrial and Technical Consultancy Organization Ltd.
GMDC	Gujarat Mineral Development Corporation
GNFC	Gujarat Narmada Fertilizer Corporation
GoG	Government of Gujarat
GoI	Government of India
GoWB	Government of West Bengal
GPCC	Gujarat Provincial Congress Committee
GPCC(I)	Gujarat Provincial Congress Committee (I)
GSFC	Gujarat State Finance Corporation
Guidance	Tamil Nadu Industrial Guidance and Export Promotion Bureau
IAS	Indian Administrative Service
IDR Act	Industrial and Development Regulation Act
IIFT	Indian Institute of Foreign Trade
IL	Industrial License
ILPIC	Industrial Licensing Policy Inquiry Committee
INC	Indian National Congress (also known as the Congress Party, after independence in 1947)

iNDEXtb	Industrial Extension Bureau
ISI	Import-Substituting Industrialization
Justice Party	South Indian Liberal Federation
I&CA	Department of Information and Cultural Affairs (West Bengal Government)
ICMS	Tax on the circulation of goods and services
IPCL	Indian Petrochemical Limited
IRIS	Center for Institutional Reform and the Informal Sector, University of Maryland
KHAM	Kshatriyas, Harijans, Adivasis, and Muslims
KMT	Kuomintang
LC	Licensing Committee
LF	Left Front
LOI	Letter of Intent
LS	Lok Sabha (Parliament)
L & T	Larsen and Tourbo
Majoor Mahajan	Laborer's Guild (in Gujarat)
MCCI	Madras Chamber of Commerce and Industry
MELTRON	Maharashtra Electronic Corporation
MGR	M. Gopala Ramachandran
MIDC	Maharashtra Industrial Development Corporation
MIDS	Madras Institute of Development Studies
MLA	Member of Legislative Assembly
MNC	multinational corporation
MP	Member of Parliament
MRTP Act	Monopoly and Restrictive Trade Practices Act
MSEB	Maharashtra State Electricity Board
MSFC	Maharashtra State Financial Corporation
MSSIDC	Maharashtra Small-Scale Industrial Development Corporation
MW	megawatts
NCDBA	National Commission on the Development of Backward Areas
NDC	National Development Council

NETSAPPE	Network on South Asian Politics and Political Economy
NIE	New Institutional Economics
NRI	nonresident Indian
OECD	Organization for Economic Co-operation and Development
PAB	Project Approval Board
PCC	Provincial Congress Committee
PEC	Provincial Election Committee (of the Congress Party)
PHDCCI	PHD Chamber of Commerce and Industry
PM	Prime Minister
PMO	Prime Minister's Office
PRC	People's Republic of China
PSUs	public-sector undertakings
RDO	Regional Development Organization (in Northeast Britain)
RSFSR	Russia (largest province in former Soviet Union)
SC	Scheduled Castes
SDP	State Domestic Product
SFC	State Finance Corporation
SIA	Secretariat of Industrial Approvals (also known as Secretariat of Industrial Assistance after 1994)
SICOM	State Industrial Corporation of Maharashtra
SIDC	State Industrial Development Corporation
SIIC	State Industrial Investment Corporation
SIPCOT	State Promotional Corporation of Tamil Nadu
SLPE	state-level public enterprise
SPIC	Southern Petrochemical Corporation Ltd.
TC or AITC	All India Trinamool Congress
TCA	Trans-Canada Airline
TDP	Telugu Desam Party
TIDCO	Tamil Nadu Industrial Development Corporation
TIIC	Tamil Nadu Industrial Investment Corporation
TLA	Textile Labor Association
TMC	Tamil Manila Congress

TNC	Tamil Nationalist Congress
TVS	TV Sundaram (a private business group based in Tamil Nadu)
UF	United Front
WEBEL	West Bengal Electronic Corporation
WBIDC	West Bengal Industrial Development Corporation
WBPCC	West Bengal Provincial Congress Committee
WIIDC	West Bengal Industrial Infrastructure Corporation

THE REGIONAL ROOTS OF DEVELOPMENTAL POLITICS IN INDIA

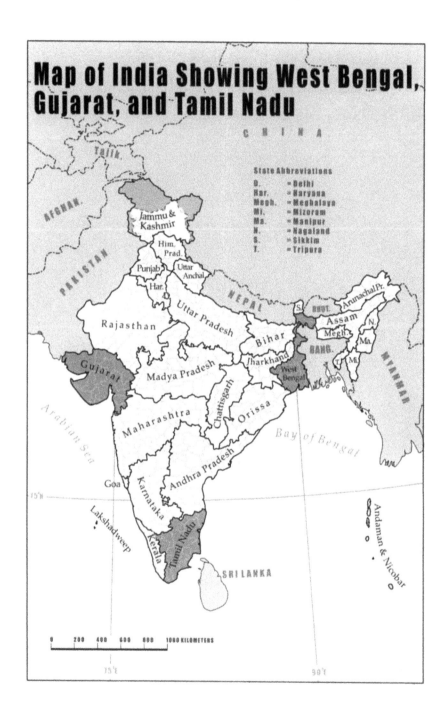

Map of India Showing West Bengal, Gujarat, and Tamil Nadu

CHINA

Tajik.

AFGHAN.

PAKISTAN

Jammu & Kashmir

Him. Prad.

Punjab

Uttar Anchal

Har.

Rajasthan

Uttar Pradesh

NEPAL

Bihar

S.

BHUT.

Arunachal Pr.

Assam

N.

Megh.

Ma.

Jharkhand

BANG.

West Bengal

T.

Mi.

MYANMAR

Gujarat

Madya Pradesh

Chattisgarh

Orissa

Arabian Sea

Maharashtra

Bay of Bengal

Goa

Karnataka

Andhra Pradesh

Lakshadweep

Kerala

Tamil Nadu

SRI LANKA

Andaman & Nicobar

State Abbreviations

D. = Delhi
Har. = Haryana
Megh. = Meghalaya
Mi. = Mizoram
Ma. = Manipur
N. = Nagaland
S. = Sikkim
T. = Tripura

0   200   400   600   800   1000 KILOMETERS

15°N

15°E

90°E

PART I

Introduction and Theoretical Framework

1 The Puzzle of Developmental Failure and Success

> If the republic is small, it is destroyed by foreign force; if it be large, it is ruined by an internal imperfection.
>
> —Montesquieu, 1750

IN OCTOBER 1997, an official from the Industry Department of the Indian state of Tamil Nadu said to me, "In the pre-liberalization days, industrialists used to chase us, now we chase them; the government intervenes as much as before, if not more." How best to create institutions that will enhance developmental outcomes is a long-standing question once again at the forefront of debate in comparative political economy. Recent scholarship confirms that the issue of effective governance over markets is caught in a fundamental dilemma: a strong state necessary to curtail perverse individual incentives and ensure investment may also act in a self-interested way. Democracy seems to make this dilemma worse, creating particularistic pressures that divert crucial public goods away from their most productive uses. This pervasive problem prompts the main question of the book: What kind of state will provide developmental governance? Given the constant enlargement of the state's function in the twentieth century, the state's role in ensuring developmental success or failure deserves serious analytical attention. Nation-states around the world have varied greatly in the extent to which they have succeeded in transforming the developmental trajectory of their societies. Some states are more successful at facilitating industrialization, managing globalization, and ensuring the well-being of their citizens than others are. Thus, the corollary question becomes important: What accounts for persistent variation in achieving developmental failure or success?

To this debate on developmental failure and success, India, a large democratic country, provides an enduring puzzle in that its developmental record is characterized by a significant gap between its ambitions and its capacities.[1] India seems to be the exception that belies the prediction of a triumphant Asian century. Amidst other relatively strong Asian states, we are confronted with contradictory images of the Indian state[2]—at once strong, soft, and interventionist. Indeed, the nature of the Indian state is an issue of intense debate not only among students of Indian politics, but also among scholars of comparative political economy. The debate focuses on the role of the state in generating wealth and in ensuring that a minimum of developmental needs of its citizens are met. India is the most celebrated case of a *failed* developmental state in that its developmental failures are attributed to a strong state that intervened too much and with too little felicity.[3] Recent success in achieving much higher growth rates is largely attributed to the ascendance of market forces attendant upon liberalization in the 1990s. Thus, the Indian model of development—during *both* its slow- and the recent high-growth periods— seems to confirm the conventional view that state failures are more crippling than market failures. However, self-sustaining regional variation in India despite the presence of a powerful central state urges a reevaluation of this conventional picture.

This book modifies the conventional view of India and of strong states by showing that the Indian state is a divided leviathan; its regional states' actions have surprising and powerful consequences. In this view, neither India's developmental failure nor its recent successes can be attributed to only the central state; rather, they are the combined product of central-local interactions and political choices by regional elites. This book, then, is an attempt to convince those schooled in the belief that the central state is responsible for India's "Hindu rate of growth"[4] or stalled, "half-hearted reforms"[5] of a different reality: that regional elites, in varying ways, have inserted and continue to insert their agendas into the central framework. Limiting analytical attention to the top-down centralized state blinds us to the crucial regional responses to that state; these responses, I show, prove to be directly consequential for investment flows and institutional changes in many countries. What is commonly understood as a strong central state's failure to perform stems, in part, from the regional states' variable responses to implement their developmental programs; it does not follow uniformly from the framework imposed by the central regime.

These arguments resonate with a larger critique of prevailing theories. Usually, economic policy is treated as "output" of a coherent state. The core argument of this book challenges assumptions regarding the appropriate roles of states rooted in both neoliberal and institutionalist accounts: the emphasis of neoliberal assumptions on a self-regulating market system is misplaced, yet arguments related to strong versus weak states are equally misleading. Market-friendly views must redirect attention to the indispensable role of the state in building markets. Statist claims must attend to variations within state institutions and coordination across geographic areas. This book argues that regional politics and national policy are inextricably interrelated. These conclusions arise from an analytical framework in which the federal and regional governments interact to determine and implement economic policy. I argue that the national framework that governs industrial change in India was, and continues to be, a combined product of central rules of the game, subnational strategic choices, and regional institutional variation. Regional politics, a product of subnationalist movements and electoral compulsions, emerges as a salient factor explaining both central-regional and horizontal interactions. These regional incentives and the institutions they produced were not solely a response to regional material conditions such as initial economic differences, ecology, technology, demography, or market access. Nor were they unique to each subnational setting; rather, they were found in different configurations across regions within India. The operation of a similar regional logic means that regional differences cannot be dismissed as idiosyncratic regional peculiarities or as inevitable, and thus they can be understood within a general theoretical framework. The argument that regional political incentives and subnational institutional variation shape outcomes must not disregard the effects of factors operating at a higher level of analysis. Rather, I insist that regional responses are shaped, in part, by central rules of the game and the possibility of central transfers as well as by regional electoral competition. This reinforces the need to evolve a disaggregated and multilevel framework to understand economic policy, development, and globalization. Such a framework must attend to local (subnational) responses toward both dirigiste states and globalization. This chapter explicates the problem of India's developmental failure. I introduce the theoretical concepts animating the study and present the argument of the book.

The Puzzle of India's Developmental State

India epitomizes an unfulfilled yet potentially realizable economic future. Despite the country's democratic achievements enviable in the rest of the developing world, Indians feel cheated economically. Born in the similar historical context as East Asia, with not only a steel-frame meritocratic state but also a well-diversified resource base, with the world's fourth-largest pool of skilled manpower, with domestic stability and a high savings rate, India was expected to perform well.[6] And yet, India grew slowly, at the proverbial Hindu rate of growth (a dismal 3.5 percent a year from 1960 to 1990), and failed to fulfill the basic developmental needs of its citizens. In 2003 India was ranked 161st, with a per capita income of $480 (current market prices) (World Bank 2004, 252). Forty percent of the world's poorest people, earning less than one dollar a day, live in South Asia (World Bank 2001). While one-third of India's population live below the poverty line, the adult literacy rate in 2001 was 67 percent in India (69 percent for men, 46 percent for women), far behind the 84 percent literacy rate in China (93 percent for men, 79 percent for women). Yet, the paradox of India remains: it is a regional power with the nuclear capability to destroy lives, but its state capacity to affect the developmental well-being of its citizens remains attenuated.

Industrialization patterns reveal a similar story of a gap in potential. India was the first country in Asia to have a modern textile industry as of 1851, preceding Japan by twenty years and China by forty years. In fact, the first cotton mill (1851), the first jute mill (1854), and the first railway track (1850) were established in India and Japan around the same time, in Japan after the Meiji restoration in 1867 and in India in the mid-nineteenth century. Asia's first stock exchange was the Bombay Stock Exchange, established in 1875, three years before the setting up of Tokyo's stock exchange (in 1878). In the twentieth century, developments in Japan and India diverged significantly. A comparison with China, a country of comparable size, becomes even more revealing. China's industrial development in the 1940s was slower than India's at independence and was debilitated by poorer transport facilities and undeveloped technology (Maddison 1995, 299). By 1995, China was one of the most industrialized countries in terms of output; its industrial value-added was forty-three times as high in real terms in 1995 as in 1952. In terms of output, China is now one of the most industrialized countries. Forty-one percent of its GDP arises from industry, compared with 22 percent in Britain and the United States and about a quarter in India (Maddison 1998, 79). Material well-being in India lags behind many comparable nations. In 1955, India's GDP per capita in 1988 prices averaged $672, while South Korea's per capita GDP was $879. In 1991, India's per capita GDP in 1988 prices was $1,251, while South Korea's was $7,251 (Krueger 1998, 190–91), almost six times India's per capita GDP. By 1996, Korea entered the OECD club as an industrialized country, while India remained a poor underdeveloped country.

This cross-national contrast has led scholars to characterize India as a *failed* developmental state, a state that aspired to, and had some important preconditions for, rapid growth but failed to realize its developmental potential (Evans 1995; Herring 1999; Bardhan 1984; Isher Ahluwalia 1985; Arrow 1998; Krueger 1974; Wade 1985). A World Bank study on India reiterates the internationally accepted consensus that India has fared poorly in growth and poverty reduction in comparison to Southeast Asia (World Bank 1997a, 1–2, 5).

While India's economic potential shows more promising results in the 1990s, what is remarkable is that a surprising consensus unites the observers of India's dramatic developmental failure as well as recent successes. The developmental failure from the 1960s to the 1980s is attributed largely to the effects of a regulatory state that intervened too much and was not flexible enough to respond to changing international conditions. Similarly, the recent economic upturn is attributed to the liberalization program, which checkmated the role of the central state. The central state is perceived to be the key lever of indifferent progress from the 1960s to the 1980s, and liberalization is seen to provide a drastic antidote to the central state. The state in India seems to be a powerful explanatory tool for all analyses.[7] One high-level official in New Delhi is reported to have told a friend, "If you want me to move the file faster, I am not sure I can help you; but if you want me to stop a file I can do it immediately."[8] Both liberal and radical scholars, as well as the international policy community, business leaders, and journalists, attribute the failures of India's developmental trajectory to its central state and constraining policy framework, embodied in what has come to be called the "license-quota-permit-*raj* [rule]" (hereafter license-*raj*). Krueger's analysis of the "rent-seeking state" originated in the Indian experience.[9] India became the model of failure that helped to usher in the anti-state, pro-market zeitgeist of the 1980s. The *Economist* characterized India as a caged tiger—its potential caged by the central state.[10] The Indian example served, in both the popular imagination and the scholarly community, to urge caution about the role of states in economic life, overturning a powerful postwar faith in state intervention. The Indian model of development seemed to confirm that state failure was more crippling than market failures. Kenneth Arrow, the father of general equilibrium analysis, noted, "Institutions seem to have played distinctive coordinating roles in different developing countries. Conservative and bureaucratic direction has guided the path of India, the coordinated building of the market that of Korea. In both cases, institutions have played their roles, though clearly with differing results" (1998, 45).

This unenviable invoking of India as an example of state failure continues despite a significant turnaround in its growth prospects. In the 1990s, India grew at the average rate of 6.0 percent per annum. While economic reforms have ushered in a more promising scenario, their success is interpreted through the old lenses. The perception of failure continues to haunt assessments of India's developmental state. In a recent international conference, T. N. Srinivasan, an eminent economist, lamented the persistence of a "wooden bureaucracy" even after the onset of reforms in India.[11] More recently, Sumit Ganguly and T. N. Srinivasan argue that India's continued slow performance after 1991 can be traced to the vested interests created by the license-*raj*.[12] The *Economist* continues to blame slow reforms on lip service paid to economic reform by India's central government (*Economist* 1995; 2001).[13] Similarly, Krueger writes of "stalled reforms" in India (2000). For others, sweeping changes are valued positively so long as they imply a drastic antidote to the erstwhile central state. *India Unbound,* a recent socio-autobiography written by an Indian industrialist, evokes the historical existence of a "bound India" and echoes Bhagwati's assumption that India must be freed of its statist chains.[14] Jagdish Bhagwati, Amartya Sen, Isher Ahluwalia, and Pranab Bardhan, scholars usually found on opposing sides of the intellectual spectrum, converge in their analysis of effects of the central state, variously described as the "third actor" or "the iron fist of controls" in suffocating the economy.[15] While they do disagree with regard to the sources of this power of the central state, they do not quibble over the fact that the central state was responsible for constraining the private sector and ensuring nonproductive use of resources.[16]

This regulatory power over the private sector embodied in the license-*raj* was designed to, among other goals, ensure some level of regional uniformity and central direction; it thus went hand in hand with the power of the central state over regional units. From 1949 onward, industrialization came to be part of the central planning endeavor and subjected provincial responsibility to central rationality. The formation of the Planning Commission in 1950, the enactment of the Industrial Development and Regulation act in 1951, and the declaration of the Industrial Policy resolution in 1956 saw the passing of control into the central government's hands. As the First Five-Year Plan put it, "It is obvious that without complete coordination of policies and timely concerted action, there is danger of waste and misdirection of efforts which may have consequences extending far beyond the responsibility of any single authority, and this, it must be recognized, places special responsibility on the *Center*" (Planning Commission 1953, 11; emphasis added). Thus, India's developmental pattern was designed to be state-led and centralized. Centralization from 1947 onward seemed to confirm the conventional understanding that the central state was responsible for India's developmental failure.

Yet an intriguing puzzle, until now considered marginal to the debate over India's developmental trajectory, confounds and throws doubt on this picture. Despite uniform central policy interventions, regional states reveal very different developmental trajectories. This raises a key question: If dirigisme is the problem, as conventional scholarly opinion concludes, what explains the different subnational developmental pathways within India? Clearly, a similar central constraint cannot explain this variation. Did successful regional states mitigate the constraining effects of the central state in their regions? And if so, how?

At first glance, the most obvious marker of regional divergence has been regional growth rates. The range in growth rates of per capita regional product (SDP) among regional states has been large, and it widened in the 1990s. Among the fifteen major states, West Bengal's real per capita SDP growth rate was 1.5 percent per annum, while Gujarat's was 3.4 percent for the period from 1960 to 1993 (Ghosh, Margit, and Neogi 1998). In the 1990s the variation was much higher, ranging from a low of 1.1 percent per year in Bihar to a high of 7.6 percent per year in Gujarat. For the 1990s, the ratio between the lowest (Bihar) and the highest (Gujarat) was as much as 1:7 (Montek Singh Ahluwalia 2000, 4). Recently, the western states of Gujarat and Maharashtra have been likened to newly industrializing countries in East Asia. Given the size of the regional states—each of them has a larger population than most European countries—and their well-developed political, economic, and cultural systems, a comparative analysis of regional states will be analytically crucial to understand Indian development patterns and the variegated responses to globalization within India.

It is difficult to establish conclusively the causes of regional growth rates within India; the sources might be diverse and difficult to pin down.[17] Rather than attempt to explain the sources of regional divergence in growth rates, I focus on private investment patterns in the domain of industrial change, a variable that is more sensitive to policy interventions than growth rates. Comparative experience attests to the fact that in high performers, investment as a proportion of GDP has been high. All growth models regard investment to be crucial.[18]

Moreover, rather than the necessarily limited comparison of all Indian regional states (twenty-eight in 2004), a closer examination of industrial change and investment patterns in a few selected regional states may be more rewarding. Such an analysis reveals a diverse array of market governance patterns across India's provinces and is the focus of this study.[19] The contrast is sharpest between eastern India and western India, with southern India falling in the middle. West Bengal, Gujarat, and Tamil Nadu, three relatively well developed states at India's independence with many similar initial conditions, show significant divergence in political and economic trajectories over time. The most obvious indicator of these regional contrasts is outputs and investment indicators, but these are complemented by political and institutional contrasts.

In terms of economic outputs, Gujarat's investment shares and industrial indicators have continued to rise since the late 1960s. In 1960, Gujarat faced political integration problems (Wood 1984a) and lost the majority of its invested capital to Maharashtra (Bombay) with the division of Gujarat and Maharashtra. Over time, however, Gujarat has continued to attract a relatively higher share of all-India investment. In the 1990s (1990–99) Gujarat's per capita growth rate works out to about 6.9 percent, the highest for India and comparable to many East Asian nations (Montek Singh Ahluwalia 2000; Reserve Bank of India 2000). Industrial patterns in Gujarat have been relatively dispersed, with central and south Gujarat, and even parts of Saurashtra (western Gujarat) undergoing industrialization.[20]

In contrast, West Bengal, located in eastern India, has declined sharply in terms of its share of all Indian investment (see Table 1.1). Despite being at the forefront of industrialization during the colonial period, West Bengal remains largely an agricultural state. State capacity in effecting changes in the agricultural sector, in instituting land reforms, as well as in implementing antipoverty policies (Kohli 1987) has not transferred to the industrial domain in improving the welfare of workers (Mallick 1993) or in the pattern of industrialization in West Bengal, which remains Calcutta-centric and dominated by large firms.

Tamil Nadu's industrial pattern has been mixed and variable over time. In aggregate terms, Tamil Nadu seems to be industrially advanced; however, commentators have noted a marked decline in its industrial indicators from 1965 onward (MIDS 1988; Swaminathan 1994; Tyagarajan 1989). This is especially reflected in the data on the average annual rate of capital formation in the factory sector; it fell from 21.58 percent in 1966 to 14.37 percent in 1974–75 and to 8 percent in 1979–80 (MIDS 1988, 200–201). By 1991, the total investment in Tamil Nadu was a mere 4.8 percent of the all-India share (CMIE 1991, xix). This change over time raises the question of what changed in the post-1965 period in Tamil Nadu. Investment data reveals the pattern shown in Table 1.1.

Even more startling is the distributional pattern of investment—an institutional feature—in different regions. Industrial investment can be separated into various categories in India: central public sector, state public sector (financed out of the regional state budget), private sector, and joint sector (combination of regional public sector and private sector). As Table 1.2 illustrates, central public ownership predominates in West Bengal and Tamil Nadu, while joint and private sectors predominate in Gujarat.

Why did Gujarat attract a higher share of investment over time, while West Bengal, a state that was highly industrialized at the dawn of independence, failed to capitalize on its initial strengths as a (private) capital-intensive state? The ownership patterns of industrial investment in the three regions are as puzzling, given the common national-level stress on the public sector. This book focuses on investment patterns and institutional organization of industrial investment as the dependent variable. Historical levels of industrialization or social modernization are not adequate to explain these patterns (see case selection in Chapter 2). How does one account for such infranational variations in investment levels and diversity in industrial governance patterns within strong or failed developmental states?[21] A deeper analysis of India's developmental failure is important for both theoretical and policy reasons. By 2015, the Indian economy could be the third largest, after China and the United States; a better diagnosis of its variegated developmental experience would be, therefore, consequential.[22]

Unpacking Developmental States: A Multilevel Framework

This book insists that the search for developmental states or models of global integration has, till now, proceeded at too aggregate a level. India is

Table 1.1. Per Capita Industrial Investment in Selected States in Rs.*

States	1978 Investment Per Person (Rs.) [Investment Index (All India Per Capita Investment = 100)]	1980 Investment Per Person (Rs.) [Investment Index (All India Per Capita Investment = 100)]	1986 Investment Per Person (Rs.) [Investment Index (All India Per Capita Investment = 100)]	1994 Investment Per Person (Rs.) [Investment Index (All India Per Capita Investment = 100)]
All India	670 [100]	677 [100]	1,234 [100]	9,177 [100]
Gujarat	805 [120]	1,142 [168]	2,302 [186]	22,776 [248]
West Bengal	428 [63]	469 [69]	927 [75]	4,376 [47]
Tamil Nadu	517 [77]	503 [74]	629 [50]	7,823 [85]
Maharashtra	779 [116]	617 [91]	1,249 [101]	12,385 [134]
Bihar	684 [102]	704 [103]	410 [33]	2,301 [25]
Kerala	361 [53]	367 [54]	504 [40]	5,174 [56]

Source: Computed from Center for Monitoring the Indian Economy (CMIE), *Shape of Things to Come*, 1978, vol. 1, pp. 1–10; 1980, vol. 1, pp. 1–11; July 1986, p. xix; and December 1994, p. xix.
*In current prices.

Table 1.2. Ownership Pattern of New Investment by States in 1978
(% of regional investment)

Sector	West Bengal	Gujarat	Tamil Nadu
Public Sector (a + b)	74	38	79
(a) Center	54	6	68
(b) State	20	32	11
Joint Sector	8	30	6
Private Sector (c + d)	17	31	15
(c) Private	16	10	14
(d) Cooperative	1	21	0
Sector Unspecified	1	1	0
Total Investment in State	100	100	100

Source: Center for Monitoring the Indian Economy, *Shape of Things to Come,* vol. 1 (Bombay: CMIE, 1980).
Note: The distribution figures of public vs. private investment by state are available only for 1976 and 1978. However, this isolated data point is approximately halfway between 1960 and 1990 and does tell something about the pattern of investment in the states. Data for 1976 conform to the above pattern.

inaccurately perceived as a failed development model or a "slow reformer" because of a mis-specification of the level of analysis. India's low aggregate rate of growth in the early years and its reversal after liberalization is seen as evidence for the inappropriateness of state intervention. However, under both dirigiste (until 1991) and liberalized regimes (post-1991), some subnational states have proven to be "high performers" in India. Questions about appropriate state intervention and appropriate adjustment to globalization can best be studied by examining the question at the subnational rather than the nation-state level. I analyze in depth three provinces within India—Gujarat, West Bengal, and Tamil Nadu—in their attempt to become developmental states and manage globalization, and I show that some regional states developed "strategic capacities" that are instrumental in reorienting ongoing market processes toward development. This approach analyzes development from below, from the perspective of regional actors and businesspersons and in a comparative frame, by analyzing three regional states. A dynamic story is intrinsic to the analysis as regional states evolve their developmental choices and patterns over time. I also emphasize that states operate within a two-tiered federal system and that the type and the extent of competition in a federal system affects the developmental output of nation-states.

Thus, politics is central to the two main arguments presented in this study. First, subnational developmental states exist despite a centralized state or globalization, and it is possible to compare their effects in a systematic way. Second, subnational developmental states are born and bred through a struggle with a dominant center and shaped by regional political competition. Globalization makes these subnational interventions even more salient as local actors seek to modify and reorder global priorities for regional ends. I study three comparatively chosen (controlling for historical and economic variables) provinces within India and evaluate subnational responses to dirigiste policies as well as globalization in a comparative frame.

Theoretically, this book develops a framework for analyzing the politics of economic policy in large and multileveled polities. The framework combines a focus on regional elites with attention to the different ways in which regional elites bargain with central rulers over the extent and terms of state intervention. The Janus-faced character of the regional elites combined with incentives created by central rules accounts for different types of subnational developmental states within nations.

Disaggregating States. Most studies of failed states or of developmental states assume a unitary actor. While traditional development economics held on to benevolent conceptions of the state (Rosenstein-Rodan 1943), recent theories have asserted more realistic assumptions about rulers, arguing that states may pursue their self-interest rather than the common public good (Levi 1988). Despite this analytical progress, the underlying notion of state in *both* traditional and public choice theories is aggregate, top-down, and blunt. Comparative political economy and historical institutionalism in its focus on national styles of capitalism and "embedded" national systems implicitly rely on a similar nation-centric unitary bias in state theory. Regional variation within common national institutions seems to suggest that we need to open up the black box of the state and analyze micro-institutional variables that may engender variable responses from the regional actors. While the statist approach to the state may suggest viewing the state as an actor or as an organization, it may be more realistic to view the state as an ensemble of institutions that allow regional states and societal actors room to maneuver. For example, in India the license-*raj* designed in the early 1950s as a autonomous system embodied multiple choice points, sequential decision making, and a joint decision-making structure that created positive incentives for regional and business actors to redirect the output of the state.[23] However, while micro-institutions of the state might provide potential room to maneuver, the theory of the state needs to be combined with a spatial perspective to generate expectations about when and how regional and societal actors deploy such institutional access points to suit their regional agendas.

Developmental States: A Region-Centered Perspective. Economic development is a spatial phenomenon; it takes place at a specific space and time. The expanded role of states in economic life links the spatial dimensions of the development process with the incentives of its rulers. The spatial consequences of growth give bureaucrats and politicians strong incentives to harness regulation for political purposes. Moreover, the spatial embodiment of development and state action means that decisions about government's role in fueling economic growth cannot be made independently from decisions about location.[24] In large-sized states and in states with some differentiated regional traditions, we should expect that regulatory policy becomes a tool for shaping the regional economic prospects; furthermore, interests of regional and national politicians may vary. Regional politicians have strong incentives to encourage development in their regions. Recognizing that the impetus for creating developmental states may also exist at the *subnational* level puts regional elites and their strategic calculations at the center of the analysis. Two dimensions of regional elites' contexts deserve analysis: (1) regional institutions that implement regional and central policies and (2) political compulsions of regional politicians. Chapter 5 outlines a way to measure the effects of regional institutions, while Chapter 6 disentangles the political and electoral compulsions that shape both horizontal strategies and vertical responses of regional elites.

A Regional-Institutional Analysis. Focusing on regional politicians and elites helps explain the possible strategies they adopt in the face of central rules of the game; in addition, the ability of the regional state to implement the strategic agendas of the regional rulers becomes important. Thus, an analysis of subnational variation must attend to a comparative analysis of regional institutional capacities. A horizontal model must complement the vertical model. What do regional or horizontal institutions do?

Regional institutions may be defined as decision-making structures, bureaucratic agencies, formal and informal rules that are responsible for "translating" national policy. In multilevel systems, regional institutions may have an important impact on investment flows and investors' decisions in three distinct ways: by affecting the certainty of transactions, by providing reliable information, and by enhancing the credibility of higher-level decisions and policies.[25] Regional institutions can compensate for the degree of uncertainty of central procedures and rules by mitigating or circumventing the negative effects of central states. Lobbying the central state on behalf of investment proposals and ensuring that the procedures of the central bureaucracy work will reduce the uncertainty faced by investors. Information is the key to investment and economic growth. In systems where economic decisions are relatively free of governmental control, information provision can be an important public good; some of that information is a "local" public good. In systems where the (central) state has a monopoly on information about economic decisions, local (subnational) institutions may play a crucial role in distributing that information or in generating new information. This will introduce some competition in information provision, and local information services may *substitute* for informational rigidities at higher levels of the system. In such contexts, the role of the subnational state in providing information will be the key to investment flows in both centralized and relatively decentralized systems. Thus, regional institutions perform important functions of reducing uncertainty, providing information, and ensuring credibility in complementary or competitive relations with the higher-level regulatory institution: the central state.

The Regional Politics of Vertical and Horizontal Choices. How can we make sense of divergent strategies toward the central regime as well as regional institutional variation? The porous character of the central state can give state leaders powerful opportunities to reregulate an ostensibly central policy; this institutional fact can help explain the *possibility* of divergent strategies but not *why* these divergent strategies were actually pursued by regional states. For that, one has to turn to an analysis of regional political incentives in a parliamentary yet divided (federal) system.

Regional political incentives are shaped by the nested nature of the two-level game in which the state elites were placed. The provincial leaders face a trade-off between central transfers and regional reelection chances. In states where the regional population *rewards* anti-center actions (as in West Bengal and Tamil Nadu), the state leaders privileged their regional reelection chances; this led them to pursue an anti-center political strategy. This anti-center strategy did have political benefits (of reelection), but at the cost of reduced investment flows. In states where the trade-off between regional incentives and central transfers was convergent, the state elites could pursue bargaining strategies leading to higher investment flows in their region. In such states the absence of strong subnationalist sentiment or a regional party made integrationist policy toward the center politically rational for regional politicians.

Institutional and Policy Outcomes, an Interactive Perspective. Regional elites and local institutions matter, yet regional elites are not leaders of nation-states and are not completely free in their choices of policies and institutions; central rules and regional constituents constrain their developmental visions and strategic calculations. A fuller explanation of developmental states requires a nested framework that links higher-level constraints and regional democratic imperatives with the necessity of enhancing regional investment flows.

The framework outlined in this book suggests that we need to pay more attention to the size and the design of the state—specifically the multilevel nature of many states. Economic policy implementation is the product of intergovernmental interaction among politicians located at different levels of the system. The choices and behaviors of regional rulers, and hence their (unintended) developmental impact on the national political economy, emerge as significant; this variable is usually not analyzed in studies of economic policy making or models of developmental states. This framework is intrinsically in-

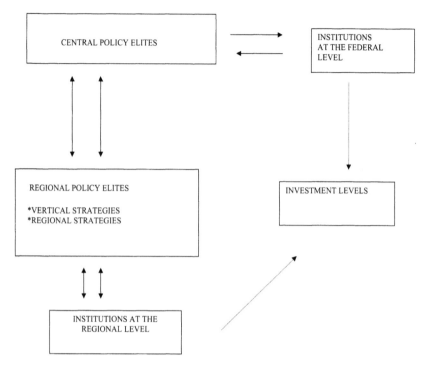

Figure 1.1. A Multi-Level Model

teractive and proposes a nested game logic between political and economic compulsions of differentially placed policy makers.[26] The framework combines a focus on regional politicians' choices of vertical strategies toward the central government with a focus on the incentives generated within the region by the operation of regional democratic politics. Taken together, these two aspects help us account for varied subnational investment flows as well as the segmented character of the national policy framework. I elaborate the framework and outline the hypothesis generated in Chapter 2. Figure 1.1 summarizes the core components of the framework.

Applying the Framework to India

The central policy framework in India, referred to as the license-*raj,* elaborated between 1947 and 1955, did not realize its anticipated effects. Rather than having a uniform effect of organizing a dirigiste model of development, it triggered variable yet coherent long-term *vertical* strategies by state-level incumbents toward the center. In the domain of the private sector, the central framework constrained private investment activity by imposing high entry costs and regulatory costs through its licensing regulations. Some regional states sought to mitigate these effects of the central state through constant monitoring, bargaining, and lobbying; others sought to oppose the central state. Investors responded to these subnational developmental models in different ways, shaped more by regional institutional contexts than by the licensing framework alone. These interactions between state and central governments resulted in a diverse array of central-local patterns across India's provinces. In addition, rather than having a uniform effect of organizing a public sector–based model of development, the central rules triggered variable models of public-private coordination in the regions. West Bengal and Tamil Nadu relied heavily on public-sector investment and Gujarat on combined public and private elements, rather than rely on the private sector alone.

The political logic in the three regional states supported these policy and institutional differences, making the pursuit of alternative strategies self-enforcing over time. Thus, I argue against a voluntarist assumption by showing how economic policies complemented by political and institutional conditions in the different regions generated an ensemble of mutually reinforcing features. In West Bengal, a narrow and regionally concentrated pattern of industrialization (based in Calcutta) limited the political support to industrialization. Political support from the agrarian sectors as well as subnationalist anti-center constituents allowed the Left Front government to be reelected. Industrial development and integration with the center were sacrificed. In Gujarat state, the politics of bargaining and integration with the center generated political support from farmers, farmers-turned-industrialists, and new investors. A combination of capital-intensive and labor-intensive industrialization in diverse sectors allowed the state politicians to win elections as well as to ensure the political and financial support of key business actors. The absence of strong regionalist traditions and integrationist political parties provided support to a pro-center strategy.

Tamil Nadu reveals a mixed pattern where a public-sector strategy paid rich dividends until the end of 1960s, with regional party leaders effectively lobbying the central state. However, the political logic of a regionalist movement —the Dravidian movement—once in power necessitated an anti-center strategy from the 1970s to the mid-1980s. The local exhaustion of the political windfalls of such a strategy by the mid-1980s led the regional leadership to pursue lobbying and cooperation with the central government.

Thus, I argue that mono-causal explanations of rapid industrial growth in Gujarat and relative decline and stagnation in West Bengal are too simple. I will show that despite the similarity of early developmental potential, post-independent regional state politics and policies encoded different "industrial orders," with varying results. These differences were politically sustained over time through institutional variation in their regional institutions, public-private

Table 1.3. The Argument

Cases	Gujarat	West Bengal	Tamil Nadu
Investment Level	High	Low	Oscillating (mixed)
Institutions of Investment	Joint (Public-Private)	Public	Public
Vertical Interactions			
Vertical Strategies	Bargaining and lobbying	Political confrontation	Mixed strategy
Central-Local Relations	Integration	Conflict	Integration and conflict at different times
Horizontal Dimensions			
Regional Institutional Capacity	High	Low	Low
Sub-nationalist movements	Weak	Strong	Strong but weaken over time

mixes, and specific central-local patterns. Regional elections and political strategies of regional elites in their respective regions made these varieties of developmental states self-enforcing. Thus, complementary sets of institutions, political incentives, and central-local dynamics provide the glue that sustains subnational developmental trajectories within India. Table 1.3 summarizes the arguments of both the vertical and horizontal models.

Globalization in India (1991–2004)

The approach to institutional variation developed here began by examining how incentives and constraints contained in the framework of economic policy led to the emergence of distinct regional responses. These regional industrial orders combined distinct vertical political strategies toward an interventionist yet porous central state as well as subnational institutions to govern industry. Analysis of this institutional variation underneath the "iron fist of controls" allows me to bring together competing perspectives on the Indian state, at once perceived as soft (Myrdal 1968) as well as strong (Isher

Ahluwalia 1985). In the framework I have laid out, the Indian state is neither a strong state nor a soft state but a divided one constrained by diverse regional industrial orders.

Beginning in 1985, but more definitively after 1991, the national framework governing industry changed. Private regulation over industry embodied in the licensing rules was scaled back substantially; international openness transformed the competitive environment for domestic capital; and the dominant role for the central state in regional policies seemed attenuated. Slowly but surely, by 2001 privatization was admitted on the political agenda, and "the commanding heights of the economy"—the public sector—stopped animating the rhetoric of politicians. While the Indian process of change is much more incremental and gradual than comparable transitions in China, the Soviet Union, and Latin America, its consequences for economic governance are not insignificant.

Simultaneously, policy and institutional innovation at the regional level has surprised many observers of the Indian reform process (Sinha 1996; Jenkins 1999; Saez 2002). Regional states have emerged as important actors mediating the process of adjustment and institutional changes. In many states, privatization has been introduced earlier than national policies, and the role of the states in attracting foreign capital has acquired independent value. Subnational economic adjustment has an independent momentum of its own. Simultaneously, central-local relations are in a state of flux. State leaders bargain openly with central rulers; federal institutions such as the National Development Council (NDC) and the Inter-State Council have become more active than ever before.

The framework outlined in this book allows me to make sense of these institutional and policy changes. In fact, this study shows that regional policy initiative in favor of reform in the mid-1990s stems in part from patterns of central-local models evolved during the earlier license-*raj* period. Those interpretations that see 1991 as a radical divide in the policy framework governing industry should attend to the historical legacies of a divided state. The logic underlying a divided and segmented leviathan affects the nature and process of economic liberalization directly.

The continuing East-West divide can be understood in light of the framework outlined in this book. Western states—Gujarat and Maharashtra—attract a larger share of private investment than the states of Bihar, Orissa, and West Bengal. Gujarat attracted about 10.6 times as much per capita private investment as West Bengal for the period 1991–2003. I show that this regional pattern has its roots in the combined logic of regional political strategies toward the center, the existing pattern of public/private-sector coordination in the regions, and institutional legacies at the subnational level, rather than in the sudden exogenous removal of policy constraints or in the greater flow of private investment, which favors some states much more than others (Rudolph and Rudolph 2001). Despite policy changes at the subnational level, regional states continue to follow the institutional and political models of the earlier period. The year 1991 seems like a radical policy divide only to those observers who view India's policy framework to be originating at the center. Regional constraints and opportunities in interaction with the central rules used to shape and continue to shape the pattern of economic policy in India.

Infranational Comparisons and Comparative Politics

This book represents an example of the subnational comparative method that compares three regional states (see Chapter 2 for the detailed research design).[27] At a very obvious level, a subnational comparative design allows us to increase variation and observations in the context of a small number of cases (small-N research design) (King, Keohane, and Verba 1994; Snyder 2001b). King, Keohane, and Verba emphasize that theories can have observational implications at many levels of analysis (208, 219, 30–31). Such a strategy may also allow us to control some explanatory variables, for example, the regime type. In addition, subnational comparisons in an analysis of the developmental state and economic liberalization offer a potential to resolve old debates in an innovative way. The debate over the appropriate role of the state in economic development has invariably been addressed through a cross-national analysis. For example, the cross-national analysis of South Korea, Japan, India, and Brazil has generated useful concepts such as the developmental state and embedded autonomy (Evans 1995; Herring 1999). However, the existence of market-enhancing developmental states at the subnational level within India raises the question of whether India has been labeled accurately as a "failed" state in such comparisons. Can we use national-level characterizations to compare countries as different in size as South Korea, Japan, India, and Brazil? Infranational differences in the nature of the state and state-economy interactions raise questions about such blunt comparisons.

A subnational research design can obviate the problems of such inaccurate coding by challenging the conclusions derived from national aggregates. Evidence presented in this book shows that we can fine-tune the coding of the Indian case if we disaggregate the experiences of its regional states. Most scholars have labeled India as an example of a failed developmental state. The reliance on national-level analysis obscured the fact that the national framework of regulation unleashed innovative market-enhancing and public-private coordination at the subnational level. In sum, in a large and regionally diverse country such as India, successful developmental states may exist at lower levels—in the provinces of India—rather than in New Delhi. Thus, a focus on subnational units can provide a basis for a better coding of the Indian case, allowing us to have greater confidence in those cross-national comparisons that attend to infranational variations. To demonstrate this claim, I undertake a cross-national comparison of four nation-states—Brazil, China, the former Soviet Union, and Russia—in Chapter 8, combining subnational and cross-national method.

However, a cautious caveat offered by Paul Peterson (1981, 3-4) may be relevant as well: "Too often city-states are treated as if they are like nation-states. . . . It is the burden of my argument that local politics is not like national politics. On the contrary, by comparison with national politics local politics is most limited. . . . The place of the city within the larger political economy of the nation fundamentally affects the policy choices that cities make." In this book, I place *relative* independence of the subnational units at the center of my explanation not only by focusing on institutional variation across regional states in those policy domains in which they have significant autonomy (industrial estates), but also by theorizing on interaction between center and regional states explicitly (in the field of licensing policy).[28] Thus, the embeddedness of subnational units within a nation-state offers the opportunity to both enhance the number of cases and reorganize the analysis of a supposed national phenomenon (e.g. economic policy) as a two-level interaction. This may correct not only for the tendency to treat lower level units as completely autonomous units, but also for the reverse tendency to view state policy as beginning and ending at the national level.

Methods of Inquiry

Questions about regional influence over regional political economies or central policy are difficult to assess in any system. Data on political relations between center and periphery are often hard to find. Regional actors find it more expedient to play up their lack of power vis-à-vis the central government than to acknowledge the influence they wield. All this contributes to the quick top-heavy and unitary model-building that characterizes most writing on economic policy making. These problems are compounded by the shortage of reliable subnational data in India. "National" statistical systems are as fragmented as the policy process that generates and implements public policy. Subnational data are not comparable in their raw form. This is compounded by most researchers' lack of interest in conducting research at subnational levels so as to compare subnational information systematically. The research design of this book grapples with some of these dilemmas explicitly. I use a comparative research design to compare states with similar economic potential.

Moreover, I chose my interviewees comparatively, focusing on similarly placed officials across diverse states. My interviews of businesspersons attempted to gauge the comparative experience of investors.

This book draws its evidence from intensive fieldwork completed in three research sites in Gujarat (Ahemdabad/Gandhinager, Anand, and Baroda), three sites in West Bengal (Calcutta, Durgapur, and Kalyani), and two in Tamil Nadu (Chennai and suburban Chennai). I repeatedly visited numerous industrial estates in each of the three states. In addition, I collected national-level information in New Delhi. The data was collected in three visits during May 1996 to August 1996, January 1997 to January 1998, and July 2001 to September 2001.

Most of the existing literature, while focusing on developmental states, lacks the perspectives of those who make policy decisions and whose choices actually affect economic outputs. This study relies on a detailed and exhaustive set of interviews with two relevant actors—businesspersons and bureaucratic officials—so as to uncover the process through which actual decisions were made. I provide a phenomenological account of what capital needs from the state. Interviews of one hundred and twenty-five bureaucrats and state government officials and about one hundred businesspersons form the main source of information for this study.

Such detailed yet comparative interviews of similarly placed government officials, which have not been done before, enable the linking up of mechanisms and actual processes operating at the regional state level. This "process tracing approach" has its own crucial advantage: it enables the researcher to tease out information about mechanisms and feedback loops that cannot be captured by more quantitative indicators. Given the context of the Indian regulatory regime where informal and rent-seeking relations were established between officials, businesspeople, and regional actors, information could be found only through detailed and persistent questioning. Such information could never appear in formal statistics even if it were possible to collect it. Moreover, large surveys usually sacrifice quality of data for quantity; long interviews conducted in this study allowed me to be more certain of the quality of responses. These interviews provided a unique perspective on how the industrial policy regime actually works in India.

The Sampling Method. Two broad social groups were the initial focus of the study: bureaucrats and businesspersons. Given the formal similarity between industrial bureaucracies of the regional states and the fact that the Indian Administrative Service (IAS) is a national service constituted by regional cadres, I followed a simple yet effective research strategy. I interviewed all top officials of the Industry Ministry in all three regional states. This included top officials of all industry and financial organizations.[29] In addition, I interviewed similarly placed medium-level and lower-level officials across three regional states. Retired IAS officials from all three regional states provided an invaluable source of historical information. In addition, I tried to procure all policy-related materials that were made available to private investors or that were matters of internal debate. Annual reports of the state organizations also provided a wealth of information. This research strategy provided comparable sources of information about subnational institutional variation across the three regional states.

The sampling method for interviewing businesspersons evolved through experimental interviewing. My initial strategy was to obtain lists of businesspersons investing in a particular state and contact a random sample within them. However, I was discouraged by refusals and unproductive interviews. Businesspersons refused to answer most questions about political connections and were not highly accessible. They did not wish to waste time with a researcher who had no clout! I turned to academic and personal connections. These consisted of other academics, acquaintances, friends, and family. Professors at the prestigious business schools in India such as the Indian Institute of Management proved to be especially useful. I discussed my project with many of them, and they kindly put me in touch with many businesspersons. One interview led to another, and I was able to find people who had invested in more than one regional state, a sample quality I would not have found listed in any directory or through any random procedures. Methodology books call this strategy snowball sampling. I also approached a number of companies without referral. I found that the success rate in such cold calling was very poor and the interviews granted were quite superficial and perfunctory. I tried to prevent bias by relying more on the academic network for interview contacts and when possible by using more than one network to gain access to one category of businessperson.

There was a tradeoff between random sampling and interview quality. If I had sought a random sample, its representativeness would be dependent upon a high response rate. Also, I was interested in institutional variation, processes linking locational decisions, and political rules and questions about corruption; I made almost no headway on these politically sensitive questions through cold interviews. In contrast, even far-removed introductions from a vague acquaintance of the businessperson worked wonders.

In selecting companies, I was guided by the need to evaluate comparative experiences of businesspersons and to develop insights about institutional effects. Thus, I used two major criteria in choosing respondents: first, those who had invested in more than one regional state or whose place of origin was different from the one in which they had a factory; second, those who had a long relationship with the relevant state administration. Through this I was able to develop a stratified sample of (a) investors having interests in more than one regional state and (b) investors primarily located in one regional state but over the long term. Most of those who had invested in more than one state were either (c) large-scale or medium-scale companies; (d) regionally based investors were usually small-scale enterprises and provided detailed information about regulation at the local level. I especially sought companies that had made conscious decisions to relocate over time. In addition, I traveled to different industrial estates in all the three states (Naroda in Gujarat, Kalyani in West Bengal, Baroda in Gujarat, and Guindy in Tamil Nadu) and talked to many investors (mostly small sector) in these specific domains. Here, I was especially interested in finding out about the infrastructural provisions across industrial estates. Repeated visits to these industrial estates allowed me to observe the quality of services and infrastructure provided by different state administrations. The overall sample was not random, but the breadth of the sample yields a good database for analyzing the consequences of regional institutional variation.

Interviewing Technique. The key to good interviews was to interest people in my project and to convince them that they could trust me. This was especially true as I was seeking sensitive information about relations of regional officials with the central government and of business actors with the political and institutional powers of the state. Personal contacts were an important advantage. Questionnaires can be very boring and are resented by businesspersons already overburdened with paperwork.[30] Their response rate can be very low. In contrast, they found it worthwhile to explain their perspectives to an interested outsider. They seemed to enjoy talking about some of the issues beyond the domain of their usual activities. Many people—both businesspersons and bureaucrats—were intrigued by the topic. A few sharply disagreed, suggesting that regional states played no role in India's centralized federation. Most felt that the role of the regional states had never been recognized but had played a major part in their decisions.

Confidentiality was vital. I explained that I was not a journalist and would keep their identities anonymous and would not report what they had said to other people. I took notes during interviews and wrote them carefully and as quickly as possible, later filling in missing information from memory. I learned to write as fast as others talked. When I used a tape recorder, I received very stilted and useless replies; realizing it was a conversation stopper, I avoided using it. I cross-checked much of the information by asking the same set of questions to many respondents.

Firm-level information and interviews with bureaucratic officials were complemented by interviews and archival work at the business associations at the regional level. I focused on Bengal Chambers of Commerce and Industry (BCCI) and Confederation of Indian Industry (CII), Gujarat Chamber of Commerce and Industry (GCCI), and Madras Chamber of Commerce and Industry (MCCI).

The interview information is complemented by macroeconomic data on the relevant regional states. While statistical information is not available in a consistent way across states and time, multiple sources have been used to provide as complete a picture as possible. For example, some information that is readily available at the national level, such as the savings rate, investment as percent of GDP, capital formation, and ownership structure, is not available for the provinces. To compensate for these shortcomings, it is important to use as wide a variety of measures as possible and to piece together fragmentary evidence from various sources and for various years. Indeed, multiple sources do give us some indication of trends. For example, this study required a measure of investment across regions. One measure of investment is statewide "gross capital formation" data. Unfortunately, no reliable estimates of these data exist. Hence, this study relied on productive capital data as well as information on the number of licenses and aggregate investment figures from a survey done periodically by the Center for Monitoring the Indian Economy (CMIE).[31]

However, interview and statistical data can be misleading if not analyzed in relation to the historical and sociological detail that provides the contextual substrata to people's statements and perceptions. The influence of historical change and of different political contexts is too complex to be captured in even the most meticulous of surveys. Hence, I have drawn liberally from a variety of other sources as well as from notable historical studies of Gujarat, West Bengal, and Tamil Nadu.

Moreover, given the lack of previous studies of regional industrial policies, and hence the absence of few usable indices, the data had to be extensively processed before it was ready for use. Thus, while this study is characterized by some degree of methodological eclecticism, I hope that it is compensated for by its empirical and theoretical results. This research strategy enables me to uncover new material about the exact role of regional state governments within the license-*raj* and equally interestingly, to reexamine old evidence and gather it into a systematic argument about the role of developmental states and center-state relations.

Plan of the Book

Comparative politics, with its cross-national emphasis and scholarship on India, focuses one-dimensionally on effects of the central state, its ideology, and regulatory structure. In contrast, I begin with a simple two-level model of state action that combines political strategies and economic compulsions of two different types of elites: regional and central-level rulers. Such a two-level model provides the requisite explanation for variation in investment patterns and is better able to identify certain fundamental processes underlying a developmental state in a multilevel democratic polity like India. The implication of this framework for an analysis of India's slow growth and slow reforms is significantly different from previous frameworks. India's "Hindu rate of growth" cannot be easily attributed to a central policy framework. Central-state influence was only one of the factors shaping the process of policy in a large multilevel democratic country like India. This also suggests a comparative insight: in large countries, successful developmental states may exist at the regional, and not at the central, level.

In this introduction I have presented the dominant puzzle of India's *failed* developmental state, describing the uneven regional pattern of investment flows in selected regional states where historical and economic explanations might suggest convergence. This provides the launching pad for detailed case studies of three states later in the book: Gujarat, West Bengal, and Tamil Nadu. Chapter 2 presents a two-level model that provides a requisite explanation for variation in investment patterns presented in Chapter 1 and outlines the empirical expectations it generates; the rest of the chapters confront those expectations with empirical material from cases within India. I also discuss the research design of this study in Chapter 2. Chapter 3 opens the black box of the central state and analyzes incentives generated by such a system, a task not undertaken to date. Chapter 4 illustrates that in response to the segmented national framework, the states evolved variable political strategies to ensure investment flows and regional political support from constituents. The various states interact and react to the national regulatory regime in widely varying ways, but each of these actions is strategic and intentional. The hypotheses generated by the vertical model are tested and confirmed here. Chapter 5 evaluates the effects of local institutions on investment within the region, confirming the hypothesis generated from the horizontal model. The analysis presented in Chapters 2–5 highlights the two-level nature of India's developmental patterns. However, the regional states' economic policies target not only other states but also business actors. How does business respond to the divided charter of the Indian state? Chapter 7 presents an ethnographic analysis generated by detailed interviews of different types of business owners at both the central and the state levels of the system. Chapter 6 addresses the question that Chapters 3–5 leave unanswered: Why do regional elites pursue the divergent strategies that they do? It explicates the regional politics in each region, outlining why and how diverse regional strategies are sustained over time. Chapter 8 asks similar questions of four other nation-states—Brazil, China, the former Soviet Union, and Russia. The concluding chapter outlines the salient findings of the empirical analysis and speculates on theoretical insights.

2 | A Theory of Polycentric Hierarchy

THE EXISTING TRADITIONS of inquiry into developmental success can be classified into three main categories: neoclassical view, statist (or developmental state) view, and public-choice (or neoliberal) view.[1] All of these current theories in economics and political science view variations in developmental success and failure through a nation-centric prism. However, puzzling regional or local contrasts within dirigiste nation-states in not only large states such as India, China, Brazil, and Russia but in smaller states—Italy, for example— challenge expectations rooted in both statist and neoliberal accounts.[2] Neoliberal theory argues that the central state's policy framework is responsible for laggard developmental outcomes. Regional differences, despite the presence of a central framework, suggest that regional political elites can *circumvent or mitigate* the effects of a constraining national environment, thereby reducing its analytical power to explain all of investment flows. Statists focus disproportionately on market failures; the high performing states within India and in many other countries are not anti-market but are market enhancing. These doubts expose an important limitation of the existing work in the political economy of development. Both neoliberals and statists have seen the state as a unified actor, which either succeeds or fails but does so coherently. Few scholars have addressed the size and multilevel character of states, leaving us, consequently, without a framework for systematically explaining variation *within* supposed strong or failed developmental states. This book provides such a framework. I argue that the political economy of growth in most, but especially large, countries must be understood with the help of a multilevel interactive model that analyzes regional actors' political choices as consequential for national policy.[3]

This model posits that the policy framework of growth in most countries may not be centrally guided but is a *joint product of central rules, provincial strategic choice, and subnational institutional variation.* The interaction between different levels of government is consequential not only for internal political conflict or central-local relations, but also for the ways in which central policy is implemented and developmental states are created and sustained.[4] Cross-national analysis, which pays no attention to infranational differences, compares noncommensurable units, throwing in doubt the validity and generalizability of conclusions about developmental states. Thus, analysis of subnational levers of economic policy becomes important. Yet subnational states are not completely autonomous and thus cannot be treated like nation-states. Rather, being located within a political hierarchy, they respond to and evolve strategies toward the central government in diverse ways. Thus, we need to both disaggregate the state *and* reorganize its units in a multilevel framework. The elements of this two-level framework are the following: incentive structure created by (central) rules of the game and regional responses and political choices (regional strategies) to that central framework; these regional strategic choices may be a product of trade-offs in spatially different political arenas (regional and national space). The strategic capacity of regional units to implement their own developmental agendas also becomes crucial in this framework.

This chapter explicates the theoretical and methodological underpinnings of the study. I show that core concepts derived from the statist and neo-institutionalist frameworks may not be adequate for understanding subnational action and interaction across levels of government in India, and in developing countries more generally. In section two, I build an alternative theoretical framework that views states as multilevel polycentric hierarchies (or polyarchies) that govern diverse regional orders. The last section describes the research design of the book.

India and Comparative Politics

India features in scholarly debates about the role of the state in the economy in a prominent way. India's experience seems to confirm the arguments of the neoliberal scholars that state failure can be more debilitating than market failures. This dominant perception cuts across the two contending approaches, neoclassical and heterodox, both of which focus on the central Indian state as the primary mechanism of slow economic growth. The neoclassical explanation attributes India's slow growth to the national regulatory state, which through its system of pervasive controls, similar to strong states of East Asia, strangled private economic activity (Bhagwati and Desai 1970; Bhagwati and Srinivasan 1975; Bhagwati and Srinivasan 1984; Isher Ahluwalia 1985; Isher Ahluwalia 1991; Basu 1992; Joshi and Little 1994). In Isher Ahluwalia's view, "the latter [Indian state] became more and more regulatory and less and less developmental, thus belying the original promise of 'channeling' growth in the desired direction" (1985, 163). This neoclassical view posits a counter-factual trajectory, where if the central state had intervened and regulated less, the developmental results would have been drastically different and socioeconomically preferable. This idea acquired international currency when Anne O. Krueger in a seminal essay (1974) put forward the notion of the "rent-seeking" state using the experience of India.[5]

The contrary view, having its lineage in the Marxian and Keynesian traditions, isolates for scholarly attention the nature and kinds of group/class interests underlying the Indian national state that, in this view, subverted its developmental role and impact (Raj 1973; Bagchi and Banerjee 1981; Bardhan 1984; Chakravarty 1987; Nayyar 1994; Patnaik 1995).[6] This view posits, as its counterfactual, a strengthening of the Indian state's role rather than its withdrawal. However, in a manner not dissimilar to the microeconomic argument, the heterodox approach sees the problem as the central state having a stranglehold on the industrial sector. In his diagnosis, Bardhan inadvertently echoes Ahluwalia (1985, 163; quoted above): "As a consequence, the autonomy of the Indian state is reflected more often in its regulatory and patronage dispensing role than in a developmental role" (Bardhan 1992, 323).[7]

Hence, the critique of the overzealous central regulatory state has become the common and most dominant understanding of India's political economy. This convergence of neoclassical and heterodox assessments is mirrored in the paradoxical expression "weak-strong" state, found in Rudolph and Rudolph (1987). Thus, India is invoked as a negative case in most comparative studies. The comparative contrast in policies is often made: "During the same century in which Russia, China, Iraq, Zaire, Cuba, Haiti, India, and many other countries engaged in disastrous economic and social policies, the United States, Western Europe, Japan, and many others engaged in policies that were successful in stimulating economic growth" (Mesquita and Root 2000).

However, it is notable that most writers on the developmental state find it difficult to characterize India as either developmental or predatory. Most scholars across approaches focus on the Indian central state but are unable to resolve the coexistence of its strong state characteristics with its weak attributes.[8] India seems to be, yet again, an inexplicable exception that baffles scholars. Peter Evans (1995), who analyzes India in comparison with Zaire, Brazil, and South Korea, categorizes India (together with Brazil) as an "intermediate state":

> Neither [the Brazilian state nor the Indian state] can be simply dismissed as predatory . . . India amassed a remarkable record of industrial growth in the 1950s and early 1960s. . . . Their internal structures and relations to society are, like their performance, hard to describe in unambiguous terms. They have been described as "strong" and as "weak." Depending on the analyst's prism, they may appear as "autonomous" or "captured."
> Analyzing internal organization and state-society relations in these cases will almost certainly require a more *complicated* diagnosis, one whose con-

tours will have to be constructed from the historical specifics of the two countries [India and Brazil]. (60; emphasis added)

Peter Evans's puzzle in categorizing the Indian state reflected the difficulty of easily applying the concept of the developmental state to the Indian state, as it possessed many of the characteristics of these strong states and deployed many similar policy instruments.[9] The following statement by Bardhan echoes "the paradox of state strength and policy weakness" witnessed in India: "It is, by now, obvious to most people that in spite of some measure of political autonomy and its direct command over vast economic resources, the Indian state is rather weak in shaping the economy" (Bardhan 1992, 323). The recent stability of the Indian economy in the face of the Asian financial crisis challenges the conventional comparison made between East Asia and India and complicates the internationally hegemonic model of a developmental state. These contradictory and divided assessments of India's developmental trajectory mirror the messy conclusions of the comparative political-economy literature regarding the role of states in development. Clearly, the existing analytical categories of the developmental-state literature do not seem adequate for the task of analyzing India. It may be necessary to build an alternative framework.

A Theory of a Multilevel Hierarchy: Territory, Divided Government, and Nested Games

The comparison to East Asia and the miracle economies always finds India in an unfavorable light; however, regional variation in growth rates and investment levels within India should give some pause to the easy conclusions that emerge from such comparisons. Quick cross-national comparisons ignore the differences in size and the political problems that internal heterogeneity creates. The question of state autonomy, or state capacity, a salient variable in the analysis of South Korea or Japan, acquires a different dimension when the state has to govern over a large, complex territory. Thus, while many of the recent theoretical advances in understanding the role of the state in economic development offer us crucial clues about how to conceive of the relationship between state and development, all the contending approaches are fundamentally flawed in three distinct yet interrelated ways.

First, the notion of the state or state capacity underlying most accounts is overly aggregate and blunt. This problem is amplified rather than resolved by cross-national bias in comparative politics. States seem to have national effects, and each country is seen to develop a national "style of capitalism" that combines a constellation of mutually reinforcing features (Shonfield 1965; Zysman 1983; Katzenstein 1985; Weir and Skocpol 1985; Haggard 1990; Steinmo

1993; Dunlavy 1994; Hall and Soskice 2001). These conceptual assumptions about states need to be modified. Public policy and state outputs are not usually produced by a unitary actor with adequate control over all resources and actors, and with a single-minded interest in the common public good (Scharpf 1997, 11). While the assumption of a common public good has been effectively challenged by the public-choice approach to the state, we need to modify the assumption that the state is a unitary ruler. In this book an attempt to develop finer-grained concepts of how the state intervenes in economic life leads me to *micro*-institutional variables and to an analysis of conflict *within* national state institutions. Conventional analysis of a state's effects presupposes a totalistic perspective on the state; rather, the state must be conceptualized in a nonaggregated way.

Similarly, the three competing arguments about the consequences of state action—the neoclassical approach to the state,[10] the public-choice view of the state, and the developmental view of the state—share one common feature.[11] While the public-choice approaches offered a more realistic and analytically superior modification to the benevolent and organic conception of the state found in both the neoclassical and the developmental state arguments, all three of these approaches view the state as a leviathan, either benevolent (developmental) or malevolent (predatory).[12] In this book, I argue that any study of the consequences of state action must attend to the incentives generated by the *internal architecture* of the state. I unite recent developments in the neoinstitutionalist literature, which focuses on the design of political institutions, and the literature on federalism with comparative politics debates on the role and nature of the state. This alerts us to an understanding of the incentives generated by the divided or multileveled structure of the Indian state.

Third, state theory takes a top-down approach that robs lower levels of government of their autonomy and capacity to have an independent or even intervening impact on economic development. States are presumed to act from capital cities and have centralized effects. Yet, different rulers, institutions, and regional governments within the national state may have different goals, preferences, and abilities to pursue national policy. In many countries, subnational governments and local institutions mediate and intervene in the process of development, enhancing, circumventing, or negating the intentions and purposes of central state institutions.[13] This variation at lower levels of the system not merely affects regional developmental outputs, but also shapes the effectiveness of national economic policy and policy change. In these states, the "national" developmental output may be the *combined outcome* of relations and interactions between levels of the nation-state.

The top-down perspective echoes the neglect of the *territorial* aspect of policy making and state impact. States originated by fixing external boundaries, and hence the territorial aspect of states was an important variable in studies of state formation (Tilly 1975; Ertman 1997). Attention to aspects of territorial politics has been, however, ignored in studies of economic policy.[14] States need to reconstitute themselves continually, and they do so in response to and in interaction with subnational units within their boundaries. State-centric literature focuses on the external territorial aspects of states, while territorial politics internal to states has not been explicitly analyzed.

The shortcomings of the top-down approach in state theory can perhaps be obviated by the recent literature on federalism, which focuses on relations between central and subnational levels of government. The economic approach to federalism examines the welfare implications of decentralization.[15] The vision of constituent units in this approach is of functional, overlapping, and competing jurisdictions that are welfare enhancing in two distinct ways: First, the governments of these constituent units face strong incentives to satisfy citizen demands as they adopt to "geography of problems."[16] Second, the provision of public goods is nationally efficient as jurisdictions (central or regional) provide those services that they are *able* to provide (McKinnon and Nechyba 1997). Similar to the neoclassical view of the state, this literature holds on to benevolent conceptions of state agents.

The recent theory of market-preserving federalism inserts rational-actor assumptions into the benevolent notion of government found in public finance literature to argue that strong states want to confiscate the wealth of their citizens. In this formulation, decentralized control over the economy by subnational governments prevents the central government from interfering in markets (Montinola, Qian, and Weingast 1995, 58). Intergovernmental competition over mobile sources of revenue also constrains individual subnational governments. Thus, for Montinola, Qian, and Weingast (1995), under certain conditions, "market-preserving federalism"[17] can both lead to high growth and be self-enforcing.

However, despite their realism, the market-preserving federalism arguments are clearly apolitical. Concerned with economic efficiency effects of centralization, this approach focuses on economic or administrative central-local relations.[18] It conflates economic development with the interests of subnational political leaders, although their interests cannot always be equated with economic development. On the contrary, I argue that regional political leaders are inserted into a two-level game in which they not only fashion relations with central governments, but also must build popular support among local constituencies.[19] In contrast to the apolitical public-finance approach, my approach demonstrates that regional politics and party dynamics shape strategies that regional leaders undertake in dealing with central governments. Regional and national party competition emerges as salient in this analysis. These political incentives are likely to create persistent diverse strategies by regional elites, an outcome not well explained by the public-finance or the market-preserving federalism approach.

A Theory of Polyarchy

The above-documented lacunas with prevailing accounts of state and economic policy can be addressed by disaggregating the state and its institutions. An infranational or subnational research design might prove very productive for such a disaggregated analysis. However, disaggregation in and of itself may not be enough. Actors within a state bargain with other actors for centrally determined economic and political rewards. We need a new framework to disaggregate the actions and political preferences of units within a state but also to generate expectations about interaction across levels. Much of the recent work in both the statist and the neoliberal traditions has focused on the impact of institutions to the neglect of multilevel or cross-level analysis. Interaction *among* these varying rulers and state institutions may be the key to understanding policy outputs and state action. This interaction is mostly strategic, shaped by rules of the game, preferences of the actors, and the territorial spread of political incentives of the actors.[20] Although many scholars have recognized the interdependence of regional orders and national policy (Schmitter 1997; Whiting 2001), few have developed explicit political theories of this interaction. Building and applying such a theory is the purpose of this book.

The distinctive element of this theory is a disaggregated yet multilevel framework that allows us to understand how different state actors located at spatially separable levels of the system evolve and react to economic policies. Such a framework must, first, reconceptualize the state. In my framework, states are not hierarchies with a unitary decision maker but *polyarchies* marked by multileveled actors and institutions.[21] Polyarchy as a concept is especially suited to understand the territorial character of and internal heterogeneity in large states. In a polyarchy, a project or policy is approved by the higher-level state agency in coordination with the lower-level state organization; decisions are joint, but the higher level agency has veto power to accept (or reject) the project. Thus, polyarchies are a combination of horizontal (within subnational units) and vertical (across levels of governments) interactions. I show that relaxing the unitary state assumption in this way generates new and fruitful observations about economic policy in comparative contexts.

Reconceptualizing the state must be complemented by a different way of analyzing interaction within such a state. I employ the theory of two-level games or nested games to understand this dynamic between central and local rulers in the domain of economic policy.[22] The notion of two-level games is prominent in understanding the interaction between domestic and international politics (Putnam 1988; Evans, Jacobson, and Putnam 1993). Many scholars have also used these two-level frameworks to understand international economic policies (Milner 1997) and wars (Bueno de Mesquita and Lalman 1992). The notion of nested games in comparative politics outlines a similar idea (Tsebelis 1990; Scharpf 1997). However, its application in comparative political economy has been less extensive.[23]

The main idea behind such interconnected games is crucial: political actors act and live in two different arenas simultaneously. While actors face different pressures and constraints from these different domains, the goals, choices, and actions of these political actors are shaped by the interconnectedness of these different arenas. Tsebelis described nested games as games in multiple arenas. Concerned with suboptimal behavior, Tsebelis argues that "what appears sub optimal from the perspective of any one game is in fact optimal when the whole network of games is considered" (1990, 7). Putnam outlined it thus:

> The politics of many international negotiations can usefully be conceived as a two-level game. At the national level, domestic groups pursue their interests by pressuring the government to adopt favorable policies and politicians seek power by constructing coalitions among those groups. At the international level, national governments seek to maximize their own ability to satisfy domestic pressures, while minimizing the adverse consequences to foreign developments. Neither of the two games can be ignored by central decision-makers, so long as their countries remain interdependent and sovereign. (Evans, Jacobson, and Putnam 1993, 437)

This idea needs to be extended to what has been termed "comparative political economy" to yield a framework of not two, but multilevel games. Critics and even the proponents of this framework have argued that the notion of two-level games is a mere metaphor and does not generate explicit theories (Putnam 1988; Milner 1997). Thus, the main idea needs to be specified further to analyze substantive thematic issues in diverse contexts.

Applying the Framework

The key to understanding the effects of economic policy is to understand how the game between different types of domestic actors is played. Certain assumptions about the structure of the game must first be specified. Size and territorial aspects of the state specify the nature of the multilevel game. In a large state, bargaining and conflict across subnational and national units are more likely. Strong regional traditions, either cultural as in India or political as in China and Brazil (historical episodes of decentralization as in the Mao period in China, or party decentralization in Brazil), will make this interaction across levels even more consequential for policy making and implementation. The formal constitutional makeup of a system—federalist or unitary—will also play a role.

Regime-type democracy or authoritarian governments will shape the specific nature of political incentives of regional actors. Thus, regional politicians' reelection compulsions will shape the nature of interactions with higher levels directly. In most federal democratic systems, regional rulers become elected through regional assembly elections as well as participate in national representation mechanisms. These democratic incentives enhance the extent and scope of intergovernmental interactions. Thus, the results of the game between regional rulers and their constituents shape the intergovernmental game of bargaining between different levels in a polyarchy.

Does this mean that a two-level analysis would be less consequential in a nondemocratic system? The framework outlined herein suggests that political incentives tied to a specific region are important, but these need not be reelection compulsions, but rather, may be *career incentives* in nondemocratic systems. Evidence from China, the former Soviet Union, and Mexico confirms the existence of career incentives within the single dominant party in shaping the nature of the nested game between regional elites and central actors.[24]

In the case of India, while economic games are played by regional states with the central government in the hope of obtaining central resources, political games primarily reside in the regional arena where regional elites must be elected and reelected. Regional rulers hold the key to both games as they are the intermediate hinge points responding to regional constituents as well as evolving vertical political strategies toward the center in the hope of greater resources. The nested game depends on three variables: strategic political choices of regional elites, regional political institutions, and central institutions.[25] In this framework the strategic political choices of the elites are themselves a function of their policy preferences and regional electoral incentives.

The nested game framework operates in two ways in an analysis of economic policy: Political choices/strategies require a trade-off between interests in two distinct arenas: the regional political arena and the central arena. Further, national policies are not exhausted at the central level but are a combined product of incentives created by central and by regional institutions. Thus, national economic policy is the combined product of central rules, subnational variation in institutions, and divergent political choices arising out of varying regional incentives. This argument implies that territorial *separation* of political incentives created by federalism and democracy has a direct impact on the nature of the national policy framework.

I show empirically in the rest of this book that the constraining framework of growth in India between 1955 and 1991 was a joint product of divergent political choices followed by its regional states. The regional states and their rulers in India are facing incentive structures in two distinct arenas: a regional electoral incentive in the relevant state and the expected payoff from central transfers, which might necessitate bargaining with central rulers. Of greatest consequence, the arena of choice differs in terms of expected payoffs from central transfers and the electoral rewards from political confrontation with the center. Of independent consequence are the institutional differences across provinces; these drive different types of regional public-private coordination and variable implementation of regionally initiated industrialization strategies across states. These two variables—central-local linkages (the vertical analysis) and institutional differences among the states (the horizontal analysis)—are able to explain the regional pattern of investment flows. This vertical model suggests two propositions about subnational political strategies in India.[26]

PROPOSITION ONE:

When regional constituents care more about central transfers than about political and culturalist anti-center actions by the regional elites, the regional state's rulers pursue bargaining and positive-sum strategies toward the center; this increases investment flows to the relevant region.

PROPOSITION TWO:

When regional constituents reward resistance behavior toward the center as a result of legacies of subnationalist movements, the incentives across the two arenas diverge, leading to zero-sum confrontational strategies toward the center leading to low investment flows.

The implication of these propositions is that regional elites may make economically suboptimal (but politically optimal) choices if the two games (horizontal game between the regional elites and their constituents and vertical center-region game) diverge significantly. These two results generate expectations about possible variations in the behavior of regional elites toward the center; these political strategies affect investment flows. Chapter 4 evaluates these theoretical expectations with case analyses of various regional states' political strategies.

While the nested framework elaborated above allows us to understand the logic of *vertical* strategies of bargaining and confrontation within a polyarchy, subnational institutions in the respective regional states perform important mediation functions for the effective implementation of these strategies. Subnational institutions and their effectiveness provide the requisite enabling conditions for private investors. Concepts from neo-institutionalism provide a way to specify the effect of institutions within the regional states and to think systematically about institutional variations at lower levels of nation-states.

Neo-Institutionalism and Regional (Subnational) Institutional Analysis

Scholars of India are confronted with an apparent contradiction: all agree that the state plays a dominant role in economic development yet remains ineffective in achieving its goals. This paradox, I suggest, might be fruitfully addressed if we moved beyond conceptualizations of state strength or weakness to a focus on institutional designs and the incentives they generate. I agree with recent advances in neo-institutional economics, which maintain that development is shaped by the manner in which institutions create incentives that affect the micro-decisions of economic and political actors.[27] Neo-institutional economics further highlight the economic significance of nonmarket institutions under conditions of market failures (Bates 1988).[28] The important contributions of this literature are in highlighting bedrock mechanisms that affect economic behavior.

Three micro-mechanisms—credibility, uncertainty, and information asymmetry—play an important role in a multilevel state engaged in formulating and implementing a dirigiste economic policy.

Credibility and Uncertainty. Macroeconomics and the neo-institutional economics literature emphasize that credible commitments play a major role in contributing to economic growth. The credibility of institutions determines both the flow and the levels of investment. The notion of credibility arises in the context of the literature on macroeconomics, specifically with regard to the time-inconsistency problem, wherein a policy is said to be time inconsistent if the policy maker has an incentive to change it in a later period, when the policy is no longer rational for the policy maker. Thus, a state might promise something, but the state agency or actor has the incentive to renege on the promises at a later time. The source of this time inconsistency is the difference between ex-ante and ex-post incentives in a situation where one actor's action, such as the decision to invest, may be, by its very nature, binding. Policy and economic processes are by their nature dynamic and take place sequentially. Thus, in this case, the government may want to announce a policy so as to invite a pro-investment action by investors. However, once investors have committed, the government has incentives to renege on its policy commitment. Knowing this, investors have no incentive to invest unless policy announcements of the government are credible, that is, unless there is some assurance that the government will carry out its policies.[29] Where institutions are credible and the policy environment is consistent and predictable, domestic and foreign investors are likely to invest and have favorable long-term expectations from the economy (Snider 1996, 7).[30] The Indian state, it might be argued, could not commit to a noninterventionist developmental policy; its licensing system instituted to facilitate investment degenerated soon into elaborate micro-level constraints on private investment (Bhagwati and Desai 1970; Marathe 1989). The Indian state was strong, but its strength created problems of credible commitment not to overregulate. How could such a strong state show itself to be credible?

Two mechanisms for credible commitment are found in the literature (Elster 1984; North and Weingast 1989). One mechanism establishes the reputation of the discretionary agent for fair play (North and Weingast 1989). However, this reputational mechanism depends upon a strong assumption that the interaction between relevant actors will be repeated or is limited by the scale and scope of the reputation system (Milgrom, North, and Weingast 1990). Moreover, in democracies the possibility of losing future elections causes politicians to discount the future. Thus, reputation may not work as a good credible commitment tool in a democracy. The second mechanism suggests that the ruler can voluntarily agree to tie her own hands by delegating some power to other agencies/institutions, in the spirit of Homer's Ulysses, who had himself tied to the mast lest he be tempted by the song of the sirens (Elster 1984). This introduces the possibility of the role of institutions as self-binding agents (Grief, Milgrom, and Weingast 1994; Root 1994).

Both neoclassical and statist accounts assume that the state is the third-party enforcer without credibility problems;[31] the neo-institutionalist accounts offer an important corrective but do not address the credibility problems created by the multileveled structure internal to the state. However, in large-sized states with a multilevel structure, different types of agents at different levels of the system complicate the credibility dilemma. For instance, the Indian central state granted a license to the investor, but the credibility of its implementation was dependent upon the actions of the relevant regional state.[32] Thus, what can be perceived as the central state's credibility deficit arose as a result of the two-level character of the regulatory state. Unilateral action by the central level could not address this problem; the regional- or local-level authority could compensate for this credibility deficit. This joint-credibility structure meant that those regional states that were able to credibly commit to implement industrial proposals received a higher share of the implemented licenses and thereby of the investment flows. In Chapter 5, I outline how these micro-mechanisms work across three regional states.

Asymmetric Information and Its Distribution. Economic theories and recent scholarly debates in development economics emphasize the role played by informational inequalities (Hayek 1945; Mookherjee 1994; Stiglitz 2000).[33]

Hayek saw the main advantage of markets versus states in decentralizing information flows. The public finance literature, similarly, assumes that local governments will have better information about market conditions and needs. In this view, centralization of authority, commonly found in strong-state contexts, would be harmful for growth by undermining informational decentralization. Given the crucial role of information in economic decision making, strong states have seen the control of information as politically advantageous in shaping development outcomes. In strong states such as India, state failure to decentralize information affects economic activities directly. The control of information by the state is seen as economically inefficient and as creating rent-seeking opportunities.[34]

This view, however, relies on a zero-sum perspective of state-market and central-local informational relations. Markets and localities are seen to have better information for development-enhancing activities. A more realistic formulation is that informational asymmetries across levels of government may exist: regional states possess local knowledge about market needs and local conditions, but central agencies may possess macro-information and have strong incentives to control information to regulate the rents that accrue from such regulation. This asymmetric access to different *kinds* of information within a polyarchy generates the prospect for conflict or cooperation across levels of government; at the very least, one may expect to see cross-level informational interaction and coordination in shaping development. Moreover, regional actors will attempt to use their informational power to counteract the power of central government.

However, competition between different kinds of state agents (central or local for example) introduces a new dimension in the "information dilemma" of a developmental state. In a centralized state, the lower-level state agents might have an incentive to withhold some information from the principal (higher-level agency). Studies of federal states, especially of the erstwhile command economies, have stressed how regional officials had an incentive to misreveal their achieved targets, fearing an enhancement of planning targets for the next year (Solnick 1996a; Bahry 1987). In a multilevel democratic system, where lower-level officials are accountable to regional constituents, this competition for information might take another form. In systems where the (central) state has a legal monopoly on economic decisions, regional-level officials, under some conditions, may play a crucial role in using local information to mitigate the controlling power of central rules.[35] This will introduce some competition in information provision and dissemination; local information services may *substitute* for informational rigidities at higher levels within the system. Thus, the role of the regional state in providing information is the key to investment flows in both nondemocratic and democratic systems, but may have different consequences for the overall extent of information distribution and competition between different types of state agents. In Chapter 5 I measure the role of information services across regional states in India.

We see that if we explicitly model states as layered entities not only dealing with functional policy problems but consisting of territorial units, then the problem of institutional design acquires a new dimension. Thus, statist and neoclassical theory of the state needs to be fundamentally reformulated to account for infranational variations and multilevel interactions and incentives in a democratic polity. Advances in the theory of institutional design and agency theory may provide some clues but also need to be modified substantially to account for the operation of democracy in a federal system.

This subnational model suggests two linked propositions (expected results) about the conditions under which the vertical strategies adopted by regional elites will be effectively implemented.

PROPOSITION 3:

If regional elites compensate for the credibility deficit of the central state (by regional-level credibility mechanisms), then investors will implement their projects speedily. The lack of such credibility mechanisms at the local level will contribute to slow and low levels of investment.

PROPOSITION 4:

In systems where the (central) state has a monopoly over economic decisions, local institutions may play a crucial role in distributing information about central rules or differential local conditions, or in generating new information. This will introduce some competition in information provision. Thus, local information services may substitute for informational rigidities at higher levels of the system.

Variation of these mechanisms across regional states in India will be demonstrated in the rest of the book. This multilevel interactive model posits that the policy framework of growth is not centrally guided but is a joint product of central rules, provincial choices, and subnational institutional variation. These assertions allow me to reconceptualize both the vertical and the horizontal aspects of "stateness." By so doing, I argue that comparative politics needs to move from a nation-state-centric framework to a regional political-economy framework that is sensitive to the multilevel structure of politics. The following two-by-two table captures both the vertical and the regional dimensions of subnational developmental states within India. I build and apply that framework to India's developmental state in the remainder of the book. Figure 2.1 and Table 2.1 lay out the causal mechanisms of the main argument.

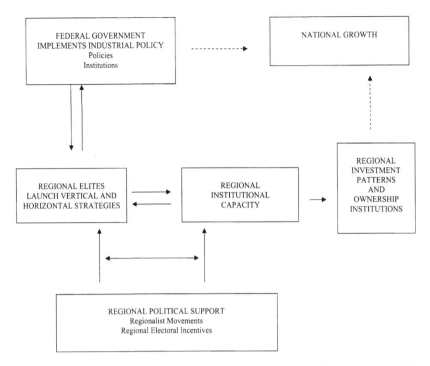

Figure 2.1. Explaining Regional Patterns of Investment and Ownership Institutions (Note: the broken lines represent indirect causal effect; the unbroken lines represent direct causal effect.)

Business Responses and Investor Behavior in a Dirigiste but Multilevel State

How are business actors affected by the institutional structure of interactions in a segmented state? How do they respond to strong subnational interventions in the economy?

The theory of the developmental state usually ignores business responses and investment choices. It implicitly suggests that business elites are politically and economically weak. Consistent with late-industrialization and "guided markets" (Wade 1990) approaches, the theory attributes business weakness to delayed industrialization in many postcolonial societies, which subordinated the business class to the demands of an assertive and autonomous nationalist state. The elites' weakness and the state's regulatory strength led the elites to evolve particularistic and rent-seeking relations with state officials, contributing to what Herring (1999) has called "embedded particularism," rather than "embedded autonomy" (Evans 1995).

These assessments render invisible the multifaceted ways in which business

Table 2.1. Vertical and Horizontal Dimensions of Developmental States

Vertical Model⇒ Regional Strategic Capacity⇓	Bargaining	Confrontation
High	A Vertically Integrated Developmental State **(Gujarat)** Outcome: High Investment in the Region	Isolationist but Productive State (No cases) Low–Medium Investment
Low	Inconsistent but Integrated State **(Tamil Nadu 1947–1967)** Low–Medium Investment	Isolationist Nonproductive State **(West Bengal) (Tamil Nadu 1967–1991)** Low Investment

actors negotiate the complex institutional architecture within a developmental or overly regulatory (as was India) state. These dominant characterizations also assume that most business actors are national and operate at the systemic level. Some of these implicit and explicit assumptions about business action need to be cross-checked with an empirical analysis of business responses to state regulation and subnational policy differences. This bottom-up micro-perspective will, at the very least, correct the statist bias of state and developmental theory while also providing a phenomenological view of the developmental process. In this book, drawing from interviews with a number of businesspersons at both national and subnational levels, I provide a micro-perspective on how the divided structure of the developmental state affected business actors. Thus, studies of development must attend to the third corner of the three-cornered triad: central state, subnational state, and business actors. Figure 2.2 highlights the importance of this interaction.

Design of Study: Selection of Cases

An important methodological question central to such a study is at what level must variance be studied? Should one focus on cities (Bombay vs. Calcutta), districts (Howrah vs. Surat) or regions (western India vs. eastern India)? Substate-level variation (district level) in investment flows is not as persistent as across-state variation in India. Moreover, the levers of political authority vis-à-vis economic policy are located at the provincial level in India, and local governments, whether in cities or in villages, lack policy power to affect invest-

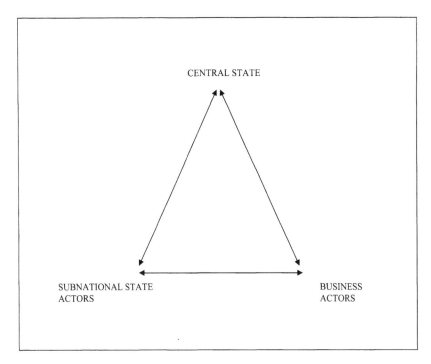

CENTRAL STATE

SUBNATIONAL STATE
ACTORS

BUSINESS
ACTORS

Figure 2.2. The Developmental Triad

ment patterns.[36] Broader units of analysis such as regions—western India versus southern region—are too aggregate to get at finer analytical distinctions. Given these patterns, the provincial level is the most appropriate unit of analysis for economic policy in India.

An important issue is that of case selection. Historical arguments suggest that initial political, economic, and social preconditions were crucial for later developments.[37] It may be argued that the regional patterns set during colonial times would have a powerful impact on later developments.[38] Economists also suggest that it is unfruitful to compare advanced (Maharashtra or Bengal for example) and backward regions (Bihar or Orissa for example); thus a comparison of the industrial and economic structure before the postulated divergence begins may be necessary to control for economic variables.

Can one find cases—provincial states—where similar initial conditions and similar industrial potential may be found? Selecting from the larger set of fifteen major regional states, I chose those cases where many initial social and economic conditions were similar and where developmental potential was clear. Following this reasoning, I found it necessary to choose those regional states that were under direct presidency rule during colonialism, and thus had experienced the economic and political effects of colonial modernization most directly. The choice of West Bengal and Tamil Nadu was clear as they were ruled by direct British rule (presidency areas). Two other cases, Gujarat and Maharashtra (as the southern part of Gujarat and most of Maharashtra was part of the Bombay presidency), suggested themselves as plausible cases for comparison.

Economically, the comparison of key industrial indicators by state at the eve of independence shows the clear "dual dominance" of Bengal and Bombay in the industrial field arising out of colonialism. Historically, the colonial pattern of industrial development predisposed the development of port towns, such as Bombay, Calcutta, and Madras, which in turn worked as nuclei for the development of Maharashtra (Bombay state till April 1960), West Bengal, and Tamil Nadu respectively.[39] On the other hand, the resource-rich regions such as Bihar, Orissa, and Madhya Pradesh lagged behind. The data on the spatial distribution of companies corroborates the emergence of dual dominance, with Madras as the third most industrially advanced state in the colonial period. In 1913–14, the total number of companies in the province of Bengal was 973 (35.4%); Bombay, 613 (22.3%); and Madras, 427 (15.6%). During 1938–39, Bengal increased its share by 6 percent at the expense of Bombay and Madras. In 1947, while Madras led in the number of registered factories, West Bengal was close behind; Bombay had the maximum productive capital employed, closely followed by Bengal, and Madras employed less than 10 percent of productive capital. The three major provinces—Bombay (which included what was to become Maharashtra and a large part of Gujarat in 1960), Bengal, and Madras—accounted for 68 percent of the total factory strength, and Bombay and Bengal alone employed 62 percent of the total productive capital. Thus, these three presidency areas were far ahead of other states in terms of industrial potential.

Indicators related to human capital—literacy rate—reveal that the literacy rate was similar across the three states in 1961 (30% in Gujarat, 29% in West Bengal, and 31% in Tamil Nadu). Urbanization levels were also similar in the three states in the early years. In 1951, all four states' share of urban population was similar: Maharashtra's share was 28 percent; Gujarat's, 27 percent; West Bengal's, 23 percent; Tamil Nadu's, 24 percent. Kerala (13%) and Bihar (6%) ranked much lower. Orissa had the lowest share of the urban population (4%). Given the relationship between economic growth and agglomeration economies generated by urbanization,[40] it is to be expected that all the four states—Gujarat, Maharashtra, Tamil Nadu, and West Bengal—had equivalent potential to attract further investment. The per capita income of West Bengal in 1955 was the highest: Rs. 319 per capita; that of Bombay (bifurcated into Gujarat and Maharashtra in 1960) income was Rs. 288 per capita, and that of Madras (later renamed as Tamil Nadu) was Rs. 233 per capita. Thus, at the eve of independence, West Bengal, Bombay (Gujarat and Maharashtra), and Madras (Tamil Nadu) were relatively well developed and industrially advanced, thus generating the expectation that all four were potential developmental states.[41]

I decided to focus on Gujarat rather than Maharashtra as its post-partition development was more unexpected. Given the dominance of Bombay city and therefore Maharashtra on the industrial map of India, Gujarat's trajectory of successful industrial management was not predetermined. It could have become a subordinate hinterland, supplying labor and raw materials (oil and lime for example) to Maharashtra. In contrast to this plausible counterfactual, Gujarat's developmental trajectory reveals that over time it became an independent center of industrial activity, building autonomous sites of industrialization in southern, central, and, increasingly in the 1980s, western Gujarat. Thus, I analyze three states: Gujarat, Tamil Nadu, and West Bengal, located in three corners of the country.[42] The choice of economic controls for the case selection implies that economic variables outlining either the different initial conditions in the three chosen cases or their different levels of industrial potential cannot fully explain the regionally divergent investment patterns across these three states in the post-independence period.

Thus, the comparative method employed in this book helps to undermine the cogency of formulations that find the roots of regional politico-economic trajectories in colonialism or initial economic structure. If colonialism or initial social and economic structure is associated with stagnant development in West Bengal, but rapid investment flows in Gujarat, the comparative method instructs us to look elsewhere for causes of regional pathways.

Controlled comparisons are not a perfect answer to the problems associated with quasi-experimental research. Scholars may quibble that West Bengal was a colonial enclave with most of its industry declining with the withdrawal of British capital. However, in Gujarat the severe decline of the textile industry in the 1960s was also a crippling blow. In 1960, when Gujarat was partitioned from the erstwhile Bombay state, most of Gujarati investment stayed in Maharashtra.

Class formation in the two contrasting cases—Gujarat and West Bengal—was also different. Historically, West Bengal's economic scene was dominated by British capital and a non-Bengali Marwari business community (whose original home province is Rajasthan), while investment in the western state of Gujarat comes from indigenous business classes (Bagchi 1972; Ray 1979). British capital was not interested in the development of Bengal, and the Indian business classes based in Bengal, it is suggested, are "mercantile in spirit."[43] Yet, this conventional wisdom of West Bengal as a classic European enclave with an unrelenting hegemony of British managing agencies has been effectively challenged in a series of articles by Omkar Goswami (1982; 1985; 1990; 1994).[44] From approximately the 1930s to the 1950s indigenous entrepreneurs dominated economies in both Bombay and Bengal states in equal measure.[45] Moreover, the difference between foreign and "indigenous" business, while politically important in the context of colonialism, is problematic for the period *after* 1947. It is difficult to argue that Marwaris are not indigenous to Bengal when they have been based in Bengal since the 1800s, or that they are "mercantile in sprit" when they have invested in industrial sectors such as chemicals and engineering since the 1930s. Moreover, there is no indigenous ethnic business class in Maharashtra, the state that attracts the largest share of investment among all states. Tamil Nadu does not lack indigenous (Tamil) business communities, yet its investment levels have been low for much of the post-independence period. Thus, while the preexisting ethnic composition (British versus indigenous) of the business classes in the different regions may play a role, it does not completely explain the decline of West Bengal in the post-1960s. While one can never get a perfect set, these cases have enough similar initial conditions to warrant comparative analysis.

In terms of political determinants, the regime types of the regional states are widely different: Gujarat and Maharashtra have been ruled by various factions of the centrist Congress party for most of their political history, Tamil Nadu 1967–96 with alternate rules of DMK and AIADMK (regional Dravidian parties), West Bengal 1947–77 under Congress rule except for 1967–69 and under Left Front coalition rule 1977–present. This allows me to examine the congruity between state-level political arrangements and central regimes, a variable of particular interest in this study. Hence the cases chosen for this study are Gujarat and West Bengal as polar contrast cases, and Tamil Nadu as a case that declines after 1965 but not as much as Bengal.

Conclusion

Theories of economic development have relied on a unitary and top-down notion of a state; in this chapter, I have argued that understanding developmental politics in multilevel territorial societies requires a more sophisticated understanding of states than we currently possess. Most states do not succeed by themselves, yet scholars have yet to integrate insights from local institutional and federalism studies. Disaggregation of states and their activities by itself, however, is not enough. We must be able to theorize how interaction *within* the state shapes economic activity. Subnational rulers' preferences and strategic choices emerge as crucial intervening variables. A theory of nested games, modified for economic interactions, yields analytical dividends in showing how competition and cooperation *internal* to the nation-state may affect the developmental prospect of a country. Subnational institutional capacities transform central capacity by enhancing (or reducing, as the case may be) credibility and informational tasks of the central state. Regional politics shape the political choices made by subnational rulers, yet the prospect of rewards from the vertical center imposes an intergovernmental constraint on the choices made by regional elites. I confirm these insights with an analysis of three initially similar Indian regional states in the rest of the book; Chapter 8 will extend the insights of this framework to four other nation-states (Brazil, the former Soviet Union, China, and Russia).

PART II
National-Level Analysis

3 | Disaggregating the Central State

NATIONAL INSTITUTIONS HAVE consequences, but they do not matter as they are intended to matter or on account of their formal and uniform effects. In the domain of economic policy, both neoclassical and statist theories tend to assume that the state is a third-party enforcer. Societal approaches—Marxism, for example—displace analytical attention onto the power of societal (class) actors to shape state action. But *all* these accounts—neoclassical, statist, and societal—fail to adequately address the agency problems generated by a multi-level structure internal to the state. When and under what institutional contexts is developmental versus predatory capture of the state feasible? This chapter deploys a rational-choice view of institutions by opening up the black box of the Indian central state, and analyzes the incentives generated by its multileveled structure. I show that the Indian state is not a strong state, but a territorially divided one. This view challenges coherent and nation-centric models of the Indian state found both in the comparative politics literature and in the scholarship on India. I unite neo-institutionalist theory with an incentive-driven explanation to outline the effects of this internal architecture on policy outputs and on responses by lower-level state units.

The assertion that the Indian state is a segmented state flies in the face of the dominant view among scholars of India's political economy. The received wisdom is that India's state was centralized, effectively denying any role to regional states. I show, in contrast, that the national state embodied crucial choice points that could be deployed by regional governmental actors to redirect development for their regional goals. Modifying the conventional understanding of India's political economy, I show that this system, in fact, created powerful incentives for regional states' leaders to defend provincial interests. The reproduction of this porous state responded to the overriding dilemma faced by *central* rulers: How can the needs of political stability in a territorially divided society be reconciled with economic growth? This chapter, then, disaggregates the regulatory state but also locates it in a larger political-economy argument, wherein the central rulers' pursuit of the twin objectives of economic growth and democratic and political continuity made that system sustainable. This approach endogenizes the central state by analyzing its existence and reproduction as a product of the interaction between central rulers and regional actors. The empirical analysis not only challenges dirigiste interpretations of the state in India but also urges a reevaluation of economic policy changes undertaken in 1991. I argue that it is historically inaccurate to characterize the role played by regional states in the recent reform experience as a product only of the 1991 policy changes. While key exogenous changes in 1991 changed the policy environment for regional elites, the elites' actions also had deeper historical roots. The legacy of a divided central state continues to offer crucial choice and veto points to regional states under the new policy regime. These conclusions are especially counterintuitive, derived as they are from an analysis of the large-scale industrial sector, a policy arena that was (and continues to be) under the legal control of the central state from 1955 onward.

This chapter begins by examining variation of investment patterns across well-chosen regional states in the large-scale private sector, a policy domain regulated by the central state. Section 2 considers a plausible competing explanation for that variation, the argument that the central government discriminated against opposition-ruled states, but finds that explanation inadequate for both theoretical and empirical reasons. In section 3, an alternative argument is presented that analyzes the internal rules of the license-*raj* and the actual workings of the license-*raj*. Section 4 argues that the specific structure of the regulatory bureaucracy was consistent with the political compulsions of combining economic growth with political stability in a large, territorially divided country. The last section completes the analysis for the post-1991 period, when policy changes abolished much of the central state's regulatory power over industry. Yet I argue that the divided structure of the erstwhile state continues to shape the nature of vertical interactions in those domains that remain with the center, such as foreign direct investment (FDI), international loans, technology transfer policies, and fiscal policy.

Regional Variation in Large-Scale Investment

The central state played a significant role in shaping developmental prospects in India. The Indian central leadership at independence (1947), in accordance with the dominant developmental wisdom of the time and as in many other developing nations, conceived of economic development as industrialization, to be undertaken through sustained and rapid capital accumulation.[1] Import-substituting industrialization (ISI) was implemented to alleviate the capital crunch in an agrarian and colonial economy through governmental allocation of scarce resources into priority areas of investment. State direction of both public and private investment in the industrial sector, it was believed, would lift India out of the "low-level equilibrium trap." The state, then, was to be the agency of the "Big Push,"[2] aiding and facilitating capital investment in heavy, basic, and capital goods industries.[3]

Between 1947 and 1955, state architects designed an institutional framework and a policy structure to fulfill their vision of development. The policy regime consisted of a two-pronged regulatory instrument: the reservation of key industries for the public sector and the state regulatory arm's control over the private sector, which was described as the "license-quota-permit-*raj* [rule]."[4] The license-*raj* was designed to achieve multiple objectives: increase and direct the flow of large-scale investments, calibrate the capacity of demand and supply of commodities, ensure a balance between efficient and equitable location of industries, and prevent concentration of economic power into few hands, all with a view to achieving rapid growth in economic output.

Two aspects of the regulatory system in India are striking. First, while many countries have licensing instruments to regulate what is produced by the private sector, the scope of Indian licensing regulations was broad, comprehensive, and aimed at expansive developmental goals. It may, thus, be better conceptualized as a "licensing regulatory regime" rather than a mere policy instrument.[5] Second, the central government had almost absolute power to make and change licensing policies. If taken alone, the de jure boundaries of rules and regulations seem to justify the perception of a centralized state in India. The ambit of the 1951 act was extended in 1956 to a comprehensive set of about thirty-eight industries, including defense, capital goods, metals, fuels, telecommunications, transport, fertilizers, chemicals, cement, timber, rubber, glass, ceramics, and a host of consumer goods such as textiles, drugs, paper, sugar, food, and leather products. The comprehensive nature of the licensing system led many scholars to argue that this policy framework imposed adverse economic costs on the private sector and affected the growth rate of the economy (Isher Ahluwalia 1985; Bhagwati and Desai 1970; Joshi and Little 1994). Was the license-*raj* as uniform, centralized, and totalizing as it appeared? Regional variation in industrial development patterns suggests otherwise.

Throughout the colonial period from 1857 until about the mid-1960s, the four regional states—Gujarat, Maharashtra (called Bombay state before 1960), West Bengal (Bengal before 1947), and Tamil Nadu (Madras before 1969)—were industrially the most advanced regions of the country; indeed, these regional states attracted the majority of Indian investment. However, in the late 1960s and definitely from 1970, West Bengal's share of licenses sharply declined. By 1984 or so, the regional development pattern had been completely reversed: Gujarat and Maharashtra's industrial potential continued to grow, while West Bengal and other eastern states became industrially less developed. The dual dominance of Bombay and Bengal states transformed into a Bombay and Bengal contrast.

It is clear that just after independence, West Bengal and Bombay were placed equally in the industrial sector. That dual dominance continued until about 1965–70 and is evident in the figures for productive capital of that time.[6] West Bengal outstripped other regional states in total productive capital invested from 1960 to 1965, thus occupying the first rank, but after 1970, West Bengal's share of productive capital declined.[7] West Bengal had the largest number of factories (1,493) in 1956, while Bombay and Gujarat together had 1,549. Tamil Nadu had half their number, about 798. All other states in India had far fewer factories. West Bengal's share of all India productive capital in 1956 was 21 percent, while Bombay state's (which included Maharashtra and Gujarat) was 30 percent.[8] Micro-project-level data—on the licenses granted by the central state[9]—confirm the dominance of three regions (and four states) on India's industrial map.[10] The data on licenses from 1955 to 1966 show that the four most advanced states did get a proportionate share of the licenses. The R. K. Hazari committee report also noted: "About 46% of the approved investment in 1959–1966 was in the three top states, Maharashtra, West Bengal and Madras" (Hazari Report 1967).

The reversal of this pattern is evident by 1973. The data for the period 1973–93/94 reveal the pattern shown in Table 3.1 and Figure 3.1.[11]A similar *divergence* between Gujarat, Bombay, and West Bengal is evident in the data on licenses after 1970.[12] Between 1955 and 1966, West Bengal received a very high number of licenses (1,649), higher than Gujarat (890) and Tamil Nadu (970), second only to Maharashtra, and significantly greater than that of the other provinces. After 1973 it received one of lowest number of licenses, showing a marked decline from 1970 to 1982; its share recovered slightly for a year in 1983–84 but then fell again after 1984 and remained low.

Tamil Nadu's data revealed a definite pattern: 1955 to 1966, high, but not the highest; 1976 to 1986, low; and 1986 to 1990, high, although again not the highest. West Bengal's trajectory over time was 1955 to 1966, second-highest share (after Maharashtra); 1974 to 1990, very low. Gujarat: 1955 to 1966, relatively low; 1974 to 1990, second-highest. Economic factors cannot fully explain this divergence that occurred in the late 1960s. Then what does?

A Competing Political Explanation: Central Discrimination

It is plausible to argue that the central state itself biased the flow of licenses toward certain regional states, especially those ruled by opposition parties.[13] The evidence harnessed in support of the view that the central government discriminated against non-Congress-ruled state governments (two of the cases— Tamil Nadu after 1967 and West Bengal between 1967 and 1969 and after 1977—have been opposition-ruled states) stresses *two types of mechanisms:*

Table 3.1. Productive Capital in the Factory Sector* by State, 1973–1993
(Percentage Distribution)

States	Gujarat		West Bengal		Tamil Nadu		All India
	Factories	Productive Capital	Factories	Productive Capital	Factories	Productive Capital	
1973–74	10.9	7.5	8.2	10.3	10.8	8.7	100
1983–84	10.8	10.2	5.8	7.3	12.3	7.5	100
1993–94	9.7	10.2	4.8	7.1	15.2	8.6	100

Source: Computed from Annual Survey of Industries, *Summary Results of the Factory Sector,* Central Statistical Organization, Department of Statistics, Ministry of Planning and Program Implementation (New Delhi: Government of India, various years).
Note: The Annual Survey of Industries and Central Statistical Organization series data are comparable across time and across states.
*The large-scale industrial firms constitute the factory sector.

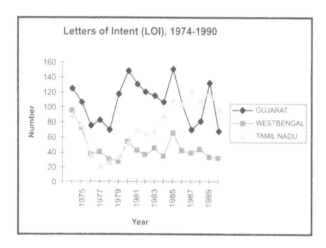

Figure 3.1. Letters of Intent, 1974–1990

(1) the uneven distribution of licenses to regional states despite equivalent locational attributes; (2) the locational distribution of public-sector spending controlled by central ministries.

Despite the popularity of this explanation, it is insufficient in explaining both private and public investment to regional states; it suffers from inherent measurement problems, lacks sufficient empirical support, and is theoretically weak. It is very difficult to establish "discrimination," because it is crucial to show that a state did not get something that it otherwise, in the normal course of events, would have received. The definition of "normal," or what would have otherwise happened (that is, the counterfactual expectation), is very difficult to establish. Moreover, for this argument to work, the license-*raj* should be biased *against* certain state governments and work *in favor* of others. However, it is interesting to note that almost *all* regional states (including those in my research universe: Gujarat, West Bengal, and Tamil Nadu) have consistently argued that they have been discriminated against by the center.[14] There seems to be a fallacy of composition in that all regional states claim to be the victims of central discrimination. Plausibly, exaggerated reports of discrimination are to be expected in a democratic federal system. In a democratic system, regional states have incentives to complain of discrimination and to argue that the central government should be held responsible for the low level of licensed investment in their region.[15] Regional elites very consciously calculated the political effect of such complaints; complaints might have had the effect of reducing discrimination by the center. As Nossiter puts it, "Left governments genuinely believe that they have been discriminated against in the allocation of resources but their very agitation to publicize the fact makes the Center more cautious, since elections are never far away" (1988, 8). Hanson's analysis of the planning system in the early stages, when central control had both legitimacy and effectiveness, confirms that claims about discrimination are likely to be exaggerated: "In a sense, the position of dependence suits them [regional states] very well. It enables them both to avoid taking unpopular measures and to attribute failures to 'circumstances over which they have no control'—in fact to enjoy the fruits of political office without bearing the full burdens of political responsibility" (1966, 334).

Moreover, it is important to offer this explanation with greater precision than is sometimes done. If one analyzes the fragmentary evidence available, central bias operated through different mechanisms at different times and was not systematically related to opposition rule. In some cases, it was district-based (Amethi, Malda, for example, not Uttar Pradesh or West Bengal) and not statewide. For example, Ghani Khan Choudhury, central railway minister (1983–85), is said to have ensured a large central government railway investment for Malda (a district in West Bengal) in the 1980s, ruled by the opposition party. In another example, Amethi, the constituency of the Nehru-Gandhi family in Uttar Pradesh, was particularly blessed. In such cases, allocation was determined by the relationship of a minister to a specific constituency, not by the ideological orientation of the state regime. Ministerial personality was equally crucial. N. D. Tewari, the industry minister in the 1980s, is said to have done more for Uttar Pradesh than any other industry minister. From 1975 to 1977, Haryana is said to have received the Maruti project through the personal intervention of Sanjay Gandhi, Indira Gandhi's son, who was at that time the president of the Congress Party.

The opposition-based discrimination argument also does not work if it could be argued that the Union government might be more willing to appease an opposition-ruled state in the hope that the ruling party at the center could win in that state's next election (Treisman 2001). Given the logic of a "political business cycle" theory, such appeasement should appear around elections. Some evidence exists to support this claim. Indira Gandhi, prime minister 1964–77 and 1980–84, in order to establish an alliance with M. G. Ramchandran, the chief minister of Tamil Nadu, is said to have promised key projects to Tamil Nadu in the hope that the Congress Party would win in the next elections. She did the same in Andhra Pradesh when it was under N. T. Rama Rao's chief ministership (in the early 1980s). Rajiv Gandhi (prime minister from 1984 to 1989) promised many projects to West Bengal in 1985. Amarsingh Choudhary, a congressman from Gujarat, is reported to have told the PM, Vajpayee, that "when Chandrababu Naidu threatened him, he immediately gave package of Rs. 1000 crore to cyclone-hit Andhra Pradesh, but because the Gujarat government belongs to his party, he has done the state an injustice."[16] Thus, theoretically, it is equally possible that opposition-ruled states would see *more, not less,* central largesse; central *appeasement* is as plausible as central discrimination.

Despite these obvious objections to this explanation, it is worth examining the evidence. We may, for instance, analyze this argument as it applies to West Bengal, the province ruled by the Congress Party from 1947 to 1967 and ruled by the Left Front from 1977 onward. Center-state relations were marked by conflict *before* the ascendancy of the Left Front in West Bengal. A case in point is the West Bengal–New Delhi dispute over the constitutionality of taking over the state's coal-bearing areas. In Supreme Court, under the Acquisition and Development Act of 1957, the West Bengal government challenged the power of the central government to acquire land rights in West Bengal. This and similar examples led Jha and Mishra to argue, "It is interesting to note that even before the CPI(M) came into power in West Bengal during Congress rule (1947-67) and particularly during the time of B.C. Roy (Chief Minister from 1948 to 1962), at times a certain tension was generated in Union-State relations" (1993, 210). A similar conclusion can be found regarding Tamil Nadu in an in-depth study of center-state relations with reference to industry in Tamil Nadu:

> A popular explanation for the industrial stagnation in Tamil Nadu after the mid-1960s is the one based on political changes. It has been argued, that since 1967, when the Congress Party lost power in the State to the DMK, [a regional party], the Congress-dominated Centre began to discriminate against Tamil Nadu, not giving its "due" share of public-sector projects and industrial licenses. At best this line of argument is naïve, and at worst, it serves as an excuse for things not done at the state level for whatever reason. (MIDS 1988, 201)

Let us further examine the two different types of central resources: licenses and public-sector allocation. In the case of licenses, a claim of central discrimination can be substantiated only if we find corresponding data for the number of *applications* for each regional state and then match the application data with the license data. Only if the number of licenses granted is disproportionate to the number of applications can a case be made that there was discrimination in their allocation. Such information is available only for the years 1956 to 1966.

Table 3.2 shows that the ratio of West Bengal's share of applications to its share of licenses is close to 1. These data indicate that there was *no* discrimination against West Bengal in the period 1955-66, which is expected since it was ruled by the Congress Party at that time. There seems to have been some mismatch with Madras; this mismatch contradicts the central-discrimination argument because between 1956 and 1966 Madras was ruled by the Congress Party and not by an opposition party.

Table 3.2. Distribution of Applications and Licenses by State, 1956–1966

States	Total Applications	Licenses Issued
Maharashtra	3,645 (25.88)	2,741 (27.37)
Madras	1,263 (8.97)	970 (4.68)
West Bengal	2,296 (16.30)	1,649 (16.46)
Bihar	688 (4.88)	517 (5.16)

Source: Government of India, *Industrial Licensing Policy Inquiry Committee Report,* Department of Industrial Development, Government of India, Main Report (New Delhi: Government of India, 1969), p. 110.
Note: The figures in parentheses are the share in %.

Table 3.3. Relative Central Public Sector Investment Ratios, Controlling
for Population

States	Gujarat	West Bengal	Tamil Nadu
1960–1969	1	6.9	4.0
1970–1979	1	2.2	1.47
1980–1989	1	1.8	1.43

Source: Computed from Bureau of Public Enterprises, *Annual Report on the Working of the Industrial and Commercial Undertakings of the Central Government,* or Public Enterprises Survey (renamed) (New Delhi: Bureau of Public Enterprises, various issues) and Census of India, various years.
Notes: Investment includes value of gross block, capital, work-in-progress, unallocated expenditure during construction and other assets.
The figures for the years 1980 and 1987/88 are taken from CMIE, *Basic Statistics Relating to the Indian Economy,* vol. 2, States, Sept. 1989, Table 9.19 (Bombay: CMIE, 1989).

However, the data on the number of applications is not available for the period after 1965. The evidence regarding divergent numbers of licenses without the corresponding data on applications does not tell us much. A low number of licenses could have been due simply to a low number of applications. Thus, the available evidence on licenses is not enough to *either* confirm or deny the claim that licenses were distributed to Congress-ruled states.

The argument of central discrimination can be examined with direct evidence with reference to central public-sector investment, which was under the full control of the central state. Table 3.3 gives the picture of central public-sector investment during the period 1964–90.[17] Table 3.3 shows that both Tamil Nadu and West Bengal[18] received a higher share of central government investment than Gujarat; both of these states received a low and declining share of total (public and private) investment. The decline over time in West Bengal's share of central investment is proportional to the decline of the total pie: central public-sector investment was shrinking over this period. The period after 1965–66 saw a sharp decline in the rate of growth of public investment at the all-India level. Moreover, the growth rates of public investment between 1971 and 1983/84 show that Tamil Nadu's share grew by 16.1 percent, West Bengal's by 13.6 percent, Maharashtra's by 35.9 percent, and Gujarat's by 19.5 percent (MIDS 1988, 201–204). In the case of Gujarat, the higher-than-average growth rate was due to a low initial base rate, so that Gujarat's share remained low, even at the end of the period. The most obvious case of increased central public-sector investment is Maharashtra, where the share rose considerably. No clear explanation can be made about the congruity between Congress-based rule and central investment, however, as many other Congress-ruled states, namely Madhya Pradesh, Uttar Pradesh, and Bihar, also had lower-than-average growth rates. Thus, central-level discrimination cannot be the only explanation for regional divergence in investment.

It is also important to remember that the largest share of investment in the central public sector was in the areas of energy and steel, and a large part of that went into exploitation of oil off the coast of Bombay city (in the state of Maharashtra), which pushed up Maharashtra's share in the gross block. Those states without the natural resources to invite such investment were not expected to receive them. As the MIDS study put it:

> Since Tamil Nadu simply does not have the natural resources as yet to attract such investment, it is not surprising to find its share coming down over time. . . . [B]ut the point is that it is difficult to sustain the argument that the regional dispersal of Central public investment has been such as to discriminate against Tamil Nadu in a major way. This does not, of course, prove that such discrimination has taken place at all; however the data do suggest that the argument of discrimination can be and has been somewhat exaggerated. (1988, 203)

Echoing my conclusions, one of the most recent and sophisticated econometric studies on the question of regional divergence has this to say on the question of the role of the central planning process:

> Even if we find some degree of divergence across the states, there is not much justification in blaming the [central] planning process. In fact there are reasons to believe that private capital accumulation has outweighed the efforts of planning and has ultimately resulted in rising regional imbalance. Our impression is that the evolution of such an outcome has been strengthened by the State's [regional states] own policies for development. (Ghosh, Margit, and Neogi 1998, 1624)

In sum, the one major explanation for the unexpectedly divergent regional growth rates in India is that the central policy framework was biased in favor of Congress-ruled states. However, this argument does not explain the various cases of discrimination *and* nondiscrimination (in Congress-ruled as well as non-Congress-ruled states). For the post-1966 period, unavailability of data on the number of applications raises questions about strong claims in favor of the discrimination thesis. No pattern emerges from the fragmentary data available on licenses. Moreover, the central-discrimination explanation fails to explain the public-sector investment flows in the two major opposition-ruled states—Tamil Nadu and West Bengal. Clearly, central discrimination does not seem to be a major factor contributing to the postulated divergence between regional states.

The implicit assumption of this powerful top-down explanation is that the central state was a centralized and unified actor, acting with total effect. But how did the licensing system actually work? I argue that it is important to open up the black box of the licensing system and analyze its decisions, rules, and procedures of operation; this will allow us to reconstruct the mechanisms that might link the pattern of license flows with institutional incentives.

I will now offer an alternative account that sheds light on the *combined and strategic interaction* between the national regime and the regional elites. I propose that, despite its formal centralism, the institutional structure of the central state had procedural and structural "choice points" (or access points), which potentially could be utilized by regional actors to redirect the flow of licenses. In response, the different regional states evolved a variety of strategies in their dealings with the national regulatory regime (elaborated in Chapter 4). In contrast to the top-down analysis suggested by the central-discrimination argument, the actual picture of the process of decision making on various projects shows a much more interactive process, where bargaining and specific actions by the regional leaders played a crucial role. These strategies arose as rational political responses to the divided character of the "strong" central state. Uniting a neo-institutionalist perspective that attends to incentives generated by the internal architecture of the state with a political analysis of democratic incentives in a large polity reveals that both structure and process evolved to sustain a multilevel state that was designed to fail in its regulatory objectives but was politically rational for *both* central and regional rulers.

An Alternative Institutionalist Explanation: The Central State Designed to Fail

In federal systems, subnational units have policy autonomy. However, in the Indian case, two countervailing features make the phenomenon of subnational activism counterintuitive. First, the legal policy framework vis-à-vis the industrial sector was centralized and hierarchical. The central government had the legal power to grant licenses, determine location, and shape ownership patterns in the private sector. Second, the Congress Party ruled at the national level and in the various states till the 1980s. Other aspects—the vertical fiscal dependence of the states on the center, the asymmetric tax structure, and the provision of the President's Rule[19]—seemed to confirm this dominant model. Since Indian federalism had well-recognized centralizing features, the role of the central government in shaping industrial policy and the developmental pattern of states cannot be ignored. Thus, evidence from India seems to confirm the macro-institutionalist arguments that national institutions have significant consequences in shaping policy choices (pro–public sector, pro–import substitution policy in India), defining interests (encouraging rent-seeking rather than developmental goals by interest groups), and even shaping the types of participants that are included in the policy process (proprietary classes in Bardhan's analysis [1984] or the demand groups of Rudolph and Rudolph [1987]). But if such vertically dependent regional rulers had no autonomy, why did we find a proliferation of state-level policies and such divergent investment flows? An answer to this question requires a disaggregated knowledge of the operation of the licensing system; the formal constitutional allocation of industry to the center, by itself, cannot explain the diverse patterns.

This alternative view of the central state is rooted in a *micro-institutional* analysis of its internal architecture. I suggest that opening up the black box of the central state might be a useful research strategy. What rules governed the granting of industrial applications? A careful analysis of the license-*raj* shows that its institutional structure was *porous,* generating opportunities and incentives for *all* regional elites to evolve political strategies of circumvention. Equally surprisingly, the regulatory structure involved *joint decision making* between the center and the regional states. Furthermore, the *sequential* character of procedural rules magnified the number of choice points and the joint-decision-making structure. These three mechanisms—choice points, joint-decision structure, and sequential decision rules—created obstructions for investment behavior but enabled provinces to adopt circumvention strategies from within the supposedly centralized state.

I demonstrate that the regulatory state is not centrally directed but involves *joint* coordination between the center and the regional states even in the domain legally under the control of the central Ministry of Industry. This structure, further, creates strong positive incentives for regional states to promote industry, necessitating conflict and not passive acquiescence in industrial policy. Thus, before 1991, the operation of the licensing system potentially allowed room for regional elites to maneuver. After 1991, when the licensing system was abolished, political openings in the structure of the government and continued shared coordination between center and states became even more obvious. This joint structure of industrial governance satisfies the political imperatives of central political elites faced with the dilemma of ruling over a large heterogeneous country and regionally inflected political challenges. This alternative explanation explains the oft-noted divergence between policy intentions and policy implementation or the coexistence of "state strength and policy weakness" (Nayar 1992) in the field of industrial change in India.

A micro-institutional explanation urges attention to formal and informal decision rules and social choice mechanisms internal to the central state, internal rules of the game, and the structure of policy making. Let me attend to each of these in turn.

Institutional Design Governing Industry: Joint and Shared

In the field of industrial policy, the political context is the institutional context, especially since industrial policy came to be implemented by the autonomous bureaucracy. Three rules of the game governing industrial change were key: (1) the constitutional division of powers between the center and the states (article 273 of the Constitution); (2) the Industrial and Development Regulation (IDR) Act, 1951; and (3) the institutional structure of the licensing system.

(1) Article 273 of the Constitution allocated various functional powers to the Union and the provinces; it is quite clear that the Constitution embodies a shared responsibility for the center and states, envisaging an independent and coordinate involvement of regional state governments in industrial policy making and management.[20] Table 3.4 confirms that the constitution embodied a shared and joint responsibility between center and states. However, this constitutional division of labor was subverted, it may be argued, by the ascendance of the planning goals of the central state. The lynchpin of this central preeminence was regulatory control over the private sector embodied in (2) and (3): the IDR Act and institutions of the license-quota-permit-*raj* [rule].

The major component of the regulatory framework was the system of industrial licensing for large-scale industries, introduced by the Industrial Development and Regulation Act of 1951. This act set up licensing regulations to direct the flow of industrial investments to desired locations and sectors, with the desired mix of product and technology. A license from the Ministry of Industry, Government of India at New Delhi was required to set up a large-scale industrial undertaking, to expand capacity by more than 25 percent of existing levels, or to manufacture a new article. The scope of the licensing controls extended to any manufacturing unit employing more than fifty workers if not

Table 3.4. Allocation of Subjects between Center and States

Policy Area	De jure (constitutional) responsibility (union, state, concurrent List)*	De facto responsibility
International Trade	Union but state in case of trade and commerce within the state	Union and state
Diplomatic and Trade Representation	Union	After 1991, trade representation is being done by provinces and by chamber associations
Entering into Foreign Treaties	Union	Changes after 1991; now state governments form independent deals with international organizations
Industries Declared by Parliament to be Necessary for the Purpose of Defense or War	Union	Union
Railways, "National" Highways	Union	Union
State Highways	State	State
Inter-State Trade, Commerce	Union	Union
Industries for "Public Interest"	Union	Union and states
Industries Except "War" Industries and "Public Interest" Provision (7 & 52 of List I)	State	State
Production, Supply, and Distribution of Goods Except "Public Interest" Goods (Subject to List III, Entry 33)	State	State

Table 3.4. *Continued*

Policy Area	De jure (constitutional) responsibility (union, state, concurrent List)*	De facto responsibility
Transfer of Property Other than Agricultural Land	Concurrent	State
Contracts	Concurrent	Union and state
Economic and Social Planning	Concurrent	Union and state
Commercial and Industrial Monopolies	Concurrent	Union and state
Trade Unions	Concurrent	State
Social Security and Social Insurance; Employment and Unemployment	Concurrent	Union and state
Welfare of Labor	Concurrent	Union and state
Education, including Technical and Vocational Education	Concurrent (added in 1976 to the Concurrent List from the State List)	Largely state
Ports (Other than Major Ports)	Concurrent	Union and state
Trade and Commerce (Entry 33)	Concurrent	Union and state
Factories	Concurrent	Union and state
Electricity	Concurrent	State

Source: Computed from Government of India, *The Constitution of India* (New Delhi: Universal Law Publishers Co. Ltd., 1996), Seventh Schedule (Art. 246). Information in column two is derived from interviews with numerous policy officials from both central government and the states, and newspaper analysis of policy implementation.

*Federations like the U.S.A. and Canada categorize the third category as "residual" and its jurisdiction falls within the provinces. In India "Concurrent List" refers to shared jurisdiction.

using electric power and one hundred workers if using electric power (referred to as the "organized" or "factory sector" in India). The purpose of the act was to regulate the entry of firms, keep industrial capacities in line with plan targets, achieve regional balance in the creation of industrial capacities, diversify the industrial base, and create a broad-based pattern of ownership. In addition, such applications were reviewed for suitability of the proposed enterprise or expansion plans from the point of "national" and economically rational objectives, such as balanced regional development, prevention of concentration of economic power, encouragement of labor-intensive technology and small-scale industry, and regulation of foreign capital and technology imports. This comprehensive power to regulate the private sector seemed almost "Leninist" in its policy scope and reach and provided ammunition for those who argued that India's economic policy was similar to that of the Soviet Union (Friedman 1998).

The central government had the statutory power to make and change licensing polices as well as to grant licenses. A licensing committee set up by the act was responsible for evaluating all licensing applications. Over time, the institutional structure of the licensing system became elaborate and the procedures detailed.

By 1970 an application would have to be filed with the Ministry of Industrial Development and Company Affairs, which had many agencies servicing it, including a Director General of Technical Development (DGTD) and a Secretariat of Industrial Approvals (SIA). The Ministry of Industry was the nodal agency for coordinating the government's policy as it pertained to the sector as a whole, while certain sectoral ministries looked after steel, petrochemicals, mines, and fertilizers. The Ministry of Industry[21] was the policy-making body for the whole industrial sector and also the main licensing authority. In these two realms it had the authority to supersede the other ministries. In 1973 the SIA was set up as a unified agency of the Ministry of Industrial Development for the processing of applications for industrial licenses, foreign collaboration, and import of capital goods. It was supposed to function under the overall supervision and guidance of a high-level interministerial committee known as the Project Approval Board (PAB).

In time, however, due to division of power between the various functional approval committees, the PAB came to lose its structural power over the SIA and became just another committee to decide upon licensing cases, albeit important ones. A form of division of labor was worked out. Within the SIA, various approval committees went into the details of the various licensing applications. These committees were the PAB, the Licensing Committee (LC), the LC cum MRTP (Monopolies and Restrictive Trade Practices) Committee,[22] the Foreign Investment Board, and the Capital Goods Committee. Hence, the functional divisions in the department were (a) the SIA, constituted of the various licensing committees, (b) the policy desk, (c) the industries division,

(d) the finance division, and (e) the administration and general division. An outline of the regulatory laws and institutional structure seems to confirm the dominant view that central agencies were the agenda setters as well as the veto actors in industrial policy. How did the complex mazelike structure and rules of the game actually work? Did its structure enable regional mediation?

A closer examination of the micro-institutions reveals that regional states had significant roles to play within these institutions. As early as 1969, the Industrial Licensing Policy Inquiry Committee (ILPIC) Report noted that:

> On the other hand there have been cases, where because of persistent pressure by the [regional] State authorities concerned, licenses have been granted for location within those States. Our case studies show that there are certain States which followed up applications for location in their territories very systematically and persistently and those States were often able to ensure that applications for licenses within their territories succeeded. (Government of India 1969, 113)

The report goes on to say:

> One difficulty in the way of licensing being effective for regional dispersal even in the few limited areas where attempts at planning were made was the pressure that was exerted on the licensing authorities, especially by State governments. . . . State governments also brought to bear considerable pressure at different levels at the Center in favor of the various State applicants. (114)

While some analysis of the role played by business actors in redirecting licenses exists (Hazari 1966), there has been no systematic attempt to document or analyze the role played by regional governments, actors with much greater institutional access and formal power. Regional governments had an institutional presence in shaping the allocation of licenses. The various licensing committees examining applications had the representation of state government officials. The meeting of the Full Licensing Committee heard from the state government's representatives when an application was being considered.[23] Usually the Full Licensing Committee considered many licensing applications in one day. The states whose applications were being considered were invited to make presentations and/or take part in the deliberations. The same application, with or without alterations, could be considered more than once by the Licensing Committee, which might defer or reject it or even reconsider it again at the request of the applicant or the state of location (Government of India 1974).

Here, requests for reconsideration by state governments were more likely to be accepted favorably than similar requests by businesspersons.[24] A Ministry of Industry official said, "After all, they are part of the government, moreover, they have many other access points to convince us—political [through politicians] and official; we prefer that they go through the official channels."[25] The role of the state representatives was even more important when the application could be rejected. Then, the state governments could defend the application and offer counterarguments.[26] The regional representatives could not veto or accept the applications but could influence the decisions taken in the Licensing Committee meetings.

Thus, regional governments lacked veto power but did enjoy access to "choice points" in the system. It is probable that the source for the gap between policy design and actual implementation in the working of the licensing system noted by numerous scholars (Marathe 1989, 17–18; Nayar 1992) lay in this role of provinces as internal to the institutional framework of the licensing system. This state government presence in the Licensing Committees stood in contrast to the complete *absence* of private business representation. While analysis of regulatory policy in India has noted that large business enjoyed informal links to the central industrial bureaucracy, the role of the structurally placed regional states deserves far greater attention. Thus, the *composition* itself of the central agencies provided greater scope for intervention from territorial regional states.

In addition to the institutional presence of regional representatives within central agencies, certain decisions and procedures unintentionally amplified the role and power of regional government actors. Decision making took place through a *sequential* process. Approval of an investment license required sequences of decisions made by both national and regional actors at different spatial locations. After the SIA received an application for a license, it would first be considered by the Capital Goods Committee and various other committees within the DGTD, depending on the technical requirements of the project, and finally by the Full Licensing Committee. It could be rejected at any of these various stages. However, given this movement through several different committees, states could infiltrate and influence the licensing process at multiple "choice points" along the way. Thus, crucial features of the license-quota-permit-*raj*—its mazelike character and sequential structure—provided the opportunity for and even invited circumvention by regional state actors. Figures 3.2–3.4 give a pictorial sense of the regulatory structure.

Even more significantly, the rules of the game necessitated much greater *coordination* between the relevant agencies. A license is only one of the clearances needed to set up production. The following order of interlinked procedures was required in order to set up a manufacturing unit. First, an entrepreneur planning to establish a manufacturing plant in the licensed sectors submitted an application for a license to the Ministry of Industry. A number was allotted to the application to acknowledge receipt. After one to three months, the SIA granted a Letter of Intent (LOI), which enabled the entrepreneur to apply for other clearances such as land, power, and capital goods clearances (if a capital goods sector), or an import license (if applicable). After receiving various clearances, the entrepreneur applied for what is known as the Conversion of an LOI to an Industrial License (CIL or IL). When the entrepreneur received the CIL, production could commence. The application for conversion could be accepted, rejected, or returned with conditions. An LOI for setting up an industrial unit was converted into an IL if the entrepreneur had taken effective steps for the implementation of the project and if all conditions indicated in the LOI had been met. Thus, obtaining clearances was an important step to get an LOI converted into a license.

An investor said to me, "The license was a like a passport—you needed it to get in the system, but it did not ensure that you had a good trip."[27] The time period between getting an LOI and an IL was a crucial period, affecting the viability of the project, its cost overruns, and hence industrial investment in the state. It is important to recognize that in the coordinate federal regulatory system, while some clearances had to be obtained by the central ministries (capital goods, DGTD, and import licenses), many others had to be obtained at the regional level. These included land acquisition, whether through private means (often subject to additional state-level regulations, as in West Bengal) or through the state government; location choice in an industrial estate; power clearance; raw-material clearance in the case of an industry that needs raw materials such as coal (that is, minable products that are in the hands of the public sector, both central and state); and environmental clearance.

Hence, while the actual grant of the license was in the hands of the central government, the speed with which an LOI could be converted into a license was a federally coordinated affair. Large-scale businesspeople admitted, "Getting the license was not enough, we had to get many other clearances from the state government and other ministries."[28] The Ramakrishna Report made this prescient analysis in 1978: "Industrial licensing is only a necessary but not a sufficient condition for setting up an industry. Rapid and sustained development can be prompted only by coordinated action on a broad front involving not only licensing policies, but also fiscal, pricing and purchase policies, incentives and reservations and the like" (35).

The problem of entry barriers engendered by the license system was not an automatic result of the "centralized" regulatory system (Isher Ahluwalia 1985) but rather a consequence of coordinate rules of the game between the center and the regional states. At the same time, if variation existed in the ability of regional states to give clearances, then those provinces that consistently gave clearances faster tended to get the maximum number of LOIs converted into ILs, affecting the extent of investment in their regional states. Figures 3.2, 3.3, and 3.4 represent the analysis presented above.

The analysis has demonstrated a crucial modification in our picture of the central state and its workings. The three micro-institutional aspects of the cen-

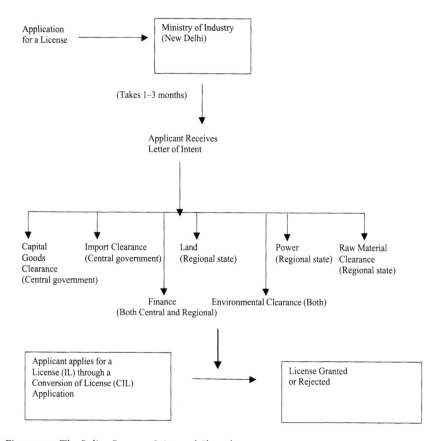

Figure 3.2. The Policy Process: Joint and Shared

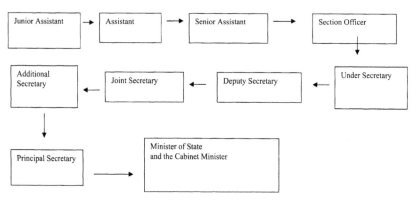

Figure 3.3. The Movement of Files and Applications within the Central State (Sequential and Multiple Choice Points)

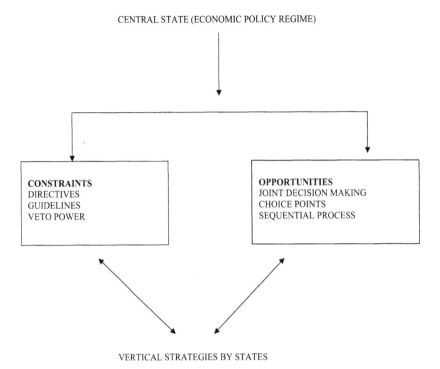

Figure 3.4. Central State: A Vertical Model

tral state—*composition, sequential decision making, and coordination between levels*—created the possibility for a far greater role of regional states from below. I argue that these crucial institutional features of the system allowed "room for maneuver" for provincial elites to redirect the location of investment in their regions. Potentially, the licensing system was not centrally directed but could be subverted from within by regional actors.[29] This bottom-up analysis of the state must replace conventional top-down perspectives of the Indian state to present a complete picture of the *interaction* between central rules and regional responses.[30]

An analysis of the micro-institutions that exist beneath a strong state reveals that the Indian state may have lost its autonomy to direct the economy over time; these porous "choice points" allowed a diverse set of actors room to maneuver within its maze and to redirect the output of the regime to their specific ends. Large-scale business actors were one such group, but regional states were even more powerful, enjoying greater structural and formal political power. Strategies from below reflect not the unilateral failure of the central state, but the combined interaction of central incentives, constraints, and regional responses.

Until this point, I have offered a neo-institutional explanation for the particular "lock-in" of India's policy regime. The joint structure of the rules of the game, sequential process of decision making, and choice points that allow regional states to maneuver mean that it is difficult to change the system. In the following section I intend to show that this joint decision structure served important political ends for its rulers. There was no attempt to reform the system from within because the evolving architecture of the regulatory regime allowed central rulers to deal with regional claims to maintain political stability in a heterogeneous, multileveled polity. The specific structure of the national regulatory regime allowed enough scope for such regional (and also business) claims to be addressed in the domain of industrial policy. The next section (and the next chapter) demonstrates that the economically deleterious regulatory system survived so long because it was politically expedient for *both* central rulers and regional actors.

Political Economy of the Divided State

As I have argued above, the structure of the central Indian policy regime moved away from the vision of an autonomous state and instead embodied multiple access points for key regional actors. It is worth asking how this segmented state benefited central politicians. An important task for political economists is to endogenize institutions in the sense of treating them as the result of strategic interaction between economic and political actors (Weimer 1997, 10). Various official committees noted many of the irrationalities of the central regulatory framework, yet there was no attempt to reform or rationalize the divided structure. The mid-1960s saw a crisis in the industrial realm, yet the regulatory system continued. Persistence of an economically irrational system, especially after a crisis, deserves explanation. Institutional inertia of an elaborate system might have made it difficult to reform the system. This negative explanation about absence of reform must be complemented with a positive argument about political conditions for non-reform. What were the political considerations within the national political economy that continued to sustain such a system?[31] The prevailing literature does not adequately address the political roots of the persistence of the license-*raj*. Bhagwati (1993) suggests that the influence of pro-state economists was the key. Other scholars have argued that big business groups acquired crucial stakes in the licensing system (Hazari 1966; Kochanek 1974).

The segmented structure was a system "designed to fail"; that is, it continued to exist precisely because its divided structure allowed the central politicians to reconcile the needs of political stability in a territorially divided society with modest economic growth. In the realm of economic policy, all national leaders in India were forced to confront the need to maintain an autonomous and centralized state, a need *contradicted* by the political requirements of ruling a large country. The divided and joint structure of industrial regulation served to accommodate regional pressures.

The two central leaders with the longest tenure between 1947 and 1984— Jawaharlal Nehru and Indira Gandhi—responded to this common problem in different ways. Nehru was forced to accommodate central policy autonomy with explicit central-local mediation mechanisms. Indira Gandhi abused these central-local political mechanisms and gave diverse regional states and business groups particularistic access to the policy regime.

This interpretation differs from the conventional reading of the two regimes in the following ways. First, I combine the economic and political dilemmas of policy regimes in one analysis. Nehru's regime, perceived to be the era of state autonomy in economic policy, faced significant challenges from regional political and party elements. He, however, dealt with these challenges through institutionalized *intra-party and intra-bureaucracy* mechanisms. Indira Gandhi dealt with similar challenges by subverting the preexisting institutional channels of central-local mediations in party politics, but she too was forced to accommodate societal (regional and functional) claims by continuing and even enhancing the segmented character of the *bureaucratic* policy regime. In both periods, thus, the regionally segmented character of the economic policy regime became stronger, while economic growth was slower than expected. This was the era of the Hindu rate of growth, when the economy grew at the aggregate 3.5 percent per annum.

For the state leadership and the ruling party in India, democratic continuity and political stability were (and are) as compelling as economic development. While the 1950s saw a remarkable enhancement in the power and prestige of the central regulatory machinery to design and implement economic policy, the continued authority of the regulatory regime conflicted with the political obligations of governing a large country. Thus, the political complexities imposed by the size of the country and its federal structure intervened to make the simultaneous pursuit of rapid economic accumulation and democratic continuity extremely problematic. First, central planning necessitated a rational, strong bureaucracy that could match targets with actual achievements and modify plans. This would have implied the rule of the state *over* the party. But the necessity of ruling and winning elections across a large country meant that political claims had to be allowed to infiltrate central autonomy. These political claims took the form of regional claims because of the federal structure of the Congress Party and mechanisms of aggregating national majorities in a two-level parliamentary system. Thus, the segmented nature of the regulatory practices (outlined above) continued and was made even more porous over time. Reciprocally, regional states and regional party units became stronger, making it possible for regional divergence in economic policy to sustain itself.

Constraints Imposed by the Structure of Democratic Politics: Central State and Party in Conflict (Nehru Regime 1947–64)

Different institutions of the nation-state embodied different principles of a modernization imperative after 1947. While the central state came to embody the principles of state autonomy in public policy, especially in economic policy, the Congress Party came to represent both the democratic (or mass) and the federal logic. The central rulers, in order to rule and ensure democratic stability, needed the party, but economic policy demanded state autonomy from societal and political pressures. This paradox, mediated by the Congress Party, gave rise to contradictory tendencies in Indian politics. I will demonstrate how the Nehru (1947–64) and Gandhi (1966–77, 1980–84) regimes negotiated the dilemmas produced by the simultaneous pursuit of democratic continuity and autonomous public policy in a territorially divided society.

As has been argued before, the centralization imperatives in matters of public policy were indispensable for the Nehruvian vision of state and nation building (Sukhamoy Chakravarty 1987; Byres 1994). Nehru sought to establish and create a predominant role for the center in the economy and policy in his efforts to ensure the domination of the executive over both the legislature and the party. However, Nehru was confronted with the legacy of the Congress Party and the political necessity of winning elections. In his struggle to establish his ascendancy and his vision of a modern state and economy, Nehru had to contend with the prevailing coalitions of political and social groups. Through this interaction, decentralization imperatives that had been suppressed under the lid of constitutional design and the planning machinery began to appear and had to be mediated by the license-*raj* and planning institutions. This effectiveness of the regional pressures to bypass or circumvent the system was shaped by the structure of the license-*raj* and the structure of the Congress Party. The following section analyzes the structure of the Congress Party.

The Congress Party since the Nagpur (Maharashtra) session in 1920 has been a territorial organization consisting of provincial congress committees.[32] The provincial committees were in turn subdivided into districts, taluq (district subdivision), towns, and villages, forming a "parallel government," with each lower body electing delegates to the committee immediately above it, and ultimately to the All India Congress Committee (AICC), the highest executive organ of the party. The importance of this regional-linguistic party structure is evident in Nehru's comments in the parliament:

> We in Congress accepted the principle of linguistic provinces 40 years ago for a very good reason. The reason applies today too. We felt that in order to reach the people it was essential to function in the language of the people, whether in respect of education or of public conferences, congresses or other activities. As a result we attached importance to the language question and therefore to linguistic areas. That was the beginning of the linguistic idea. (Nehru's speech, "The Right Approach," in the Lok Sabha [parliament] August 30, 1961)[33]

This structure gave independent power to the provincial congress committees not only during Nehru's time but also during the tenure of Indira Gandhi. Marcus Franda's study of the provincial-central party relations in West Bengal confirms this argument:

> The independence of the state Congress party from influence by central party leaders rests not only on the state-based, close-knit organization that has been created, it is also encouraged by the formal structure of the party itself. . . . [T]he pivotal group within the Congress party organization has been, since the 1920s, the Pradesh Congress Committee (PCC), which generally organized the party within state or provincial boundaries. The PCC determines the number of local district and *mandal* Congress committees that shall be organized within the state, and it is almost solely responsible for bringing these locally organized units together. Control of local units obviously gives the state party leadership a great deal of influence with party membership, and as a result, an important role in the maintenance of the electoral position of the state ministries and the central parliament. (1968, 207)

Similarly, Robin Jeffrey is worth citing here:

> To connect with the third category of the party—the party in the electorate—it seemed essential during the Nehru years to have a functioning party organization. . . . In its idealized form, it heard, translated, and mediated *local* disputes; interpreted government programmes to *local* supporters; gave aspiring individuals or groups a channel by which to influence government. (1994, 167–68; emphasis added)

The central state's institutional dominance in economic policy confronted the political compulsions of a hegemonic party in electoral and democratic management. Even more so, the central plan had to be implemented by regional state governments and state-level party units (Appleby 1953; A. H. Hanson 1966). Thus, democratic and administrative compulsions led to decentralist pressures within the party-state and the bureaucratic state. As a result, the role of the state governments and regional party units became stronger, providing the political context for "choice points" within the license-quota-*raj* and the possibility of provincial strategies from below.

How did the regional states and their incumbents respond to the unprecedented autonomy wrested by the central state between 1947 and 1956? In 1961, the Industry Minister of the Government of India, Manubhai Shah, complained in frustration,

> I have been assuring throughout the country that, during the Third Five-Year plan period, every State is going to have the establishment of a major public sector engineering undertaking. I cannot do anything better than that. . . . There is from every State, deputation after deputation, representation after representation and misrepresentation after misrepresentation of various types of things. Every time the newspaper says the heavy electrical plant has already been located in some State, another State comes forward and asks whether that is correct. (1961, 314)

Even the Planning Commission, designed as an autonomous organization, was forced to deal with the central-local dimension of planning. In 1963, thirteen years after the formation of the Planning Commission (established in March 1950), Nehru acknowledged that it was not a supra-executive body vested with supreme autonomy, but rather a mediator. Nehru addressed parliament, saying:

> [The] Planning Commission has performed an essential task; without it we could not have progressed. . . . We are a federal structure and it has served to bring the various states together and have integrated planning. If it had not been there, the central government could not have done its job because immediately difficulties would have arisen that the central government was encroaching on the rights of the States. (Lok Sabha Debates, quoted in Fadia 1984, I: 129)

A. H. Hanson's magisterial analysis of the Planning Commission for the period 1947–67 confirmed that the planning process was a negotiated process:[34]

> Federalism is invariably a headache to the central economic planner. Whether India has a "genuine" federal constitution, in view of the fact that the constitutional states of the Union can be abolished or divided by fiat of the central legislature and made subject to "presidential rule" in an emergency, is a question on which pedants will continue to spill ink. The facts are that in normal times the states possess and exercise certain autonomous powers and, what is more important, are politically self-assertive units whose interests and views the central government cannot afford to ignore. Some of the juridical essentials and much of the vital spirit of federalism are therefore present. (1966, 311–12)

These political pressures from the regions had a direct policy impact. In the third five-year plan (1961–66), regional dispersal and questions about location were acknowledged to be salient factors in shaping national policy.

Industry has tended to concentrate in the States of Bombay and Bengal. Irrigation had developed mainly in Madras, Uttar Pradesh and Punjab. This was the result of the operation of free enterprise and provincial autonomy. So long as the government of India did not embark upon a planned economy, there was no particular feeling of injustice and bitterness [among states]. Now the position has been reversed. There is a strong feeling that somehow or other industries should be set up in all States, that irrigation should be developed irrespective of cost and social services should be brought to the common level. (*Eastern Economist*, 7 May 1958, Special Plan Supplement, ix. Cited in A. H. Hanson 1966, 313)

The report of the Administrative Reforms Commission in 1948 proposed that the National Development Council be upgraded and visualized as a supreme political body (constituted by the chief ministers of regional states), giving broad guidance relating to national planning. In direct response to political pressure from the regions, the government set up a number of committees and, subsequently, new policies to deal with the demands of various states, especially the more backward states. Such committees and their reports included the Small-Scale Industries Board, *Report of the Committee on Dispersal of Industries*, 1960; Planning Commission, *Economic Development in Different Regions of India*, 1962; Planning Commission, *Resource Development Regions and Divisions of India*, 1964; Report of the Working Group, Planning Commission, *Identification of Backward Areas*, 1969 (Pande Committee); Small-Scale Industries Board, *Fiscal and Financial Incentives for Starting Industries in Backward Areas*, 1969 (Wanchoo Committee); and Planning Commission, *National Commission on the Development of Backward Areas* (NCDBC), 1980.

Richer states were able to influence the system by identifying poorer districts within their states rather than encouraging cross-state allocation of resources. In 1971, the central government initiated a new capital investment subsidy scheme. Under this scheme, new or expanding units in selected backward districts (identified by the regional governments) were entitled to a subsidy of 10 percent of their total fixed-capital investment. Such schemes as the industrial estate program started by states in the 1950s received central approval and enhanced prestige in the 1970s.[35]

These policies and policy deliberations reflected a concern for regional dispersal in response to the political pressure enjoined by many regional states on the central policy regime. At the same time, in licensing policy (the large-scale industrial sector), the license-*raj* acquired a divided structure and the sequential choice points described previously. The porous structure of the license-quota-*raj* enabled the central state to retain formal policy-making powers yet allowed states and the private sector to interact with the licensing machinery on mutually advantageous terms. Effectively this compensated for the formal rigidity of the system and allowed decentralized efforts by states to circumvent the license-*raj* in favor of their respective regions. As the government of Gujarat recognized recently: "The 'license-regime' imposed certain limitations in the [our] approach and this resulted in each State competing with other States in the country for attracting more investment to that state" (Government of Gujarat 1995, 1).

Nehru certainly realized the value of the party organization and the role that the regional leaders played. His detailed letters to the chief ministers reveal his recognition that they were important "hinge points" in party politics and policy implementation, as well as in the democratic functioning.[36] This view is confirmed by many scholars of Nehru, who have noted that Nehru played the role of a mediator par excellence but refused to be dictatorial. Jeffrey goes on to say, "Such a functioning party helps to explain Nehru's appreciation of regional leaders whom he not merely tolerated but encouraged (1994, 166)."

In summary, during the Nehruvian period, the central state successfully won control over economic policy.[37] State-centered industrialization (embodied in licensing and public sector–led development) became one of the crucial pillars of the modern Indian state, shaping both party competition and intergovernmental relations. In its original design the public sector–led strategy and the license-*raj* was visualized as a rational response to the resource constraints faced by the Indian economy. As successive regimes mediated the relationship between autonomy in economic policy and the demands of federalist democracy, in actual economic and political practice, licensing and the public sector became a hybrid of policy and patronage.[38] Simultaneously, the operation of the industrial economic policy regime—licensing and public-sector regime—came to accommodate decentralizing pressures and intergovernmental bargaining.

In retrospect, the statist development strategy created political patronage so that the regional party units could be incorporated in the national winning coalition. The Congress Party, organized regionally, encouraged the regional leaders to make claims on the central public sector. Tamil Nadu and West Bengal, ruled by the Congress Party till 1967 (as was Gujarat), followed this strategy. Paradoxically, it was precisely the dominance of the central state in industrial policy making that made regional demands on the central state so urgent. From the perspective of the national rulers in the Nehruvian period, insisting on the strength of the central state and allowing regional satraps to make claims on it and infiltrate it from within were not contradictory, but politically complementary, strategies.

This was evident in the formation, in 1952, of the National Development Council (NDC), created to give the chief ministers of the states an opportunity to review and recommend social and economic policies and targets for the National Plan. Most crucially, the licensing system over time evolved in such a way that, despite its centralist initiative, it had "choice points" within its structure that could be used by states to direct licenses toward their regions. The organization of the economy was centralized, but it was not a hermetically sealed centralization; rather, the provincial state governments were loosely linked to the center through bargaining and patronage. This political argument, then, accounts for the seemingly contradictory combination of a strong central state and state-level divergent strategies toward that central state.

Indira Gandhi (prime minister from 1966 to 1977 and 1980 to 1984) faced a similar dilemma of reconciling regional pressures with the need for central autonomy in economic policy. Her centralist initiatives were a direct response to territorial pressures from below and had only partial success in subverting the pressure from regional elements within the Congress Party or from regional states.

Populism and Centralism in Economic Policy during Indira Gandhi's Regime (1966–77, 1980–84)

Most analyses of Indira Gandhi's regime seem to agree that she ruled through personalized control at the center. Moreover, she sought to deinstitutionalize the national party and state-level party units (Kochanek 1968, 1976; Brass 1982; Rudolph and Rudolph 1987). As a descriptive model of Indira Gandhi's regime this is accurate. However, most explanations of the transition from the Nehruvian period to one of soft authoritarianism attribute it to Indira Gandhi's personal proclivities. In this section, I argue that the change in governance strategy at the national level from 1969 to 1977 was not a matter of personal style of the ruler. Rather it was the necessary outcome of an attempt to reconcile state autonomy in economic policy with democratic stability *but under a changed structure of intra-party competition and federalism*.

It is well established that economic policy after 1969 took a "leftist" turn.[39] It seemed to signify an ideological struggle between conservative and rightist factions within the Congress and the Nehruvian ideals embodied in the Socialist Forum within the Congress Party. In my opinion, this turn to the left represented a more enduring struggle between the regionally inflected party and the executive and an attempt by the central state to reclaim initiative over public policy.

The power vacuum created by Nehru's death (prime minister 1947–64), the succession battles, and Shastri's tenure (prime minister 1964–66) exacerbated provincial dominance over the central state. The food crisis in 1965–66 led the regional states to make further demands on the central state and insist on a liberalization of agrarian strategy. This period increased the domination of regional interests over economic policy. Thus, Shastri's rule and Indira

Gandhi's early regime let the party and regional party units take over. This period witnessed a shift to the right in direction of economic policy from the Nehruvian strategy of public sector–led planned growth. Shastri's and Indira Gandhi's economic policies between 1964 and 1967 were in fact conservative, designed for political survival in a situation of economic crisis and political transition. In 1966, the rupee (the Indian currency) was devalued and foreign exchange liberalized. In agriculture, a Green revolution strategy, composed of price incentives to farmers and the availability of key farm inputs such as seeds and water, epitomized the liberalization of agriculture (Varshney 1995, 48–80).

However, from about 1969 onward, Indira Gandhi changed her tack radically in industrial and welfare policies and followed a populist and ostensibly "socialist" direction. The first indication of this was on July 16, 1969, when Mrs. Gandhi relieved Morarji Desai (the economically "conservative" leader from Gujarat) of the finance portfolio. This led to his resignation, as his inclusion in the government had been based on the pact that he be given the portfolio of the finance minister, a post second only to the prime minister in status. Then, in direct contravention of a party decision not to do anything about bank nationalization, and forty-eight hours *before* the Lok Sabha was supposed to meet, the government announced that fourteen of the large commercial banks were being nationalized by presidential ordinance (Frankel 1978, 420). This added to prime-ministerial prestige in delineating economic policy that was progressive (421). On February 1970, a new licensing policy was announced, reversing the trend toward decontrol started in the mid-1960s. Previously granted exceptions from licensing requirements were withdrawn from forty-one industries, and applications from large business houses were to be specially screened. In addition, the Monopolies and Restrictive Trade Practices (MRTP) Act was enacted for the first time in 1969 to ensure that monopolies were not formed; it set up a Monopolies and Restrictive Trade Practices Commission appointed by the central government to advise the Ministry of Industrial Development on questionable applications. In September 1970, legislation to terminate the privy purses and privileges of former princes was passed in the Lok Sabha, but did not make it through the Rajya Sabha (upper house of parliament). This led the cabinet to hold an emergency meeting to recommend that the law be passed by the president through an ordinance. In 1973, the Foreign Exchange Regulation Act (FERA), an act regulating foreign exchange, was passed. At the same time, antipoverty policies and welfare measures were announced.

I argue that this ideological turnaround by Indira Gandhi reflected her attempt to frustrate an *intra-party* threat that had solidified on the basis of regional divisions within the Congress Party and to deal with the emergence of an *extra-party* threat from regional parties and the emergence of opposition-ruled governments in the states. Thus she, not unlike Nehru, was forced to deal with the dilemma of reconciling democratic and regime stability with autonomy over public policy in the context of federalism and the necessity of weaving together a national coalition in a territorially divided society.

Given the regionalized structure of the Congress Party and the complexity of governing a country of such proportions, Indira Gandhi resolved the problem of national regime stability through three mutually reinforcing strategies. She tried to (1) undercut the power bases of regional leaders; (2) bring about an ideological transformation toward "populist socialism" in economic policy; and (3) reorganize the social bases of Congress Party units in states toward Muslims, the poor, and the Adivasis (indigenous groups), creating vote-banks[40] rather than pre-constituted provincial state units.

Two elements of the changed circumstances between 1966 and 1969 are crucial to understanding her response. Indira Gandhi faced a regionalized and highly differentiated party in which the regional leaders played key mediator roles, but *without* having the legacy of the nationalist movement behind her. Moreover, she faced more direct challenges at the state level than Nehru had faced.[41] Her strategy of taking control of the central state and the party was therefore shaped by her changed circumstances. Between 1964 and 1967, the regionally based mediators-arbiters not only asserted their claims on democratic and organizational aspects of the party-state but sought to shape economic policy and control the prime-ministerial candidates, namely Shastri and Gandhi. Thus, for her, central-local relations had become central to questions of governance, which she could not ignore. Also, her own political and charismatic resources were thinner in 1966 than Nehru's had been in 1947. Thus, she faced a strongly regionalized party and had *fewer* inherited resources to deal with the task of reorganizing the federal democratic state. Hence, for Indira Gandhi the question of stability came to be defined narrowly and overwhelmingly in terms of regime stability and personal continuity.

She resolved the regional problem within the party by "centralizing a federal party" (Kochanek 1976, 98) and appointing state leaders without independent power bases. The Parliamentary Board of the Congress Party became stronger and intervened in party affairs such as recruitment of candidates, arbitration of disputes, and selection of chief ministers in Congress-ruled states (Kochanek 1976, 99–100). President's Rule was used frequently and for narrowly political ends (Dua 1979).[42] Between 1967 and 1977, article 356 was used thirty-nine times. Gandhi attempted to gain control over the central organs of the party such as the Central Working Committee (CWC), the Parliamentary Board, the post of the president of the Congress Party, and the Central Election Committee (CEC). Her policy took a leftist direction. And she reorganized the ideological and social axes of power within the Congress in a such a way that she could appeal to voters and ordinary party workers without the mediation of intermediate party leaders, "the mediator-arbiters."[43] Thus, appealing to ideologically defined vote-banks—the poor, the Muslims, the SC (Scheduled Castes, also known as Harijans), and the Scheduled tribes (indigenous communities)—made sense.[44] These groups represented *horizontal social cleavages* in society and were orthogonal to the organization of the old Congress. In the old Congress system, at the provincial level, the party cleavages reflected societal cleavages, but the aggregation of all party units at the national level meant that it was the provincial/regional principle that dominated national party politics.[45] Indira Gandhi's regime sought to change that dynamic to curtail the power of established regional mediators.

However, her attempts at centralization were partial and incomplete: after 1980 she was forced to rely on many regional incumbents to craft a national majority coalition. In the 1980s, each (Provincial Congress Committee) leader delivered the members of parliament from his or her state to the national majority. Any national leader who hoped to put together a national majority in the Lok Sabha looked for each state leader to deliver his or her state rather than individual seats. For example, after the general election of 1980, "Madhavsinh Solanki [the Congress leader from Gujarat] having regained control of the GPCC(I) presidency and having '*delivered Gujarat*' in the general election [parliamentary election], was now in a position to determine who would be Congress (I) candidates in the sure to follow [provincial] Assembly elections" (Wood 1984b, 210; emphasis added).

The role of the state-level leaders was to ensure that all the MPs from their state stayed in the Congress Party by bargaining with the central command to give them party tickets for the next elections. Zwart confirms the importance of state leaders to the Congress Party. "Before the elections of 1985, Madhavsinh Solanki—just like in 1980—was handled with kid gloves by Delhi [the national-level party], in the sense that nearly all those people he had proposed actually got party tickets" (1994, 89).[46] Sharad Pawar and A. R. Antulay in Maharashtra have performed similar roles. Mostly the "high command" accepted the recommendation of the state chief minister for the post of the PCC(I) and nomination of candidates.[47] Similarly, Maharashtra leaders' ability to deliver the "sugar lobby" was crucial for their power within the Congress Party.[48] The prime minister was anxious after 1980 to strengthen the hands of the Congress chief ministers rather than encourage factionalism within state Congress units.[49]

In the realm of economic policy, Indira Gandhi's populist socialism instituted an "economy of favors," well described by Bardhan (1984, 1992) and the Rudolphs (1987) as a form of demand politics. The regime and the central state continuity allowed competing groups to make demands and claim doles/subsidies, even with declining central public investment. The central regulatory structure during Indira Gandhi's regime became more porous as many licensing regulations were relaxed. Paradoxically, despite centralization in macroeconomic policy, the licensing policy was made more flexible, not in a systemic or general way, but on a case-by-case basis, strengthening circumvention strategies by states within the bureaucratic state.

The twenty-point program (a policy program initiated by Gandhi in the early 1970s) allowed, as one of its points, the entry of larger private-sector houses in certain areas that earlier had been off-limits. The application of the MRTP Act was substantially modified to allow large houses to be constructed within medium and small-scale developments. Thus, behind the appearance of centralization, the regulatory regime under Gandhi made room for ad hoc, particularistic, and flexible mechanisms that compensated various social groups and the regional states for the costs of authoritarian centralism.

The net result, however, was that the Indian economy became an elaborate network of patronage and subsidies responding not only to economic pressure groups but also to regional interests, well embedded within the hierarchical yet porous system. Despite its efforts to counteract the effect of regional claims over economic policy, Indira Gandhi's regime was forced to deal with the political necessity of incorporating regional pressures. Her policy regime could not fully undercut the power of the regional pressures over economic policy. In fact, progressive segmentation of the license-*raj* enhanced the power of regional (and functional) interests to circumvent the system from within. By 1980, when her political base was stronger, Indira Gandhi relied on regional Congress leaders to deliver states to her national majority coalition, augmenting their role in national economic policy, but in a circumventing way.

Liberalization and the Central State in India

In July 1991, under intense exogenous fiscal pressures, the policy regime governing industry was reformed. Many of the licensing regulations were abolished. How did this policy shift change the institutional relationship between central and regional elements? Many of the constraints imposed by the central states—veto power and directives and the power to issue licenses—have been scaled back, although not completely abolished. However, many of the access opportunities—choice points, sequential decision making, and joint decision making—remain.

Moreover, the *political* executive has become much more porous with the incorporation of strong regional elements in the government itself. Thus, the crucial change in central policy has not undermined the segmented character of the central state; rather, the political logic of regionalized coalition governments has *increased* the choice points within the central state. However, with a reduction in veto and regulatory powers, regional states have *less* need to access the central state; when they do so, they continue to rely on internal choice points.

Changes in Central Constraints after 1991

In 1991 and subsequently, significant changes in the role of the central state vis-à-vis large-scale industry reduced the institutional weight of central constraints over provincial agendas. In 1991, industrial "capacity" licensing was abolished for all industries, irrespective of levels of investment, except for a short list of specified industries. In 1991, eighteen industries needed compulsory licensing, reduced from thirty-eight in 1956,[50] and by 1998, only seven industries needed licensing.[51] In addition, the items reserved for the public sector were reduced from seventeen items in 1956 to eight items, of which two more were de-reserved in 1993. An entrepreneur does not need to apply for a license to the Ministry of Industry, except for a short list of items, but needs merely to submit a memorandum to the central ministry and then seek financial, land, and infrastructure-related clearances, most of which are obtained at the regional level. The Ministry of Industry forwards the relevant applications to the regional state's industry department for local consideration. Thus, the veto and directive power of the central government remains attenuated, but the joint structure of its decision making continues to require central-regional coordination in many matters.

Continuity vis-à-vis Institutional Opportunities within the Central State

Bureaucratic choice points have been supplemented by political choice points in post-reform India. Also, central-regional interaction in some policy domains has decreased, while it has increased in some others. Industrial policy does not need vertical interaction anymore, but an enhancement of global interactions in such policy domains as foreign direct investment, export, technology transfer, and international loans[52] and fiscal policy has increased central-provincial interactions. In these domains, a joint structure of decision making and regionalized coalition government continues to demand coordination across levels of government. The internal structure of the state becomes even more salient in this changed scenario, and the decision rules of the game and sequential choice points factor in.

Moreover, coalition governments at the national level have introduced another dimension to the segmented nature of the Indian state. Two aspects of the coalition government enhance the multilevel character of the post-liberalization regulation regime. First, the national government operates not as a traditional prime minister's government, with the Prime Minister's Office (PMO) dominating policy making, but rather, as a government where different ministerial heads enjoy equal power and policy-making authority. This gives autonomous policy space to different departments, augmenting the "decentered"[53] nature of the governmental structure. Many of these department ministers, in addition, are the representatives of regional or state parties and thus pursue the developmental interests of their respective regional states aggressively. Thus, choice points within the central state have become increasingly regionalized, allowing the officials and politicians from regional states to pursue regional agendas.

Ever since 1996, the regionalization of national governments has reintroduced political choice points in the central state. The general election of 1996 saw the seat share of regional parties go up significantly. Table 3.5 demonstrates the growing strength of these parties in the national parliament since reforms began in 1991. It might be argued that in an executive-dominant system, legislators play a less important role than the cabinet. Thus, we must attend to the issue of regional representation in the cabinet. Table 3.6 shows that the representation of regional parties in the Indian cabinet has increased significantly.

The dominant view argues that coalition governments harm the reform process. Mehgnad Desai argues, "A sustained reform package would require a government at the Center with a substantial majority. This government would have to have its party in power in a large number of States. It would help if it were led by a nationally recognizable PM rather than one who has a fragile regional base" (1995, 94). In contrast, I argue that the preconditions for economic reform in a large, territorially divided federal country are significantly different from those in a small unitary country. In a large country, reform coalitions must be able to represent diverse regionally based interests; aggregation across different levels of government is more important than autonomy or state strength measured in terms of policy consistency. Coalition government with strong regional representations may be important to this process of aggregation. The existence of coalition governments in 1996, 1998, and 1999, with strong roots in the regional parties, has helped the reform process in India. Opposition against reform is unable to coalesce around one single power center as there are multiple power centers within the present government. While the coexistence of numerous parties in the national government may give the appearance of conflict and inconsistency, given a broad consensus on reforms, all the allies pursue reforms on their own and with autonomous credibility.

Under Rajiv Gandhi (prime minister from 1984 to 1989), all policy initiative flowed from one source, and reforms could be initiated only by the PMO.

Table 3.5. Share of Regional Parties' Seats and Votes in the Parliament in the 1990s (in Percent)

Lower House Election Year ⇒ Parties ⇓	1991		1996		1998		1999	
	Seat %	Vote %	Seat %	Vote %	Seat %	Vote %	Seat %	Vote %
Congress	42.7	36.5	25.8	28.8	26.0	25.8	21.0	28.3
BJP	22.0	20.1	29.6	20.3	33.4	25.6	33.5	23.8
Other National (Multi-State) Parties	20.9	24.7	18.8	20.0	11.8	6.6	13.3	14.1
Subtotal of National Parties	**85.6**	**81.3**	**74.2**	**69.1**	**71.2**	**58.0**	**67**	**66.2**
Regional (Single-State) Parties	**6.9**	**9.3**	**20.4**	**17.7**	**26.3**	**26.4**	**26.8**	**23.5**

Source: Author's calculations from David Butler, Ashok Lahiri, and Prannoy Roy, *India Decides: Elections 1952–1995* (New Delhi: Books and Things, 1995), election commission website: eci.gov.in; and G. V. L. Narasimha Rao and K. Balakrishnan, *Indian Elections: The Nineties* (New Delhi: Har
Anand Publications Ltd., 1999), p. 44.

Note: These figures don't add up to 100% as many small parties and independents are not included.

Regional and Single-State Parties: Telugu Desam, Samajwadi Party, Shiv Sena, DMK, AIADMK, Biju Janata Dal, National Congress Party, Trinamool Congress, Rashtriya Janata Dal, PMK, Indian National Lok Dal, J& K National Conference, MDMK, and RSP.

Other National (Multi-State) Parties:

1991: JD (Janata Dal), JP (Janata Party), LKDB (Lok Dal-Bahugana), CPM, CPI, ICSS (Indian Congress Socialists)

1996: CPM, CPI, Samata, Janata Dal, AIIC (Tiwari), and Janata Party

1998: CPM, CPI, Samata, Janata Dal, and BSP

1999: CPM, CPI, Janata Dal (U), and BSP

Table 3.6. Expression of Regional Parties in the Coalition Governments of
1996, 1998, 1999, and 2000

Year of new cabinet→	1996	1998	1999	2000
National or state/regional parties ↓				
% share of regional parties in cabinet	52.6 (20)	51 (22)	24 (10)*	23 (17)*
% share of national parties in cabinet	42 (16)	44 (19)	68 (28)	73 (52)
% share of Independent in cabinet	5.2 (2)	4.6 (2)	7.3 (3)	2.8 (2)
Total cabinet members	38	43	41	71

Source: Author's calculations from Government of India, *India: An Annual* (New Delhi: GOI Press, various years).
*The role of regional parties in the 1999 and 2000 cabinet is an underestimation of their role in the executive; TDP, a regional party that supports the central government from outside and is completely necessary for the government to survive. Also, somewhat invisible in the formal representation are the alliances that BJP formed with regional parties in various states; this allowed it to win more seats overall.

Now, in contrast, multiple centers of power pursue reforms with competitive vigor. The railway minister, the commerce minister, and the industry minister all vie to take part in the reforms and allocate reform spoils to their respective states.[54] Karunanidhi, the erstwhile chief minister of Tamil Nadu, was convinced by the prime minister to give up claims to the Finance Department's portfolio in the 1999 government. At that time he said, "We want finances for our state and not finance (portfolio at the center)."[55] M. Maran, the DMK (regional party from Tamil Nadu) representative, was allotted the commerce and industry portfolio. It is clear that Mursoli Maran, the industry minister of the UF (United Front) government in 1996 and commerce and industry minister in the BJP government of 1999, played a crucial role in directing investment toward Tamil Nadu. Fax messages between the Tamil Nadu government and the industry minister kept their industry department informed of any new investment coming in, even before the central cabinet knew of it.[56]

Andhra Pradesh's TDP also has utilized these choice points within the central state effectively. Andhra Pradesh (AP) was the first state to benefit from a new type of state-focused lending by the World Bank. A loan of US$543.2 million was approved in June 1998 for the multi-sectoral Andhra Pradesh Economic Restructuring Project. This was followed a few months later by a US$1 billion commitment for a series of loans for restructuring AP's power sector.[57]

Conclusion

An analysis of the rules, membership, and organizational structure of the licensing system as well as the post-1991 state shows that the central state in India is porous and has "choice points" that generate opportunities and incentives for regional states to evolve political strategies of circumvention of the central state. Certain rules, such as the *composition* of the Licensing Committees, the rules of *sequential* decision making, and the *coordination* necessitated with provincial industry ministries, are analyzed to build a detailed microanalysis of the regulatory state and the incentives generated.

This analysis contends that a formal legal institutionalist approach to the study of industrial policy, one that focuses only on macro state institutions, is deeply flawed. I suggest an approach that focuses on the incentives generated by the actually existing rules of the game internal to the regulatory regime (administrative rules as opposed to legislative intentions). Such an approach is able to reconcile the conventional assessment of India as a strong but slow-growing state with the coexistence of regionally diverse investment patterns. For a study of Indian federalism and regulatory policy, this analysis highlights the weakness of the argument that India was a highly centralist federation.

The analysis also generates insights about the macro nature of governmental institutions over time. Usually, as in presidential federations, the operation of political institutions such as the national legislature may play an important role in the relationship between government agencies. If legislatures fail to act as arenas for the expression and accommodation of local and regionally-based interests—as in India—intergovernmental bargaining and negotiation *within* the central state may become more important.[58] Between 1947 and 1996 the central bureaucracy was the main policy maker in industrial policy, and hence the central-local conflict was located within its structure. After 1996, with the onset of regionalized coalition governments, central-regional conflict has been displaced to the national cabinet.

This micro-institutional analysis reaches two new conclusions. First, the regulatory state is not centrally directed, but involves joint coordination between the center and the regional states even in domains legally under the control of the central Ministry of Industry (licensing between 1947 and 1990 and international loans and FDI [foreign direct investment] after 1991). Second, the operational rules within the central state allow room for regional elites to maneuver. Crucial choice points internal to the central bureaucracy or the central cabinet are key to this process. Thus, the various strategies adopted by the regional leadership and documented in the next chapter are a rational response to the central rules of the game.

PART III
Subnational Variation Mapped

4 | Regional Strategies toward the Dirigiste State

THE PREVIOUS CHAPTER showed that rules internal to the central state provided room to maneuver for regional states. In this chapter, I show that some regional states exploited the structure of the license-*raj* to satisfy regional investment hunger, and pursued regional developmental strategies. I describe variable but consistent strategies toward the central state adopted by rulers in the three states of Gujarat, West Bengal, and Tamil Nadu. The regional states interact and react to the national regulatory regime in widely varying ways, but each of these actions is strategic and intentional. Such vertical strategies allow some state elites to circumvent or mitigate centralist regulatory rules, thereby ensuring investment flows and regional political support from their regional constituents.

In Gujarat, regional rulers attempted to mitigate the constraining effects of the central rules by *bureaucratic* pressure, lobbying, and monitoring internal to the regime. Investment flows were quite high as a result. In West Bengal, however, *political and public* channels were employed to evolve a rhetoric of conflict and confrontation. Tamil Nadu rulers, in an opportunistic vein, followed the swings of the electoral cycle; anti-center rhetoric and lobbying efforts were followed at different moments. As a consequence, investment flows under the control of the central machinery languished in West Bengal and oscillated over time in Tamil Nadu. Central-local relations emerge as significant determinants of investment flows. Thus, the national policy regime is a combined outcome of strategic choices by regional states and choice points internal to the central state.

Table 4.1 lays out the diversity of the strategies adopted by the states. The main argument is that central policy framework engendered persistent diversity of vertical strategies rather than convergence. The table captures this diversity; the rest of the chapter explains the nature of these vertical strategies and their impact on investment flows. Most of the Indian states followed three different strategies, some of which enabled greater investment flows, whereas others had an adverse impact on regional industrialization. The three strategies are bargaining, confrontation, and populist protectionism.[1] Gujarat and West Bengal embody bargaining and confrontation respectively, and an analysis of Tamil Nadu provides support for the third strategy, populist protectionism.[2]

Bureaucratic Developmentalism in Gujarat

The actions of Gujarat's bureaucracy embodied the classic developmental role of "guiding markets." This market-guiding role of the subnational state evolved through strategic action against the central state. The subnational state was faced with a constraining central state, a constraint of relevance not only to the private sector but to the subnational state, which had an independent stake in regional development. Strategies of *mitigation* to counter the barriers to entry posed by its rules, of *circumvention* to bypass those rules that could not be mitigated, and of *enhancement* of some policies such as the joint sector concept to enhance the public-sector bias of the central government were evolved over time.

Gujarat's rulers and leaders chose to bargain with central rulers; they monitored the output of the central bureaucracy to ensure a larger share of investment locations for Gujarat, and circumvented its constraints by institutional innovation. In doing so, Gujarat's political elites adopted a radically different strategy than West Bengal's and Tamil Nadu's elites in face of the rules and regulations of the license-*raj*. Rather than position themselves against it, as did West Bengal, Gujarat's bureaucratic and political elites evolved tactics of nibbling at and circumventing the licensing system from within. These tactics were principally of *bureaucratic* infiltration, rather than a *partisan* (party-based) strategy, to ensure that the licenses came Gujarat's way. This enabled Gujarat to evolve a "bureaucratic-liberalism" model of strategic interaction with the center. Its essence is described evocatively by Gujarat's finance minister, and by a former Gujarat cadre bureaucrat:

> It is known that Gujarat today [1970] symbolizes an image of progressive liberalism. . . . We have framed our industrial policy on the foundations of the basic character of the State. Our industrial policy, therefore, has had the attitude of complementarity at its core. We have not functioned on mutually excessive alternatives. (Jashvant Mehta, Minister of Finance and Industries, 1970)[3]

> Our [Gujarat government officials'] motto was "necessity is the mother of invention"; the license-quota-*raj* was a constraint and it led us to innovate around it. (N. Vittal, December 1997)[4]

This "bureaucratic infiltration" strategy had three main characteristics. First, it countered a highly rigid system in New Delhi with constant bureaucratic pressure. Second, flexible alternatives such as the "joint-sector" route effectively enhanced the emphasis on public-sector development at the center in favor of joint control by public and private sectors at the state level. Third, state bureaucrats employed informal informational channels to succeed at

Table 4.1. Three Strategic Models of Center-Regional Linkages and Their Political Correlates

	Bureaucratic Liberalism	Political Confrontation	Populist Protection
Cases	Gujarat	West Bengal	Tamil Nadu
Vertical Strategies of Regional Elites toward the Center	Bureaucratic entrepreneurial strategy	Confrontational strategy	Populist strategy that oscillated between alliance formation and oppositional regionalism
Main Actors	Bureaucratic	Political	Political
Mode of Action	Bargaining	Confrontational opposition and eschew bargaining	Lobbying and/or regional protest
Channel of Access	Central bureaucracy	Public sphere and media	Political sphere and electoral alliances
Timing of Action	Long-term and consistent	Long-term and consistent	Episodic and inconsistent (varies with the electoral cycle)
Type of Action	Monitoring and information gathering of the output of the central bureaucracy	Absence of monitoring; rhetoric of regionalism	Absence of monitoring; rhetoric of regionalism but declines over time
Institutions	Creation of agencies for the above functions (institutional innovation)	Absence of bargaining agencies; rather the creation of partisan agencies (institutional innovation)	Absence of bargaining agencies; rather the creation of cultural agencies (institutional innovation)
Regional Correlates	Absence of linguistic subnationalism	Linguistic subnationalism	Linguistic subnationalism
Types of Politics	Nonpartisan, integrationist politics	Partisan	Opportunistic
Type of Center-Region Relationship	Pragmatic integration	Ideological regionalism	Pragmatic regionalism

these tasks; in a highly regulated system, information was at a premium. The aggressive search and use of information introduced some competition within a highly hierarchical and noncompetitive system.

The first aspect of the strategy was evident in the constant and careful monitoring of the licensing process in New Delhi, a form of "industrial espionage."[5] Initially (in the mid-1950s) many regional states, especially West Bengal and Bombay, began to evolve strategies of infiltration.[6] Gujarat perfected its tactics over time and consistently followed them despite changes of government in Gandhinagar (the capital of Gujarat state) or New Delhi.

Since the late 1960s, but most consistently in the 1970s, the officials of the Gujarat government located in New Delhi established contacts with key Ministry of Industry officials, seeking information as well as support for Gujarat-specific licensing applications.[7] This involved procuring information on future projects, allotment of licenses, and the status of licenses granted for Gujarat, as well as following up to ensure that the applications for Gujarat were implemented effectively and quickly. The Ministry of Industry had a list of all license applications (Letters of Intent, or LOIs). The task of getting information about the list of prospective private-sector companies and their preferred choice of locations was an important one. Three sets of information were valuable: one about the Gujarat applications, another about those who had not stated a preference, and a third about those license applications that were in direct competition with Gujarat applications. Information about Gujarat's (but only that state's) LOIs, after they had been granted, came to the Ministry of Industry in Gujarat as a matter of licensing procedure;[8] the central Ministry of Industry sends one copy of the license application to the relevant state government for their recommendation. Armed with this prior information, Gujarat government officials contacted the private parties who had specified Gujarat as a location, in order to ensure that they actually invested in Gujarat.[9] The promptness with which the regional agency responded with its recommendation played some role in the final grant of the licenses. Interviews revealed that Gujarat generally responded immediately by sending a reply to the central government as well as sending a letter to the concerned private party "expressing thanks" for their interest in investing in the state and also inviting the investor to examine various locations. Thus, the response of the Gujarat industry department played a crucial role in implementing the projects faster. Many businesspeople admitted that they had been very surprised to receive a letter from the Government of Gujarat (GoG) soon after they had applied for a license.[10] These organized follow-up and promotional efforts were crucial in enabling the regional state to implement their LOIs. Constant support by the state government proved to be very useful in the mid-1970s, when it became increasingly difficult to get licenses.

However, the other two types of information were not available in the normal course of things. Information regarding investors who were *not* investing in Gujarat and those who had not marked their locational choice and fell under the category of "others" in SIA (Secretariat of Industrial Approvals, Ministry of Industry) data was crucial information. Gujarat officials contacted these businesses as well, in order to show potential sites in Gujarat (at the expense of Gujarat government) and to offer various incentives to persuade these investors to finally locate in Gujarat.[11] This information about those investors who were in the category of "others" was classified information and hence difficult to obtain. Bureaucratic camaraderie, payment under the table, and social networks of informational access were various mechanisms used to garner this information.[12] Interviews suggest that Gujarat started this practice around 1965–66 and continued to follow the practice on a consistent and systematic basis from 1970 onward.

My own observations in the Gujarat government industry office confirmed that monitoring of investment projects was taken seriously. A huge chart on one of the walls of the industry office lists in great detail the number of applications received by the central ministry, their current status, the extent of investment and employment envisaged for each project, and their locations. The official in charge of the "monitoring cell" told me that the chart is updated monthly, allowing them to keep track of changes over time.[13]

Obtaining crucial and usually informal information was key to the process. How many projects would the central government allow in any one sector? Information about prospective sectoral priorities of the central ministries would allow the Gujarat government to propose "good" projects.[14] Informal information about matters such as the licensed capacity, the industry preferred by the Licensing Committee, and other states that had applied for the same license that Gujarat was applying for allowed the state's representatives to be better prepared if the cases came up in the official meetings.[15] One IAS (Indian Administrative Services) official of the Gujarat cadre said to me,

> In order to stay ahead of our competitors, we as officers of the Gujarat government needed to do a lot of industrial research. I used to regularly read industry magazines like *Chemical Industry*, etc. to figure out what kind of project was feasible, what technology would require low import content and what would the government [central] approve. Also, we had to constantly pick the brains of bureaucrats in the various ministries so that we could know what kind of projects they would support. Our IAS networks came in useful to do this. I used to try to find out through informal channels what were the objections, if any, to any of Gujarat's projects. Then, we would do research to find counterarguments.[16]

These efforts allowed the Gujarat Industry Department officials at Licensing Committee meetings to build a coherent defense. As a result, a large majority of Gujarat licenses were approved. This is confirmed by the data on licenses for the period 1974–90 presented in Chapter 3 (Figure 3.1).

Moreover, even when industrial capacities were frozen for the private sector, the SIA could and would approve public-sector projects. The Gujarat Industrial Investment Corporation (GIIC) applied for these licenses, and after getting the license, brought in a private industrialist as a joint-sector partner.[17] This tactic bypassed the central rule of discouraging the private sector.

All these tactics were possible as a departmental wing in Gujarat's bureaucracy called the Licensing Monitoring Cell was created in 1969–70. These efforts to monitor licenses became more institutionalized when an informal Industry Department "Tea Club" that had begun at the initiative of the industry secretary as a social forum soon became regular. A few IAS officials started to meet in an official's home to discuss plans to increase investment to the state. This became further institutionalized in 1977 when iNDEXTb,[18] an autonomous and promotional agency, was formed within the Department of Industry, Government of Gujarat, to ensure the flow of investments to the state.[19] The institutional creation of an independent agency dedicated to attracting investments was in itself an index of "credible commitment." Its mandate and sources of authority were uniquely designed to keep it independent of political and even bureaucratic influence. This was done by making its financial source independent of the state budget. The initial capital was provided by contributions from three state industry corporations: the Gujarat Industry Development Corporation (GIDC), the Gujarat Industrial Investment Corporation (GIIC), and the Gujarat State Finance Corporation (GSFC).[20]

I did not find evidence that this conscious targeting and monitoring of the licensing system and of potential private-sector investors was pursued and implemented by any other state.[21] Maharashtrian officials felt that their state did not need to "encourage (investment) consciously" as various natural factors were favorable for investment in Maharashtra.[22] West Bengal did introduce some bureaucratic infiltration in the mid-1950s but soon began to favor a more partisan approach.[23]

Liaison offices of many state governments in Delhi oversaw this systematic monitoring of the central government output. They operated like embassies and coordinated state government actions toward various ministries of the central government. Gujarat had a definite presence in New Delhi. An office of the GIIC worked as a liaison to the central government Industry Department.[24] The GoG "embassy" in New Delhi kept in regular touch with various important central government bureaucrats.

In contrast, West Bengal's Delhi office had low priority, in that it a lacked a higher-level official.[25] The West Bengal Administrative Reforms Committee (1983) said the following regarding West Bengal's office in the capital (despite this recommendation no such office was established in New Delhi at this time):[26]

> The State government [West Bengal] has to maintain a major presence in the nation's capital. It has been the experience of other State governments

that an effective liaison office in New Delhi facilitates dealings with the different ministries. Such a liaison office can speed the release of funds from the Ministry of Finance and other ministries, and keep the Members of parliament informed on issues concerning the State, which might be raised on the floor of the parliament. . . .

The condition of the liaison office the State government [West Bengal] at present maintains in New Delhi is disappointing. Although there is a Special Commissioner for liaison work with the rank of the Secretary, he does not even have jurisdiction over the staff of, for instance, the departments of Information and Cultural Affairs, Transport and Public works located in New Delhi. This arrangement needs to be radically changed. The commissioner for liaison work should be placed in charge of all personnel of the State government working in New Delhi irrespective of departmental affiliations; all activities in the nation's capital should be carried out under his guidance and coordination. The office needs considerable augmentation of staff. Apart from the Commissioner, it is important that another official is placed with the office who had held tenure in New Delhi either with the Ministry of Finance or the Ministry of Industry, and can therefore maintain regular contacts with these two ministries. The office should set up a proper filing system so that detailed information of all cases and problems, which need to be discussed in New Delhi, in addition to general facts, and information pertaining to the State are available on tape. . . .

It is desirable that the liaison office is attached to the Chief Minister's office. . . . The Liaison Commissioner will have to maintain contacts not just with the Union Ministries but also with other State governments, and sometimes with the representatives of foreign missions too. . . . Unfortunately, the quality of hospitality accorded by the State government to representatives of the Union government, representatives of other State governments, members of parliament, legislators from other States as well as foreign dignitaries leaves a great deal to be desired. . . . We should be at par with what other [state] Governments are capable of offering. (Government of West Bengal 1983, 25–26)

In contrast to the failure of West Bengal to ensure intra-level linkages within the license-*raj*, Gujarat's strategy was to work slowly but persistently at building channels of political access inside the bureaucracy. Partisan channels were relatively neglected in favor of bureaucratic channels. This "industrial espionage" meant that GoG officials were in constant touch with various layers of the industrial bureaucracy in New Delhi. As noted by a retired industry secretary of Gujarat,

I did not have any ego in meeting a junior officer (Deputy Secretary or Section Officer in New Delhi) in his office. IAS officials from other States would have thought twice about doing so. This also meant that the junior official went out of his way to help me. Can you imagine an Industry Secretary of a state visiting the office of a junior officer rather than calling him to his office? Whenever I was in Delhi, I made it a point to meet the relevant officials. I would get a lot of simple information if not much more else. In addition,

when Gujarat cases came up in the Licensing Committee meeting, these officers had some informal knowledge about the cases as well as a stake in de-
fending them. I made it a point to urge and encourage other GoG officials to
continue this practice.

Alternative Hypothesis

It could be argued that this strategy of "bureaucratic liberalism" was
merely an offshoot of the congruity of Congress rule in Gujarat and at the
center since 1947. However, a careful analysis of the center-state relations between Gujarat and the central Congress Party shows that the relationship had
been marked by conflict. Very strong leaders—Sardar Patel, and later Morarji
Desai—have held office in Gujarat; they did not merely toe the center's line.
This leads me to argue that the state's strategies toward the center, rather than
party congruity, were (and are) the crucial variable in determining investment
flows. What the states managed to obtain from the center depended upon the
bargaining power of the state's leadership and the strategies they adopted, irrespective of party affiliation. An analysis of the central-local relations between Gujarat and the center shows that despite the existence of a conflict-
ridden intra-party relationship between the two, what became crucial was the
strategy Gujarat's leader adopted to deal with that conflict.

In terms of center-state party relations, Gujarat, despite being ruled by
the Congress Party for most of its political history and despite the role of its
leadership in nationalist history (Mahatma Gandhi, Sardar Patel, and Morarji
Desai were all from Gujarat), has not enjoyed a very close relationship with
the Congress regimes in New Delhi. In the 1960s, for example, the Gujarat
Provincial Congress Committee (GPCC) retained an independent stance relative to the central party (Sheth 1976a, 85). "The entire list of candidates presented by the PEC [Provincial Election Committee] was to be approved by the
CEC [Central Election Committee] so much so that even Nehru was not allowed to open the issue of the ousting of the Jivraj ministry in the Congress
executive meeting. This was because the GPCC was devoid of any faction and
Morarji's position as the supreme leader of Gujarat was accepted as such" (85).
The inharmonious relationship between Morarji Desai and Indira Gandhi
was reflected in the relations between Gujarat and the central government in
the early 1970s despite the selection of the chief minister, Ghanshyam Oza, by
the PM in 1972. Prime Minister Indira Gandhi tried unsuccessfully to break
the Congress (O) (a breakaway faction from the Congress Party) government
during 1969–70. In 1974, when Mrs. Gandhi declared president's rule in
Gujarat following a series of riots and student agitations, Chimanbhai Patel,
the leader of the legislative party in Gujarat, refused to step down from the
leadership position and resigned from the assembly. Patel was subsequently

suspended from the party for six years. Thus, intra-party relations between Gujarat and the center have not been very congenial. These alliance dynamics have led to widespread complaints that Gujarat has not been given fair treatment by the center in central grants and the location of public-sector sites. The Nav Nirman movement in Gujarat was a testimony to oppositional relations evolving into violent and "extra-parliamentary opposition" (Wood 1975). Wood's analysis of the 1974 Nav Nirman movement in Gujarat is worth citing:

> As suggested in the beginning, Central interventionism had a negative impact on the autonomy of state political development. Especially in Gujarat and Bihar, the imposition of a Chief Minister [Ghanshyam Oza] dependent for his authority on New Delhi solved no intra-Congress disputes, and lent an atmosphere of illegitimacy to the State government. Secondly, in matters where central control of state-affected economic decisions was salient, the political relationship between central and state regimes became extremely important. In the case of Gujarat, the absence of a spokesman in the central cabinet after Morarji Desai's departure left many Gujaratis feeling that their legitimate interests—especially with regard to the Narmada project—were being ignored by the Center. (332)

It is clear that the mere presence of ruling party congruity in the center-state does not preclude center-state conflicts. I argue that the crucial element is the *strategy adopted by the state leadership in the face of conflicts*. It is important to note that despite the nature of center-state party conflicts, "the Congress government . . . adopted a gentle style in dealing with the Center and pursued its case with a low profile, patience and forbearance" (Sheth 1976b, 86). Other researchers working on Gujarat have also noted the "pragmatism" of Gujarati politics. John R. Wood had this to say of Gujarat:

> Several notable features of Gujarati politics reveal the pragmatism inherent in Gujarati economic activity. First, Gujarati politics has never been ideological or separatist. . . . There have been no strong regional parties in Gujarat. . . . The Maha Gujarat Janata Parishad, which agitated between 1956 and 1960 for the creation of a separate Gujarat, disappeared soon after Maharashtra and Gujarat were carved out of Bombay State in 1960. Gujaratis identify strongly with all-India politics and usually seek to influence, not oppose, New Delhi. Clearly their stake in India's economic development is instrumental here. Despite a lack of powerful representation in New Delhi, the post–World War I habit of Gujarati involvement in national politics continues. (1995, 26)

West Bengal: The Strategy of Partisan Confrontation

West Bengal and Tamil Nadu chose alternative strategies despite center-state conflicts that were similar to those found in Gujarat. Regarding West

Bengal, I establish two propositions. Conflict between the parties that ruled West Bengal (Congress (I) and Left Front)[27] and the national ruling party (Congress (I)) has been a continuous feature of West Bengal politics. Despite different partisan ideologies, the Congress Party and the Left Front in the state have pursued confrontational strategies toward the center. Furthermore, these strategies have differed significantly from those pursued by Gujarat's and Tamil Nadu's elites.

The West Bengal Provincial Congress Committee (PCC) and the Left Front have both had conflictual and oppositional relations with the center. In that sense, the vertical components of the ideologies of the regional units have been very similar. After 1947 West Bengal, despite being very important to the national-level Congress Party and despite the close relationship between Nehru and B.C. Roy, felt itself to be treated unfairly. The unique problems of West Bengal after 1947—the second partition, the refugee problems— compelled its leaders to demand, largely for legitimate reasons, special attention from the Center (Weiner 1967; Franda 1968; Saroj Chakravarty 1974). While the hostile relationship between central governments and various Left Front governments (1967–69 and 1977–90) in West Bengal has been the focus of much political commentary and journalistic ink (Chaudhuri 1976; Kohli 1984), such difficult center-state relations preceded the coming of the Left in West Bengal. An important set of correspondence between Nehru and B.C. Roy, the chief minister (CM) in the 1950s, shows that Roy did have important differences with Nehru, which he was not afraid to voice. These differences related to a wide range of issues: the choice of a national anthem, the fiscal policy of the Government of India, the resignation of a state cabinet minister after a by-election electoral reversal, and the issue of central grants for the refugee problem in the regional state (Saroj Chakravarty 1974, 101–104, 105, 122–25, 140–42). The following exchange between B.C. Roy and Nehru gives a snapshot of the conflict:

> Allow me to repeat what I have said more than once that when Bengal was partitioned, West Bengal started with a deficit balance of 2½ crores still unpaid. We were badly treated by a Centre which took away a part of our share of Income tax and Jute Tax allotments and distributed the income tax moiety to other provinces and appropriated the Jute tax share for themselves. . . . [W]e were informed in March 1948 that our share of the income tax receipts has been reduced from 20% to 12%. . . . The remaining 2½ crores was distributed to other provinces. See how iniquitous this new arrangement proves to be: Bombay with a population of 21 million received an additional share from 20 to 21% whereas Bengal with the same population or perhaps a little more got her share reduced from 20% to 12%. And yet West Bengal and Bombay contributed the same amounts towards the income tax pool. . . .
> I fully realize the tremendous difficulties which the Centre has to face having been myself responsible for industrial and other constructive schemes. I

know—I am convinced—that these difficulties are due to the vacillating policies of the Centre. They have no definite vision and method of executing a scheme; the individual components of the Centre do not act in a team. You are wrong when you say that the difficulties of the Centre are greater than those of the provinces but we may agree to differ on this point. (Letter from B.C. Roy to the Prime Minister, December 1, 1949)[28]

Later, in response to Nehru's reply, Roy reiterated his point:

[I] felt that I should emphasize two points, namely, firstly, to point out that there was not much cohesion between the different departments of the government whether Central or Provincial, and secondly, there is not much of cooperation and coordination in matters of common interest between the Centre and the provinces. (Letter dated December 8, 1949)[29]

Franda's seminal study of center-state relations during the Congress period reiterates my conclusion:

The evidence from these case studies indicates that political leaders and groups in West Bengal were not constrained to accept central government decisions concerning either state matters or constitutionally central matters, even during that period when the Congress party was in power at both central and State levels. (1968, 6)

Another instance of center-state conflict is the creation of an industrial complex at Durgapur by the West Bengal government (Chanda 1965, 282). The government's memorandum to the Third Finance Commission put forward a forceful argument on behalf of other states that central expenditure was relatively greater on state subjects than on those in the Union List (Chanda 1965, 283–84; Franda 1968).

The difference in terms of center-state relations between the Congress rule in West Bengal (1947–67 and 1971–77) and the Left Front rule (1977–onward) lay not in the ideological positions of the two parties, or in the existence of center-state confrontation on many issues (which existed in both periods), but rather in the political routes the parties used to oppose the center. Despite the perceived conflict of interest between West Bengal at the time of B.C. Roy's chief ministry and the central government, the hostility was not allowed to spill over into agitational politics (Jha and Mishra 1993). B.C. Roy adopted a tough but constitutional route that can be called "intra-party bargaining" to address the interests of West Bengal in its dealings with the central government. In contrast, what distinguishes the Left Front rule is not its ideological differences from the central government but rather the choice of a political strategy that stresses *inter-party zero-sum confrontational bargaining.* As stated by Chaudhuri,

It [CPI(M)] took the State along the path of ideological hostility to New Delhi during UF rule and made itself a vehicle of Bengali regional sentiment.

> ... The Chief Ministers do not normally lead "struggles" against the Centre. But in a state with a built-in "politics of scarcity" the successful Chief Minister is by necessity a bargainer par excellence for more food aid, financial grants and assistance at New Delhi. If the State's "client status" is emphasized thereby, this is perhaps an inescapable part of the federal process. (1976, 384)

While the Communist Party of India (Marxist) [CPI(M)] retreated from most of its radical "socialist" stances after 1977, there was continuity in its anti-center policy. The Left Front made its anti-center stance an ideological plank in itself. In the field of industrial policy, the Left Front government has argued that it has been discriminated against by the center. In response, the Congress government of Indira Gandhi has continued to argue that the CPI(M) is irresponsible and creates problems of law and order.[30] The failure of the Left Front to attract investment has been laid at the door of its class-based politics, which, it is argued, creates an atmosphere of confrontation and class hostility. To counter this attack, the Left Front government from West Bengal has been specifically vocal in its political argument that it has been discriminated against in public-sector allocation and the granting of licenses on account of the ideological nature of its rule. The CPI(M) followed its anti-center policy with strong political and institutional commitment. This is evident from the following four pieces of evidence:

First, the mere *volume* of official public press output on the question of center-state relations in West Bengal is considerable. This output served to ensure continuous attention to the question of central discrimination. The political and electoral issue space has been successfully redefined by the ruling Left Front. Approximately 75 percent of the documents released by the Department of Information and Cultural Affairs (I&CA), GoWB (Government of West Bengal), are on center-state relations. No other opposition party government (DMK in Tamil Nadu, TDP in Andhra Pradesh, AGP in Assam, or Akali Dal in Punjab) makes center-state relations such a regular focus of attention. One of the major tasks of the I&CA department has been to disseminate information on the question of central discrimination in industrial development. Some of the documents that raise the issue of confrontational center-state relations released by the I&CA department are "A Study on the Industrial Scene in West Bengal," "A Note on Haldia Petrochemicals Project and Bakreshwar Thermal Power Project," "Industrial Progress and Rural Development in West Bengal," "The Left Front Government: Its Performance and Significance," "Industry in West Bengal: Perspective and Present Position," "Some Aspects of the Seventh Plan: West Bengal's Views," "Industrialization in West Bengal: More Facts," "Address of Jyoti Basu to the Ninth and Tenth Finance Commission," "Jyoti Basu on Industrial Policy of the Left Front Government," and various budget speeches of the finance ministers.

Two things are clear from an analysis of these documents. First, industrialization was a clear priority of the Left Front government, and thus the goals were similar to the goals pursued in Gujarat and Tamil Nadu. Second, despite these goals, there was a conscious strategy to highlight the role of the central government in discriminating against West Bengal and thereby evolve a consistent strategy of opposition against the central government.[31]

Second, almost every public statement of key ministers on center-state relations is published and circulated widely. A notable example is the publication of two volumes that contain most of the chief minister's letters to the prime minister and industry minister.[32] These letters relate to development schemes, problems, law and order, and the Assam situation.[33] The ones relating to problems of law and order adopt an extremely critical and threatening tone and criticize the West Bengal Congress (I)'s actions to the president of the Congress (I). The CPI(M) is criticizing the West Bengal Congress Party to the prime minister, who is a member of the same party. Some of these criticisms are worth citing.

> It is reported that Shri A. B. A. Ghani Khan Chowdhury, Union Minister for Energy, Power and Coal, in a statement on the floor of the Lok Sabha on 9.7.80 accused the government of West Bengal of indulging in "smuggling and earning tonnes of money." This matter was discussed in a meeting of the Council of Ministers of this [the West Bengal] government today. The Ministers were distressed to find that such wild allegations could be leveled by a central Minister against a state government without making any attempt to verify the facts. The council of ministers unanimously decided to lodge a strong protest against the reported statement and urge you to direct him immediately to either prove the allegations or to express an unqualified apology.[34]

> I take this opportunity to inform you both as a leader of the Congress (I) and the Prime Minister, that according to information with us a section of the Congress (I) in West Bengal, being in a hurry to have our government dismissed, are making desperate attempts to disturb the peace and create a law and order situation, and to lay the blame for any violence that they indulge in on the CPI(M). . . . All of us should feel concerned about the law and order situation in all States whichever is the party that runs the government. I think that it will be useful to compare from time to time the law and order situation in all States including the centrally administered ones so that we can learn the proper lessons.[35]

These letters are the embodiment of the partisan confrontational strategy: the purpose is not to achieve a solution to the problem but to be *seen* as agitating against the Congress Party and the center.

Third, the commitment of West Bengal's leadership to the pursuit of a partisan confrontational strategy was evident from the establishment of and the key role played by such institutional and political agencies as the I&CA

department, GoWB; *Ganashakti,* the Bengali newspaper of the CPI(M); and *People's Democracy,* another CPI(M) newspaper; as well as the support given to various cultural and educational agencies such as Nandan (the institute that has become the center of cultural life in Calcutta). These cultural and political organizations served to corroborate the state government's positions and offer the state government substantial political support. In addition, this support signaled to investors and the central government alike that the political elite was interested in sustained and committed opposition to the center, thus making its strategy credible. In contrast to such public and political channels utilized by West Bengal, Gujarat raises issues of center-state differences from within the bureaucratic channels and through bureaucratic agencies such as the iNDEXTb. Both strategies, although contradictory to each other, were extremely successful because they were both credibly sustained by the state's political elites and corresponding institutions.

Fourth, the Left Front government successfully molded public opinion on the question of central discrimination.[36] Almost every public statement on economic issues by the Government of West Bengal raised the issue of central discrimination. One hundred percent of the public statements on industrial issues refer to various perceived instances of central discrimination. Such cases as the much-delayed Haldia Petrochemicals Project, the Bakreshwar Thermal Project, and the Freight Equalization Policy form the folklore of party and public opinion across classes and castes. Interviews reveal widespread and consistent information dissemination on the question of center-state relations across party lines. Most illiterate and literate people, supporters and opponents of the regime, upper and lower castes, know about various instances of central discrimination. Rhetorical tactics abound. One of the most famous examples of rhetorical flourishes is the blood donation camp organized to raise money for the Bakreshwar project despite the absurdity of the idea that a blood donation camp could raise adequate money for a thermal power project! The Left Front managed to achieve extraordinary unity on the question of center-state discrimination, cutting across class lines, and enhanced the linguistic-regional divide. Even more so, the Left Front government took initiatives at the national level in raising the issue of center-state relations at various public forums.[37] In addition, it attempted to organize other regional states, especially the opposition-ruled states, in coalitions that could organize their action against the central government. The 1980s saw many national-level conferences of states organized under the initiative of the Left Front.[38]

This evidence all points toward the fact that West Bengal pursued a consistent and successful strategy of partisan confrontation against the center. Paradoxically, this critical posture was predicated upon a dependent developmental strategy that relied on the central public sector to solve most of West Bengal's problems. In that sense, the Left Front regime after 1977 was strikingly similar to the Congress regime of B.C. Roy (1948–62). This strategic model of confrontational opposition led the state government to abandon any state-level attempts to infiltrate the license-*raj* from within.

Mixed Vertical Strategy in Tamil Nadu: Anti-Center Mobilization (1967–77) and Opportunistic Alliance Formation (1980s)

This ascendance of cultural subnationalism in the 1950s and 1960s and its circumcision to "populist rather than empowerment populism"[39] over time also shaped the developmental strategy adopted by the state's ruling elites toward the center. Lobbying of the license-*raj* and pressuring for public-sector projects from the center was abandoned in favor of anti-center rhetoric. Yet at various times the parties also flirted with alliance with the center. Thus, Tamil Nadu's elites oscillated between anti-center mobilization and opportunistic alliance formation with the Congress Party, when it suited their regional reelection chances.

Tamil Nadu elites' strategy toward the license-*raj* changed over time, partly to coincide with electoral cycles and the extent of anti-center mobilization in the province. In the 1950s and 1960s, like other regional states' leaders, they tried to get as many public-sector projects and licenses as possible. However, the tactic of influence employed by *all* regimes in Tamil Nadu differed from those employed by Gujarat's government. All governing elites used political, partisan, or public channels in their attempt to reregulate and influence central policy. From 1950 to 1967, at the time of the Congress regime in Tamil Nadu, partisan, party channels rather than bureaucratic infiltration were used to direct the licenses toward Tamil Nadu. DMK and later AIADMK (regional parties ruling Tamil Nadu after 1967) ignored an intra-party strategy, opting instead for episodic bargaining at the time of elections to secure big and prestigious projects. Yet the regional parties in the state also employed public channels. Thus, the strategy of Tamil Nadu under the Dravidian parties was one of "populist regional protection," which implied opportunistic bargaining at key electoral moments and anti-center invectives at other moments.

Tamil Nadu from 1950 to 1967 tried to procure as much central public-sector investment as possible through political lobbying and bargaining. Regional leaders such as Kamraj (of Kamraj Plan fame) and R. Venkataraman (state industry minister in the 1960s and later the president of India), as state Congress leaders, played an important role in lobbying for the allotment of the maximum number of central public-sector projects. This strategy was instrumental in pushing Tamil Nadu ahead as a regional beneficiary of the public sector–dominated growth in the 1950s and the 1960s.[40] In this period, West Bengal too, led by Dr. B.C. Roy (from 1950 to 1962), benefited as a result of central public-sector investment in the state. In the period from 1950 to 1969 most states tried to get as much central public-sector investment as possible and established state-level public-sector units as a complementary strategy. A very senior IAS official from Tamil Nadu who later became the Reserve Bank governor said in an interview, "In those times (before 1991), we used to first lobby for a certain sector/industry to be in the public sector. After that had been achieved, senior leaders like R. Venkataraman[41] used to make the case for its location in Tamil Nadu. Tamil Nadu got many projects by using this strategy."[42] Tamil Nadu thereby followed an explicitly party-based or partisan route to industrialization. Since the central government in power was also the Congress Party with close ties with regional leaders and control over the allotment of the public-sector investment, the public sector became the preferred channel for securing investment.

After 1967, Tamil Nadu was ruled by DMK and AIADMK regional parties, which had their historical genesis in a regional populism of anti-north and anti-Hindi agitation (before 1991). After the rise of Dravidian parties, the strategy of lobbying with the central government came into disfavor. The governments at this time adopted a public, partisan strategy of strong anti-center one-upmanship against the Indira Gandhi regime. Yet the decline of confrontational subnationalism within Tamil Nadu in the late 1970s and the onset of alliance politics initiated by Mrs. Gandhi led M. G. Ramchandran, the chief minister of Tamil Nadu from 1977 to 1987, to move between radical anti-center posturing on the one hand and opportunistic bargaining and alliance formation with Indira Gandhi on the other.

The Phase of Anti-Center Strategy

The DMK (more than the AIADMK) made north-south domination and center-state conflicts over economic policy a major ideological issue in its party program. When it came to power (1967) it pressured the central government to give more autonomy to the state governments to pursue industrial development.[43] For example, the DMK throughout its mobilizational phase and after coming to power "charged the Congress with bad management of State-owned industries, corruption, and dictatorship" (Barnett 1976, 137). In July 1967, the chief minister, Annadurai, wrote to the prime minister, Indira Gandhi, and the cabinet transport minister urging them to stick with the original plan of making Tuticorin a major port. Apprehensions had been raised that Tuticorin could be developed only as a fishing harbor. The state minister for information, Satyavanimuthu, said in Tuticorin that the project should not be given up and the state government should do everything to make that project possible.[44] Explicit partisan pressure was used to get projects for Tamil Nadu. This implied that the DMK was concerned with industrialization of the state. However, its stress on "Marwari" and northern "rich" domination of southern economy meant that outside investment did dry up during the 1960s and the 1970s.[45] The DMK's rhetoric argued that "Tamil Nadu was being cheated by New Delhi" (Washbrook 1989, 252) and that greedy Marwaris had robbed Tamil Nadu. Given this hostility, the so-called northern and Marwari investors were hesitant to invest in Tamil Nadu.[46] Independent policies to attract Tamils or to encourage small-scale investors within the state were nonexistent. Thus, the consequences for investment in Tamil Nadu from the late 1960s onward were mixed, contributing to advancement in some spheres, such as industrial infrastructure, industrial estates, and power/energy, but weakness in other spheres, such as investment from outside Tamil Nadu and efforts to ensure a high number of licenses. This contributed to Tamil Nadu's occupying an intermediate position in terms of industrial indicators after the 1960s.

Alliance Formation and Opportunistic Bargaining with the Center

Subsequently, MGR (M. Gopala Ramchandran, the chief minister of Tamil Nadu from 1977 to 1987) and the AIADMK (All-India Anna Dravida Munnetra Kazhagam)[47] embraced a pan-Indian nationalism and sought to downplay the strident regionalism of the DMK regime. While seeking some continuity with the Dravidian and Tamil nationalism tradition, MGR indicated that he never "favored anti-Brahmanism and that the ADMK would oppose ethnic exclusion" (Subramanian 1999, 265). He moved the AIADMK party's ideology against Tamil revivalism and sought to depoliticize the educational policy of the government by claiming that the question of the medium of instruction could be left for educationists to decide (Subramanian 1999, 265). Policies associated with the AIADMK and MGR moved further down the social end of the continuum. AIADMK's support base expanded to include poorer people—fishermen, rickshaw pullers, poor and destitute women—and, crucially, leadership of the party units in many districts was given to non-Tamils. He is credited with the extension of social security provisions targeted toward certain occupational groups, basic needs programs, and a massive food program known as the Noon Meal scheme. Thus, MGR instituted extensive and regular welfare policies targeted to the poorer segments of Tamilnad society such as the AdiDravidas (untouchables) and poor women, in an attempt to widen the electoral base of the ADMK. However, he displayed some ambivalence toward backward caste reservations and the interests of farmers (Swamy 1996, 181). In terms of center-state and north-south divide, he inaugurated a period of alliance politics with Indira Gandhi and Congress downplaying the conflictual relationship that had marked the DMK rule.[48] Thus, his strategy was partisan but pragmatic. This did lead to the location of some industrial projects in Tamil Nadu during this period.

These oscillations over time had repercussions on Tamil Nadu's incorporation into the national regulatory regime. The lack of an explicit politico-economic strategy with a politically opportunistic bargaining strategy in alliance formation with the ruling party at the center (1977–88; 1991–96) meant that Tamil Nadu lost out in the public-sector allocations, while the lack of an independent state-level strategy like that of Maharashtra, Gujarat, and Karnataka was reflected in the regional economic decline that was apparent between 1970 and 1990 in Tamil Nadu (MIDS 1988; Swaminathan 1994).

Suresh Krishna, the CEO of a Madras-based automobile company called TVS, felt very strongly that the Tamil Nadu government did not lobby enough with the central government in the 1970s and the 1980s. His writings about the automobile industry reflect that frustration. He suggested that in the 1970s the regional balance in automobile industry shifted toward the north of India, although the south, specifically Tamil Nadu, had many strong companies involved in automobiles and auto components. Krishna's suggestions to the Tamil Nadu government in 1984 are worth quoting:

> As a first step, the Tamil Nadu government should establish close liaison with the Center so that its existing strengths can be capitalized on for locating any new manufacturing unit. It needs to be emphasized what it has to offer by way of skilled labor and ready avenue of auto components, and the largest auto ancillary base in the country. It should also take urgent steps to back up this effort by offering substantial improved fiscal and other incentives to attract future entrepreneurs. The incentives should be better than those offered by any other State and there can be no justification for the existing vehicle manufacturing in Tamil Nadu having to look elsewhere for better terms and opportunities due to lack of initiative by the home State.[49]

I asked Mr. Krishna in an interview if he thought that the Tamil Nadu government had done some of what he suggested in the 1970s. His answer was: "No, not really, it's only after 1994 or so that auto manufacturers have begun to come back to Tamil Nadu. Throughout the 1970s and 1980s we did no lobbying towards the center in an effort to attract auto industries."[50]

Vertical Interactions in Pre-1991 India

The core as reflected in the central licensing regime and the periphery as reflected in the vertical strategies of regional political elites are joined politically in very different ways across the Indian states; the three states chosen for study in this book represent three models of such central-local linkages.[51] Differences in their local-national political linkages are fundamental to understanding the diverse investment and licensing patterns across states. But contrary to common understandings, it was not merely ideology that dictated the linkage. The ideology of anti-centrism was a strategic choice in the federal equation rather than a determining factor in itself. The political tactics and instruments that I document in this chapter arise out of typologies of politico-economic strategies that the states' political regimes adopt toward the national state over time. They fall into three broad patterns of intergovernmental bargaining. First, bureaucratic liberalism depended upon covert lobbying and non-zero-sum bargaining and was pursued by Gujarat and Maharashtra.[52] Second, the regional populist strategy was reflected in a kind of opportunistic bargaining when Tamil Nadu oscillated between opposition to the center and electoral alliance formation with the Congress Party from 1977 onward. Third, the partisan confrontational strategy brought together the pursuit of a zero sum and confrontational bargaining with the center, which West Bengal's Left Front did very successfully.[53]

The behavioral correlates of *vertical competition* implied that states did not compete against each other directly. Given the dominance of the central regime, all competitive strategies were formulated with a view to get crucial resources (economic or political) from the center. Given the regulatory licensing regime that allocated both public- and private-sector "goodies," there was competition between the states for these allocations, but the competition was mediated through the central government. Until 1966, when investment in the central public sector was on the rise, the competition was aimed toward getting central public-sector projects. Each and every state (even Bihar, whose share of central government investment was very high: 22.2% in 1971–72, 13.3% in 1983–84) complained of central discrimination. Each tried to get as many centrally allocated public projects as possible. Given the cap on capacity and declining public-sector resources, it was intense competition over a small number of significant projects. There was competition between states during the license-*raj*, but this competition was mediated through the center. A statement by the then industry minister, Manubhai Shah, in the Lok Sabha on April 10, 1961, clearly reveals the vertical competition over central public-sector projects:

> I have been assuring throughout the country that, during the Third five-year plan period, every State is going to have the establishment of a major public-sector engineering undertaking. I cannot do anything better than that. Therefore I would humbly beseech hon. [honorable] Members [of parliament] that the atmosphere of "economic divide" in which each one is arguing to get a project for his State should be avoided and we should try to

recognize and highlight the national character of these public-sector under-takings, whether they are located in Bengal, Punjab, Maharashtra, Gujarat, Madras, or Andhra. They are national projects. They are not some regional aspirations to be satisfied and we should not create something like an inter-nal feeling of irritation and bitterness, because some of us have become so much pressurized from all parts of the country. There is from every States, deputation after deputation, representation after representation and mis-representation after misrepresentation of various types of things. Every time the newspaper says the heavy electrical plant has already been located in some State, another State comes forward and asks whether that is correct. We say, "It is wrong." They say that is likely to be located in their State. Again another friend wants it to be contradicted.

. . . [Y]ou [will] find that every project is sought to be located in a dis-persed manner, avoiding those places where already they were lucky due to various reasons to get heavy industrial undertakings in the public sector. I should welcome and request the cooperation of this House [Lok Sabha] in avoiding regional tensions on the location of these public-sector under-takings. (Shah 1961, 313–14)

The political consequence of this vertical competition on the structure of intergovernmental politics was that asymmetric one-to-one bargaining relation-ships were established between regional leaders and the central ministries. In these bargaining relationships state leaders were not mere supplicants but could be also agenda-setters. As outlined by a senior IAS officer from the Tamil Nadu cadre, "We would first try to ensure that a particular project should be the responsibility of the public sector and then senior Congress lead-ers in the party persuaded that they should be allotted to Tamil Nadu."[54] The ability of political leaders from the states to carry the state with them and de-liver Lok Sabha seats to the Congress Party at the national level made a crucial difference. The rules of the game, that is, the structure of an interrelated and elaborate regulatory regime with important choice and veto points, made this asymmetric bargaining necessary and possible.

Vertical Interactions in Post-1991 India

In 1991 the central government changed the regulatory regime, scaling back many of the veto powers enjoyed by the central state. The central govern-ment's approval is no longer needed to set up industries; location is now deter-mined by the relevant regional state. How did this exogenous change affect central-local interactions and the vertical strategies adopted by regional states? In this section I show that this change in the central rules of the game has reduced the need for circumvention strategies by the regional states. Thus, ver-tical interactions have diminished in importance although not vanished. The regional states continue to need the central government approval for large foreign direct-investment projects, international loans, and central transfers through the planning mechanisms. In these domains, the regional states rely on the legacies of their previous vertical strategies: Gujarat continues to pursue a *bureaucratic* route to ensure central resources, while Tamil Nadu and West Bengal rely much more on *partisan and political* routes. Moreover, while Bengal has reduced the confrontational stance adopted earlier, it continues to complain about discrimination by the center. However, with the reduction in the power of the central government over states' industrial prospects, such a strategy of confrontation is not as credible in the eyes of regional voters. Thus, in the 1990s West Bengal's incumbents carved a somewhat contradictory strategy of bargaining with the center and making complaints against the center. In Tamil Nadu, positive-sum vertical interactions in the 1990s were facilitated by Tamil Nadu's regional parties' increased political influence within the central government. Thus, Tamil Nadu's rulers continue to rely on partisan channels of vertical influence after the onset of economic reforms.

Gujarat: The Strength of Continuity

The skills of monitoring the pre-1991 licensing system have allowed Gujarat to monitor both the central Ministry of Industry and the individual investors since 1991. The Gujarat agencies modified, not abolished, the earlier policy of consistent monitoring of the central licensing system. The targets of attention began to include foreign investors as well as the domestic private sector apart from the central government.[55] A 1995 memorandum from the Gujarat government to the central government indicates a continuation of its practice of monitoring the central government and the private sector in order to reduce the delays involved in implementing projects:

> The time gap for forwarding [a] copy of applications from Department of Industrial Development to the state government has increased substantially.
> As per the GOI [Government of India] procedure, we are to examine these applications on the locational aspect and forward the reply to the department in case the application is not in order. Thus we can start follow-up of applications only after a gap of 2 months or more. I therefore request you to expedite the process at the Department [of Industry, New Delhi] so that the time gap in forwarding the application to the state government can be reduced to minimum.[56]

Thus Gujarat continues to use intra-bureaucracy channels in monitoring the central state and the investors directly.

Policy Shifts in West Bengal in the 1990s

In West Bengal the ruling political party, the CPI(M), initiated politically risky policy shifts in favor of private, foreign, and even multinational investment in the early 1990s. In 1994, a new policy regime—policies and institutions—came into being in West Bengal. It included a new emphasis on involving the private and foreign sector in the state's industrial development, provision for incentives, infrastructural and governmental support for the development of the private sector, and institutional changes to implement the new policy intentions. Some of these shifts had begun during the earlier regime, in 1985 in a fragmented form, but in 1994 a new policy statement, institutional changes, and systematic governmental attention encompassing most departments of the government heralded a systematic policy shift.[57] A new policy statement announced in 1994:

> The State government welcomes foreign technology and investment, as may be appropriate, or mutually advantageous. While the state government considers the government and public sector as an important vehicle for ensuring social justice and balanced growth, it recognizes the importance and key role of the private sector in providing accelerated growth. . . . [T]he state government would also welcome private sector investment in power generation. Alongside the public and private sector, the State government looks upon the joint and assisted sectors[58] as effective instruments for mobilizing necessary resources and expertise in important areas of economic activity.[59]

Involvement of the private sector in the infrastructure sector, in growth centers, and even in social infrastructure such as education, health, and hospitals became governmental policy for the first time.[60] Institutional changes involved the reorganization of the West Bengal Industrial Development Corporation (WBIDC) and the upgrading and revival of an escort service within the WBIDC, the Shilpa Bandhu.[61] Simultaneously, the chief minister appointed as the chairman of the WBIDC a senior CPI(M) leader—Somnath Chatterjee—who was given a free hand to evolve the state's new policies and plan for the industrial development of the state.

Studies of liberalization usually focus on policies in terms of objective output intentions and policy instruments. The experience of subnational liberalization in West Bengal reveals that equal attention must be paid to the way in which these policy changes were framed in the discursive moral economy of the state.[62] In framing its policy to the public, the government of West Bengal faced a peculiar problem: the public's and the investors' widespread skepticism about the government's policy intentions, given its earlier claims that the center was responsible for industrial decline. Thus, West Bengal's political leadership had to walk a fine tightrope, attempting to evolve a new strategy in favor of the center's new liberalization policy, but one that retained the subnationalist critique of the center perfected during the license-*raj* period. Jyoti Basu, then CM of the state, explained his stance on the central policy of liberalization that sought to walk this tightrope:

> In 1991 the New Economic Policy of the GoI was announced. While disagreeing with many items in this policy we welcomed its two aspects, viz. the de-licensing and discontinuance of the freight equalization scheme. . . . With the removal of regulation and controls, we have got the opportunity to plan for the industrial development of our state. In this new situation, we are making efforts to restore West Bengal status as a leading industrial state. . . . We have made it clear that our government has no hesitation in welcoming foreign technology and investment in selective spheres and on mutually advantageous terms. Since the "mixed" economy has been in operation in the country, the public sector, the private sector, and joint sector are required to play their required roles. As a state government, we are to function within its economic milieu and therefore endeavors need to be stepped up for all concerned quarters to bring about the industrial resurgence of West Bengal.[63]

Comments by Somnath Chatterjee, the newly appointed political head of the revived WBIDC, also reflect this dilemma:

> The most serious problem is one of image — an image that nothing happens in West Bengal, nobody works here, there's no power, no water, and the government is run by the Mafia, the industrial sector is full of all sorts of irresponsible people. That's the image that has been very assiduously created [by the press and center]. . . . Even now, even three, four, or five years back. There was deliberate action on the part of the Centre to deny licenses, persuade people to move people from here. . . . But I say, forget the past, except to learn from the past. We have hopes for the future and we have to work for it.[64]

At other times, the anti-center rhetoric of the 1970s and the 1980s was revived. Speaking to reporters on his return from a foreign trip in 1995, Chatterjee said:

> The Centre has assiduously cultivated a negative image of West Bengal abroad. I am amazed at the level of ignorance among Embassy officials about West Bengal. While I cannot declare a war against the Centre, I would ask these people, who have no stake in West Bengal, not to play with its future.[65]

Simultaneously, and in contrast to the 1970s and 1980s, Bengal's leaders did seek the center's help for Bengal's liberalization. Thus, the state commerce and industry minister lobbied with the central finance minister for financial help for incentives and for central funding for the Haldia project.[66] In 1996, coinciding with the onset of elections, the same minister declared:

The fruits of the Centre's economic policy have not percolated down to the state even five years after the process of liberalization began. . . . The Centre has in no way helped in developing the infrastructure of the state, an essential prerequisite to industrialization. . . . Even the removal of the freight equalization and licensing policies cannot compensate for the ill that has been already done. Our port system at one time was the largest in the country. But it has been years since the Centre has volunteered any modernization scheme.[67]

Thus, West Bengal's rulers, in their attempt to implement a pro-liberalization agenda, continue to draw upon the legacies of their preexisting vertical strategy of partisan confrontation; in doing so, they attempt to balance an anti-center strategy with a pro-liberalization agenda.

Tamil Nadu after 1991

Tamil Nadu's regional elites' dilemma is less troubling, as its pre-1991 strategy was one of opportunism; in the post-1991 period its regional leaders continued this strategy, using their central influence to ensure a large share of private investments. Between 1991 and 1996 the AIADMK party supported the Congress ministry of Narasimha Rao and exploited that linkage to launch a regional strategy of liberalization. Since 1996 the Ministry of Industry, and after 1999 the newly combined Ministry of Commerce and Industry, have been controlled by Mursoli Maran, the representative from the regional party DMK.[68] Maran plays a major role in informing Tamil Nadu's officials of potential sources of information about potential investors, even to the extent of faxing details of possible projects before the central cabinet has had occasion to consider the proposals.[69] This central influence combined with institutional innovation allows Tamil Nadu to attract a significant share of investment. Since 1995–96 Tamil Nadu's rank in the race for investments has ranged between third and fourth, after Gujarat and Maharashtra.

Conclusion

In the domain of the large-scale private sector, the existing theoretical and empirical literature expects the *least* amount of policy autonomy by regional states in India (and elsewhere). I, in contrast, have demonstrated that the regulatory system gave room for regional elites—bureaucratic and political—to maneuver. There was more scope for state elites to exercise influence than is commonly believed. Equally significantly, the strategic models adopted by different states parceled out the central regulatory framework in such a way that the problem of the national developmental state in India became not its alleged "strength" that "failed" to be strong enough (Isher Ahluwalia 1985; Chakravarty 1994, 143), but rather its porous character. The strategies adopted led to a segmented nation-state divided regionally. In response, the respective states tried to fashion their own models of developmental states at the regional level through enhancing or mitigating the constraints they felt had been imposed by the central state. Various types of developmental states took shape at the margins of the national developmental state, while the core was federally segmented and divided. Thus while the central state was "weak," it had strong and nimble fingers.

My analysis contends that a formal, legal institutionalist approach to the study of industrial policy is deeply flawed. In contrast, I suggest an approach that focuses on the incentives generated by the actually existing rules (administrative rules as opposed to legislative intentions) of the game internal to the regulatory regime. Such an approach is able to reconcile the conventional assessment of India as a strong but slow-growing state with the coexistence of regionally diverse investment patterns. For a study of Indian federalism and regulatory policy, this analysis highlights the weakness of the argument that India was a highly centralist federation. Usually, as in presidential federations, the operation of political institutions such as the national legislature may play an important role in the relationship between governments. If legislatures *fail* to act as arenas for the expression and accommodation of local and regionally based interests—as in India—intergovernmental bargaining and negotiation may become *more* important.[70] This chapter confirms one of the main arguments advanced in this book: national economic policy is the aggregate product of regional political strategies and institutions given a certain set of centrally imposed constraints. In this view, slow national growth from 1960 to 1991—the Hindu rate of growth—as well as the rapid growth of the 1990s can be better understood as an aggregate of divergent regional growth rates rather than as a coherent national model that failed.

5 | The Subnational State as a Developmental Actor

> In Gujarat, a bureaucrat behaves as if he were a businessman, while in West Bengal a businessman acts like a bureaucrat.[1]

SCHOLARS OF FAILED developmental states are confronted with an apparent contradiction: all agree that such states play a dominant role in economic development, yet remain ineffective in achieving their goals. This has been true of China at different historical moments, of Brazil, of Russia, and certainly of India. This paradox might be resolved if we move beyond aggregate conceptualization of state strength to a focus on micro-institutional characteristics of states and the incentives they generate at different levels of the system.[2] This focus on incentives generated by micro-institutional variables must be combined with an attention to subnational or infranational levers of state action; in large and weak national states, subnational states may compensate or provide substitutes for (or aggravate) failures at higher levels of the system. The regional level is not inconsequential for understanding national economic policy patterns. Chapters 3 and 4 explicated the contours of central-local, or vertical, interactions; this chapter focuses on a comparative analysis of institutional effects at the regional (infranational) level.

Provinces in large and multilayered countries such as India are Janus-faced in the pursuit of industrial policy. Looking one way, they confront the center; looking the other, they act within their regional boundaries. Simultaneously, regional states feel compelled by the strong developmental imperatives experienced within their respective provincial boundaries. These two factors—the preeminent control of the center over investment flows and strong regional imperatives—fuel the demand for investment among regional states. This investment hunger necessitates vertical coordination with the center in industrial governance. Regional states adopt diverse vertical strategies to reregulate central industrial policy. Despite the influence of these common vertical compulsions, state-level institutions mediating central policies and investors' choices not only affect the level and pattern of investment flows to the relevant region, but may create new investment performing crucial entrepreneurial roles. Thus, regional actors not only translate central policies, but also give birth to new institutions to satisfy regional investment hunger. Globalization, somewhat counterintuitively, makes this imperative more urgent, requiring renewed sub-national developmentalism (Sinha 1999; Oi 1999) or subnational reregulation (Snyder 2001a).

This chapter provides a comparative measuring stick for assessing "good industrial governance," at the subnational level, which I then apply to an empirical analysis of Indian regional states. Subnational developmentalism is as much about ideas as it is about institutions; hence, I analyze both developmental ideas and institutions across three regional states: Gujarat, West Bengal, and Tamil Nadu. The matter of private versus public modes of coordination affects investment behavior and regional economic development prospects, as does institutional performance. This chapter analyzes both regional developmental *strategies* (ideas about the allocation between public and private sectors for example) and the *implementation* of these strategies by local institutions. This analysis will, therefore, outline the within-region aspect of the subnational developmental states in India. This chapter focuses on what subnational governments *want* and what they *do,* as well as *how* they do it. In other words, the focus is on institutional effects and the creation of new institutions at the subnational level in India.

With the reduction of central regulations over industry and investment in 1991, subnational institutions have acquired increased importance since liberalization policies were initiated in that year. Recent evidence and scholarly assessments reveal that central state shrinking has enhanced, not reduced, the demand for subnational governments in India (Sinha 1999). Simultaneously, acceleration of regional variation in economic outputs (income, infrastructure, welfare services) has led to growing economic disparities between rich and poor states after liberalization. However, the institutional underpinning of regional economic disparity after liberalization is less analyzed or understood. Institutions in India's regions may compound the trend toward regional disparities: in its efforts to attract different type of investors after globalization, Gujarat clearly benefits from better micro-institutions developed during the license-*raj* era, while institutionally weaker states (Uttar Pradesh, Bihar, and Orissa, for example) are hurt by both economic and institutional factors. Yet, institutional diffusion across Indian regional states is not impossible in the new scenario: Andhra Pradesh and Madhya Pradesh, for example, are trying to leverage their states by rapid institutional innovation. Later in this chapter I assess the effects of subnational institutional capacities on the new economic policies initiated by regional states in the 1990s.

Why Are Regional Institutions Important, and How Do They Matter?

A businessman said in an interview, "The license [central approval] was like a passport; you needed it to get in, but it did not ensure that you would have a good trip. Many projects with licenses failed."[3] He went on to document how interactions with the regional state administrations affected centrally approved projects. State theory tends to analyze the effects of either national rulers (Levi 1988; Horn 1995) or national bureaucracies (Tilly 1990; Krasner 1984; Evans, Rueschemeyer, and Skocpol 1985). Most of these accounts fail to attend to infranational variation in state effects or to analyze coordination (or conflict) between regional and national rulers. A disaggregated picture of the state that analyzes local and regional institutions and their effects independently can yield a better theory of the state.

In a unitary system, regional institutions may play mediating roles in translating central policy goals. Policy interdependence in multilevel systems, however, is much more consequential and systematic. In multilevel systems, regional institutions impact investment flows and investors' decisions in three distinct ways: by ensuring complementarity between contradictory organizational (hierarchical and horizontal) or ownership (public and private) forms, by providing (un)reliable information, and by enhancing (or reducing) the uncertainty and credibility of higher-level decisions and policies. Each of these effects—complementarity, information, and credibility—requires not only effective implementation but also the creation of new institutions.

First, regional institutions may span the great divide between states and markets or public-private institutions, leading to complementarity between these diverse principles.[4] Complementarity can be said to exist when two or more different organizational principles come together to form a mutant and different institutional form, but one that is more effective than either of the two principles alone. Among Indian regional states, the joint sector was one such organizational form embodying complementarity at its core. While the central rulers stressed the preeminent role of the public sector, some regional states evolved new hybrid forms.

Second, regional institutions, being closer to society and markets, may play a crucial role in providing information; information is the key to investment and economic growth. In strong states, governments may attempt to use their control over economic information in the economy to control rents accruing from such control; in such circumstances, subnational institutions may play a crucial role in providing alternative information sources or in generating new information. This will introduce some competition into information provision. Thus, local information services may *substitute* for informational rigidities at different levels of the system.

Third, politicians are subject to contradictory pressures and trade-offs; moreover, ex-ante desires to promise will conflict with ex-post incentives to renege. Thus, policy instability and lack of credibility will affect investment and, thereby, economic growth. Policy credibility is an important issue at all levels, but regional institutions implement national policies *after* they have been formulated at the center. Regional elites thus can increase or decrease the credibility of a policy by assuring the investors that they will or will not keep their part of the implementation chain. We need to be able to measure the degree to which regional states ensure *complementarity and credibility, and provide adequate information* at the local level.

Empirically, the starting point must be the analysis of the Indian civil service: it implements the regulatory policies regarding investment. The civil service (Indian Administrative Service or IAS) while characterized by a corporate identity (Potter 1996) and trained nationally, is constituted regionally; that is, it is constructed by provincial cadres. Each member of the civil service has a home-state cadre, which determines his or her promotions, transfers, and other career trajectories. Most importantly, the role and performance of different state cadres of the "national" civil service differ across regional states, shaped as much by regional political and social conditions as by national rules and training. Thus, for both theoretical and empirical reasons a study of regional institutions deployed to manage investment becomes important.

Developmental Strategies in Indian Regional States

This chapter starts with an assessment of subnational developmental strategies, especially with reference to how state rulers thought of and implemented the relationship between public and private sectors in their regional political economy. The evidence presented here shows that rulers from the three regional states pursued state-led development, but the proportional role of the public and private sectors differed across the three states. In the second section I develop a comparative framework to measure institutional capacities across regional states. I focus on three different elements of institutional performance: policy outputs, policy implementation, and informal institutional effects. In the third section of the chapter I focus on subnational institutional reforms after India initiated liberalization policies in 1991.[5]

All regional leaders sought to achieve industrialization in their provinces during the 1950s and 1960s. As an illustration, in early-1960s Gujarat, there were extensive debates among the political and bureaucratic leadership about the possible trajectory of development that Gujarat should follow.[6] The debate centered on the possibility of agrarian modernization or an industry-led growth path. In the face of competing viewpoints about the trajectory of Gujarat's development, the

> state government decided to pursue *rapid, orderly and systematic* industrial development. I thought and told the CM [Chief Minister] that this was an opportune moment to develop Gujarat because agriculture could not be the basis of development in Gujarat. So industry was the only option. Myself

and others at that time saw it as a unique opportunity rather than as something distressing. I told the CM so. (Italics added)[7]

The example of Bombay served as a model, and the political leadership sought to replicate the success of Bombay in Gujarat. Agrarian modernization, however, could not be ignored. The first chief minister, Jivraj Mehta, was concerned about the stagnant food economy. Constraints of the natural agro-economy meant that food crops would always be deficient. In addition to encouraging food crops the political leadership decided to explore the option of encouraging cash crops.[8] Nonetheless, the overall consensus tilted in favor of rapid industrial development in Gujarat.

Imperatives toward industrial development were common across West Bengal and Tamil Nadu too. The next issue was one of using state versus markets as allocation mechanisms. National authors of India's developmental plans firmly believed in a state-led strategy of industrial development. How was this to be achieved? Nehru, India's first prime minister, considered the public sector to be a primary instrument of development. Most of India's regional satraps shared Nehru's vision of state-led development but differed in the specific public-versus-private-sector choices they adopted to achieve their goals. Moreover, the unique way that some states fused the public and private sectors—the joint sector—reflected a commitment to "market-enhancing" state intervention.[9] These specific *micro*-institutional differences proved to be more consequential than state-versus-market allocation choices.

Ideas favoring the public sector were widely prevalent among the regional leadership at this time. None of the chief ministers of Gujarat, West Bengal, or Tamil Nadu was a strong believer in the free market (Erdman 1971; 1973). In Gujarat, for example, the government was ruled by the Congress Party, which maintained a strong commitment toward the public sector. The chief ministers of Gujarat from 1960 to 1975—Jivraj N. Mehta (May 1960–August 1963),[10] Balwantrai Mehta (September 1963–August 1965), Hitendra Desai (September 1965–April 1971), G. Oza (March 1972–June 1973), and Chimanbhai Patel (July 1973–January 1974)—were strong public-sector supporters.[11] Similarly, in West Bengal, the chief minister, Dr. B. C. Roy, a staunch congressman, believed in a self-reliant public sector for his state. Tamil Nadu's chief ministers in the 1960s and 1970s were also firm believers in public sector–led strategies.

In Gujarat, the state's elites' approach toward the public sector differed from other regional states in three distinct ways: First, within the public sector, the government focused more on regional public-sector undertakings. Second, it involved the private sector through partnerships with firms owned by the state government; this took the form of joint-sector firms. Third, all public-sector firms were encouraged to perform efficiently and incorporated private-sector entrepreneurs in their decision-making structure.

While *central* public-sector investment in Gujarat was low, its share of the public-sector undertakings (PSUs) financed from the regional budget was very similar to West Bengal's and Tamil Nadu's in the 1970s and 1980s. Gujarat and West Bengal had similar number of PSUs: forty-four in Gujarat and forty-six in West Bengal in 1984–85.[12] A better indicator is the share of regional investment devoted to regional public versus central public sector. Table 5.1 shows that the percentage of regional (not central) investment devoted to the state sector in Gujarat was higher than the share of regional investment devoted to the regional public enterprises in West Bengal and Tamil Nadu.

The table shows a remarkable picture: In 1978, the share of public investment in West Bengal's regional investment was 74 percent; in Tamil Nadu, 83 percent; and in Gujarat, only 36 percent. A few other things deserve note. First, the share of central public investment in the three regional states varies greatly, with Gujarat having the lowest share. Second, while Gujarat had a larger share of the private sector, it also had a much larger share of the joint sector, the state sector, and the cooperative sector, in which the role of the state bureaucracy was important and strategic. Thus, Gujarat's private investment-led strategy was not anti-state but rather employed state-led efforts in partnership with the private sector.

In the early years, while the number of PSUs and the regional public-sector investment was roughly equivalent across the three states, the various leaders from Gujarat insisted that the public sector should be as efficient as the private sector. In a statement made in 1961, the chief minister of Gujarat put it thus: "I am not for a moment minimizing the importance and necessity of these [public-sector] undertakings showing the same efficiency or profits as private undertakings" (Mehta 1961, 403). One Gujarat government official told me in an interview, "We tried to run the central public sector with as much efficiency as we could. From early years (1960s) there developed a tradition of noninterference in the affairs of the central public-sector units located in the state. This was true, for example, of IPCL (Indian Petrochemicals Ltd.). As a result, the public sector in Gujarat has generally functioned efficiently."[13]

Moreover, in Gujarat, chief ministers encouraged more *hybrid* forms of organizations. This led to the evolution and persistence of joint-sector units within Gujarat, a more efficient and productive public sector, and incorporation of key private business actors within the state sector.[14] Regional private actors and the joint sector were incorporated into the state's development strategy. Moreover, the Gujarat Congress leadership diversified its reliance away from the central public sector. The first chief minister, Jivraj Mehta, insisted that the government of Gujarat become more self-reliant. Debates over

Table 5.1. Ownership Pattern of Industrial Investment by States, 1978–1986 (in Rs. Million and Percent of Regional Investment)

	Public Sector (a + b)	Center (a)	State (b)	Private Domestic	Joint Sector	Cooperative Sector	Foreign	Total in State
Gujarat 1978	6,640 (36%)	6,280 (34%)	360 (2%)	3,250 (17%)	4,210 (23%)	4,540 (24%)	None	18,640 (100%)
Gujarat 1980	16,600 (42%)	2,300 (5.9%)	14,290 (36%)	3,430 (8.8%)	11,090 (28%)	7,680 (19%)	None	38,800 (100%)
Gujarat 1986	22,310 (28%)	20,590 (26%)	1,720 (2.1%)	18,900 (24%)	34,250 (43%)	2,690 (3.4%)	100 (0.1%)	78,270 (100%)
West Bengal 1978	9,860 (74%)	5,770 (43%)	4,090 (31%)	2,070 (16%)	1,310 (10%)	N/A	None	13,240 (100%)
West Bengal 1980	20,720 (80%)	14,400 (55%)	6,320 (24%)	3,130 (12%)	1,270 (4.9%)	80 (0.3%)	590 (2.2%)	25,810 (100%)
West Bengal 1986	35,140 (68.9%)	34,840 (68.3%)	300 (0.5%)	1,090 (2.1%)	13,790 (27%)	0.0 (0%)	900 (1.7%)	50,940 (100%)
Tamil Nadu 1978	13,650 (83%)	11,490 (70%)	2,160 (13%)	1,820 (11%)	620 (4%)	260 (2%)	None	16,350 (100%)
Tamil Nadu 1980	20,810 (86%)	16,690 (69%)	4,120 (17%)	950 (3.9%)	990 (4.1%)	90 (0.3%)	1,280 (5.3%)	24,140 (100%)
Tamil Nadu 1986	9,530 (31%)	8,290 (27%)	1,240 (4.1%)	6,120 (20%)	14,200 (47%)	110 (0.3%)	200 (0.6%)	30,180 (100%)

Source: Center for Monitoring the Indian Economy, Shape of Things to Come (Bombay: CMIE, 1978, 1980, 1986).
Notes: Industrial Investment includes investment in mining, quarrying, and manufacturing industries.
The figures for share (in percent) have been rounded off; thus the total, 100%, is not always the exact sum of the other share numbers.

the Gujarat State Fertilizer Company, a profitable firm controlled by the state government in the 1960s, showed that the government of Gujarat recognized the need for an efficient public sector within Gujarat. "[T]the GoG wanted to have the fertilizer plant operate in a businesslike fashion, and the 'poor track record' of central public sector plants further militated against reliance on GoI" (Erdman 1973, 35). As Jashvant Mehta, the industry minister of the GoG, said in 1970,

> It is known that Gujarat today [1970] symbolizes an image of progressive liberalism. . . . We have framed our industrial policy on the foundations of the basic character of the State. Our industrial policy, therefore, has had the attitude of complementarity as its core. We have not functioned on mutually excessive alternatives. We have felt that sectoral alignments in the industrial organization are primarily functional. We have felt that expertise from the private sector and the prudence of the public sector can be mixed in ideal proportion. In framing the corporate network, which to our mind is about the widest in the country, we have functioned on this principle. Each corporation we have set up has on top of it a trusted and experienced non-official and the Boards have a liberal sprinkling of talent from both [public and private] sectors.[15]

Moreover, the decision-making structure in the joint sector differed substantially in the three regional states. The managers of these manufacturing units in Gujarat were largely left free to pursue business decisions. Many of these joint-sector units flourished; firms such as Gujarat Narmada Fertilizers Corporation (GNFC), Gujarat Heavy Chemical Corporation (GHCL), and Gujarat State Fertilizers Corporation (GSFC) were among the top fifty most efficient companies in India in the 1970s and 1980s.[16]

In contrast, West Bengal continued to regard the central public sector as crucial to its developmental strategy during both Congress and Left Front rule. While Dr. B.C. Roy, the first chief minister of West Bengal from 1947 to 1962, was keen that this state should develop industrially, he also insisted that the Government of West Bengal (GoWB) should leave major organized industries to "be looked after by the central government on the national level or by the private sector [and not the regional public sector]" (Franda 1968, 315). This *dependent expectation* of the West Bengal government in regard to the central government continued to characterize the relations between the two during successive central governments, even after the Left Front came into power (1977). However, it was transformed into a confrontational dependence. Successive West Bengal governments, both under Congress rule and under Left Front rule, argued vociferously that they had been discriminated against but also relied on the center for heavy investments in the public sector. In response to the central government's urging to put in a part of the money for a railway project, Jyoti Basu refused, arguing that it was the center's responsibility (Profulla Roy Choudhury 1985).

In contrast, the Government of Gujarat's officials decided to use state government's equity participation in many central projects to attract more investments. The experience of the formation of the GSFC provides an illustrative contrast between the strategies of the two regional governments. Soon after its formation, Gujarat's Industry Department wanted to set up a fertilizer unit to increase its agricultural production. It contacted the central government to urge it to allocate a fertilizer central project in Gujarat.[17] The Government of India was not very encouraging, because it "had to balance many different needs, but it did not reject the idea out-of-hand."[18] The GoG decided to go ahead and set up a fertilizer manufacturing unit on its own: the Gujarat State Fertilizer Corporation, which began as a state public enterprise but later became one of the most profitable joint-sector firms established by any state government. The chief minister of Gujarat had a strong preference that "Gujaratis should demonstrate what they could do to develop their own State and others related this to the alleged neglect of Gujarat by the Government of India in the matter of central public sector undertakings" (Erdman 1971, 35).

Tamil Nadu and West Bengal, in contrast to Gujarat, tried to get as many of the central public-sector projects as possible. Historically, the strategies of Tamil Nadu's and West Bengal's political leadership made sense, because the developmental strategy followed by India's national rulers was a public sector–led strategy. Thus, I am not suggesting that Tamil Nadu and West Bengal did worse by depending upon the central public sector. However, given the *decline* of central public-sector investment in India from 1965 onward, Gujarat's strategy of reliance on the joint sector and the private sector proved to be *unintentionally* sensible in the longer run. With the decline in fixed-capital formation in the public sector to 5.5 percent of the GDP per annum after 1965, West Bengal and Tamil Nadu were competing for a share of a shrinking pie.[19]

This contrast in policy is evident in the various policy statements of the Left Front during that period. In 1978, the then recently elected Left Front coalition government in West Bengal came out with an industrial policy. Its goals, "keeping in mind some principles of the Left Front," were to "stop the rising unemployment, encourage small and cottage industries and to reduce the control of monopoly capitalists and MNCs [multinational corporations] in the state's economy." The gradual expansion of the public sector and indigenous technology was seen to be a crucial goal of the Left Front, as was the control by actual producers, that is, the workers, over the industrial sector.[20] "We are not going to allow any monopoly capitalists or MNCs to set up any new industry here, because it is against the LF policy. The old ones may run if they do not violate any law and compete with the cottage and small-scale industry. Our first priority is the cottage and small-scale industry."[21] The support for the public sector was a clear priority in 1978:

> Whether for encouraging indigenous technology or for offering stimulus to small scale operations or for providing basic inputs to crucial sectors, it will be necessary to rely more and more upon the instrumentality of public undertakings. The public undertakings must become the channel through which the goals of production, investment, surplus generation and income distribution are achieved. They should be utilized to promote activities that private enterprises do not engage in, to supplement activities engaged in by private enterprises in a limited scale, or to replace private enterprises that have somehow proved themselves undesirable.[22]

And, vis-à-vis the joint sector:

> Till now the joint sector has been a mere cover for expanding the jurisdiction of private enterprise with the help of public funds. This situation must change, but the prior condition for that is an effective and ideologically oriented public industrial sector.[23]

Around 1985 there was an extensive debate within the Left Front about the role of the joint sector.[24] The problems faced by the Haldia Petrochemical Project led the Left Front government to seek private-sector participation (from the Goenka business family) for the project. However, strong criticism of that "shift in policy" from within the government and the party led the Left Front to pursue the encouragement of the joint sector halfheartedly. Nothing came of the expected Goenka participation in the Haldia joint-sector project at that time; it was only in the mid-1990s, almost ten years later, that the Haldia project took off, this time with private-sector equity participation. This episode of attempted policy change after eight years (in 1985) is revealing, for it shows that the Left Front abandoned a policy shift toward the joint sector after considering it. In 1986, the Left Front government, in the face of strong criticism, defensively said about the joint sector:

> But it should be made very clear that the state government has full control of the joint sector projects. The state government has a 26 percent share, the private entrepreneur has a 25 percent share, and the remaining 49 percent are from public issues. The state government has a majority in the board of directors of the joint sector company, and all important decisions of the company are subject to the approval of the state government.[25]

In Gujarat, in contrast, the state government adopted the joint sector as a core part of its developmental strategy and encouraged effective and active private-sector participation. From 1968–69 onward, Gujarat diverged from Tamil Nadu and West Bengal in following a much more market-based but state-led strategy (and not a market-led strategy). It focused attention on getting the maximum number of licenses from the center, offering independent encouragement to the private sector and the joint sector, and building industrial infrastructure for the private sector, both small and big. Moreover, it encouraged the joint sector (participation of the state government equity up to 26 percent) as a truly independent and autonomous wing of the public sector, which had few parallels in India. Thus, partly by design and partly by accident, Gujarat's policy makers responded to the decline in central public-sector investment by diversifying their state-directed "investment portfolio."

One does not see a corresponding shift in strategy in Tamil Nadu and West Bengal. In fact, at about the same time (1968–69), a partisan strategy took shape in Tamil Nadu and West Bengal that put much more emphasis on making the regionalism question a political issue. The question of central discrimination in the allotment of public-sector funds became the crucial fulcrum around which such mobilization occurred. The government of Tamil Nadu came out with the Rajamannar Committee Report (Government of Tamil Nadu 1971), the first such report by any state government; it was highly critical of the central government. Similarly, West Bengal, from 1977 under the Communist Party of India (Marxist) [CPI(M)], opted for an explicitly confrontational stand vis-à-vis the center. Thus, Tamil Nadu and West Bengal made the question of center-state relations the focus of a political and electoral battle, both within and outside their states.

Another set of evidence also reveals this. If one looks at the regional state-level public enterprises (SLPEs), they play two different roles. Some regional state-level enterprises are government companies (registered under the Companies Act), engaged in commercial activities and producing manufacturing goods. In addition to these SLPEs, other state enterprises deal with the establishment of infrastructure, the procurement of raw materials, or the provision of credit. Such SLPEs are promotional, because their impact on investment flows is indirect although no less essential. Sankar, Mishra, and Nandagopal (1994) categorize all the various regional state-level governmental organizations into these two types—commercial (that is, manufacturing firms) and promotional—as Table 5.2 illustrates.

Sankar, Mishra, and Nandagopal conclude:

> The study of typology in terms of the number of the SLPEs points out that the relative importance of different kinds of SLPEs differed in the various States in view of their economic strategy. For example, the States such as West Bengal and Kerala set up more manufacturing enterprises in view of their strategy to participate in directly productive activities. As opposed to this, states such as Gujarat and Maharashtra and Tamil Nadu preferred to set up more promotional enterprises in view of their strategy to accelerate the pace of economic development through helping the private sector enterprises. (1994, M-115)

Table 5.2. Categorical Distribution of State-Level Public Enterprises (SLPEs), by State in 1992

	Number of Commercial Enterprises (a)	Commercial Share of Total SLPEs (%)	Number of Promotional Enterprises (b)	Promotional Share of Total SLPEs (%)	Total Number of SLPEs (a+b)
Gujarat	20	44	25	56	45
West Bengal	29	78	8	22	37
Tamil Nadu	40	59	28	41	68
Kerala	71	68	33	32	104
Maharashtra	12	28	31	72	43
Total (All India)	436	49	439	50	875

Source: Computed from Sankar, Mishra, and Nandagopal, "State Level Public Enterprises in India: an Overview," *Economic and Political Weekly* 29, no. 35 (1994): M-115.
Note: The data for Bihar are not available.

While it would be premature to conclude that the two emphases are mutually exclusive, because all states had a large number of commercial enterprises, it can certainly be said that those states that employed a very small fraction of their SLPEs for promotional purposes had negative consequences for the flow of investment to their boundaries. Out of Gujarat's forty-five state enterprises, twenty-five are promotional, while out of West Bengal's thirty-seven SLPEs, only eight are promotional. Tamil Nadu puts its SLPEs to both production-related and promotional uses, but, as in West Bengal, the promotional enterprises are fewer in number (twenty-eight out of sixty-eight).

Thus, we see a curious pattern in the three regional states' horizontal strategies. Gujarat pursues a state-led strategy that encourages joint public-private partnerships. Within its share of public investment, the regional-level public sector dominates, and a greater number of state public enterprises are employed in the service of promotional rather than production-related activity. In West Bengal and Tamil Nadu, the central public sector is dominant, and the role of the regional, private, and joint sectors is relatively small. Most of the SLPEs are manufacturing units serving employment rather than promotional goals.

In this section, I have documented the policy shift toward the private and joint sectors in response to declining central public-sector investment in the mid-1970s. Arguably, all states could have emphasized a policy shift toward the private and joint sectors in the face of declining central public investment. In Gujarat, a definite policy shift toward encouragement of the private and joint sectors was evident in the number of license applications by state-level agencies for joint-sector projects and in the decline of lobbying efforts toward the allocation of central public sector in the regional state. In Tamil Nadu a similar policy shift led the state government to encourage a few joint-sector projects with genuine autonomy for the private sector, but lobbying to get central projects continued to soak up the political energies of regional politicians. In West Bengal the political leadership's dependence upon central public-sector investment continued without recognition that this investment was declining. In response to declining central investment, the regional leadership adopted a strident critical attitude regarding the declining *share* of central public investment in West Bengal. They struggled to reinstate and to protect the central public-sector units. Thus, state politicians across the three regional states differed in the role they accorded to public versus private sectors and in the experimentation with new and hybrid organizational forms. These differences contributed, in an unintended way, to greater reliance on joint and private sector in Gujarat and on the central public sector in Tamil Nadu and West Bengal. Macro-allocation differences, such as state versus markets, do not capture the complementarity that existed between the public and private sectors in Gujarat or the tension that persisted in West Bengal and Tamil Nadu.

A discussion of subnational developmental states is incomplete without assessing whether these strategies are effective and consequential for investment and industrial indicators. Thus, the following section evaluates variation in institutional performance across the regional states, focusing on how organizations ensure complementarity between different organizational forms, enhance credibility of state agencies, and provide information to investors.

Institutional Capacities in India's Regions

Policy choices or policy ideas are implemented by organizations, and we must be able to measure their institutional effects. In addition, a significant gap between laws or policies and outcomes urges attention to the mediating power of institutions. Institutions must be analyzed with reference to three different aspects of the policy process: policy outputs, policy implementation and process, and informal institutions. Two of these refer to more formal aspects, while institutional quality affects outcomes through subtle mechanisms, which are more difficult to measure.

Policy Outputs in Regional States

Evaluation of regional institutional performance must start with *what* governments do. This section examines the policy pronouncements and policy outputs of each regional state. The focus is on policy outputs and not on policy outcomes. The reason, as noted by Putnam and by Eckstein, is that policy outcomes are the results of more than governmental action (Eckstein 1971; Putnam 1993). Investment flows, for example, may be the result of a combination of economic conditions, investors' choices, exogenous shocks, or governmental policy. I focus on governmental priorities, policies, and policy outputs. Investment flows are sensitive to different types of policy mechanisms; I focus on three: (1) the policies' categorization as supply-side or demand-side; (2) the existence of disciplining mechanisms; and (3) policy innovation, that is, the ability to introduce new policies to attract a larger share of industrial investment.

Formal Organizational Structure of Industrial Governance in Regional States

In the mid-1960s almost every regional state instituted similar organizations with the intention of implementing central industrial and regulatory policy. While some organizations were formed explicitly under central guidance, other organizations emerged when regional states began designing their own industrialization strategies in the 1960s and 1970s. It was these organizations that implemented central licensing policies, created new policies, and implemented the region-specific incentive and dispersal policies. Hence, these organizations were important mechanisms for the attraction of investment to regional states. Analysis of their functions and capacities can prove useful in mapping out the contours of the subnational developmental states in India.

The first regional industrial development corporation was set up in Bihar in 1960. Soon thereafter Andhra Pradesh established its industrial development corporation, and by 1971 every state except Manipur and Tripura had set up its own corporation (Commerce, 1973–1974). The central guidelines suggested in the 1950s that states would have to administer the loans for the small-scale and the medium-scale sectors, which might be provided by the National Developmental Banks, the National Small Scale Sector Bank, and the All India Financial Institutions. Thus, under the SFC Act of 1951 most regional states established state finance corporations (SFCs) to administer assistance to large- and small-scale industry in the relevant regional state.[26] In addition, state industrial development corporations (SIDCs) were established to provide matching term loans to medium- and small-scale units, while a separate small-scale industrial corporation was set up to govern other matters pertaining to the small-scale sector. However, once formed, these SIDCs were employed in the service of the regional industrialization strategies, whose goals and means could differ from central goals. In time, most of the regional states came to evolve their own industrial policies. These "industrial policies," while not designated as such, covered both supply-side and demand-side policies for attracting both large- and small-scale industries, as well as their regional distribution. Density, not scarcity, of regional industrial institutions is evident. How do we assess the impact of these state-level institutions on the level and extent of investment flows?

Supply-Side versus Demand-Side Policies

Did regional states have their own industrial policies? Did these policies merely redistribute investment or attempt to create new investment? The creation of new investment or new markets, "attention to the demand side of the equation" (1988, 9), distinguishes what Eisinger calls an entrepreneurial state from a traditional state (12).

While supply-side instruments aim at reducing the production-factor costs through government subsidies of capital and land through tax cuts, demand-side arguments assert that growth is promoted by discovering, creating, and expanding *new* markets for local goods and services.[27] The main focus of the supply-side policies is on *relocating* (or retaining) established mobile capital; demand-side policies focus on *creating* new kinds of capital and expanding new business formation. More generally, supply-side efforts tend to rely on competition with other jurisdictions for the same investment and therefore have a zero-sum quality. In contrast, demand-side policies tend to encourage the growth of indigenous business and to involve social groups and sectors that are new to the production of goods and services. Simultaneously, the government may support and itself participate in the growth of the "leading" and "high-risk" sectors rather than limit itself to low-risk undertakings and leaving the growth of high-risk industries to the decentralized decisions of the market. Finally, the role of supply-side government is to "follow and support private-sector decisions about where to invest, what businesses will be profitable, and what products will sell" (Eisinger 1988, 12). In contrast, a more entrepreneurial state's role is to "help identify investment opportunities that the private sector may either have overlooked or be reluctant to pursue, including opportunities in new markets, new products, and new industries" (Eisinger 1988, 12).

Eisinger's analytical distinctions are especially valuable in sorting out the role of regional states in India; most provinces combined *both* supply-side and demand-side policies to shape industrialization within their regions from the 1960s onward. This finding is surprising in the context of the general supposition, in the literature on India's economic policy, that industrial policy—both supply-side and demand-side—was the domain of the center.[28] Some regional governments were clear leaders in designing industrial policies, but all major regional states evolved various kinds of industrial policy instruments.[29]

These policy instruments were implicitly competitive, drawing investment away from other states by providing locational incentives to both large and small firms and ensuring infrastructural facilities.[30] Policies oriented toward backward-area development attempted to match incentives provided by the center to backward districts. Many regional states vied with each other to characterize their districts as "backward" to be eligible for central funds.

Many of the supply-side policies are generally incentives of the following types: (a) land at a concessional rate; (b) power at a concessional rate; (c) water at a concessional rate; (d) sales tax refund schemes/sales tax loans; (e) exemption from octroi;[31] (f) subsidization of feasibility studies; (g) supply of scarce raw material; (h) price preferences; and (i) supply of finance at concessional terms. Demand-side policies were aimed at development of land and sectors and an attempt to increase the size of the market in the region. Some states also attempted to create new entrepreneurs. A detailed analysis of these policies for Gujarat, West Bengal, and Tamil Nadu can be found in Tables 5.3–5.5.

This careful cataloging of subnational industrial policies challenges a commonly accepted view that economic policy in India was centralized. Differentiation of policies as supply-side and demand-side reveals the intense involvement of regional states. The purposes of subnational policies in the pre-reform period are very similar to those of the post-reform (1991) period: infrastructural development and locational incentives. Subnational liberalization in the recent post-reform period (since 1991) is at its core similar to reregulation during the license-*raj* era.

Disciplining Mechanisms

Even more, these subnational policies reveal a developmental purpose as defined by Amsden. Amsden characterizes a "developmental versus predatory" policy as *"Getting the Prices Wrong" but in the right way!* She puts it thus:

> In late-industrializing countries, *the state intervenes with subsidies deliberately to distort relative prices in order to stimulate economic activity.* This has been true in Korea, Japan and Taiwan as it has been in Brazil, India, and Turkey. In Korea, Japan, and Taiwan, however, the state has exercised discipline over subsidy recipients. *In exchange for subsidies, the state has imposed performance standards on private firms.* Subsidies have not been giveaways, but instead have been dispensed on the principle of reciprocity. (1989, 8; emphasis in original)

In the case of the subnational states within India, I did not find their disciplining efforts to be what Amsden describes—the imposition of direct performance standards on *export* targets. However, constant and regular monitoring of the implementation of the projects by some regional states had the unintended effect of imposing a certain kind of discipline on the firms; these firms had to meet their *"project targets"* to qualify for the subsidies provided.

To clarify this issue, I sought the opinion of those affected by such monitoring. Interview data of eighty-three businesspeople from three states give us some sense of whether subnational states were imposing this discipline even if the central state was not. In response to a three-part question—Were the subsidies conditional on any action on your part? If so, on what basis were the subsidies granted to you by the state administration: by payment of bribe, political and social connections, or meeting of certain project-specific targets? And, if so, in which state was this more true?—85 percent of the investors who had invested in more than one state said that it was in Gujarat that the "project achievement targets" were most rigorously enforced. Many firm owners said that Gujarat issued a form on which they were forced to report their production progress regularly, and subsidies were conditional on the basis of the responses recorded there. Firms owners with comparative experience in Tamil Nadu and West Bengal were not subject to monitoring. I also asked the same

Table 5.3. Supply-Side and Demand-Side Policies of Gujarat, 1970–1990

	Supply Side	Demand Side
Gujarat	*Fiscal Concessions* *Tax Incentives* (1) Sales tax exemption for the first 5–7 years on the purchase of raw materials, etc. (2) Sales tax deferment for 12 years (3) Interest-free sales tax loan	*Development of Land* (1) Acquisition of land for the development of industrial estates. By 1982, 80% of Gujarat was eligible for "special" incentives by one criterion or another. (2) Development of infrastructure such as roads, sheds, provision of water, power, etc.
	Subsidies (1) Added cash subsidy of 5% to the 15% central subsidy: a total subsidy of 20% of the fixed-capital investment for small industries in notified backward districts (2) Another 15% cash subsidy for large- and medium-scale industry (3) Special subsidies for GIDC estates	*Thrust/Pioneer Industry Development* (1) Development of electronic estates with special subsidies (2) Special incentives to engineering industries (3) Pioneer industries get special subsidies
	Finance (1) Incentives for preparing a feasibility report equivalent to 80% of the cost of the report (2) Term loan facility (3) Working capital loans	*Development of Local Markets* (1) Sales tax exemption for the first 5–7 years if the raw materials, consumables, packing, and processing materials used for manufacturing are purchased from within the state (2) Sales tax exemption on finished goods produced in Gujarat.
		Development of Local Entrepreneurship (1) Training for new entrepreneurs under the EDP (Entrepreneur Development Program)

Source: Drawn from iNDEXTb, *Gujarat's New Package of Financial Incentives, 1977–1982* (Ahmedabad: iNDEXTb, 1977); iNDEXTb, *Gujarat Presents a Winning Combination: Attractive Incentives + a Congenial Industrial Environment 1982–1987* (Ahmedabad: iNDEXTb, 1982); iNDEXTb, *Gujarat Like Nowhere Else in India, 1986–1991* (Ahmedabad: iNDEXTb, 1986).

Table 5.4. Supply-Side and Demand-Side Policies of West Bengal, 1970–1990

	Supply Side	Demand Side
West Bengal	*Fiscal Concessions*	*Development of Land*
		(1) Acquisition of land either
	Tax Incentives	for specific units or for devel-
	(1) Sales tax concessions and	oping growth centers
	sales tax loans based on loca-	(2) Housing scheme for new
	tion	industrial units
	(2) Entry tax relief	(3) Subsidy toward acquisition
		of sheds in estates
	Subsidies	(4) Subsidy toward rents on
	(1) 15% of fixed capital in-	land
	vestment	
	(2) 75% of the cost of the	*Thrust/Pioneer Industry*
	feasibility study is available as	*Development*
	unsecured loan	(1) Special incentives for elec-
	(3) Interest-free loan	tronics and pharmaceutical
	(4) Subsidy on purchase and	units
	installation of captive power-	
	generating sets	*Special Policy for Small-Scale*
	(5) Power subsidy of 30%	*and Cottage Industry*
	rebate on electric power tariff	(1) A separate policy docu-
	for five years	ment announced in 1977
	(6) Employment subsidy for	
	three years for the employ-	
	ment of additional workers	
	Finance	
	(1) State contribution toward	
	the cost of feasibility and proj-	
	ect report	
	(2) Term loan from WBIDC	
	(3) Underwriting of shares	
	(4) Working capital loans	
	(5) Developmental loan to	
	meet stamp duty paid or	
	transport or electricity charges	

Source: Drawn from Commerce and Industries Department, *The West Bengal Incentive Scheme, 1971* (Alipore: Government of West Bengal Press, 1971); Government of West Bengal, *Industrial Policy, 1978* (Alipore, West Bengal: Government of West Bengal Press, 1978); Commerce and Industries Department, *West Bengal's Incentives and Opportunities for New Industries in West Bengal, 1984* (Alipore, West Bengal: Government of West Bengal Press, 1984); Government of West Bengal, *Guidelines for Cottage and Small-Scale Industries* (Calcutta: Cottage and Small Scale Industries Department, GoWB, 1977); PHD Chamber, *State-Level Incentives* (New Delhi: PHD Chamber, 1985); Indian Investment Center, *West Bengal: Potential for Industrial Investment* (New Delhi: Indian Investment Center, 1972).

Table 5.5. Supply-Side and Demand-Side Policies of Tamil Nadu, 1970–1990

	Supply Side	Demand Side
Tamil Nadu	*Fiscal Concessions* *Tax Incentives* (1) Sales tax waiver for backward areas (2) Sales tax deferral *Subsidies* (1) Capital subsidy (2) Power tariff concessions *Finance* (1) Incentives for preparing a feasibility report (2) Term loan facility (3) Working capital loans (4) Concessional finance from financial institution and 20% deduction in income for industrial units in certain districts (5) Interest-free sales tax loan	*Development of Land* (1) Developed land with infrastructure facilities available to industries for outright purchase, on installment basis, as long-term lease, or as industrial estates *Other Infrastructural Facilities* (1) In industrial estates, up to 400 gallons of water a day supplied free of cost (2) Power tariff: new units using HT power charged a concessional tariff for 5 years *Thrust/Pioneer Industry Development* (1) Certain industries (petrochemicals, automobiles, bicycles, ceramics, etc.) designated as industries encouraged by the state (2) Special investment subsidy for electronics, leather, etc. *Development of Local Entrepreneurship* (1) Financial assistance to the extent of 100 percent is given to technocrats for the purchase of machinery and work sheds.

Source: PHD [Punjab, Haryana, and Delhi] Chamber of Commerce and Industry, *Incentives to Industry: An Inter-State Comparison* (New Delhi: PHD Chamber of Commerce and Industry, 1985); Government of Tamil Nadu, *Incentives* (Madras: Government of Tamil Nadu, 1989); Guidance, *Incentives of Tamil Nadu* (Madras: Government of Tamil Nadu, 1994).

question of those who had invested only in Tamil Nadu or West Bengal or Gujarat. A larger proportion (80 percent) of those who had invested only in Tamil Nadu said that in Tamil Nadu the rationale was bribes and/or political connections most of the time, while in West Bengal, 70 percent said that distribution of subsidies was implemented badly irrespective of either bribes or connections. Thus, monitoring in respect to subsidies served as a substitute "disciplining mechanism" in Gujarat but not in Tamil Nadu and West Bengal. So, we see that subnational policy regimes are well developed and show diverse activity even during the license-*raj* period; moreover, analysis of policies allows us to sketch the variations across the three regional states.

Institutional Creation, Policy Innovation, and Diffusion

Developmentalism is also indicated by policy innovation. In India, the rigidity of the central framework constrained innovation. Is that confirmed at the subnational level as well? Policy innovation in the domain of export policies during the license-*raj* is a crucial test case of subnational policy innovation, as export promotion was the responsibility of the central government.

Gujarat State was a clear innovator in export policy. Gujarat set up an export-oriented corporation called the Gujarat Export Corporation Ltd. in 1965 to assist and foster the development of export trade, with special emphasis on meeting the requirements of small-scale and cottage industries. This corporation was given a merit award by the Engineering Export Promotion Council for its outstanding performance in 1969–70.[32] The Gujarat government entrusted the corporation with the task of surveying all industries in Gujarat in regard to exports. The corporation's execution of orders of the value of Rs. 1.24 crores during 1973–74 clearly indicates that it was quite active during that time.[33] West Bengal or Tamil Nadu did not establish a separate agency for export promotion at this time, nor were policies for export promotion a priority.[34] In most other regional states, export was seen to be the central government's responsibility, left to the central commerce ministry in New Delhi. In 1972, the Gujarat Perspective Plan also noted the need to harness the great export potential that would be generated with the industrial growth planned in Gujarat (Government of Gujarat 1972, 40). This led to the strengthening of the Gujarat Export Corporation Ltd. by adding local offices and foreign offices. In addition, participation of Gujarat export companies in fairs and exhibitions and the institution of an export potential survey and technical cell contributed to a coherent policy on export promotion, a policy domain enumerated in the Union List in the Constitution and ignored by most regional governments.[35]

The creation of new institutions (apart from policy innovation) is the ultimate test of policy commitment toward industry. In 1972, an informal group began as a weekly social ("tea") meeting in the Gujarat industry commissioner's house. Usually frequented by the chief secretary, the finance secretary, and the managing directors of various SIDCs, it initiated a discussion of ways to attract investment from neighboring Maharashtra. Out of these weekly meetings came the idea of a collective organization that might collect information and, if possible, give clearances at one place. S. J. Kyulu, who was the industry secretary (the top civil servant of the Industry Department at the regional state level) in the early 1970s, may have first floated the actual idea. Jay Narayan Vyas, a state-level official, simultaneously broached the idea of an organization that might specialize in gathering "industrial intelligence" in order to provide it to potential investors. Moreover, an international cell was formed in the early 1970s within the Industry Department to attract NRI (nonresident Indian) investments into Gujarat. Through such regular but social meetings, with a view to encourage the flow of investments from NRIs, emerged an idea to formalize and coordinate the actions of various state agencies. As a result, in 1977, an agency called Industrial Extension Bureau (iNDEXTb) was formed in Gujarat.[36] Its finances came from contributions of GIDC, GIIC, GSFC, and the Industry Department commissioner so that it would have some autonomy from the political budgetary process. Its deputed head was Jay Narayan Vyas, who was given wide powers to shape the organization as he saw fit.[37]

The initial impetus of such an organization was clearly a competitive one: it sought to identify "potential entrepreneurs" both within India (Bombay and Calcutta at that time) and abroad (East Africa at that time) in competition with Maharashtra's government efforts. Moreover, a consciously mitigating strategy was adopted vis-à-vis the central government as early as 1972. The rules of the license-*raj* were perceived to be obstacles that the state government in Gujarat needed to obviate and compensate for. The perspective plan for Gujarat recognized this need in 1972:

> The major contact points for identifying and adopting entrepreneurs at the present juncture are *Bombay, Calcutta and East Africa.* Another point of contact for official relationships is *Delhi.* Most entrepreneurs find it time-consuming, embarrassing and even annoying to get their matters sorted out with the concerned ministries and department in Delhi. Any service that would iron out these problems to a satisfactory resolution would be one of the most effective ways of convincing the entrepreneurs of the state's ability to support their industrial activity. A senior-level officer of the rank of the secretary to the state government should be appointed as a liaison officer at Delhi. It is only at this level that the state's interaction can be effective and fruitful. A lower status would ruin the purpose.
>
> An officer at a fairly senior level (not below the rank of joint director of industries or deputy secretary to government) should be appointed at

Bombay for establishing contacts with entrepreneurs. In Calcutta, a local Gujarati resident with adequate business and social status with a small supporting staff could adequately serve that purpose. In East Africa, a local nonresident Indian with adequate business and social status with some supporting staff could be considered. (Government of Gujarat 1972, 36–37; emphasis added)

Almost simultaneously, in Maharashtra a similar organization came into being in 1979. Udyog Mitra[38] was conceived as an agency that would house officials of all the state departments from whom investors needed clearances, thus expediting the licensing process.[39] Udyog Mitra housed officials from Maharashtra State Electricity Board (MSEB), Maharashtra Industrial Development Corporation (MIDC), Maharashtra State Financial Corporation (MSFC), Maharashtra Electronic Corporation (MELTRON), and Maharashtra Small-Scale Industrial Development Corporation (MSSIDC). Similar to iNDEXTb, these organizations and their output had no legal sanction or legal status, but they evolved informal arrangements to avoid red tape at both the central and the regional levels. While they had no power to force any single state agency to do its job, they mediated among all the relevant state agencies.

In a federal system, one would expect a high diffusion of institutions initiated by one region, and then adopted by another. However, before 1991, institutional diffusion was rare. During the license-*raj,* certain regions were consistent leaders or laggards as institutional innovators. A measurement of institutional diffusion yields a powerful index of regional developmentalism. I measure this by developing a simple metric. I consider four possible domains of institutional diffusion: an investor promotion service, an industrial estate law, an entrepreneurship development program (EDP) for new investors, and a joint-sector program.[40] In each domain I give scores to states: (a) a score of 50 for having that service or law (thus, for example, Gujarat, West Bengal, and Maharashtra get 50 for having an investor promotion service, while Tamil Nadu gets 0); (b) a score of 50 for the time lag with which the service was copied by other states (Gujarat gets 50, because it was the first to start the service, and Maharashtra gets 40, because it started the service one year after Gujarat; West Bengal started a similar service in 1985 and hence gets 20, and Tamil Nadu gets 0); the total adds up to 100. Each state receives a score.

Given the lack of institutional diffusion across states, no other state instituted similar organizations till 1992. West Bengal did institute a wing within WBIDC, Shilpa Bandhu, in 1984, which was based on the single-window idea, but that department did not function effectively until it was revived and restructured substantively in 1994. Tamil Nadu had no similar agency or department till 1992, when Guidance was formed. Innovation and institutional diffusion vis-à-vis the industrial estate program was similarly *asymmetric,* with Gujarat copying verbatim the Maharashtra Industrial Estate Law of 1961 in

Table 5.6. Measuring Institutional Diffusion and Innovation during 1960–1990

States ⇒	Gujarat	Maharashtra	West Bengal	Tamil Nadu
Investor Promotion Service	100	90	70	0
Industrial Estate Law	90	100	80	80
EDP	100	70	0	0
Joint-Sector Program	100	70	70	90*
Average Diffusion Score across the Four Domains	97.5	82.5	55.0	42.5

Source: Author's estimates drawn from annual reports, memorandums, and interviews.
*These scores for Tamil Nadu arise as a result of its attempt to replicate the joint sector as developed in Gujarat, as in the experience of SPIC (Southern Petrochemical Industries Corporation).

1962. West Bengal's industrial corporation was registered under the Companies Act in 1967 and governed many different industrial development programs. Also, GIDC was structured similarly to MIDC, while WBIDC was a state financial corporation with a department that looked after growth centers.[41]

In terms of the EDP (entrepreneurship development program), Gujarat was the frontrunner, and it was Maharashtra that copied the program with considerable lag and reduced effectiveness.[42] Table 5.6 illustrates the extent of institutional diffusion across four states.

Policy Process and Implementation: How Do States "Do" Industrial Policy?

How well were the announced policies implemented? One investor said to me, "What does it matter what policies exist on the books? What matters is *how well* whatever little is promised to us is made available."[43] A Gujarat cadre official related a metaphorical story to convey a similar point:

It appears that a cat was harassing a rat. It went for advice to the owl, the legendary wise bird. The owl said, "You have been harassed because you are a rat, whereas your opponent is a cat. If you also become a cat, then there be no problem." The next day the rat went to owl again and said: "I agree in principle that if I were to change from a rat to a cat, I would have no problem. But could you please tell me how I could become a cat?" The owl then pulled himself to his full professional length and said, "I am here to give you policy directions and advice; implementation is your problem!"[44]

The question of how well policies are implemented is extremely important in studies of institutional evaluation, especially for achieving the goals of economic development. It spans the difference between promise and performance, a gap of much consequence to investors on the ground and more meaningful than vacuous promises. For economic development, various issues of "how" can be crucial. For example, does the industrial bureaucracy deliver on its promises in a timely manner? Time has a direct impact on the expected cost of a project and hence on its rate of return. And, how clear and simple are the procedures of implementation?[45]

Implementation of Supply-Side Policies

Gujarat and West Bengal lie at two extremes of the implementation of supply-side and demand-side industrial policies. In Gujarat, information about the available incentives was found in collated and clear form, and their disbursement was, on average, effective and timely.[46] For example, capital subsidies were usually made available before production started, ensuring that they were available when the investor needed them. There was corruption involved in getting some incentives, especially disbursement of term loans, but all investors said that once they had given the bribe money, the response from the bureaucracy was fast.[47] Term loans from the GIIC were easily available and promptly delivered.[48] The existence of a specialized agency in Gujarat—iNDEXTb—that was responsible for making the information regarding the state's industrial policies available to all investors facilitated the implementation of the various incentives. One investor told me, "As soon as I decided to set up a manufacturing unit in Ahmedabad, the government gave me a lot of brochures that laid out what I was supposed to do, which office I was supposed to go to, what clearance I needed, and at what stage. The procedure, while extremely cumbersome, was clearly laid out in front of me."[49]

Many Gujarat government officials whom I interviewed suggested that the governmental bureaucracy vigorously implemented the incentives on the basis of policies announced by the state government during the 1970s and 1980s. One official said, "We paid a lot of attention to them [incentives], because their results were easy to measure. We could enter how many loans we had sanctioned, how many feasibility studies we had subsidized, etc. [Moreover], the results in terms of investment flows were direct. It's a myth that incentives don't affect investment. Most investment is sensitive to tax cuts, etc."[50]

Another GoG official, reinforcing the claim that the implementation of incentives was autonomous from any central intervention, said, "All the various tax incentives were very important in our [Gujarat] government's strategy. It was the means through which we could ensure small-scale and labor-oriented industry. Most Congress governments [in Gujarat] wanted us to have results, and incentives were good for getting direct results. For licenses we had to go to the center, but within Gujarat we used the concessions to attract investments."[51]

In West Bengal, in contrast, even the formally available incentives such as capital subsidies were never available on time. Information regarding incentives was not coherently presented or made available to investors.[52] There was no specialized agency that collated all the information regarding incentives. I asked investors about Shilpa Bandhu, a departmental wing of the WBIDC, which had started operations in 1984–85. Most did not know of its existence. One investor told me, "The state agencies move very slowly to give us what they have promised. I no longer make my decisions in Bengal on the basis of what concessions the government promises."[53] Another said, "The sales tax concessions are there only in name. I have had to run to the district office so many times, I have given up."[54] Another official from Kalyani, an industrial estate, said, "If one could count how many industries came here because of incentives but then failed because they were not given the incentives, the majority of the failed units would be because of that."[55] And yet another official said to me, "The incentive policies in West Bengal were not designed well. No research was ever done to assess the needs and demands of actual investors. No attempt was made to attract industries to backward areas in the state. No careful and coordinated planning was done to make the incentives most effective."[56]

Tamil Nadu's state agencies perform well, but there are significant gaps between implementation by higher-level officials and by field offices. In addition, in Tamil Nadu the implementation of policies was idiosyncratic, with active and effective implementation in some periods followed by indifferent implementation in other periods. No specialized agency existed to make the information on policies available in a coherent form. Lack of information was compensated for by regular and routinized action by organizations such as Tamil Nadu Industrial Development Corporation (TIDCO), but it was heavily dependent on the quality of leadership in the relevant organization.[57] The actual disbursement often depended on the person heading the organization.[58] Most investors were happy with organizations like the State Promotional Corporation of Tamil Nadu (SIPCOT) and TIDCO. However, many complained that it was very difficult to get any assistance from lower-level officials. One bureaucrat said to me, "Bureaucracy at the higher level is quite good in Tamil Nadu, but low-level officials are very inefficient. This slows down the process of disbursement."[59] Another investor complained of the lack of availability of information in Tamil Nadu. He said, "No one seems to know what we have to do to get these incentives. It's a prestige thing. Rather than being our right, the officials see it as their might. I found it very difficult to get my loan dis-

Table 5.7. Relative (General) Infrastructure Development Index: 1980-81 to 1993-94 (All India = 100)

	1980-1981	1985-1986	1989-1990	1993-1994
Gujarat	123.0	124.8	116.8	122.4
West Bengal	110.6	100.5	96.3	94.2
Tamil Nadu	158.6	148.5	147.4	144.0
Bihar	83.5	84.2	83.1	81.1
Kerala	158.1	149.2	153.2	157.1
Maharashtra	120.1	116.8	111.0	107.0

Source: Centre for Monitoring the Indian Economy, *Profiles of States,* March (Bombay: CMIE, 1997), p. 7.
Note: This index is comparable across states and across time. This index prepared by CMIE is a weighted one totaling 100 percent. The components of the index include: transportation facilities (weight, 26 percent), energy consumption (24 percent), irrigation facilities (20 percent), banking facilities (12 percent), communications infrastructure (6 percent), educational institutes (6 percent), and health services (6 percent).

bursed even after it had been sanctioned."[60] Also, corruption in the disbursal of incentives was very high in Tamil Nadu. This seemed to have discouraged quite a few investors.[61]

Implementation of Demand-Side Policies

Good infrastructural facilities are very important for investors, and their impact on future demand and agglomeration economies is most compelling. Infrastructure consists of physical infrastructure (such as roads, ports, railway, and energy) and social infrastructure (such as educational, communication, and health facilities). In India, infrastructure is inadequate in all regional states, but relative differences have mattered (and continue to matter). In the mid-1960s and 1970s, when incentive policies were few and poorly administered, the provision of industrial infrastructure (irrespective of its quality) and the availability of power on a regular basis were enough to distinguish regional states from each other. Variation in the provision of infrastructural facilities across regional states is significant. Table 5.7 captures the measure of "general" infrastructure.

However, an anomaly is apparent. Tamil Nadu and Kerala, states in south India, have a very high infrastructural index, but investments have been low there. This puzzling finding leads me to an important distinction: *General* or *common* infrastructure does not seem to affect locational choices as much as the availability of *specialized* and *concentrated* industrial infrastructure. Businesspeople confirmed that infrastructural development in the industrial sector, not only general infrastructure, was extremely important in their decisions to invest. I asked business actors what type of infrastructure is more important for them? They clarified that industrial infrastructure such as the provision of industrial land, the quantity and quality of power, and the provision of industrial sheds, telephones, and specialized roads makes more difference to locational decisions than general infrastructure such as banking facilities, road length, railway length, educational facilities, and health facilities. For example, businesspeople said that they looked at the quantity and quality of energy that was currently available and the capacity of what was to be installed in the future, and the state of industrial infrastructure within industrial estates. One investor in Maharashtra said in an interview, "The government of Maharashtra offers 'five-star infrastructure.'"[62] Another small-scale investor from Calcutta who had decided to invest in Gujarat in the early 1980s said, "It's a honor to set up a unit in an industrial estate in Gujarat; most of them are so good."[63] This seems to suggest that the actual flow of investments is more sensitive to *industrial* infrastructure than to general infrastructural facilities.

How do we measure specialized or industrial infrastructure? The capacity of installed electricity in Kerala (1,484 megawatts [MW]) is much lower than that of Gujarat (4,935 MW), as is the per capita consumption of power (Kerala: 207 MW; West Bengal 156 MW; Tamil Nadu 364 MW; Gujarat 520 MW; Maharashtra 443 MW). Industrial estates, comparatively known as special economic zones, give us a sharper sense of industrial infrastructure.

Industrial Estates: Specialized Industrial Infrastructure

Industrial estates represent "state effort in its most concentrated form" (Gorter 1996, 2), as the setting up of estates involves coordination with the Power/Electricity Ministry, water authorities, Pollution Control Board, the Industry Department, and the Land and Revenue Departments. Moreover, the goals of industrial estates were wide-ranging and diverse, and their successful establishment can go a long way toward industrialization of the region. It has been found that industrial units inside estates are economically more viable than those located outside the estates (R. L. Sanghvi 1979). In the Indian context and especially in the pre-1991 period, the various state governments used industrial estates to encourage the development of small-scale investors. Industrial estates also provide the opportunity for regional states to offer not just general infrastructure such as roads or electricity, but also specialized functional infrastructure such as storage plants, high-technology parks, and the like. In many cases these are custom-made to specific sectoral requirements. Moreover, the goals of backward areas' development and regional dispersal overlap with the development of the small-scale sector, making the success of the industrial estate program in India a litmus test for three sets of goals: rural industrialization, small-scale private sector–based employment generation, and regional dispersal across the nation.

Given the federal structure of regulation, industrial estates also represent provincial efforts to harness state power for regionally specific political and economic ends. In contrast to the policy domain of licensing, where the central rules dominate, the industrial estate program represented a policy arena in which central control was minimal.[64] In this policy domain, the states attempt to *enhance or augment* resources provided by the central government as well as evolve independent policies. In the process of doing so, they may transform or even contradict national goals. The central government attempted to encourage the establishment of industrial estates for achieving regional dispersal of development across India. The states, however, conceived of industrial estates as achieving employment-intensive industrialization and used industrial estates to provide services to the small-scale sector. Moreover, estates' location was not always according to the central guidelines. An evaluation report on the backward-areas development noted, "In addition to central incentive schemes [for backward-areas development], a wide range of incentives/facilities were being offered by the State governments, appearing to vie with each other, to attract the industrial units."[65] The regional states also linked their industrial estate program with other policies, which, in fact, increased regional inequalities. For example, the central government has attempted to "develop" the backward areas of the country by providing capital subsidies. Some regional states transformed these capital subsidies into an instrument of investment attraction. Moreover, they augmented the central resources by developing industrial estates in the districts that were eligible for the capital subsidies. As a committee report on backward-areas development said:

> It is clear that the benefits of the Central subsidy (which is applicable to 101 district/areas) have accrued to a small number of districts. With the exception of Solan, all the top districts are in the West or the South. Only 3 of the 15 districts are in States-UT's [Union Territories] which were classified as industrially backward by the Pande Committee. . . . Many of the Districts that have benefited have large industrial estates or areas promoted aggressively by state-level agencies, e.g. Hosur in Dharampure, Rampet in North Arcot, Aurangabad town in Auragabad [district].[66]

A comparative analysis of industrial estates across regional states, thus, can be useful to measure subnational developmentalism. Table 5.8 gives us a comparative picture. Gujarat had the highest number of estates—68—and the highest number of industrial sheds (3,007). Tamil Nadu, the state ranked sec-

Table 5.8. Industrial Estates in States in 1975

	No. of Estates (1)	No. of Sheds Occupied for Production Purposes (2)	Total Number of Manufacturing Units in the Sheds	Employment
Gujarat	68	3,007	3,596	53,114
West Bengal	6	123	83	2,031
Tamil Nadu	36	605	603	30,613
Kerala	19	480	231	4,467
Bihar	13	334	122	1,476

Source: Computed from Sanghvi, *Role of Industrial Estates in a Developing Economy* (Bombay: Multi-Tech Publishing Co. 1979), pp. 23–24, 26–30. Also see R. K. Bharti, *Industrial Estates in Developing Economies* (New Delhi: National, 1978), pp. 178–231.

ond, had almost half the number of estates (36). The total number of manufacturing units across regional states also varied significantly. The provision of specialized or customized infrastructure correlates highly with the regional share of investment. Gujarat's specialized infrastructure was far more extensive than other regional states'.

Affecting the Choices of Investors through the State-Level Licensing and Approval Process

Chapter 3 demonstrated that industrial regulation in India was and continues to be joint and shared. The regulatory rules at the center in India were formal and rigid; subnational developmental states, thus, felt compelled to compensate for these entry barriers. Subnational variation in institutions, rules, and styles of that compensation was consequential for investment flows at the local level.

The license-*raj* can be disaggregated, at least, into a two-stage game, one with the central Ministry of Industry in New Delhi, which served as an important and necessary decision-making point. But, of equal importance was the second game with the regional state administrators and with what can be called the "licensing and approval administration" at the state level. *Two* aspects of this process are crucial: (1) persuading new investors to apply for licenses for a particular state, and (2) ensuring that those who had received licenses for that state from the central government implemented them. The second problem was especially crucial, as *preemption* of licensed capacity (when entrepreneurs with licenses would refuse to start production) was an important and regular feature of the licensing process, contributing in no small measure to the slow growth in India in the 1960s and the 1970s.

Variation in subnational licensing approval institutions—directed to investors both before and after the licenses had been granted—should affect the implementation of licenses. The committee on licensing analyzing the data for the period from 1956 to 1966 (Government of India 1969 [ILPIC report]) noted that the number of licenses being implemented in some states was extremely small. This report provides information on very few states and does not include the states I have chosen for study. But it does tell us something about the actual working of the licensing system and its regionally diverse effects. It shows that in Assam, the percentage distribution of implemented licenses was 48.7 percent, compared to 71.3 percent in Maharashtra. In the case of the pulp and paper industry, despite attempts to balance regional allocation, the implementation varied widely.

> Only 30 percent of the licenses granted were implemented in the northern region, 42 percent in the western region, 35 percent in the southern region and 46 percent in the eastern region. Thus the western region and the eastern region although already well-developed in this industry became more so, not only because they got a larger share of the licenses but also because implementation of licenses was better there than in the other two regions. It may be noted that, in this period (1956–1966), Bengal obtained as many as 48 licenses and implemented 28 of them, thus maintaining its dominant position in the paper industry. (Government of India 1969, 112)

This report came to the conclusion as early as 1969 that licensing is only one of the mechanisms for achieving the goals of development. "Only when there is a detailed plan for region-wide industrial development, covering both private and public sectors, can the licensing system help to implement it. Moreover, a great deal depends upon the initiative of State governments in providing the infrastructure [in the states] without which any development of industry is impossible" (Government of India 1969, 67).

Regional states differed in their ability not only to acquire licenses for their states but also to implement them *after* they had been allotted. How can we measure this ability to acquire licenses? The total number of licenses in a year refers to those LOIs that were converted into ILs from the total number of LOIs granted in the earlier years. To get an objective measure of the "ability to get licenses" we need to calculate the *rate* at which the LOIs were converted into ILs in one year, by state. Some fragmentary unpublished data can be computed on the question of the rate of conversion of LOIs into ILs. This conversion rate measures regional capacities. While this data is not completely reliable as it is calculated out of rough CIL registers, every attempt was made to check for its verifiability. It does provide a rough guide to the patterns but should not be taken to be a precise measure. Unfortunately the CIL registers for Tamil Nadu were not available. Gujarat had a quite high conversion rate for the period 1977–85, around 60 percent, while that of West Bengal was considerably lower at around 42 percent. Moreover, West Bengal's conversion rate declined rapidly over the 1980s, reaching a low of 9.5 percent in 1986. This conversion rate is a rough estimate of the states' ability to use the choice points inside the license-*raj* to their benefit, and did differ across Gujarat and West Bengal.

Thus, Gujarat was most systematic (even more than Maharashtra) in monitoring letters of intent and ensuring their conversion into licenses. An analysis of the process of such conversion can be instructive. The state government procured from the central government the list of the LOIs allotted for Gujarat. Then, the Industry Department of Gujarat used to send a letter to the relevant investor, inviting them to Gujarat to see possible sites. In addition, a simple monitoring form was sent to the investor that urged them to report the "application status": whether the project was implemented/under implementation/not pursued or dropped/cancelled. If it was under implementation, then the "milestone status" was asked for: Approved/Applied/No progress/Not applied/Not required/Rejected. If the application was pending, the investors were required to specify "pending with whom" and the date. This enabled iNDEXTb to pursue the matter with the agency with whom the application was pending and in turn made for speedier granting of the approvals.[67] Table 5.9 summarizes these comparative observations.

Information in a Centralized State

In a textbook private economy, all information is conveyed by price signals, leaving no room for information gathering by firms or states. However, informational uncertainty is a very serious problem in most real economies (Stiglitz 2000). The problem of information flow and uncertainty acquires a special character in centralized command economies like the former Soviet Union and China and, to a lesser degree, India. In India, the centralized state did have the ability to monopolize industrial information. In such a centralized system, local institutions could play a crucial role in distributing information or in generating new information, introducing some competition into information provision. Thus, local information services could *substitute* for informational rigidities at the central level.

Some regional states compensated for the informational rigidity and uncertainty at the central level by providing information about both state-level

Table 5.9. Comparison of State-Level Approval Process (1960–1990)

Score	States	State-Level Investment Approval Process
4	Gujarat	—Constant monitoring of licenses allotted for the particular state by a promotional state agency —Detailed and independent information gathering about the investors who had expressed interest in investing in the relevant state —Regular follow-up action on the part of the state agency vis-à-vis the central government on the licenses allotted — Independent road shows conducted in other metropolises (Calcutta, Madras, and Bombay) to attract small- and large-scale investment —Attempts to attract NRI and overseas business investment
3	Tamil Nadu	—Lobbying efforts toward the center to ensure the flow of licenses toward the state, but no institutional mechanism within the state to make it effective and systematic
2	West Bengal (1947–1967)	—Defense of licenses for that particular state in the licensing committee meetings but no implementation at the state level
1	West Bengal	None of the above; let the normal and slow licensing process work itself out

Source: iNDEXTb, *Agenda Items* (Ahmedabad: Government of Gujarat, 1996); GoG, *Overseas Indian Business and Technology Exposition at New York, USA: Tour Report of the Gujarat Team* (Ahmedabad: Government of Gujarat, 1989); GoWB, *A Review of Industry in West Bengal* (Calcutta: Government of West Bengal, n.d.); interviews with iNDEXTb officials; interviews with businesspeople who were affected by the state-level approval administrations.

and central-level regulations to investors and by generating local-specific information for regional planning; this was shared and made available to other state agencies. The Indian states exhibited considerable variation in the scope and breadth of available information services. Both Putnam and Stoner-Weiss give importance to the role of statistical services in their studies of democratic governance (Putnam 1993, 67; Stoner-Weiss 1997, 101), but such services are even more important in any study of economic governance, because information can be crucial to the decision to invest and the expected rate of return therein.

The comparative analysis of information services revealed that Gujarat by ad hoc experimentation and trial and error designed institutional mechanisms to collect industrial information and then disseminated it selectively to industrial entrepreneurs. In its effort to ensure investment flow from Bombay, Calcutta, and East Africa (in the early years), it had to *generate* databases of the various entrepreneurs existing in the various locations that were the potential targets of its competitive efforts. Initially these databases were stratified on the basis of ethnicity, because the Gujarat bureaucracy felt that it would be easy to attract businesspeople of Gujarati origin. This provided one rationale for the creation of a specialized body engaged in data and information collection: iNDEXTb. Even more significantly, in an explicit effort to develop leading sectoral strength—chemicals in the 1960s and 1970s and electronics in the 1990s—iNDEXTb and other industry agencies began to collect industry-related information about many sectors.[68] In addition, information about government rules at both the central and the state level was collated in one place because of the state agency's comparative advantage to fetter out such information in a state-dominated economic regime.[69]

The Industry Departments in both West Bengal and Tamil Nadu did have access to information about central rules or sectoral information, but this information was dispersed and not found in a coordinated and collated form. Moreover, these organizations during the pre-reform period did not attempt to generate new types of industrial intelligence nor did they distribute information to potential investors.[70] I visited the office of the Industry Department in each of these states and did not find any similar internal studies or any information-gathering or data-producing institutions as in Gujarat. In Tamil Nadu, the Statistical Department collected industrial data, but it was only in 1992 that independent attention was given to the task of systematic *production and distribution* of that information to target groups. Similarly, in West Bengal and most other states, a statistical department existed but was not linked with the task of producing and disseminating information from and for industrialists.

Informal Institutional Effects (Autonomy, Credibility, and Coordination)

Informal aspects of institutions—the extent of political interference, coordination across agencies, the credibility of the institutions' policies—are deeper-level variables, and crucially affect investment flows. Regional institutions in a multilevel polity could significantly enhance or negate coordination or credibility of central rules and institutions; their measurement requires a fine-grained analysis of the rules and decision-making structures internal to formal institutions.

Level and Extent of Autonomy vis-à-vis the Political Leadership

The organizational structure of the SIDCs was usually as follows: It was headed by a chairman, who was usually a political appointee of the current political regime. He was aided by a board, consisting of IAS officials and other state-level officials, that looked after various activities specific to the relevant SIDCs. If it was a financial term-lending institution, as in the case of GIIC, TIDCO, WBIDC, and SICOM (State Industrial Corporation of Maharashtra), then a member of the All India Financial Institution was also part of the board. The chairman's role was a perfunctory one, and he was not supposed to intervene in the everyday operation of the SIDCs. The political party in power saw this position as a patronage appointment, a reward to its supporters. This structure was the convention across most states.

Logically, political interference could occur through the role of the chairman and through direct or indirect orders of the managing director (usually second in command in an SIDC) or industry ministers to these SIDCs. Despite this uniform organizational structure, the extent of political interference in the everyday operations of the SIDC varied across the regional states. Sudhir Mehta, vice-chairman of Torrent, a pharmaceutical company, said, "It is best for our growth here [Gujarat], because the bureaucracy is positive, business-oriented, and understands the importance of making quick decisions. And there is no government interference, even in the joint-sector projects."[71]

However, the extent of political interference varied over time in the various states according to the political leadership in power. Hence, this variable is not very reliable as an index of comparative state institutional performance. Moreover, it is not clear that political intervention is necessarily harmful; in a democracy some political interference may be desirable. As an example, after 1991 the only way the WBIDC could be revived was through the appointment of a "dynamic" politician (Somnath Chatterjee, member of Parliament) who has, by all accounts, breathed a new political energy into the once moribund organization. Thus, this variable should be treated with caution.

One way in which this variable affects policy output is that informal "rules of the game" develop that enable the political space for economic policy making irrespective of political instability. As an illustration, the absence of interference by the political regime in Gujarat for the first thirty years of its history led to the conventional norm that political leaders would not interfere even when leadership changed. Thus, three different changes in the government in Gujarat between 1994 and 1998 did not affect the negotiation of a loan for public-sector restructuring that took place during those changes. Although it is not clear whether a lack of political interference is good or harmful for private investment flow, an analysis of the various states shows the pattern in Table 5.10.

Table 5.10. Measure of Political Interference across States

Scores	States	Measure of Political Interference
4	Gujarat (1960 to 1989)	— Almost no decision has to be ratified by the chairman, and he has only formal powers — Most policy and procedural decisions are taken by the managing directors — Operational autonomy for the board to manage the IDC — No interference by either the chief secretary, the industry secretary, or the industry minister
3	Gujarat (1990 to 1999), Tamil Nadu	— Most policy decisions are taken by the managing directors and his board of directors, and operational autonomy was prevalent; however the chairman could overrule on major issues
2	West Bengal	— Managing director and his board of directors had operational autonomy but interference from the political wing was regular
1	Bihar	Almost every decision had to be ratified by the political wing of the government

Source: Detailed and confidential interviews with the various officials and heads of GIDC, WBIDC, MIDC, and TIDCO.

The Extent of Coordination across Organizations Governing Industry

In Gujarat and also Maharashtra, certain active channels of communication and information flow were established across different types of state agencies; these channels were used to coordinate policy decisions and evolve coordinated plans whose individual aspects would be worked out by the individual agencies. Some of these channels worked through the overlapping memberships of the various boards of the SIDCs. Also, as in the case of Gujarat, since each SIDC "owned" part of iNDEXTb, and iNDEXTb acted on behalf of each and every organization in the public realm, it acted as a coordinating agency. As the public face of the Government of Gujarat, iNDEXTb represented all the government agencies in a coordinated fashion, providing information about each agency to others in the group and interacting with them to get clearances. In turn, iNDEXTb became a forum wherein all the agencies found institutional overlap and where each of them coordinated its action with the others. The budget of iNDEXTb was "shared" by Gujarat Industrial Development Corporation, Gujarat Industrial Investment Corporation,

Gujarat State Finance Corporation, Gujarat Mineral Development Corporation, and Gujarat Small-Scale Industrial Corporation.[72] On one hand, this made iNDEXTb independent of the state's budgetary process, and on the other, each agency had a stake in participation and coordination of its functions.

The second aspect of the institutional structure in Gujarat that contributed to coordination among the industrial agencies was their "specialized interdependence." In contrast, in West Bengal and Tamil Nadu, West Bengal Industrial Development Corporation (WBIDC) and Tamil Nadu Industrial Investment Corporation (TIIC) had separate departments that looked after the industrial estates and the disbursement of incentives. This structure, however, led to a neglect of the needs of the separate programs. In Gujarat, industrial estates were handled by a completely separate agency, as were the financial needs of medium-sized and small firms. This kind of *specialization* gave institutional power to the separate programs and provided the relevant state agency the incentives to coordinate with other agencies.

The seeming self-sufficiency of the various agencies in West Bengal, wherein each agency had separate departments handling all aspects of the industrial policies of the state government, insulated the organizations from each other, contributing to institutional fragmentation. Moreover, the organizational structure of SIDCs in West Bengal and Tamil Nadu seemed to encourage duplication of effort. In West Bengal, for example, WBIDC handled the industrial estates, but WIIDC (West Bengal Industrial Infrastructure Corporation) looked after growth centers. This led to duplication and institutional jealousies, because the agencies could interfere with each other's authority, thus preventing coordination rather than contributing to it. Similarly, in Tamil Nadu, TIDCO handled industrial estates as well as the financial needs of large- and medium-sized enterprises, but SIPCOT handled industrial estates too.

In terms of information flow, iNDEXTb was the formal nodal and recognized agency of all the SIDCs to collect industrial information and to communicate it to other agencies. With the power as well as the accountability to ensure information flow to other agencies, iNDEXTb contributed to regular communication among the various organizations.[73] In West Bengal and Tamil Nadu, each organization collected its own relevant data, which led to greater turf protection as well as a close guarding of information and unwillingness to share it across agencies.

Extent of Institutional Credibility

The macroeconomics and neo-institutional economics literature emphasizes that credible commitments play a major role in contributing to economic growth. Credibility of institutions determines both the flow and the level of investment. In Gujarat, the formation of an agency that specialized in attracting investment was the state's rulers' direct signal of their credible intentions to private investors. Gujarat also involved the private sector in key organizational and official positions within the joint sector and in state institutions, so that the political rulers could be *bound* against interfering in its functions. The presence of private investors as board members in the state agencies, such as GIDC and GIIC, contributed to the "Ulysses and the sirens effect," enhancing the credibility of state rulers vis-à-vis the private sector (Elster 1984). In the 1960s and 1970s in Gujarat, eminent industrialists were regularly part of state enterprises, the joint sector, and governmental state agencies, giving these state organizations greater prestige and credibility in the eyes of investors as well as keeping the political leaders from interfering too much. For example, Hari Vallabbhai Das, Dr. Vikram Sarabhai, and K. Lallbhai regularly played a role in state agencies and the joint sector in Gujarat. These industrialists were highly regarded for their business acumen and independence, and their presence within the industrial bureaucracy and manufacturing units such as Gujarat State Fertilizer Corporation was a source of credibility.[74] In contrast, in West Bengal the rulers treated the private sector as antagonistic competitors and kept them at arm's length. They could not evolve the mechanisms of self-curtailment that Gujarat's political leadership seems to have evolved by ad hoc experimentation.

The above section has measured policies, their implementation, and informal institutions affecting industrial investment across Indian states as evolved from 1960 to 1990. In 1991 central regulations were abolished, and institutional reform was initiated at the subnational level. How are we to understand the role of subnational institutional effects in this recent period? In the next section, I analyze changes in the role of subnational institutions from 1991 to 2000.

Sticky Institutions in West Bengal, Gujarat, and Tamil Nadu after 1991: A Comparative Institutional Analysis

The liberalization of central policy in 1991 enhanced the role of regional institutions in three distinct ways. First, the till then covert functions and roles played by state government became more visible to investors, policy makers, and scholars. This amounted not to a real enhancement of policy autonomy but to an increase in the public *attention* to preexisting roles and regulative capacities. During the licensing regime, the regional states were implementing and initiating new policies regarding, for example, regional dispersal, land allocation, infrastructure development, and environmental clearances; they continued to do so after 1991. The abolition of the central license-*raj* in 1991 has not *created* the inspector-*raj* at the state level, but rather made it *visible*.[75]

Second, state institutions at the provincial level attempt to adapt the new economic policy (1991 policy) to suit their specific regional conditions in the same way they had reregulated the licensing policies of the 1950s. For example, some regional rulers (for example, Madhya Pradesh's chief minister, Digvijay Singh) saw in the centrally sponsored liberalization a mandate for greater emphasis on human and social development relevant to their provincial realities, while others (for example, Naidu in Andhra Pradesh) articulated their regional policies within a "Washington consensus" paradigm.[76]

Third, regional states also initiated new rules and policies, and engaged in administrative reform in the face of a regulation vacuum created by central state withdrawal. The e-governance policy, where all the governmental offices are linked through computers, initiated by Andhra Pradesh in 2000 and followed by West Bengal in 2001, is one such example.[77] Thus, some new policy initiatives originated at the state level after 1991, and in such cases, regional policy de facto becomes national policy (Herring and Mohan 2001). For example, power (electricity) sector reforms first designed in Orissa have become a template, a "model," for national policy.

The net outcome of these changes is greater impact of institutional capacities of regional states on both domestic and foreign investment flows. In this section I argue that despite the enhanced role of regional institutions in effecting industrialization after 1991, the effectiveness of these organizations was largely determined by their pre-1991 capacities and skills. I elaborate this argument through a detailed analysis of post-1991 institutional capacities and changes in Gujarat, West Bengal, and Tamil Nadu.

Gujarat

The skills of monitoring the pre-1991 licensing system (elaborated in Chapter 4) have also allowed Gujarat to monitor both the central Ministry of Industry and the individual investors after 1991. The policy of consistent monitoring of the central licensing system before 1991 was modified, not withdrawn, after 1991 by the Gujarat agencies. The targets of attention began to include foreign investors as well as the domestic private sector apart from the central government.[78] The strategic capacities that had proved useful during the license-*raj* were equally beneficial after its abolition. The erstwhile "monitoring cell" in the regional Department of Industry monitors every investment proposal. This constant monitoring of investment applications by the promotional state agency helps to account for the fact that the ratio of implementation to proposed investment is the one of the highest (in comparison to other

Table 5.11. Distribution of Industrial Investment by
Implementation Status (in %)

	Under Implementation	Announced	Proposed	Total
Gujarat	60	13	27	100
West Bengal	35	34	31	100
Tamil Nadu	27	39	34	100
Maharashtra	40	28	32	100
Andhra Pradesh	37	31	32	100

Source: CMIE, *Profiles of States,* March 1997 (Bombay: CMIE, 1997).
Note: "Announced" refers to declaration or announcement. An investment intention is defined as "Proposed" when the Investment Entrepreneur Memorandum exists. "Under Implementation" refers to a situation where many clearances have been granted, such as procuring land or finances, and/or manufacturing has begun.

states) for Gujarat. Table 5.11 gives a sense of the comparative implementation capacity after 1991. Gujarat's implementation capacity is the highest among all regional states.

Monitoring the investors is as important. The Department of Industry in Gujarat continues to collect detailed and independent information about those investors who express an interest in investing in Gujarat. Regular follow-up action on the part of the state agency vis-à-vis the central government and the promoters has remained a regular feature of industrial governance in the state.[79] An investor described the approach of the industrial bureaucracy in Gujarat: "The state bureaucracy has developed a killer instinct when it comes to wooing investors."[80] Outlining the working of the Gujarat power corporation, a vice-president said, "What the corporation does is after identifying the area in which the project can be developed, it acquires land and begins to get clearances. By the time the competitive bidding for the project takes place, every clearance has been bagged [by the Gujarat government]."[81]

The "investment promotion" functions of the state agencies depend upon regional information services. In the liberalized scenario prevalent after 1991 the information-gathering capacities of the state agencies have become an important institutional variable helping to determine success in attracting investment.

Again, Gujarat's state agencies' pre-1991 experience in collecting information related to industry has proved extremely useful in fine-tuning that "killer instinct." In the post-1991 period, the state agencies in Gujarat deploy these information abilities to attract, and then to effectively implement, many industrial projects. As the main promotional organization of the Gujarat government formed in 1978, iNDEXTb has continued to play a crucial role in collecting information about new investors and disseminating that information to potential investors after 1991.

West Bengal

In West Bengal similar roles of investment promotion have been performed by the WBIDC after 1994, although there is no systematic system of monitoring different types of units—large or mid-size—as in Gujarat. Historically, in West Bengal no monitoring of the license-*raj* was institutionalized. After 1994, the investors have not been required to submit any implementation status form or any similar documentation. The state agency does keep track of some of the industrial proposals, and some regular follow-up action is evident. However, disproportionate attention is directed to large-scale prestigious projects. The Industry Advisory Committee considers and evaluates the progress made on these projects, but many mid-sized and smaller projects are not carefully monitored. The revived promotional organization—the Shilpa Bandhu—is the designated "single-window agency" of the WBIDC but helps only those investors who come to it with problems. In contrast, various promotional agencies in Gujarat have institutionalized procedures for proactively seeking investors even before they begin to have problems.

Regarding information provision, after 1994 the industry department in West Bengal began to provide information to investors, but no information- and data-producing institutions comparable to those in Gujarat exist in West Bengal. Thus, while Gujarat had established a separate agency with the responsibility of information gathering regarding industrial issues as far back as 1978 and this agency remained responsible for information gathering after 1991, in West Bengal this role is ostensibly performed by the WBIDC, but it does not have any specialized departments for gathering industry-related information. Interviews with entrepreneurs in West Bengal revealed that information related to industrial matters is still fragmented and not easily available.[82] Gujarat's iNDEXTb conducts extensive data collection about central policies, new projects technology, and international trends. Moreover, iNDEXTb provides some of this data to private investors in systematic ways through pamphlets and policy guidelines. While information dissemination has also been attempted in West Bengal after 1994, not many investors know of WBIDC's role in providing information.[83] The investors in Gujarat are fully aware of iNDEXTb's role as an information provider and as the single coordinating agency of the Gujarat government. The long-standing experience of Gujarat's iNDEXTb in gathering industry-related information leads to greater competence and quicker responses, while newer organizations like the WBIDC are still learning the ropes.

Thus, different institutional aspects of the two regional states—the state-level approval process and informational capacities—show that institutional differences going back to the pre-1991 regime persist and affect investors' decisions, and hence investment flows, since 1991. Gujarat has benefited by the significant continuity in policies, but also by the continuation of the pre-1991 institutional framework underlying its regional industrial strategy. Institutions are sticky in both Gujarat and West Bengal, contributing to greater divergence than can be predicted by those models that generate the expectation that wrong policies, if corrected, will set these economies onto more prosperous trajectories.

Tamil Nadu

Tamil Nadu has shown significant institutional innovation in reorienting its bureaucratic agencies in the service of monitoring and implementing investment proposals speedily after 1991. Since 1993 Tamil Nadu has emerged as one the prime destinations for foreign investors among Indian states. The share of Tamil Nadu in the total investment in the country was 10 percent as of January 1998, and it stood third among Indian states. This is the highest share recorded by the state since 1970. In 1997 the total outstanding investment in the state increased by 37 percent.

Institutional reform, aggressive promotion of the state to the media and to private investors, and the use of central influence to attract foreign and domestic investment have played a significant role in this transformation of Tamil Nadu from a middle-range state during the period 1960–90 to a state having one of the highest shares of investment flows after 1993. New policies have been accompanied by institutional creation and reform. The industry minister of Tamil Nadu put it thus: "We are initiating far-reaching structural reforms to lead the industry in the State away from a regulatory and protective regime to a free market–oriented competitive and globalized environment" (Speech to the CII–Southern Committee meeting, August 27, 1996).

The single most important component of the institutional reform was the creation of a single-window agency in July 1992, intended to be the first-point contact for all investors. It was called the Tamil Nadu Industrial Guidance and Export Promotion Bureau (or Guidance). Guidance was given independent resources and powers to serve as a service agency for investors and entrusted with the task to attract and "sell the state to potential investors."[84] Interestingly, it was instituted after an explicit analysis of the promotional agency in Gujarat, the iNDEXTb. Tamil Nadu's government officials studied the organizations in Gujarat and Maharashtra and were most impressed by the Gujarat model of iNDEXTb.[85] Guidance's success in attracting investment into Tamil Nadu after 1992 has been notable. From its formation in 1992 till 1994, for example, it handled three hundred inquiries, a high number.[86] Guidance's role in the collection of information has been key to its success in ensuring a high level of investment flow after 1993. The office keeps track of potential investors through diverse methods—Internet, embassy contacts, regular conferences, and foreign trips—and ensures a regular and effective follow-up of these contacts.[87] However, the organization size is very small—just four to five people—which limits its ability to emerge as a nodal coordinating agency.

Conclusion

This chapter accomplished three tasks. First, it demonstrated that it is possible to measure a diverse array of institutional dimensions, both formal and informal, across subnational units. An analysis of three regional states yields a comparative framework that should be applicable in other states within India as well as elsewhere. Some states evolved hybrid organizational forms—the joint sector, innovative mechanisms for the incorporation of the private sector in the state sector (business representation on the board of many public-sector firms), and creation of innovative promotional state agencies—which created a dense network of regional organizations and institutions. This comparative framework stresses similar causal mechanisms across institutions, organizations, and regions: complementarity and coordination, credibility, and information production and distribution. Three different dimensions of institutional capacities—policy outputs, policy implementation, and informal institutions—are analyzed and measured.

Second, this analysis of regional institutions allowed us to build a more complete picture of India's developmental state as well as to contribute to the theory of the developmental state. Regional institutions are not mere translators, but are indispensable for enhancing, transforming, and mitigating the effects of central policy.

Third, the chapter showed that some regional states have better institutions than others do. While Gujarat has produced comprehensive and long-term plans and created effective mechanisms and institutions to carry them out, Tamil Nadu made comprehensive plans available, but their implementation proceeded slowly and in fits and starts. West Bengal has produced very ambitious plans for public-sector protection and small-scale development, but the capacity to implement them is weak; and in regional states like Bihar and Orissa, neither the plans nor the institutional mechanisms were adequate to the demands of attracting investment. Even more important, these institutional legacies crafted under conditions of central constraint (1960–90) continue to facilitate investment flows even after a change in central rules (since 1991). Institutions, both formal and informal, are sticky in all three of the states examined—Gujarat, Tamil Nadu, and West Bengal—contributing to greater regional divergence in investment flows than can be predicted by the radical shift in policies in the 1990s.

6 | Divided Loyalties
The Regional Politics of Divergence

CHAPTERS 4 AND 5 mapped the nature and structure of regional developmental states in India. Despite the centrist, uniform, national policy framework in New Delhi, the regional states responded with *divergent strategies* toward the central regime and their regional institutional structures differed widely. This variation in vertical strategies and regional institutions contributed to divergent investment rates in the large- and small-scale private sector as well as different infrastructural conditions for industry in the respective regions. This persistent regional variation in policy, institutions, and outcomes raises a set of deeper and interrelated questions: Why and how did the provincial regimes evolve the divergent strategies toward the national state and vis-à-vis the regional economies? What kind of regional politics sustained divergent strategic capacities across regional states? Reframed in another way, how and why were Gujarat's bureaucratic elites successful in pursuing its "bureaucratic-liberal strategy" while West Bengal's political elites pursued a very different strategy — "political confrontation"—successfully, albeit with negative economic consequences? This chapter addresses these deeper questions.

In order to answer these questions an analysis of the regional political dynamics and the incentives confronting state-level incumbents becomes necessary. Regional political elites are driven by electoral compulsions (motivation toward reelection in the province) and developmental aspirations (developmental goal); these motivations operate differently across the three states, given different popular pressures and varying support from socioeconomic groups. In this context, it is important to explore the role of each state's socioeconomic groups in supporting or opposing industrialization. The accommodation of social classes and caste groups into the regional *political regime* is as important for the pursuit of long-standing developmental strategies. Ruling political parties incorporate socioeconomic coalitions in each province into the regime, and thus, an analysis of their relations with dominant socioeconomic actors will also be instructive. These factors, in combination, contribute to the political support necessary to build strategic capacities and design institutions conducive (or not) for industrialization in each of the regional states. The roots of subnational developmental state can, thus, be traced to the regional coalitions that supported pro-center vertical strategies and pro-investment regional strategies. Legacies of subnational political mobilization (or the lack of such legacies) and the neighboring context also create varying political incentives for each state's regional politicians. Thus, the four variables that might explain the rise and persistence of subnational developmental states are: (1) the dominant social coalition and its role in the industrialization of the state, (2) the relation of the developmental coalition to the relevant ruling party-state in the state, (3) the extent of popular subnationalist pressures, and (4) the nature of the neighboring regional context. Table 6.1 summarizes the arguments, fleshed out in the rest of the chapter.

Gujarat: The Roots of Classic Competitive Capitalism

Gujarat embodies a classic capitalist developmental state; its regional state pursued growth-oriented industrial policies implemented in a flexible and effective manner by its bureaucracy.[1] What led its regional incumbents and political regimes to pursue industry-friendly policies and institutionalize a subnational developmental state, at a time when the national state was moving in an overly regulatory direction and when other states were implementing populist, anti-growth programs?[2] The salience of developmental politics in Gujarat is the result of a fortuitous combination of entrepreneurial resources in the shape of an artisanal and trader base, well-developed linkages to the external world, and most crucially, the transformation of a farmer-Patidar caste into an industrial capitalist class. However, these class-based characteristics, while crucial, were not sufficient in themselves. The distinctiveness of Gujarat's industrial growth lies in the incorporation of a wider base of upper castes, intermediate castes, and lower groups into the Congress Party, albeit in an inferior position, at a crucial and initial period of the state's development (1960 to 1975). These societal and political classes were transformed into a pro-developmentalist coalition by the regional party-state that fused preexisting elements in the political economy of Gujarat (traders and artisans) with a new class of capitalist farmers (Patidars) and disenfranchised social groups (indigenous groups and small farmers). All these groups acquired political and economic stakes in rapid but labor-intensive industrialization.[3] In the development of this political coalition, the regional party-state was a crucial catalyst. Moreover, the lack of a serious political competitor to the Congress Party meant that the potential opposition from the industrial workers and the agricultural laborers to the pro-growth strategy could not find an alternative political voice. Class divisions among the lower classes encouraged by capitalist development in Gujarat fragmented the potential for unified opposition. The

Table 6.1. Regional Political Economy of Divergence

	Gujarat	West Bengal	Tamil Nadu
I. Support of the dominant productive (socioeconomic) group for industrial development	High	Low	Low
Size and nature of the supporting coalition	Size: Large	Size: Small	Size: Small
	Nature: A pro-industry coalition that achieved caste unity in the crucial formative stage	Nature: Divide between the pro-industry and the hegemonic, Bhadralok coalition	Nature: A Tamil, non-Brahman, social and cultural coalition
Spread of the supporting coalition in rural and urban areas	Dispersed in rural and urban areas	Concentrated in urban areas	Dispersed in rural and urban areas
Link to productive (agrarian or industrial) activities	Strong	Weak	Weak
II. Power of the dominant productive classes	High	Low	Low
Link to the ruling party	Strong	Weak	Weak
Participation in the ruling regime	Yes	No	No
III. Subnational mobilization	Low	High	High but declines over time

Extent of subnationalism	Passive	Intense	Intense but weakens over time
Nature	Integrationist and pragmatic	Social and cultural	Cultural and charismatic
Support for anti-center strategies of the regional incumbents	Lack of support	Strong support	Strong support but changes over time
IV. Neighboring context	Competitive (pressure from Bombay city)	Absence of competition (no pressure from Bihar or Orissa)	Competitive (pressure from Karnataka and Kerala)

regional party-state was politically successful because a large coalition of social groups belonging to the upper- and medium-level social scale derived benefits from its pro-growth strategy and the losers could not find an alternative political voice. Thus, the political support provided by regional social forces and the ensuing political coalitions led to the rise of a competitive developmental state in Gujarat. The lack of a strong subnationalist political mobilization created further support for integrationist pro-center policies, rather than reward confrontational anti-center actions as in Tamil Nadu and West Bengal. This coherence of a pro-developmentalist coalition gives the appearance of a consensus to the state's pursuit of industrial development. A scholar of Gujarat notes:

> The economic and the industrial aspect of the political happenings have been deliberately sidestepped [in this book] except for passing references. This is not to underestimate the importance of economics. . . . *But in Gujarat's public life, there has been a total and continuous agreement about such issues and hence they have ceased to be political.* (Nagindas Sanghvi 1996, v; emphasis added)

I show below that this consensus was crafted and carefully sustained by the regional party-state in conjunction with crucial coalitional forces in the state. The apparent depoliticization of economic policy was only a mask covering a deep *unity* of political and economic power and coherence among its capitalist classes. This regional political-economy framework to understand the rise of the developmental state in Gujarat lays stress on three variables not stressed in earlier studies: (1) the formation of a social coalition from 1960 to 1974 constituted by capitalist farmers, farmer-industrialists, and trader-industrialists as well as small-scale industrialists; (2) their incorporation by the ruling Congress Party into a developmental political and electoral coalition. These two variables provided the political basis and political capacity to the state in Gujarat to evolve the *bureaucratic liberal* strategy in the 1960s and then continue it in the face of competing pressures in the 1980s. The absence of social democratic parties and the exclusion of anticapitalist ideas in the moral economy of the state further precluded any challenge that could constrain or humanize capitalist development in the regional state. Further, (3) the *absence* of a subnationalist anti-center popular force allowed the regional elite to pursue growth-oriented lobbying with the center without political sanctions from its populace.

The political economy of Gujarat can be broken into two major periods: 1960 to 1975 and 1980 to 1990. The period from 1960 to 1975 proved to be the most consequential period in designing the bureaucratic liberal strategy both toward the center and within the state. It was in this period that a distinctive and coherent developmental strategy and a corresponding institutional matrix took shape. The policy preferences and the institutional context that evolved in this period were to shape the developmental strategy of Gujarat well after the specific coalition that supported the policy initiative in the 1960–1975 period had disintegrated. In that sense, the bureaucratic-liberal strategy of Gujarat was "sticky" and was followed even after significant shifts in its coalition base. Hence, it is crucial to understand how the strategy came to be adopted and maintained.

The Rise of a Developmental State: 1960–1975

Existing analyses of political developments in Gujarat demonstrate the role of Patidar-Kanbi[4] caste domination in the politics of the state till the 1970s and its transformation toward the KHAM strategy in the 1970s and the 1980s.[5] It is argued that the dominant caste groups—Kanbis and Patidars in the 1960s through 1970s and Kshatriyas in the 1980s—lay claims on state patronage and attempt to capture the state for their ends.[6] Electoral compulsions of the ruling party, given a certain social structural frame, make the relevant caste domination in the state politics possible. This account leaves unanalyzed a crucial part of Gujarat's development: its rise as an industrial state from 1960 onward. How does the domination of these caste groups relate to the politics of industrial development in the regional state?

Starting in the 1960s, diverse class factions within Gujarat acquired explicit stakes in regional industrial development. Even more importantly, these regional socioeconomic groups developed explicit linkages with the party-state and successive regimes. In addition, subnationalist popular mobilization in Gujarat was and continues to be traditionally weak; this provides support for the pursuit of a pro-center rather than an anti-center political strategy on the part of its political elites. This fortuitous combination of factors provided the social and political preconditions for Gujarat's political elite to pursue a state-led developmental model that privileged industrial growth and evolved new institutions to support such an intervention and the redirection of licenses granted by the center. Environmental problems attendant on rapid industrialization were neglected and equity considerations bypassed; yet, industrialization in Gujarat became more spatially dispersed and diffused among lower classes, who started small-scale ventures encouraged by the state government's liberal policy of incentives, loans, and infrastructural development. Increase in employment and decline in poverty was the result. This process created support for further industrialization, setting in motion a dynamic process of accelerated growth and capitalist development. Let me elaborate on the social-structural and political conditions that made possible the pursuit of regional (local industrial strategies and institutions) and vertical (directed toward the center) political strategies followed by Gujarat's elites.

The Regional Developmental Coalition in Gujarat (1960–1975)

Three class factions with specifically regional and caste features supported successive regimes' industrial agendas. Different caste groups dominated the three class groups, but together these three groups formed the basis of a widely dispersed coalition in favor of rapid and labor-intensive industrialization.[7] (1) A trader-merchant class transformed a historically rooted mercantilism in Gujarat into industrial capitalism.[8] (2) A caste of farmer-capitalists ushered in the development of agrarian and urban capitalism in south Gujarat by moving some of their financial and human capital into manufacturing.[9] Simultaneously, the deepening of agrarian capitalism in rural Gujarat created a vast market for intermediate industrial goods. (3) Most importantly, the creation of new small-scale industrialists and technocratic capitalists encouraged by explicit state government policies was instrumental in creating dispersed and employment-intensive capitalism in south and central Gujarat.

Thus, a regional developmental state interested in industrialization of Gujarat after 1960 was possible as a result of the formation of a regionally located and overlapping socioeconomic group of traders, artisans, industrialists, and capitalist farmers. Some of these were traditional elites—Brahmans, Banias, and Patidars—but other groups (small-scale entrepreneurs) were created as part of the effort by the political and bureaucratic elites to pursue a labor-intensive industrialization in an aggressive manner.[10] The structure and nature of industrialization in Gujarat, while elite-led, involved, albeit in an inferior way, previously disenfranchised groups of people: small artisans, small traders, backward castes[11] such as Lava Patidars,[12] some groups of the Kshatriya caste, which were lower in class status in Gujarat, and many lower-middle-class people. For many of these groups becoming a small-scale business-person was their first venture into industry. These groups came to form a political vote-bank for the Congress Party in addition to its traditional supporters (Patidars-farmers, Banias, and Brahmans). The electoral success of the Congress Party (undivided Congress) till 1969 lay in being able to forge alliances with both the Patidars (the dominant caste) and the Kshatriyas (the backward caste in Gujarat but not so in many other states) in the face of other contenders for their support (for example, the Swatantra Party). Thus, what was comparatively distinctive about the social base underlying industrialization was its socially and geographically dispersed character, especially relative to West Bengal and Tamil Nadu. Gujarat's industrialization received the economic and the political support of not only the economic elites such as larger farmers and businesspeople but also socially disadvantaged groups that moved into industrial activities and received employment benefits as an offshoot of a labor-intensive industrialization.[13] This ensured support for the political elite in the face of plausible redistributive claims on the state. Extensive state supports for the small-scale sector in the form of concessional credit, tax incentives, infrastructural support, and training worked in a redistributive way. This formed a new breed of entrepreneurs and industrialists created by the state (Gorter 1996).

Yet, the role of traditional social and caste groups must be kept in mind while analyzing Gujarat's industrial development. The role of Patidars is crucial both for Gujarat's industrialization and for the political coalition of the Congress Party between 1960 and 1975 and is worth analyzing in some detail.[14] The term "Patidar" refers to a confederation of various small castes and subcastes, some of which are upper castes while others are middle and backward castes (K. D. Desai 1965; Pocock 1972).

Two economic characteristics of the Patidars are crucial for their salient role in the political economy of Gujarat. One, traditionally they were farmers. The majority of the farmers were located in the context of commercial agriculture prevalent in central Gujarat. Gujarat's food cultivation has been very stagnant, but the extension and growth of commercial and cash crops such as vegetable oils, cotton, groundnut, peanuts, and tobacco into central, south, and west Gujarat gave economic power to the farming community dominated by the Patidars.[15] They form a strong farmers' lobby. Second, social reform movements among the Patidar subcastes led, in the early twentieth century, to upper-caste Patidars (usually Patel subcaste group) educating their children and sending them abroad.[16] The general social pattern after 1960 was for one Patel child to go abroad while the others looked after farms in their villages in central Gujarat. Usually, the child who went abroad maintained links with his hometown village, and was likely to come back to set up a small-scale industrial venture (Streefkerk 1979; Breman 1985).[17] This external linkage created investment resources, but even more important was the social capital mechanism through which farmers of traditional caste groups started industrial production especially in engineering and chemical industries after 1960. By 1989, the dominance of Patels in almost all (except textile and hosiery) industry segments is significant. Shinoda's analysis shows that by 1989, Patels held 53.6 percent of small-scale firms in food products, 20.7 percent in cotton textiles, 45.4 percent in wood products, 26.5 percent in chemical products, and 20.3 percent in machinery and parts (Shinoda 2000, 3207), clearly dominating many sectors of the state's economy. All these dimensions meant that farmers and the landholding class in Gujarat were *not* economically or socially conservative;[18] rather, they formed the vanguard of an industrial revolution when the state government came forward with credit and infrastructural facilities.[19] Rutten's (1995) research on central and south Gujarat shows that farmers in central Gujarat diversified their economic interests into trading and industrial activities in the 1960s and 1970s. This phenomenon is clearly unexpected given the general supposition in the literature that farmers rarely invest in nonagricultural activities. Thus, Gujarat's industrialization was facilitated by a fortuitous linkage between the agricultural and industrial sectors of the economy that failed to happen in many other states.[20] As Rutten argues,

> My own findings on the economic diversification among the large farmers and small-scale industrialists in central Gujarat illustrate the specific ways in which the agrarian and non-agrarian sectors of the household economy re-integrated and influenced each other. Economic diversification among the large farmers and small-scale industrialists suggests that capital flows in both directions between agriculture and non-agriculture business. . . . Agriculture, trade, industry and other economic activities are closely intertwined in these regions. For the rural elite, they are not contradictory but complementary occupations. (1995, 358)

Streefkerk's earlier study, while emphasizing the merchant capital route to industrialization in Gujarat, also found that the post-1950s industrial expansion among members of artisan castes in Bulsar (in the Valsad district of Gujarat) was due to their favorable location vis-à-vis a fertile agricultural region that organized production on commercial lines.

> The second condition, principally responsible for the post 1950 industrial development among artisans was the orientation of production toward the agricultural sector. This was made possible by the fertile agrarian surroundings of Bilmora [in central Gujarat] and the more modern, capitalist way of production there. The more advantageous political-administrative contacts of artisans-entrepreneurs in Bilmora were a by-product of gearing production for agriculture. (Streefkerk 1985, 257–58)

The efforts of the Gujarat Industrial Development Corporation (GIDC), in its first stage from 1960 to 1970, also led to unintended spatial decentralization of industrial activity. The Gujarat Industrial Development Corporation set up many industrial estates that provided land, power, roads, and other infrastructural facilities in south and central Gujarat in the 1960s and 1970s (see Chapter 5 for data on industrial estates). It is worth noting that many of these industrial estates were established in rural areas, enhancing the linkage between rural populations and industrial activity. Industrial activity in Gujarat is a rural phenomenon and extends to previously unindustrialized parts of the state, such as Saurashtra.[21] This spatial dispersion has continued after liberalization in 1991. Twenty-one percent of new investments have gone to Saurashtra in the post-1990s period (Hirway and Terhal 2002). While the dominance of central and south Gujarat on the industrial map of Gujarat is unchallenged, many small industrial centers have developed over the years in western and central Gujarat.[22] Table 6.2 confirms that five of the nine rural districts in Gujarat are industrialized.

In Gujarat, then, both the agrarian capitalists and the urban industrial houses have a strong regional base; a state government attempting both to differentiate itself from Bombay and to replicate Bombay's industrial success encouraged the further development of these classes.[23] Thus, there was a clear synergy and overlap between agrarian capitalists, the urban business houses, and the state-led efforts to create new entrepreneurs in Gujarat, contributing to the formation, after 1960, of a strong *regional capitalist class.*

What is notable is that this regional capitalist coalition was not challenged by worker-oriented and lower class–based parties despite significant exploitation and poor working conditions at the factory and farm level.[24] Thus, the presence of potential conflict within the various social and economic groups could not coalesce into organized opposition against an industrial capitalist trajectory. As the economy of Gujarat expanded and political mobilization of farmer-castes solidified into institutionalized federation of caste-groups, the dominant caste and the dominant class (Patidars, farmers, and industrialists) were not challenged from below. While there was clear *socioeconomic* conflict between classes, *politically,* the lower classes, backward castes, indigenous people, and industrial laborers continued to vote for the Congress Party. Three politico-economic modalities contributed to the incorporation of lower classes, lower castes, and the indigenous communities into the hegemonic coalition rather than encourage them to rebel against the prevailing politico-economic order.

First, *caste hegemony* among the Patidars and later the Kshatriyas across competing class divisions served to undercut such challenges, and many social groups from "below"—indigenous people, small artisans, and traders—were more concerned to ensure access to the industrial concessions given by the entrepreneurial state. Second, the nature of industrialization was itself more labor intensive and hence had a much wider base than in West Bengal, for example. Many of the small traders, artisans, and small farmers in south Gujarat moved into small-scale industry, which affected a larger section of the population than in other states.[25] Third, and most important, deprived and oppressed classes lack a political voice to channel their preferences and protests. No political party or social movement voices their concerns. The weakness of the labor movement in Gujarat has meant that most workers, despite bad treatment and exploitation, cannot appeal to any political party or union against the Congress regime. They can only vote for the Congress Party or the Bharatiya Janata Party (BJP) in the hope that these parties would fulfill their promises toward "trusteeship"-type relations between workers and employers.

Table 6.2. Extent of Urban-Industrial Symmetry in Gujarat

Districts	Percentage of Urban Population		Percentage of Main Industrial Workers Population
Urban Districts		Industrial vs. Agricultural Districts (I or A)	
Jamnagar	40	I	13.6
Rajkot	47	I	19.7
Surendranagar	30	I	14.8
Bhavnagar	35	I	23.8
Junagadh	32	A	8.7
Kachchh	30	A	10.0
Gandhinagar	40	I	13.2
Ahmedabad	74	I	27.5
Vadodora	42	I	15.1
Surat	50	I	31.5
Rural Districts			
Amreli	21	I	16.7
Mahesana	22	I	11.7
Kheda*	22	I	9.1
Bharuch*	21	I	10.4
Valsad	24	I	18.4
Banaskantha	10	A	7.2
Sabarkantha	10	A	4.4
Panchmahals	10	A	4.1
Dangs	11	A	2.5

Source: Calculated from Census of India, 1991.
*The figures for main workers underestimate the extent of industrialization in Kheda, Jamnagar, Mahesana, and Bharuch; these can be classified as industrial. Bharuch (similar to Burdwan in West Bengal) has many public-sector units, making it clearly an industrial area. Kheda, Mahesana, and Jamnagar have a large number of small-scale units, making the classification as an industrial district more appropriate. Also see Dupont's study (1995) of Jetpur (a city in western Gujarat) which concurs with this conclusion about Jamnagar and western Gujarat.
Note: I define a district as industrial if the share of main industrial workers exceeds 15 percent, and a district as urban if the urban population is more than 25 percent. Main industrial workers are defined by the census as those workers who have managed to work more than 183 days in a year in either household or nonhousehold industry.

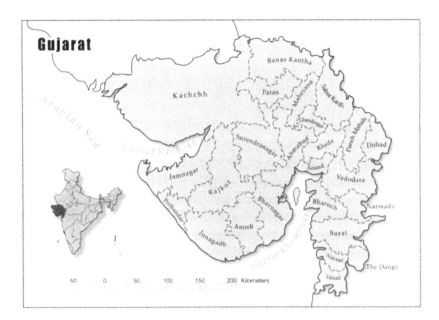

This means that any opposition to the dominant pattern of industrialization is inchoate and dispersed.

First is the issue of caste hegemony. The formation of a "Patidar community" in Gujarat is a recent twentieth-century phenomenon going back to the nationalist movement against colonialism. The Patidars had different socioeconomic interests; south Gujarat Patidars were wealthier, while the northern Patels were essentially landless peasants. Earlier in the twentieth century, Patidars were considered rural and backward; known as "Kunbis," "Bhabhas," and "Kaliparaj" (literally, black people) in some areas, the word "Patidar" was hardly used. In 1908 *Patidar Yuvak Mandal* (Patidar Youth Association), a social reform organization, was formed in Surat, aiming at the "total" uplift of the Patidars; this saw the beginning of social reform within the Patidar community and their unification. Caste journals such as *Patidar Hitechhu* (Welfare of Patidars) and its later incarnation, *Patel Bandhu* (Friend of Patidars), along with regular conferences (held in 1910, 1913, 1914, and 1917) and educational institutions such as a boardinghouse established in 1911 carried forward the task of social reform, unification of disparate subcastes, and infusion of nationalist ideas.[26] The nationalist movement saw further development of caste hegemony. The Indian National Congress under the leadership of Sardar Patel was able to unify many fractions of the middle and lower subcastes—till then—known as Kolis, Kanbis, and Patidars. "The solidarity was particularly marked among the middle and lower castes. It was a popular expression during the movement that the 'four Ks' under the leadership of Sardar Patel organized three other 'Ks,' namely the 'Kubbis' (Patidars), 'Kolis' (a lower caste) and the 'Kaliparj' (Scheduled Tribes)" (Bhatt 1970, 331). Integration of many economically opposed castes into the nationalist movement modernized the traditional castes, created diverse social institutions at the local level, and brought them together under the national movement. Bhatt further argues, "Thus, if caste was useful in the mobilization of support for the satyagraha, the satyagraha in turn integrated and secularized caste" (Bhatt 1970, 331).[27] Shah confirms: "Thus the *patidars,* who were in the forefront of the nationalist movement between 1919 and 1947, invoked caste sentiments to develop horizontal unity at the level of ideology among patidars of different social status" (Ghanshyam Shah 1990, 75) and, even more important for my analysis, different economic classes. This caste hegemony served to unify economically divergent groups and undercut the potential opposition that could have emerged on class lines.

Second, the relatively successful implementation of the land reforms in Gujarat, coinciding with a Ryotwari system during the colonial times, meant that the "class of *small* farmers has become very large and widespread. In 1961, 72 percent of landowners were small farmers, only 10 percent owning more than 30 acres" (Sheth 1976a, 79). The land reform legislation was also implemented relatively effectively in the tribal areas of south Gujarat so that the landed classes "lost the bulk of their estates to their adivasi (indigenous communities) tenants" (Hardiman 1987, 215). In Gujarat these large groups of small farmers have participated actively in politics and have been a strong backbone of the Congress Party for much of the 1970s and 1980s. Moreover, their movement into small-scale industry has meant that industrialization has received the support of a more widely dispersed social group.[28] In contrast to the immobility of Adivasis in many other states, in Gujarat, richer Adivasis, the beneficiaries of the early land reform legislation, moved into money-lending in the 1950s, and their descendants moved into government service, contracting, and small-scale local industry (Hardiman 1987, 216). In many other states, farmers and indigenous communities have opposed industrialization and remained within the agriculture sector; class divisions within the indigenous and oppressed communities and widespread mobility have served to undercut mobilization on class lines.[29]

Third, industrial labor in Gujarat has been weak and votes for the Congress Party. Moreover, leftist parties don't exist in the regional state, and mainstream parties hold leftist ideas in contempt. While analyses by Breman (1974, 1985, 1990, 1993, 1996, and 2003) and Streefkerk (1985) document the extensive exploitation of workers, this exploitation did not coalesce into political opposition against the pro-investment strategy of the Gujarat government.

One reason for this acquiescence is that the history of the labor movement in Gujarat is influenced by the Gandhian tradition of peaceful collaboration between the workers and the employers (Patel 1987).[30] The Textile Labor Association (TLA), locally known as the Majur Mahajan (Laborer's Guild), symbolizes the tradition of collaboration and was associated with the INTUC (the Congress-sponsored trade union). Sujata Patel in a recent analysis compares the pre-independence tradition of labor-capital interaction in Gujarat to societal corporatism in Europe, but one which "later . . . incorporated them in a patronage relationship that worked to displace rather than enhance or enlarge those [workers'] rights" (Patel 2002, 97). Moreover, the Congress Party after independence encouraged many social welfare institutions, which co-opted these groups within their fold. "The social welfare institutions organized for their [workers'] uplift by the Gandhian workers since the last five decades and supported and at times, influenced by the erstwhile Congress Party helped maintain their relationship undisturbed. In elections also this situation helped the ruling party to get their support to ward off the onslaught of the Swatantra party (Sheth 1976a, 78)." Streefkerk's analysis of industrial transition in south Gujarat, the center of capitalist exploitation of workers, explicitly discusses the *absence* of class-consciousness or protest movements in south Gujarat; this absence is facilitated by class divisions amongst the laborers themselves (Streefkerk 1985, 211).[31] Breman shows (1985) that despite extensive exploitation by a capitalist production process in agriculture in Bardoli (south Gujarat), the landless laborers do not organize and protest politically. First, they do not have any political group to take up their grievances; and second, "The Gandhian doctrine, which had earlier obtained a footing in the tribal area, prevented the indigenous population from adopting a more violent form of resistance against social and economic subordination. Harmony and reconciliation by adapting a model imposed from above also characterized the way in which Gandhian workers tried to promote the upliftment of the Halpatis (Breman 1985, 368)."[32] In a follow-up study of south Gujarat in 1997, Breman reconfirms that organizations that claim to "liberate agricultural workers from bondage" adopt nonpolitical and nonconflictual modes of action inspired by Gandhian ideas (2003, 94).

Moreover, the high share of migrant workers in the economy of south Gujarat and the easy circulation of workers from agrarian to nonagrarian (industrial) occupations imply that workers have many alternative options.[33] Massive immigration of industrial and agricultural workers into Gujarat from Uttar Pradesh, Bihar, Rajasthan, and Madhya Pradesh makes lower-class unity difficult; it even exacerbates intra-class conflict.[34] The absence of a Left party or Left unions and the strong Gandhian roots of the existing labor movement make it difficult for these workers to organize. Breman admits in his later work: "What are the prospects for the huge army of seasonal migrants to convert their massiveness into power politics? Probably even more crucial than their transient status is the fact that they are split into numerous gangs that have little to do with one another and which show little social cohesiveness due to the fact that they come from different regions and castes" (1994, 115). And, "In contrast to this mobilization among the rural bourgeoisie, the landless are still hardly aware of their class identity" (Breman 1994, 312).[35] Thus, the consolidation of caste hegemony of the Patidar community has submerged the economic differences amongst them, a relatively successful land reform has created relatively equitable conditions in the countryside, and the absence of an opposition party to take up the interests of the working and subordinate classes made worse by the ideology of trusteeship in the union movement meant that the industrialization-based strategy affected wider sections of society than in West Bengal and political mobilization against exploitation was inchoate and nonexistent.

Party Politics and Industrialization in Gujarat: The Congress Party and Industrialization (1960–1975)

The initial period of 1960 to 1975 is especially crucial for laying the *political basis* of sustained industrialization in Gujarat. It was in this period that an overlapping developmentalist coalition was formed, as shown above. Yet, what is crucial for Gujarat's industrial strategy is the incorporation of various sections of this coalition into the regional *party system* in the 1960s and early 1970s. Streefkerk's study of Bulsar argued that "in many cases entrepreneurs and local politicians helped in promoting each other's interests" (Streefkerk 1985, 257–58). Extending his intuition, I argue that Gujarat's pursuit of a bureaucratic liberalism strategy was predicated upon *the political incorporation of the artisan–small-scale industrialists and farmer-industrialists into the party system at a crucial stage of the state's development*. Thus, the consolidation of caste hegemony of the Patidar-Kanbi caste group, the movement of farmer-Patidar capital into industrial activities, and the incorporation of Patidars into the ruling Congress Party meant that industrialization and growth-oriented policies were on the agenda of the ruling party in Gujarat and pro-growth strategies had "ceased to be political."

However, the Congress Party needed electoral support of a wider section of people than the caste elites to win elections. The ruling regime evolved a strategy of growth that was designed to garner the support of a regionally and socially diverse cross section of people. Its first component was an aggressive strategy of investment attraction from large-scale industrialists of Bombay, Calcutta, and the central licensing regime. This ensured investment and taxes but did not directly add to their electoral support. However, an increased flow of investments and attendant tax revenue could underwrite incentives, tax giveaways, subsidized loans, entrepreneurial training, and the provision of industrial infrastructure to newly emerging industrialists in south and central Gujarat. This flow of large- and medium-scale investment also helped support a welfare system privileging scheduled castes, scheduled tribes, and Muslims in the 1970s and 1980s. The targeted groups for this state-guided fiscal support were artisans, traders, small farmers, backward castes, and even scheduled castes (untouchables) and scheduled tribes (indigenous communities). In addition, from across the border with Maharashtra, both small-scale and large-scale industrialists were targeted. Geographically, while the focus of the strategy in the 1960s and 1970s was south and central Gujarat, the initial domination of Saurashtrians in the first cabinet of Gujarat (1960 to 1963) meant that Saurashtra (western Gujarat) too received significant public infrastructure, and some industrial enterprises were set up. Thus, labor-intensive industrialization in Gujarat extended to central, south, and western Gujarat.

The initiative of bureaucrats to establish industrial estates in south Gujarat soon after the formation of Gujarat, the provision of extensive credit facilities to small-scale businesspeople especially in Vapi, Kheda, Bulsar, Bilmora, and other villages in central and South Gujarat, entrepreneurial training, and easy loans from GIIC (Gujarat Industrial Investment Corporation) and GSFC (Gujarat State Finance Corporation) helped the Patels and other medium castes to further consolidate their control over the economic life of the region and also helped the Congress Party to win elections in the assembly elections of 1960, 1962, 1967, and 1972. While Patels are about 20 percent of the population, they have consistently held 20–26 percent of the seats in the Gujarat assembly from 1960 onward. No other social group held a higher share of the seats in this period. Their share of the seats increased from 19.6 percent to 26.0 percent in 1972 (Sheth 1976a, 74). In 1973 Chimanbhai Patel became the chief minister. This led Sheth to argue:

> [T]he Patels have consistently held their dominant position. This landed gentry, which came to the forefront in the national movement spread its influence in industrial and agricultural fields and came to exercise impact on politics as a distinct and dominant group. Even in the new radical phase of "Indira age," they are not adversely affected as the Kshatriyas are. (1976a, 74)

While the landowning Patidars were naturally dominant in the pre-independence and post-1960s Congress Party, the landless peasants in north Gujarat also supported the Congress Party as a result of the caste hegemony built by key Patel leaders during the anticolonial struggle (Hardiman 1981; Bhatt 1970).[36] This submerged the structural conflict between the peasants holding land and the landless Patidars of north Gujarat under a caste-based endogamy.

The *ideological structure of party competition in the 1960s* in Gujarat facilitated the formation of a pro-growth strategy. The main opposition party in

Gujarat, the Swatantra Party, was formed out of the rural landowning class and thus represented the rural and urban rich (Erdman 1967). It gained significant vote share in both the Lok Sabha (parliament) and state-level assembly elections in 1962. In the 1962 Lok Sabha elections, it won 25 percent of the vote in Gujarat, and for the 1962 assembly elections its share was 24.43 percent, the highest vote share out of all states (Erdman 1967, 274, 277). In 1967 it increased its Gujarat vote share to 39.9 percent in the Lok Sabha elections and to 38.2 percent in the Gujarat assembly elections (Butler, Lahiri, and Roy 1995, 174–75). Its policy positions have been to the right of the national mainstream as well as of the Congress Party in Gujarat. This challenge from a dominant rightist party kept up the pressure on the Congress Party to ensure policies that favor the rural and urban rich. The policy space in Gujarat, certainly till the 1970s and even later, was more rightward than in West Bengal and Tamil Nadu, and no party with an egalitarian or leftist orientation could emerge in Gujarat. Simultaneously, the electoral dominance of the Congress Party in terms of seats won and vote share after the initial challenge by the Swatantra Party meant that the pursuit of growth-oriented policies was unchallenged in the political arena.[37]

Institutionally, the successful running of the Panchayat system and the cooperatives in the rural areas by the Congress Party meant that backward and indigenous communities participated in the "Congress coalition" in contrast to opposing the coalition. In contrast, in West Bengal, a strong association of the Zamindari landlords with the Congress Party de-legitimized the rural community structures and allowed the Communist Party (CPI) to gain support of the sharecroppers. In contrast, in Gujarat:

> It was Congress [party] under Hitendra Desai [CM in 1960s], which largely controlled the Panchayati-raj institutions of the State and skillfully used them in various elections. . . . The Panchayats in the backward areas of South Gujarat have also functioned as agents of political socialization and recruitment for the Adivasi community. It is through these structures that Adivasi leadership has been groomed and trained, some of which have now begun making itself felt at the level of state politics. Jhinabhai Darji [Adivasi leader], the President of Surat Zila Panchyat and now the president of the ruling GPCC [Gujarat Provincial Congress Committee] is not just an isolated case of rural elite assuming power but it deserves to be treated as symbolic of the phenomenon of a new emerging rural elite in the wake of Panchayati-raj which has potential for upward political mobility. (Sheth 1976a, 77)

The political elite of Gujarat encouraged and tolerated the autonomy of the industrial bureaucracy because the industrial bureaucracy competently delivered a spatially wide-based vote-bank to the ruling party in the form of small-scale and medium-scale industrialists in south Gujarat, the artisans of

Surat (for example those in the diamond trade), the textile workers of central Gujarat, and the indigenous people who worked in many industrial units, as well as the tax and financial support of the large-scale industrial capitalists. In addition, the efficient and economic functioning of the joint sector and the state industrial corporations (PSUs) meant that regular dividends flowed into the state and party treasuries.[38] These regular dividends provided the incentives to maintain the autonomy of the various joint-sector units and the SIDCs. With time the supposed independence and autonomy of its PSUs and joint sector became a matter of political pride for the political elite, an issue to be talked about during elections.[39]

The KHAM Strategy and the Politics of Industrialization: 1980 to 1990

Beginning in the 1970s but consolidated only in the early 1980s, the regional pattern of political coalition was transformed by national developments. After Indira Gandhi's Congress succeeded in splitting the Congress in Gujarat in 1971 (much later than in other states), Patels deserted the Congress (Indira) to join and support the remnants of the old Congress in the form of the Janata Dal.[40] This led the Congress (I) to shift its strategy toward a KHAM strategy in Gujarat (Wood 1984b; Ghanshyam Shah 1990). This strategy, an attempt to form an alternative electoral coalition to the dominant Bania, Brahman, and Patel hegemony, was constituted by Adivasis, Lower Kshatriyas and other backward castes, Harijans, Muslims, and lower Patels as well as the Kolis in the coastal areas. This solidified the alienation of the Patidars-Kanbi group from the Congress Party after 1980.[41] These KHAM groups were recruited into the Congress (I) Party in large numbers with the promise of party tickets and party positions. This strategy was a conscious top-down effort to realign the social basis of the party system in Gujarat. What did it mean for the industrial strategy of the regional developmental state? Did a shift in the political basis of the Congress Party have a corresponding shift in industrial strategy?

I argue that, by 1975–1980, when a two-pronged cleavage between the erstwhile supporters of Congress and the beneficiaries of the industrial strategy —the Patel-Kanbi castes and the newly mobilized KHAM groups—crystallized, the ruling Congress regime had acquired an independent stake in the benefits of efficient and dispersed industrialization. The various SIDCs paid regular dividends to the chief ministers, and regular taxes and dividends flowed into the state exchequer from the private, state, and central public sector. The labor-intensive nature of industrialization provided crucial vote-bank support to successive regimes in Gujarat. It was this financial and political support that provided the buffer for Madhav Solanki's government, which despite introduction of pro-reservation policies in favor of the KHAM coalition and some anti-reservation riots in 1981, did not face any challenge from 1980 to 1985.[42] Moreover, Solanki could evolve a potentially contradictory strategy well described by Wood:

> Solanki's government was the only government the State has had which completed its five-year mandate (1980–1985). That it survived so long is remarkable for several reasons. The first is that this was the first government in Gujarat whose members held political power but proportionately little social and economic influence. Elsewhere in India (Bihar, for example) such governments . . . were toppled. This did not happen in Gujarat mainly because the Solanki government did not launch any major legislative effort, which would disturb Gujarati capitalist interest or seriously undermine the economic situation of large cash crop farmers. In fact, under Solanki's stewardship, Gujarat became the second most industrialized State in India, as his government, in cooperation with the private sector, launched many projects in power development, electronics, fertilizer and many other industries. In addition he introduced welfare schemes such as free midday meals for primary school children, free education for female students up to university completion and distribution of food grains to families with annual income under Rs. 5000 (1995, 157–58).[43]

Ultimately, the threat to the political power of Patels could not be compensated by economic and industrial concessions, and despite the landslide victory of Solanki's government on March 5, 1985, riots and violence led to the fall of his government later in the year. The crisis in 1985 showed that economic and social power was not enough for the hitherto dominant economic and political elite of Gujarat; they also wanted unlimited political access to the state, which they had enjoyed in the 1960s and 1970s. Although Solanki's nominee (an indigenous person, Amarsingh Choudhary) was appointed as Solanki's successor, Choudhary announced various concessions to the medium and high castes, and the political balance of power was restored with the inclusion of three high-caste members as cabinet ministers (Wood 1995, 164). However, it must be noted that the dominant coalition formed in the 1960s could not displace an emerging populist and pro-KHAM political regime through the ballot box; extreme measures and brute coercive forces had to be resorted to precisely because the politico-economic coalition behind the twin strategy of "bureaucratic liberalism" and selective welfarism had massive and widespread political support.

Also, it must be noted that the world of political parties and elections in India does not reflect the interests and political power of the economically dominant class, especially of the urban/industrial sector. The modes of power and channels of influence utilized by the industrialists in most states operate backstage, and behind closed doors. What is notable for Gujarat is that the period from 1960 to 1975 was an exceptional one in which industrialists of various types had direct policy influence; after 1980 Gujarat's politics returned to the nationally normal case of representing distributive politics in the formal political space. However, by then, the productive politics of growth and industrialization was so well entrenched in the political administration and in the material interest of politicians that it was insulated from distributive challenges most visible in the electoral arena. Thus, to observe politics of industrialization in India one needs to go behind the direct and highly politicized stage of electoral and party politics and analyze the relative power of bureaucrats, industrialists, and politicians *between* electoral cycles.

The invisibility of industrial issues in explicit public discussions in Gujarat noted by N. Sanghvi at the beginning of this analysis was a reflection not of indifference by its political elite but of a remarkable coherence regarding industrial strategy across diverse and otherwise contradictory sections of society. Nevertheless, it must be acknowledged that it was the economic success of that strategy that provided the most important rationale for its continued pursuance; nothing succeeds like success. Once the industrial strategy was in place, and definite advantages began to flow from it, no group wished to see it go *despite* changes in the political balance of power that initially supported it. Wood puts forth an even stronger claim: "One is led to conclude that it is Gujarat's prosperity, stimulated by the Solanki government's economic pragmatism, which allows the KHAM strategy to continue; in a less affluent state the higher caste backlash would be much more severe (1984b, 221)." Bureaucratic liberalism, then, is not an oxymoron, at least, for Gujarat. The distinctive industrial strategy followed by Gujarat was supported by a distinctive political and social coalition led by the regional party-state. This support allowed the bureaucracy enough political room to design policy and institutional instruments that favored a state-led but private sector–based industrial strategy. This pursuit of a regional developmental state was further bolstered by the absence of strong subnationalist pressures within the province; this allowed state officials to pursue bargaining and lobbying with the central government.

Horizontal Competition and the Absence of Subnationalism in Gujarat

In contrast to many other states of India, Gujarat lacks a strong millennial regionalist sentiment or popular movement against the center. Its politics has been integrationist rather than confrontational, and its parties prefer to lobby rather than build popular movements against the diktats of New Delhi. This absence of subnationalism as a political force leaves room for its political elites to lobby the center's ministries and to seek advantages from within the system, whether they be licenses, FDI approvals, or joint-sector approvals. The roots for this politics of integrationist strategies lie in the post-independence politics of the state's formation. The pursuit of Gujarat's development strategy was shaped by the competitive pressure provided by the loss of Bombay city in 1960.

In 1947, Gujarat existed as a cultural and linguistic social fact, but its political boundaries were fuzzy and its territories claimed by diverse claimants.[44] The developmentalism of Gujarat after 1960 was conditioned crucially by this historical legacy, its immediate regional context (presence of Maharashtra and Bombay as its neighbor), and the nature of Gujarat's formation out of Bombay Presidency. At independence (1947), what is now Gujarat state (formed in 1960) consisted of a large-sized Baroda state (a princely state), 395 other princely states and estates (four-fifths of current Gujarat), and a part of Gujarat under direct British rule (one-fifth of current Gujarat). The British-ruled districts were Ahmedabad, Kheda, Panchmahals, Bharouch, and Surat districts of Bombay Presidency.[45] Labeled a "political geographer's jigsaw puzzle" by John Wood, the tasks of integration alone were multifarious and complex (Wood 1984a, 67). The two types of territories—British and princely—presented contrasting political, economic, and ideological legacies and unique integration problems (Wood 1984a).

What is also crucial is the relationship between the Gujarat part of Bombay state and Bombay as a whole, a relationship that became salient between 1956 and 1960 and in the decade after 1960 when Gujarat was hived off Greater Bombay to form the Gujarat state with its current boundaries. Bombay city was dominated by people from the Gujarat area.[46] Mallison (1996, 76) writes:

> Bombay was the cradle of modern Gujarat. . . . Owned by the Portuguese and handed over to the English crown in 1665, Bombay, at that time composed of seven islands surrounded by unhealthy marshlands, was given to the East India company in order to consolidate its position. As early as 1687 the city . . . in process of being settled by Parsi and Gujarati Banias thanks to the initiative of Gerald Aungier . . . was chosen to succeed Surat as the company's headquarters in Western India. . . . During this entire period a Gujarati speaking population moved to the city in a steady stream. The new township of Bombay, although situated beyond the Gujarat border, attracted the Gujaratis because of the economic opportunities it offered.

The eighteenth and nineteenth centuries saw a massive Gujarati trader immigration to Bombay; Gujarati population (Meghnad Desai 1995; Pocock 1972) to a large extent constituted the fourfold increase in Bombay's population between 1820 and 1864. In contemporary times, between 1948 and 1956, Gujaratis played a prominent role in the Bombay state government. After the 1952 election, four out of nine members of the Bombay cabinet were Gujaratis, including Morarji Desai, who came from Surat and was the chief minister of Bombay (Wood 1984a, 77–78).

Gujarat was formed as a state in 1960, under the pressures for the second wave of linguistic reorganization, carved out of the hitherto existing Bombay state and by combining Saurashtra and Kutch. The formation of Gujarat in 1960 constituted both an achievement and also an unsettling tearing of the social and economic fabric of Greater Bombay. Till then, Bombay had been seen a part of one subregional entity. A great deal of ambivalence (in terms of party-based support and popular opinion) existed about the Maha-Gujarat movement and the necessity of forming a separate Gujarat state (Sanghvi 1996, 146–50). Politically and administratively, a strong Gujarati identity had not emerged by 1960. What became Gujarat was a disparate and inchoate blend of hundreds of princely states in the Saurashtra region, a self-conscious princely province (Baroda), the Kutch region, and lastly, the Bombay Presidency region. Given this disparate blend of political and administrative experiences, nationalism and hence subnationalism had not developed in the whole Gujarat state (except central Gujarat, where the influence of the Congress was strong and trend setting) as it had in other Indian states.[47] In 1960, Gujarati people and the political elite were forced to turn inward to deal with this splintering. Gujarat's political leadership was forced to rethink ways to insert its new identity and new socioeconomic unity onto the national scene.

Moreover, the strong association of Gujarati culture with Bombay and the proposal to include Bombay city into Maharashtra was especially troubling for residents of central and south Gujarat. Nobody wanted to lose Bombay city, as it was the center of Gujarati cultural and social creativity as well as Gujarati mercantile and industrial capital (Mallison 1996; Sonal Shukla 1995).[48] Separate statehood could mean the loss of Bombay state's larger budgetary resources and the loss of the externalities associated with Bombay city (Wood 1984a, 80). Hence, the bifurcation of Gujarat from Bombay and the formation of the twin states of Maharashtra and Gujarat in 1960, with Bombay becoming the capital of Maharashtra, was received by the newly formed state's elite and the popular opinion within Gujarat with mixed feelings.[49] Part of the bargain settled between Gujarat and Maharashtra was that Maharashtra would provide finances for the development of a new capital city located in the outskirts of Ahmedabad (the important commercial city) to compensate for the loss of Bombay. It was an acknowledgment of the legitimate grievances of the newly formed Gujarat state.

This formed the historical matrix that shaped the "ideology of developmentalism" in Gujarat at a crucial originary moment. Almost all state bureaucrats, businesspeople, and politicians whom I interviewed narrated the role that Bombay played in fashioning an ideology of competitive developmentalism in 1960. Said one senior IAS officer on being asked why the state (Gujarat) leaders pursued development in Gujarat, "Bombay had been taken away from us, we had to replicate that here." Another said, "Bombay was ours, and it was taken away. We had to show to the world that we could surpass it and do better."[50] Thus, the loss of Bombay city to Maharashtra provided the regional context for the competition between Gujarat and Maharashtra; this became the salient motivation for Gujarat's developmental strategy. In the mid-1980s, by which time Gujarat had gained ground, reverse competition began to operate in Maharashtra. A policy maker from Maharashtra complained in an analysis of Maharashtra's future,

> The dream of an average Maharashtrian is to finish his educational career with good marks, take up a good job in a large company and then try to fulfill his other ambitions of life. . . . The tendency not to take any entrepreneurial risk is the first obstacle, which needs clearance. . . . Take the case of neighboring Gujarat. The entire governmental machinery is today working in a systematic manner to promote entrepreneurship. They have started EDP [Entrepreneur Development Program] and all the government departments are working in close liaison to remove any obstacle in the setting up of industries in Gujarat. I will not be surprised if in the next 4 to 5 years Gujarat overtakes Maharashtra and is in the first place as the most industrialized State in India. (Sarwate n.d., 92)

In response to the competitive pressure that Bombay generated, Gujarat evolved a state-led and interventionist strategy of private-sector and joint-sector development. It used the competitive and well-developed presence of the Bombay-Pune belt to extend the territorial boundaries of the market toward its borders, and sectorally emphasized the growth of chemical and modern industries. Both these strategic moves meant that industrial growth was rapid in Gujarat in the 1960s and 1970s. The competitive context led Gujarat to initiate "investment attraction" visits to Bombay as well as to Calcutta (West Bengal) in late 1960s and 1970s. These two cities were specially chosen as they had a large number of Gujarati businesspeople residing in them. In aggressively attracting capital from outside as early as the late 1960s, Gujarat was a precursor to the recent "road shows" organized by most Indian regional states. In the 1960s through 1970s the purpose was to attract "Gujarati" entrepreneurs to reinvest part of their profits back into their "home state"; after 1991, the purpose is to attract capital of any ethnicity. Moreover, in the 1970s they were relatively quiet affairs with no media blitz accompanying them. However, the credible commitment of the Gujarat state was evident from the fact that a permanent office was established in Bombay city with the purpose of liaisoning with Bombay businesspeople and with the explicit task of providing them with all information about Gujarat's industrial policies. A Gujarat Bhavan office was established in Calcutta around 1978–1980. In addition, regular visits were made by either the industry minister or the industry department's officials to hold special sessions in Bombay to which all businesspeople were invited. This led the industry department of Gujarat to maintain a systematic database of Bombay- and Calcutta-based industrialists. Gujarat, for example, copied the structure of Gujarat Industrial Development Corporation (GIDC) from the Maharashtra Industrial Development Corporation (MIDC). A retired IAS official said, "The GIDC act was an exact copy of the Maharashtra Act; even the typographical errors were copied! After we copied it, we proceeded to attract industrialists from Bombay!"[51]

The competitive nature of such "investment attraction" visits is evident from the fact that the Gujarat bureaucracy made judicious use of adverse "domestic" conditions in Bombay to attract capital. The first wave of the Shiv Sena movement started in the late 1960s. The sons-of-the-soil aspect of the Shiv Sena (literally, "army of Shivaji," a political party based in Maharashtra) movement created some apprehensions in the minds of the Gujarati population[52] although in its first wave, Shiv Sena directed itself to the "South Indians."[53] Thus, the first stage of Gujarati investment from Bombay was in response to the real and perceived discriminations against Gujarati people as a result of the rise of the Shiv Sena movement.[54] Later in the 1970s, the rise of a new stage of labor militancy in Bombay under the leadership of Datta Samant stimulated another wave of capital flow into neighboring Gujarat. The south Gujarat corridor initially designed in 1962 by the GIDC really took shape by 1968–1969. South Gujarat, then, was the beneficiary of both stages of capital flight from Maharashtra. The notable fact is that Gujarat's leadership accelerated their efforts in the city of Bombay to attract capital during these episodes.[55] Similarly, in Calcutta, special efforts for investment promotion took place when, in the late 1960s, labor militancy was high. As a senior official told me in an interview, "We saw that period [labor trouble in West Bengal] as a propitious time to convince businessmen, especially the Gujarati businessmen, that they should invest in their home state; of course, other businessmen were also interested and we exploited every opportunity [to attract them]."[56]

In addition, the Gujarat government worked on an extensive plan to encourage small-scale industrialists in south Gujarat, just on the border with Maharashtra. Many industrial estates were planned and incentives designed to attract Bombay-based industrialists. In the late 1960s, various industrial estates equipped with factory sheds were built in this region with the explicit task of attracting Bombay capital (GIDC 1971-72).[57] Streefkerk's comments (1985, 262) are worth noting:

> In the late 1960s the Gujarat government acted to stimulate the development of small industry in the southern part of the state. . . . By themselves these estates do not seem to be the results of conscious efforts to decentralize small-scale development. They were primarily intended to draw Gujarati capital and entrepreneurs from Bombay to Gujarat. The state government moreover, agreed to the wishes of Bombay entrepreneurs who were eager to invest in Gujarat, preferably at sites as close as possible to Bombay city.

Gorter's study confirms my results:

> Vapi GIDC and other estates in South Gujarat represent official attempts to draw capital away from neighboring Maharashtra. . . . During the first years, the GIDC offered land at throwaway prices and promised the entrepreneurs a "favorable" production climate. Labor in the rural areas was not organized and the government had no intention of becoming strict in terms of pollution control. (Gorter 1996, 28)

Gorter further said, "[T]his [Vapi] estate was meant to draw industrial capital away from Bombay by offering subsidies, tax holidays, cheap and organized labor as well as a free hand in terms of pollution control" (Gorter 1996, 44). The existence of Maharashtra and Bombay on its borders also meant that the Gujarat state could enjoy the financial flow of resources of Gujarati and Parsi capital into Gujarat without having to provide for their location in Gujarat. The tax that flowed into the state's treasury from the investment of large amounts of capital in south Gujarat was partially used to give credits, land, and infrastructural support to small industrialists and to design industrial estates.

West Bengal: Politics of Vertical Confrontation and Regional Protection

At independence, the counterfactual expectation was of West Bengal's industrial advancement; the state was expected to attract a high share of total investment. In contrast, by 1965, a sharp industrial decline had set in, and West Bengal's share of industrial investment by 1980 was a mere 3.5 percent of all-India investment. In fact, the decline began, albeit slowly, in the mid-1950s. Between 1961 and 1971 the growth of per capita income in the state was very slow (0.5 percent). Chapter 4 demonstrated that West Bengal's political leadership followed a strategy of "political confrontation" toward the licensing system that did not seem to "want" to lobby and work pragmatically to obtain licenses and industrial investment. This contributed to the drastic decline in the number of new licenses for West Bengal as well as a low share of small-scale investment. Correspondingly, regional institutions of industrial governance were inactive and passive (see Chapter 5). What made this strategy politically rational for the regional actors? The conventional understanding of industrialization in West Bengal has been that of capital flight induced by the ideological predisposition of the ruling party in power from 1977 and the leftist ideological structure of its public and political space at least since 1967. Capital, it is argued, flees a Left government that espouses anticapitalist rhetoric. This argument is plausible but incomplete and one-dimensional and raises another more important question. Why was it politically rational for West Bengal's government to ensure the credible success of this political rhetoric?

In order to address this question, it is important to understand the ideological discourse of the dominant Left parties in the state as a conscious *choice variable* rather than a determinist one. Thus, first, the Left Front was not ideologically anti-industry. Rather, it was unable, for political and socioeconomic reasons, to support the flow of new industrial capital into West Bengal. This line of inquiry would urge attention to the socioeconomic coalition base that supports or hinders industrial development. Second, the combination of ideological reformism vis-à-vis regional industry and radicalized political confrontational strategy vis-à-vis the center was aimed at winning regional elections. In my argument, then, the industrial decline in West Bengal was not historically inevitable, dictated by the ideological nature of its rule, but a product of regional choices (to privilege Bengali subnationalism, for example) and regional political-economy constraints (narrow spatial dispersion of industry, for example).

Other scholars also emphasize the ethnic origins of its entrepreneurial class; "non-Bengali capitalist dominance," it is believed, is partially responsible for the failure of capitalism to become an integral part of Bengali social structure.[58] The relative neglect of Calcutta by moneyed urban interests, and the tendency of capital to move away from Bengal at the first sign of trouble, it is suggested, are both related to the non-Bengali nature of its economic classes (Kohli 1990, 376). Yet, the "non-Bengali" nature of its economic classes was matched by the nonproductive character of its ruling elites, the Bhadralok, who were removed from productive activities in both agriculture and industry in the early twentieth century. These socioeconomic factors could have been mitigated to some extent (but not fully) by an entrepreneurial state—a classic developmental state as in Japan and Gujarat—capable of circumventing these constraints. Such a state was lacking in West Bengal (see Chapter 5 for details).

The regional political-economy argument developed in this chapter lays stress on three variables. First, the hegemony of the upper Bhadralok castes in social and political life but its separation from the productive sectors of the regional economy meant that the elite of the state was removed from industrial development.[59] Moreover, the incorporation of the Bhadralok by the ruling parties into the party-state ensured that the dominant regime was divorced from regional industrial possibilities. Further, a noncompetitive neighboring context and strong subnationalist political culture created strong political incentives for aggressive popular mobilization against the center by all political parties; this reduced the lobbying imperative necessary to ensure high investment in the region. Thus, the characteristics of the social coalition in West Bengal and its role within the electoral politics of the state meant that the institutions and the policy process in favor of industrialization were deficient. Its electoral success—given the highly effective strategy of anti-center mobilization—ensured that industrial decline, despite being on the government's policy agenda after 1977, was never a popular strategy. These variables, together, provided the political basis for the political leadership of West Bengal to evolve the "political confrontation" strategy and then continue it in the face of competing pressures in the 1980s.

The Role of the Dominant Socioeconomic Group in the Industrial Development of the State

The social, cultural, and political (not economic) hegemony of the Bhadralok, primarily a Bengali-speaking Hindu elite from the three dominant castes, Brahmans, Kayasthas, and Vaishyas, and its unique insertion in the regional political economy holds one of the keys to understanding Bengal's industrial decline. The upper Bhadralok castes in West Bengal occupy a position similar to the role of the Patel-Kanbi caste groups in Gujarat's political economy.[60] Three related aspects of the Bhadralok castes deserve mention.[61] First, their domination in Bengal goes beyond partisan, party lines. All parties, most notably the Congress Party and the Communist Party of India, draw their leadership and also much of their middle-level party cadres from the Bhadralok. Second, the Bhadralok moved from the then productive sectors of the economy—in agriculture—and were transplanted into the urban, radicalized milieu of Bengal after acquiring Western education, access to governmental professions, and middle-class status. These transitions created a divide between the dominant elite and the productive life of the region. Third, a minority amongst them were at the forefront of modern cultural (based in Bengali literature, culture, and an amalgam of radical political ideas) renaissance and nationalist fervor in Bengal that radicalized the ideational structure of their discourse toward Marxism, revolutionary nationalism, terrorism, and a form of Westernization.[62] This turn toward more radical ideologies by a dominant cultural elite reduced the room for conservative ideologies in the high culture of Bengal that might have supported pragmatic economic policies. This cultural renaissance and further politicization came together in a uniquely regional way to form the core of Bengali self-pride and identity.[63] This subnationalism created room for mobilization on regional lines, but its consequences for industrialization in the state were negative. Each of these points deserves some elaboration.

The middle class and the Bhadralok castes constituted the fulcrum of the social coalition that undergirded both the Congress regime from 1947 to 1967 and the leftist forces from 1967 onward. While originating in a landed background in pre-independence India, over time, the upper castes of Bengal came to be removed from productive activities in both agriculture and the urban sector. Principally, the caste groups of Brahman, Baidya, and Kayastha derived rents from the land, but their real social distinction and power in Bengali society came from their access to education, especially English education and cultural and literary hegemony. Thus, the same Bhadralok who received rents from the zamindari system in the eighteenth century "supplied sons to Government service and the learned professions" (Broomfield 1968, 7) during the colonial era. By the second half of the nineteenth century, the Bhadralok had captured crucial positions arising out of advantages of colonial modernization: European trade, the permanent settlement, the bureaucracy, and the professions (Chatterjee 1997, 70). In time, they came to exercise great social and cultural power over the urban life in both Calcutta and other urban centers and indirect hegemony over rural Bengal.[64] By 1901, for example, 80 percent of senior government appointments were held by the three Hindu writer castes, which made up just 5 percent of the population (Nossiter 1988, 116).

Their social and cultural importance was mirrored in political life. Politically, the Bhadralok held sway over most political formations in West Bengal. Before independence, both the moderate wing and the revolutionary wing of the Congress Party were constituted by the high-caste Bhadralok (Chatterjee 1997). The social structure of Bengal was such that no coherent and geographically uniform middle-caste groups (Mahisya in West Bengal) existed throughout the state to offer a challenge to the hegemony of the upper castes. By 1947,

> Indeed, the entire provincial leadership of the Bengal Congress including all its factions was until 1947 a citadel of *Bhadralok* politicians, almost wholly upper caste, with strong support from the upper-caste *Bhadralok*-dominated district congress committees of eastern and northern Bengal. This was a leadership which, in terms of the specific interests shaping its political activities, was very much a representative of "middle class" interests in Bengal—protection of rentier landed property, and preservation of educational privileges, jobs, municipal administration and, of course, "nationalism." (Chatterjee 1997, 79)

The leadership of the Communist Party also originated from among the literati, the middle-class Bhadralok, and "the leadership of the movement has been drawn from rich, influential, and highly respected Bengali families, and its most consistent followers have come from groups that are relatively well-established in the social structure" (Franda 1971, 6). The Bhadralok or the middle class constitutes about 65 percent of the membership of the Communist Party of India (N. C. Bhattacharya 1967). Myron Weiner's study of political leadership in West Bengal confirms that 46 percent of the political elite (a sample of 408 leaders of four different parties in the state) came from high castes of Bengal—Brahmans, Kayasthas, and Voidyas.[65] Of these, the percentage who had been to college or beyond was 76.3 (Weiner 1963, 181).[66] In 1969, 72 percent of the CPI(M) state committee members were from the three highest Hindu castes, and all had gone to college and came from wealthy and respectable families (Franda 1971, 14).

The second distinguishing feature of the social and political life in Bengal and one that made Bengal unique was that "the upper caste *bhadralok* have comprised the bulk of the urban Bengali population in and around Calcutta which no longer has any ties of material interest with the land" (Chatterjee 1997, 81). This meant that

> [T]he highly vocal and articulate *bhadralok* intelligentsia have not judged the issues as insiders in a struggle between contending agrarian parties. . . . Rather, the *bhadralok* have viewed such questions from a distance, from the perspective of urban consumers of agricultural products, and issues of agrarian relations, land reforms, food prices . . . have been seen in terms of much more "objective" categories: landlord, rich peasant, middle peasant, small peasant, agricultural laborer, distress sales, terms of trade between agriculture and industry etc. (81)

Thus, the most dominant section of Bengali society did not represent the commercial interest of either the agrarian or the industrial sector. This character of the dominant social group has had profound consequences for West Bengal's industrial economy. Moreover, unlike other fertile regions of the country, West Bengal does not have a separately organized political articulation of the so-called kulak (rich peasants) interests (Chatterjee 1997, 82).[67] Bangla Congress, formed briefly in 1965–1967 from the Congress Party, represented the rich peasants of southwestern Bengal, but it did not mature into a political force of any significance. It paled in political significance soon after 1967, and no other political force arose to represent the agrarian productive interests.

Further, this nonproductive hegemonic elite was radicalized by the Bengali renaissance, the nationalist movement, and Marxism-inspired ideas in the pre-independence period, which contributed in some ways to the post-independence mobilization of Left forces in the state. The ideological discourse within West Bengal had shifted toward different forms of radicalism ever since the nineteenth century and was transformed into Marxism's inspired radicalism in the late 1930s. In the nineteenth century, a cultural renaissance modernized the Bengali language, and created a corpus of modern Bengali literature, art, political commentary, and economic thinking. Franda notes this remarkable development: "By the end of the (19th) century Calcutta was second only to London among the great cities of the British Empire, Bengali poets and writers were distinguished as leading international literary figures (Tagore won the Nobel prize in 1913), and Bengalis were prominent among the Indian professional classes and in government circles in regions as distant as Sindh in the northwest and Burma to the east" (Franda 1971, 8). These cultural advancements were transformed into an intellectual movement as Western ideas of nationalism and Marxism entered the regional political culture in the early twentieth century; to Tagore's universal humanism was added M. N. Roy's socialist internationalism. Simultaneously, nationalist ideas and mobilization took a violent turn to form a strong antiestablishment idiom, and the use of violence in political life became more acceptable than in other regional states.[68] These strongly oppositional and leftist tendencies meant that, in a manner mirroring Gujarat's exclusion of left-of-center ideas, ideas of a conservative and pragmatic provenance were and continue to be excluded from its political culture. In West Bengal, neoliberalism or pro-market perspectives are as absent as are pro-labor and pro-social-justice ideas from Gujarat's political discourse. These factors in combination—the nonproductive character of the dominant Bhadralok elites, their sway over political and social life of the state, and the displacement of conservative ideologies by more radical left-of-center ideologies—meant that industrial development was not pursued by any important social or economic coalitions.

This argument challenges the conventional understanding of Bengal's decline in terms of the nonorganic character of its industrial class put forward by Bagchi (1982), Banerjee and Ghosh (1988), and Markovits (1996) and confirmed by Kohli (1990). This conventional understanding isolates the non-Bengali character of the business classes of the region—the Marwaris—as being responsible for industrial decline. I have argued above that it is not only the outside character of the dominant business class—the Marwaris—that was responsible for the lack of industrial dynamism in West Bengal.[69] Alternatively, the absence of a coherent socioeconomic coalition and the political *divide* between the politically salient and economically necessary social groups meant that there was a lack of *congruence* between the business class of the region and the Bhadralok castes.

More significantly, the material interests of a business class concentrated in a region are not constituted a priori. As an important illustration, if one analyzes the positions and activities of the Bengal Chamber of Commerce and Industry (BCCI), the chamber that historically represented the foreign and

British-European capital interest in Bengal—the most nonorganic business class if there ever was one—one finds that it has defended the regional interests of West Bengal's political elite. The BCCI has consistently argued that West Bengal has been discriminated against by the center.[70] The BCCI notes that this is especially true for the period after 1966. The BCCI was very critical of the equalization of steel prices and the subsidization of coal prices, which, it argues, took away West Bengal's locational advantage. Similarly, it accused the center of discrimination in the distribution of aluminum and cement. The BCCI argued that the Industries Regulation Act should be reconsidered and modified so that states become autonomous in industrial policy. It continued to criticize the licensing policy of the Government of India and put forward a position very analogous to the Left Front's position (BCCI 1975, 25, 47–49). Mukherjee also came to a similar conclusion:

> It is interesting to note from the above statements of the BCCI that inasmuch as it represents to a large extent a regionally located capitalist interest, it voices some of the main grievances of organized public opinion in West Bengal, principally led by the Left parties in the state, about central discrimination against West Bengal and also supports the demand for greater economic autonomy to the states within the federal structure. (1983, 8)

Clearly, the material interests of the business class are shaped by the political dynamics of their location and not their origin—ethnic or otherwise. Moreover, most political regimes in Bengal—the Left and the Congress Party—have looked after the interests represented by the BCCI (Mukherjee 1983; Profulla Roy Choudhury 1985; Mallick 1993). This analysis of the positions of the BCCI—a nonorganic business class—suggests that it was the domination of middle and upper caste in Bengal's political life and the nonproductive location of its hegemonic Bhadralok class that might have played a greater role in shaping the potential for rapid industrial development in the state than has been recognized.

Yet, ideological exclusions and social-structural characteristics must, to be effective, be accompanied by the incorporation of material interests of that persuasion into the party-state; in contrast to Gujarat, the structure and nature of parties in West Bengal were not conducive to incorporate any business class—organic or otherwise—into the party system. I analyze that next.

Accommodation of Socioeconomic Groups into the Party System in West Bengal

The social basis of both the dominant parties in West Bengal—the Congress Party ruled till 1967 and the CPI(M) has been in power after 1977—has been rooted in middle-class and Bhadralok background; the industrial and business class of the region, thus, became outsiders to the party-state during both Congress Party and Left Front regimes. The non-Bengali background of the business class was a necessary, but not sufficient, variable in West Bengal's decline.[71] If all other conditions had been favorable, that factor in itself would not have been enough. This is evident from the fact that after state-induced liberalization of 1994, many of those same non-Bengali investors have begun to invest back into West Bengal.[72] This change suggests that the crucial variable is the incorporation of the industrially relevant class into the party-state system, rather than the nonorganic character of the business class. Cabinet members during both Congress Party regimes and Left Front regimes are predominantly drawn from the Bhadralok castes of Brahman, Kayastha, and Vaishya. During 1952 to 1962, 78.1 percent of cabinet posts went to these three castes, while 88.9 percent of the cabinet was from these three castes in the Left Front governments from 1977 through 1982 (Kohli 1990, 374). Most business classes in West Bengal support the Congress Party, but from the outside, which has been out of power since 1967 and then from 1977 onward when the CPI(M), in coalition with other like-minded forces, came to power.[73]

CPI(M)'s social base came from the rural peasantry and the urban working class, largely organized in the numerous public-sector factories located in West Bengal. This social base, rather than the ideological color of the political regimes, contributed to a politics of "protection" rather than to a politics of "productivism" in West Bengal. The CPI(M) and its partners' policy outputs and party strategies were driven to protect its traditional supporters, such as public-sector unionized workers and the agricultural sharecroppers. This is evident if we analyze an important episode of policy change initiated from 1977 to the mid-1980s by the newly elected CPI(M)-led Left Front government. Despite significant policy and ideological change in 1977 in favor of private sector–sponsored industrialization, the policy proved ineffective. At that time (1977–85), the Left Front was defeated by a "policy change" dilemma confronting all leftist parties: how to reconcile ideological change, which hurts its traditional support base, with ensuring electoral victory.

Soon after the Left Front ministry was sworn in (June 1977), the United Kingdom's high commissioner visited the CPI(M) headquarters. In 1978, Jyoti Basu visited London at the invitation of the British PM, Margaret Thatcher, to attract investors and to assure them that the Left Front government was not against industrialization in the state.[74] In 1977, Chief Minister Jyoti Basu announced that industrialists were keen to invest as much as Rs. 2,630 million in the state. The late 1970s saw the promised investment for the Titaghar power project by the private Calcutta Electric Supply Corporation, the British transnational Vickers and Babbcock's demands were heard, and another transnational giant, Phillips, decided to start a new project in West Bengal (Choudhury 1985). On December 21, 1978, Calcutta hosted the Eastern Region Conference of the Federation of Indian Chambers of Commerce and Industries (FICCI). Jyoti Basu, while inaugurating the conference, said that all should try their best to avert strikes and that there was need to come to compromises (Choudhury 1985). It might be argued that in a typical doublespeak Basu was speaking with two voices in two forums: the first, foreign actors and businesspeople; the second, party and the trade union movements in the state. However, an analysis of the various statements and speeches by him in the party newspaper *Ganashakti* suggests that he was speaking in a similar way to the party cadre and to the party faithful. On July 2, 1977, Jyoti Basu commented on the governor's speech in the legislative assembly after the new ministry had been sworn into office:

> We have to work within a capitalist framework. On the one hand there are monopoly capitalists, big landowners, moneylenders, on the other hand, there are laborers, farmers and common people. We have to work to help the common man. But that does not mean that we are going to discourage the wealthy, monopoly capitalist to have business in West Bengal.

Further he said,

> We are asking the big industrialists to invest in West Bengal to build up new industries. That will help employment for your youth. Production will go up. But that does not mean that they will chain the workers denying their fair and justified share.

Responding to the debate in the assembly, Basu reiterated,

> We are in favor of PSUs. But that depends . . . on central government policies. In the meantime, we are requesting the moneyed class to invest here, keeping the worker's cause as a priority. We do not want to deprive the worker's right to strike, but what we can do is to settle or try to settle disputes amicably so that no such strike occurs.[75]

These statements reveal careful rethinking amongst the top leadership of the CPI(M) about the role of the CPI(M) and the Left forces in the context of a parliamentary capitalist system. It was recognized that the Left Front had to operate within a nation-state, get elected, ensure industrial growth, and provide employment to its people. This meant changing its erstwhile "ideological" positions in favor of the so-called monopoly capitalists and against "quick and hasty strikes." Thus, after 1977, the ideological position of West Bengal's top leadership was in favor of attraction of investment and policies to encourage industrialization.[76] As Kohli notes,

> Having forsaken organized "land grabs" and therefore the more destabilizing aspects of "class struggle" in the countryside, as well as having discouraged militant labor activities in Calcutta and elsewhere, the CPM has now

become a more acceptable government to the socially powerful than in the earlier years. As a matter of fact representatives of some of the Chambers of Commerce within West Bengal have requested Mrs. Gandhi to let the CPM rulers continue in power. They have argued that the CPM is [more] likely to initiate greater labor militancy when in opposition than when in power. (1984, 98)

Mallick's important but critical study of the Left Front government reveals that after coming into power, the Left Front was forced to reform its ideological position in favor of business and monopoly capitalists. Criticizing the ideological reformism of the Left Front, Mallick says, "From being a party committed to removing the multinationals from India, the CPM Left Front Government has become their spokesman, arguing that since socialism cannot be created in one state, foreign corporations can be used to achieve development and employment opportunities in the State" (Mallick 1993, 189).[77]

However, this policy came into serious conflict with its electoral strategy and the traditional support base. The CPI(M) could not threaten and reorient its traditional supporters, the unionized workers especially of the PSUs, who insisted upon continued protection. Thus, it continued to support the public-sector workers. Moreover, the party cadre and the leaders of the various district committees were not willing to change their local policies and strategies. Interestingly, the spatial spread of the support base of the party is rural, while industrialization is an urban phenomenon in West Bengal (in contrast to Gujarat and Tamil Nadu, for example).[78] The spatial pattern of industrialization in West Bengal is highly concentrated around Calcutta. Noted by Krishna Bhardwaj as well as Kundu,[79] this pattern has continued to persist. Between 1991 and 1995, 74 percent of *new* industrial applications and 60 percent of proposed new investment was for five districts—Calcutta, Howrah, Hooghly, South 24 Parganas, and North 24 Parganas—all of which are clustered around Calcutta (see map of West Bengal).[80] Midnapore (the location of Haldia Petrochemical plant) and Burdwan shared about 13 percent of applications between them. This concentrated band of industrialization narrows the political support for renewed industrialization and thereby liberalization to the relevant constituencies. Simultaneously, about 75 percent of assembly seats are located in rural districts and about 57 percent of the seats won by the Left Front in the 2001 assembly elections are from rural districts. Thus, the Left Front disproportionately depends upon the political support of the rural sector. This spatial narrowing of the political support in favor of liberalization is enhanced by the urban-rural divide, which maps symmetrically onto the agricultural-industrial divide in West Bengal. All the districts that are urban are also the most industrially developed (except Nadia and Murshidabad); rural industrialization is almost nonexistent in the state.[81] Table 6.3 demonstrates the symmetric character of the urban-rural and agricultural-industrial divide in West

Table 6.3. Extent of Urban-Industrial Symmetry in West Bengal

Districts	Percentage of Urban Population		Percentage of Main Industrial Workers Population
Urban Districts		Industrial vs. Agri-cultural Districts† (I or A)	
Calcutta	100	I	26.5
Howarh	49.6	I	36.7
North 24 Parganas	51.2	I	25.0
South 24 Parganas*	13.3	I	15.6
Hooghly	31.2	I	22.5
Burdwan*	35.1	I	14.1
Darjeeling	30.4	A	7.2
Rural Districts			
Nadia	22.6	I	17.2
Murshidabad	10.4	I	17.9
Midnapur	9.8	A	10.1
Coochbehar	7.8	A	7.1
Jalpaiguri	16.3	A	7.1
Bankura	8.2	A	8.3
Purulia	9.4	A	8.1
Birbhum	8.9	A	8.2
West Dinajpur	13.3	A	5.9
Malda	7.0	A	12.3

Source: Calculated from Census of India, West Bengal Tables, 1991. I define a district as industrial if the share of main workers exceeds 15 percent, and a district as urban if the urban population is more than 25 percent. This definition is used consistently across Gujarat and West Bengal. Main industrial workers are defined by the census as those workers who have managed to work more than 183 days in a year in either household or nonhousehold industry. I employ the same definitions to analyze Gujarat later in the paper.

*South 24 Paragans can be classified as an urban district given its proximity to Calcutta. Burdwan is categorized as an industrial district because of the location of Durgapur within it.

†The classification of industrial versus agricultural districts must incorporate multiple dimensions; here I use only one criterion--the number of main workers engaged in industrial activities —for which comparable district-wide data is available.

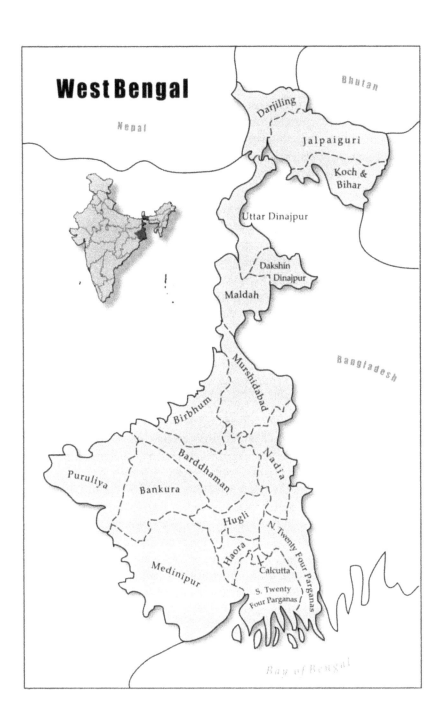

Bengal. The district-wide map of West Bengal gives a sense of the location of industrial areas and their clustering around Calcutta.

This shrank the potential support for industrialization in the state and meant that the policy change from the top in 1977 was not pushed by the local party cadre with enough effectiveness and political motivation. While Jyoti Basu insisted upon reorienting the CPI(M) and the Left Front government toward industrial and even monopoly capitalists from 1977 to the mid-80s, his efforts were not successful because he could not manage the full effort of the party apparatus behind him. Despite a significant reorientation of the West Bengal CPI(M)'s ideology toward greater reformism, it was very difficult to translate that ideological shift into an effective party and governmental program of action.[82] This meant that at the ground level investors continued to face obstacles and delays in the setting up of industry.[83] Thus, the contradictions faced by the party owing to its urban and geographically narrow support for industrialization, and the criticisms of its traditional public-sector workers in the urban areas, introduced an unwitting inertia into the administration, the ruling parties, and the industrial governance process.

Strong Subnationalism and Partisan Confrontation in West Bengal

In contrast to Gujarat, in West Bengal, a strong subnationalist—Bengali—culture, and simultaneous popular mobilization around regionalism supports an anti-center political rhetoric and political strategy. The ruling party since 1977, the CPI(M), has transformed its ideological leftism into a partisan and confrontational subnationalism. A strong pillar of CPI(M) political strategy is an anti-center regionalist policy based in Bengali politico-cultural hegemony (see Chapter 4 for details on the strategy toward the center). It was West Bengal's socioeconomic coalition based in nonproductive middle-class hegemony that provided the opportunity for "Bengali regionalism to combine with anti-capitalism and communism, without creating a split along class lines. The communists could thus find support from virtually all classes of Bengalis" (Mallick 1993, 27). Atul Kohli notes:

> Political significance of this regional identity lies in the fact that Congress rule in West Bengal has often been viewed suspiciously as an extension of Hindi domination. The CPM as a regional party has thus benefited from the sentiments of regional nationalism. The CPM is conceived of not only as a communist party; it is also a Bengali party ... The CPM's repeated harping, for example, not on "enemies" within West Bengal, but on Centre-State relations, only makes sense when interpreted from this standpoint of political support that the party generates from its regional identity. (1990, 375)

My empirical evidence (presented in Chapter 4) suggests a stronger claim: The Left Front crafted a long-term, coherent political strategy aimed at enhancing and stabilizing this regional sentiment and regionally located popular support. Since 1977, West Bengal's Left Front has followed a consistent and stable political strategy of *mobilization* of Bengali sentiment. The Left Front has successfully tapped into an essentially regional subnationalist political culture in shaping this "political confrontation" strategy. Its strong anti-center stance was a product of a history of middle-class Bengali hostility to the mainstream northern and moderate Gandhi nationalist legacy (Weiner 1963, 229–30). While it is true that the Left Front found the choice of a "political confrontation" strategy to be in line with its leftist commitment, the choice of this strategy was directed more at the electoral advantage of a regional elite than the politics of a socialist principle. The "confrontational opposition" of the CPI(M) had as much basis in *Bengali subnationalism* as in class hostility; the ingenuity of the Left Front lay in crafting an ideological structure (and corresponding institutions) that weaved in elements of both with great effectiveness. Dwaipayan Bhattacharya comments:

> The CPI(M)'s rhetoric of government as "instrument" against the bourgeois [central] state reinforced the opposition between the two. "While the state in New Delhi collects substantial revenue from the people of West Bengal, very little is re-invested in the state" was the standard Marxist argument in this period. West Bengal was discriminated against and exploited, yet the government was helpless because the state in new Delhi was constitutionally empowered to destroy it if it was considered as a threat to law and order. . . . Therefore, while the [central] state was shown as coercive, the state government in West Bengal presented itself as more dispersed and decentralized, concerned with the management of the population, and ultimately its welfare. . . . Such perceptions helped to create an image of the LFG [Left Front government] as a genuinely struggling coalition which needed the support of West Bengal as a whole. (1999, 205)

The consequences of this mobilization for industrial activism were negative; such a political strategy contributed to regular political and electoral support but declining licenses and domestic industrial investment. Rather than attempt a reorientation of the central licensing mechanism or lobby the central government, the Left Front government continued a confrontational stance toward the center (see Chapter 4 for details). Choudhury notes in his analysis of the second Left Front government (elected in 1982): "As days went by, the emphasis shifted more and more from the urgent issues and problems facing the state and its people to attacks on the centre. Anti-centre utterances became more and more strident" (1985, 175). Das Munshi, a prominent Congress Party member in the state, said revealingly after the defeat of the Congress in 1987 that they had relied on Rajiv Gandhi's flying visits to dazzle the voters but "the people in the state more than any other state do not want anything from Delhi."[84] Thus, anti-center strategies of the Left parties made political sense, given the nature of regional social groups (nonproductive elites) and the presence of an activist subnationalist popular tradition. A self-defeating economic strategy was politically rational.

The CPI(M) is a regional party having a national ideology.[85] This is further evident from the fact that the support base of the Left Front, till recently, has been linguistically divided. While Congress strength is principally amongst Hindi, Oriya, and Bihari groups, most Bengalis support the communists (Weiner 1963, 242). Thus, its regionally conscious strategy earned the Left Front important electoral successes in assembly elections as well as the parliamentary elections. The continued electoral success of the CPI(M) throughout the 1980s by following the Bengali subnationalism card meant that Basu's attempted reorientation of party ideology was isolated within the party and even the government till about 1993–1994, when the Left Front came to face serious electoral challenges in its traditional constituencies. As a consequence, industrial strategy after 1977 till 1993 came to be characterized by an apparent ad hoc nature. Despite Basu entreaties throughout the 1980s, the business class refused to be convinced of West Bengal's attractiveness as a location of investment. This made for a very inconsistent and non-credible policy program in favor of industrialization. While many continued to live in Bengal (especially the Birla family), their new investment all went to western India.

This account of the social basis of industrial decline in West Bengal has allowed me to integrate previously fragmentary explanations of West Bengal's decline into a political-economy argument that suggests that both the horizontal and the vertical political strategies adopted by the Left Front and the Congress Party were conditioned by a crucial regional electoral logic, the nature of regional coalitions, and popular support for Bengali subnationalism. To this regional political-economy account, one must add the potential for competitive pressures from the neighboring context, which can prove beneficial for the formation of subnational developmental states.

The Horizontal Regional Context in Eastern India

In contrast to the regional context of Gujarat, West Bengal and Calcutta were themselves the regional core from which their neighbors—Bihar and Orissa—could have benefited. In eastern India, West Bengal and Calcutta enjoyed such definite preeminence; Orissa and Bihar could have used the presence of West Bengal on their borders as a spur, but West Bengal itself did not have any real regional competitor. Given the initial presence of one advanced subregion within a larger region in three parts of the country (east, west, and south), two possibilities were possible: either the till then backward region (Bihar and Orissa) could become the poor hinterland of the advanced region (Calcutta) or the till then undeveloped subregion (Gujarat) could integrate itself with the market and agglomeration effects of the more advanced region (Bombay) and, in time, surpass that region. As it happens, these two theoretical possibilities in the development economics literature were both utilized in *different* regions within India. Comparative development theory presents alternative possibilities (Senghaas 1985): Gujarat could have become a backward hinterland of Bombay, providing it labor and raw materials; in contrast it utilized the competitive presence of Bombay to surpass its performance in chemical industry and infrastructural development. Gujarat could utilize the positive agglomeration effects (both market and infrastructure development) of Bombay and south Maharashtra, while West Bengal lacked any such competitor in the east. Given the lack of any systematic policies by the Bihar state to develop the infrastructural linkages between Bihar and Calcutta, it could not utilize the agglomeration effects of being the hinterland of Calcutta. Such a development might have benefited, through a reverse externality effect, West Bengal and Calcutta.

West Bengal, itself, could also have employed the externality effects of being in the proximity of the rich mineral belt of Bihar and Orissa. If, similar to Gujarat, industrial estates had been set up extending from Bihar to south Bengal, it is possible that industrial investments would have flowed in. In that sense the regional policies of successive governments in West Bengal were a complete failure. In 1975, 93 percent of registered factory employment was concentrated in 15 percent of the geographical area of the Calcutta-Howrah-Asansol-Durgapur belt. It is argued that West Bengal's proximity to the mineral-rich resources of Bihar was negated by the freight equalization scheme that allowed coal to be carried at equivalent prices all over the country and the transport of steel to be subsidized. Thus transport cost was not an advantage for steel units setting up plants near Bihar or in West Bengal. Despite this disadvantage, no new steel plants were set up in western India till the 1990s. The public-sector steel plants set up after 1947 are located in eastern India: Durgapur (West Bengal), Rourkela (Orissa), Bokaro (Bihar), and Bhillai (Madhya Pradesh); the private ones (TISCO and IISCO) are in Bihar (Jamshedpur). Moreover, if West Bengal lost out in terms of coal, it gained in terms of the transport costs of oil, which also could be transported all over the country at equal prices. Thus, the effects of the freight equalization scheme on the industrial decline of West Bengal have been exaggerated.

More significantly, Calcutta remained the dominating magnet that attracted labor from Bihar, Uttar Pradesh, and Assam and entrepreneurial talent from Marwar, Gujarat, and Bombay, but Calcutta's infrastructural decline over time contributed to West Bengal's decline. Calcutta's disproportionate role in West Bengal's economy worked to the detriment of West Bengal, as Calcutta was itself not doing too well. The contrast with Bombay's role in both Gujarat's and Maharashtra's development is significant. Thus, the horizontal competitive effects operated in very different ways in eastern India, contributing in no small measure to West Bengal's inability to utilize the historical advantages of being the center of colonial modernization. After independence, Calcutta could potentially have been what Bombay was to the western region; West Bengal and Calcutta failed to perform that competitive role, contributing further to its own decline.

Tamil Nadu: Cultural Subnationalism and Industrialization

Tamil Nadu is an intermediate case, which performs quite well on some industrial and growth indicators (number of factories and state domestic product per capita) but declines over time (till 1993) in terms of capital formation, investment figures, and its industrial structure.[86] After 1993, it shows signs of definite recovery, especially in terms of industrial investment figures.[87] Before 1991, its industrial trajectory can be divided into two distinct phases: 1947 to 1967 and 1967 to 1990. Most analysts agree that most industrial growth fundamentals revealed a decline from about the late 1960s–early 1970s till the early 1990s (see Chapters 1 and 3 for detailed evidence). It is argued that this decline is related to the fact that the ruling party at the center discriminated against regional parties—the DMK and the AIADMK—that continued to dominate Tamil Nadu after the late 1960s. The evidence presented in Chapters 3 and 4 raised doubts about that argument. In contrast, Chapters 4 and 5 showed that regional parties adopted certain strategies toward the national policy framework and Congress dominance at the center; this was not inconsequential in shaping the regional industrial governance process and the investment output in the state. This chapter goes deeper into the regional political economy of industrialization and suggests reasons that led the regional political elite after 1967 to pursue a "protectionist populist strategy"[88] vis-à-vis the center and an inconsistent and at times nonexistent industrial policy in the region.

I argue that the displacement of political strategy in favor of Tamil subnationalism and its important corollary, anti-north, anti-center sentiment, diminished the effort needed to bargain and lobby the central government. Most important for the regional political economy, an emphasis on symbolic politics and leadership-centered politics led to a neglect of the institutional conditions necessary for economic development and industrial advancement. In the later phase of Dravidian rule (1980s), AIADMK sought to renew electorally motivated alliance-building with the national ruling party—the Congress Party;

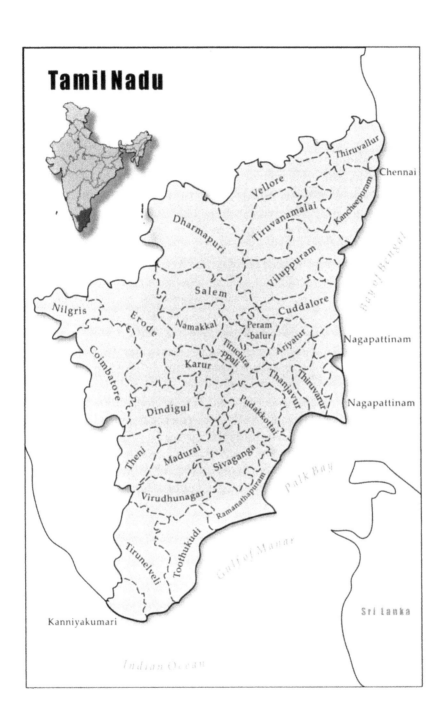

this made for an inconsistent oscillation between an anti-center and pro-center rhetoric. At this time, some central largesse flowed to the state, but the continued focus on cultural and discursive mobilization within the regional state had a negative impact on industrial development.

However, a note of caution is warranted. One cannot relate the political economic developments directly to Tamil Nadu's intermediate position; there is no direct relationship between its precise ranking among other states and the political-economy developments. Yet, the socioeconomic coalitional base and the ascendance of a regionalist cultural nationalism in Tamil Nadu make for contradictory and oscillating strategies toward center and regional industrial governance. My analysis will only point toward certain dominant tendencies in terms of industrial development, enjoined by the cultural logic of the dominant social coalition, its incorporation in the party system, and the neighboring context.

Tamil Nadu's recent political history has seen the rise to state power and the ideological hegemony of the Dravidian movement and Dravidian parties of different hues.[89] How does their rise contribute to the politics of industrial development in the state? In terms of social cleavages, the two regional parties represented slightly different constituencies: the DMK (Dravida Munnetra Kazhagam, a political party formed in 1949) represented the petty bourgeoisie, while the AIADMK represented poorer groups and especially women. Similarly to West Bengal, both parties excluded productive classes within their fold, although the DMK, over time, did benefit from support from the local business groups. Despite this lack of congruence between the social coalitions and the party state, the most important element that shaped the potential of industrial development in Tamil Nadu was the hegemony of cultural subnationalism with attendant emphasis on individual-centric, discursive, and cultural mobilization. This culture-centric politics based in linguistic (Tamil) and spatial (south) cleavages neglected the ideological and institutional preconditions for rapid industrialization and a positive animus against "northern" investors, and the Hindi-dominated center discouraged large-scale private investment and investment by outsiders.

The Social Coalition Base of Tamil Subnationalism

Ruling parties changed in a regular alternation of power in Tamil Nadu: Congress ruled from 1947 to 1967, followed by DMK (1967 to 1977) and then the AIADMK (1980s). From 1967 onward the regional parties, DMK and AIADMK, have dominated the electoral and political space, with the Congress Party playing second fiddle to them. The social coalition supporting the ruling governments since the late 1960s has been a combination of non-

Brahmans, backward castes, the youth, the rising urban middle class in the 1950s and 1960s, the educated unemployed youth, "the middling (film-going) farmer usually also of the backward castes" (Barnett 1976, 99–100), and poor people.[90] While the leaders of the DMK were, interestingly, intellectuals and elite non-Brahmans, many of whom had been landlords in the countryside and were mobilized into the Dravidian movement as a result of a sense of relative deprivation, the DMK appealed to the lower-caste non-Brahman and defined the party as the party of the "common man, the middleman, the ordinary Dravidian" (Barnett 1976, 100). Moreover, despite representing distinctly urban themes and issues, by the late 1960s and early 1970s the DMK had managed to extend its support to both rural and urban areas, cutting across economic differences (Barnett 1976, 146); the formation of a horizontal community, at least at face value, was complete. This social extension accompanied the transformation of a Dravidian non-Brahman party into a linguistic and subnationalist political formation. Swamy puts it thus: "Over the 50s, accordingly, the movement's defacto transformation from a South India (Dravidian) to a Tamil vehicle became formalized; an anti-Brahmanism, now irrelevant given the paucity of Brahmans in the Tamil Nadu Congress became less pronounced" (1996, 176). This transformation had profound consequences for industrialization in the state.

From Non-Brahman to Tamil:[91] *The Imagining of Tamil Nationalism and Its Consequences for Industrialization in Tamil Nadu*

In the post-independence period, what began as a non-Brahman movement against the Aryan and Hindu caste system was transformed into a subnationalist political party aiming to unite the horizontal community of Tamils (Brahman and non-Brahman) against the north and Hindi domination (Barnett 1976; Swamy 1996). What were the consequences of this transformation for industrial policy? One perception of Tamil Nadu's politics is that welfare populism (midday lunch schemes, for example) led successive governments to neglect growth-oriented industrial policies. This account fails to attend to the positive albeit unintended consequence of these welfare programs for the development of human capital potential of the population, and therefore, industrial development. Rather, I argue that what was crucial for Tamil Nadu's indifference toward industrial policy was a regionally specific form of cultural populism rather than welfarism per se. A culturally oriented political style meant that Tamil Nadu's economic policies oscillated between "empowerment and protection populism" (Swamy 1996) and did not invest in systematic political or institutional support for industrial development.

Thus, three elements of Tamil Nadu's political economy concern us here.

First, the movement away from non-Brahmanism to Tamil nationalism cemented a regional identity that provided enduring electoral support to the regional parties ruling the state; second, the predominance of cultural policy, personality-driven cultural politics, and ideological agenda within the Dravidian parties relegated development and industrial policy issues to the back burner; and third, the institutionalization of an anti-center, anti-north, and anti-Marwari (business interests) political rhetoric within the state discouraged the entry of non-Tamil or outside investors into the state. Thus, cultural subnationalism trumped radical social reform, in the process creating conditions for an indifferent industrial policy. I elaborate each of these three points.

Economic policy and economic culture (which includes administrative practices and administrative culture) in Tamil Nadu are marked in very specific ways by the ideology and practice of the two regional parties: DMK and AIADMK. Ideologically, the Dravidian movement in its varying incarnations (DK, DMK, AIADMK, Tamil Nationalist Party) moved between three overlapping but distinct issue-spaces:[92] (1) an anti–caste system position in religious practice and social reformism;[93] (2) an anti-Brahman and pro-non-Brahman backward castes social basis;[94] and (3) linguistic and cultural subnationalism against a dominant Hindi-centered "Indian" nationalism.[95] By the time it came to electoral power (1967), it had embraced the third—Tamil subnationalism—although it continued to invoke the others as part of its continuing ideological structure. Swamy says,

> The Dravidian movement is India's pre-eminent example of a political ideology, which synthesized diverse sources of peripherality and relative deprivation into a single doctrine of empowerment. The doctrine of Dravidianism included challenges to orthodox Hindu religious practice, and the role of Brahman priests in officiating over worship; challenges to the ideology of caste; demands for affirmative action policies; and linguistic nationalism. Taken separately each of these challenges was quite distinct and addressed a different constituency, a fact that was to produce repeated tensions within the movement. Taken together, however, the doctrine of Dravidian identity provided a plausible link among diverse grievances, centered on the twin antipathy to Brahman and northern domination that together constituted the alien Aryan. (1996, 155)

Yet, the consequences for industrial development of the state were negative. Certain material, social, and ideological cleavages became central to Tamil Nadu's political economy in the late 1960s, contributing to the strategy of "populist protection" in the state, which neglected to build an independent industrial strategy. Cleavages organized initially around the central horizontal cleavage of non-Brahman were transformed into an emphasis on "Dravidian Tamils" with a simultaneous spatial mapping of the moral economy of the state in terms of north versus south and Hindi versus Tamil. Thus, the Aryan-

Dravidian distinction was displaced onto the north-south and Tamil-Hindi cleavage. These transformations served two purposes: One, the reduction of conflict on caste grounds within Tamil Nadu (Subramanian 1999) and consolidation of a more diffuse but encompassing Tamil, a linguistic and spatially located (south Indian) community. Subramanian notes: "The DMK's ideological shifts changed the focus of opposition from Tamil Brahmans (and other local inhabitants) to the state and central governments, containing Dravidianism's potential to provoke conflict within Tamil society. . . . The DMK's vision of the Dravidian community was overtly homogenous, including all Tamils/ South Indians" (1999, 136). He further observes: "The DMK differed from such organizations as it incorporated caste and other categories within a vision of a popular community, which gave it broader potential base and more strategic flexibility, and therefore greater and more durable success" (1999, 142). A more critical comment by Washbrook confirms the move toward unity of all Tamils: "brilliant manipulation of values, culture, and history to convey simple messages which identified villains and promoted unity against them across many of the artificial lines of caste and class" (Washbrook 1989, 252–53). Two, the emphasis on Tamil identity allowed the coming to the forefront of an anti-center political strategy. The northern and Hindi domination also began to be identified with the Aryan Brahman and Marwari economic domination.[96] The resulting neglect of growth-oriented issues within the state took place despite the fact that DMK's initial ideological statement had emphasized that "Tamilnad" was suffering in terms of economic development. Moreover, many non-Brahman and wealthy industrial interests supported the two Dravidian parties in their cultural policies. Thus, indifference toward industrial policy was not historically necessary. However, the coalition base of Dravidian electoral logic and the nature of ideological culture in Tamil Nadu implied that a strong locally driven industrial policy would be weak, inchoate, and ad hoc. Barnett's comment on the Annadurai (CM of the state from 1967 to 1969) era is worth quoting here: "Ideologically, the DMK attempted to manage its industrial labor difficulties by blaming Delhi for the economic ills of the state. The ideological approach was a temporary method of coping with the lack of an industrial and labor policy" (1976, 256).

Second, what is relevant to the question of industrialization in the state is that the Justice Party, the DK, and the DMK mobilized and based themselves on social and cultural cleavages in society rather than economic ones. Simultaneously, the individual-centered mobilization of both parties, the prevalence of charismatic rather than rational-legal authority, led to the neglect of stable institutional preconditions of industrial development. Cultural reform and institutionalization of identity politics in the regional state was the main purpose of the movement. The public policy implication of this language- and space-oriented political competition was that social policies, cultural demands, and linguistic mobilization were the core public policy achievements of the DMK rule from 1967 to 1972, and industrial and economic policies were ignored. Symbolic politics was pervasive. Anti-Hindi agitators were released from prison, quotations by Thiruvalluvar (an ancient Tamil sage) were hung in state-owned buses, ministers used symbols of Tamil greatness, state government functions began with a song to "Mother Tamil," rather than a prayer song, and Tamil Nadu hosted the World Tamil Conference with great fanfare (Barnett 1976, 249; Subramanian 1999, 222–23). The cultural hegemony first established by the DMK enjoined a certain "mode of political communication": "Ornate Speeches, and elaborate and garish party rallies" (Rajadurai and Geetha 1996, 553) and paternalist top-down populism were its dominant elements. Within two years of taking office, the DMK acted on many of its cultural policy promises.[97] The state was renamed from Madras to Tamil Nadu, a commission for the implementation of reservations for the backward castes was appointed, and the DMK government forced the center not to implement the three-language formula which required reading Hindi in schools (Swamy 1996, 178; Barnett 1976). Barnett discusses this in the following way:

> The DMK used cultural nationalism as an alternate base of support in a time of crisis. . . . Cultural nationalism proved to be an open ideological category usable by any party or group to serve its own ends. Unlike an economic development ideology, where the achievement of the ideological goals requires an institutional structure and an organizational base, cultural nationalism can be articulated freely by autonomous individuals and organizations. Thus, a party, which depends primarily on cultural nationalism as a base of support, must constantly protect and reinforce its image. (1976, 247)

Cultural nationalism demands continuous and similar repertoires of symbolic and cultural acrobatics. The preeminence of culturalism was evident in the elaborate film culture and in the emphasis on discursive innovation and mobilization. This hegemonic culturalism imposed certain crucial limits on the industrial policy framework and, more crucially, on the institutional preconditions of industrialization.

This culturalism was further exacerbated by an individual-centric, charismatic leadership style in Tamil Nadu. Leadership-centered politics of the state was evident in the power of such figures as Periyar in the Dravidian movement, but culminated in the role played by and the reverence commanded by Karunanidhi, MGR, and Jayalalitha in the political culture of the state. Karunanidhi, although never as popular as MGR (M. G. Ramachandran), over time came to embody a strongly individualistic and authoritarian orientation in the party, which was exacerbated with the rise of the MGR challenge. For example, upon assuming the leadership of the party in 1968, Karunanidhi sought to undermine the power of state-level challengers. Those opposing him were either expelled or assaulted (Subramanian 1999, 235). After 1971 (when

DMK came to power with an overwhelming vote), he attempted to undermine MGR's political base and tried to "turn the party into his patrimony" by encouraging his son to act in MGR-like roles in films and establish fan clubs in his name (Subramanian 1999, 243–44). MGR represented the high point of such obsession with personalities at the cost of institutional change. "MGR had carried personality-oriented politics to its ultimate degree, keeping his party in control by making it almost completely dependent on him for votes."[98] The role of films and cinema in the politics of the state magnified this tendency.[99] In his films, MGR played a romantic hero who liberates the poor, is brave and courageous, and uses his words and songs to convey political messages (Forrester 1976; Sivathamby 1981; Widlund 2000). Individualized and constructed acts of charity, personality-driven state largesse, and active fan clubs further cemented the idealization of the man, his film roles, and his values and their identification with state policy.

While cultural policy demands such charismatic-style politics, industrial policy can be harmed as a result. Industrial policies and the creation of new institutions to govern industry and mitigate the effects of the license-*raj* were neglected. Even more importantly, the administrative machinery of the state atrophied, and at times was interfered with, as during Jayalalitha's and MGR's reign. A report in *India Today* in 1987 observed that the state government in Madras worked according to the whims and dictates of the chief minister without much predictability.[100] Kohli found "a deeply dispirited bureaucracy" in his interviews (1990, 163). Overcentralization and arbitrary decision making, a bane of industrial decision making, proved to have negative consequences for industrial investment. Entrepreneurs interviewed by the author repeatedly insisted that Tamil Nadu's ruling structure has become extremely arbitrary, ad hoc, and corrupt.[101] Thus, a deep-seated culturalism, emphasis on cultural policy to liberate and institutionalize a Tamil identity, and a charismatic personality-driven politics in the state led to the active neglect of infrastructural and industrial development. Yet, the neighboring context was quite conducive: the ascendance of leftist politics in the state of Kerala and some positive pressure from across the border in Karnataka led to industrial development on the border of Karnataka and Kerala.

Horizontal Competition in South India: Kerala and Karnataka as Neighbors of Tamil Nadu

Tamil Nadu (named so in 1967) benefited in two distinct ways from its two regional competitors, Karnataka and Kerala. While Karnataka, Tamil Nadu's northwest neighbor, provided important entrepreneurial and location competition, Kerala's troubled labor struggles encouraged both laborers[102] and entrepreneurs to flee toward Tamil Nadu. Thus, similar to south Gujarat, the presence of regional competitors in the south fueled both state-led effort and capital inflow. Yet, Tamil Nadu's government was not as proactive as Gujarat's government in using the competition to attract Tamil "sons of the soil" to its province.

Karnataka, with a long tradition of industrial development before independence, was a natural competitor to Tamil Nadu's effort to industrialize.[103] Thus, Hosur industrial complex, located in Tamil Nadu, was developed in 1973-1974 over an area of 1,200 acres on the national Highway No. 7, about forty-five kilometers from Bangalore (the capital of Karnataka), and more recently became the "silicon valley" of India. Until 1970, industrial activity was completely absent, and the district of which Hosur is a part, Dharmapuri, was extremely backward. By 1980, however, three industrial estates opened by the state government led to the establishment of 113 industrial units (Bharathan 1985, 17). As noted by Bharathan, "Hosur's proximity with Bangalore—only 35 km away—has been one of the major factor influencing the decisions to invest in the area" (1985, 17). However, Tamil Nadu's efforts were relatively more inward-looking than Gujarat's, and the state government did not set up any office in Bangalore to attract entrepreneurs from there. It concentrated on establishing good infrastructural facilities and providing key incentives, and was able to attract crucial big industrialists to locate there. Such companies as Askok Leyland, Easun Reyrol, Asia Tobacco, Best and Crompton, and Reckitt Colman set up industries and found the industrial estates to be well run.[104] In 1988-1989 an additional area of 500 acres was acquired in Hosur to meet the growing demand for sheds in that area. Known as Hosur II, it aimed to encourage electronics and software industries in a conscious attempt to be competitive with Karnataka.[105]

The second source of inflow of labor and capital has been from Kerala. M. A. Oommen's study, "Inter Shifting of Industries from Kerala," found that Tamil Nadu has been a major beneficiary of capital outflow from Kerala.[106] This capital outflow has taken place even from Kerala-based agro-industries such as Beedi and cashew nuts. Tamil Nadu in the early 1970s had a mere 8 cashew industries, which by the early 1980s mushroomed to around 170, mostly run by Keralites in Tamil Nadu. This capital inflow into Tamil Nadu was induced by conditions in Kerala such as the implementation of labor legislation, and facilitated by the incentive policies of the Tamil Nadu government. The regional context in south India was competitive, providing the stimulus to Tamil Nadu (and Karnataka and Kerala) to design spatially contextual industrial and infrastructural policies. The evidence suggests that Tamil Nadu did take advantage of the positive externalities provided by its regional competitors but was more passive than the policies followed by Gujarat's elites in the 1960s.

In conclusion, Tamil Nadu's story is a mixed one, with the horizontal context supporting an aggressive and pro-investment strategy, while the effects of the political coalition are mixed and vary across different regimes. While the first DMK rule was hostile to rich and northern business interests, later DMK regimes have been more supportive. The AIADMK period is marked more by indifference toward industrial policy rather than by deliberate animus. Moreover, the close alliances between the Congress Party in New Delhi and MGR (chief minister from 1977 to 1987) did lead to some investment flowing in but in an ad hoc fashion. No conscious targeting of investors or of bureaucrats in New Delhi was done. Moreover, the coalitional structure of the DMK and the AIADMK predisposes it toward social and cultural issues to the neglect of institutional preconditions of industrialization. In addition, as revealed in Chapter 5, corruption during the MGR period affected the institutional health of the industrial bureaucracy. The nature of incorporation of "Tamils" into the regional parties *enhanced* the strategy of cultural and social populism followed by both parties. Yet, the neighboring context provided for some positive incentives for industrial development in the bordering regions of Kerala and Karnataka (especially Coimbatore and Hosur). Pragmatic alliance-building with the ruling party at the center also contributed to a larger share of centrally directed investment in the 1980s. Thus, the mixed consequences of these sets of variables meant that while industrial growth in Tamil Nadu was not as poor as in West Bengal, it did show a decline over time.

Conclusion

A comparative analysis of the three states reveals that the nature of the dominant political coalition, its incorporation into the regional party system, the pressure for anti-center subnationalist popular mobilization, and competitive pressures from the immediate neighboring context produced varying political capacities for the pursuit of regional industrial policy and vertical strategies toward the central state.

The nature of the dominant socioeconomic coalition in the regional states played a major role in providing the political conditions for varying state action toward industry. In Gujarat, three different class-caste factions within Gujarat—capitalist farmers turned industrialists (Patels), traders and artisans, and technocratic and small-scale industrialists—were joined by outside investors from Bombay and Calcutta, and later in its development, by nonresident Indians. Simultaneously, a spatially dispersed pattern of industrialization created a broader support for industrialization. In West Bengal, the dominant cultural elite—the Bhadralok—was removed from the production process in both agriculture and industry; a rich peasant class was absent, and the Marwari and

British investors resident within the state were alienated from the industrial governance process. Crucially, a narrow band of industrialization around Calcutta reduced the political support for industrialization in the state. In Tamil Nadu, the rise of regional parties embedded in a strongly culturalist and populist political idiom created an "imagined" horizontal community of Tamils; this transformed an internalist, and potentially divisive, cleavage of caste into one emphasizing language. Attendant mobilization against Hindi domination and the "north" allowed the regional political incumbents to credibly pursue an anti-center strategy that was politically popular in the regional state. Secessionist trajectories were abandoned, but pragmatic and lobbying tactics were also abjured. Outsiders and "Marwaris" were, therefore, hesitant to invest in Tamil Nadu.

Industrial policy is the policy domain of the regional regime; regionally specific class or structural variables were activated or rendered mute by the precise incorporation of these social groups into the state and the party system. In Gujarat, an early pre-independence affinity between the ruling Congress Party and the capitalist farmers was further sealed when after independence, the state ensured credit, infrastructure, and other industrial facilities to many first-generation, small-scale, and medium-scale industrialists. Despite the transformation in favor of the KHAM alliance, the ruling state continued to favor industry and capitalist farmers; in fact, a mutual exchange made this alliance enduring. The losers of this inevitably unequal process—workers, small peasants, and indigenous communities—lacked any political organizations that could take up their issues; in economic policy, the political and discursive space in Gujarat was and continues to be right-of-center. In West Bengal, the socially dominant elite classes were incorporated in all the ruling formations, and the party-state was alienated from the producing classes. In Tamil Nadu, the state oscillated between "paternalist and assertive populism" (Subramanian 1999) toward its core social base; simultaneously, cultural policy dominated economic policy.

In a dirigiste state such as India, regional states' strategies toward the center were very crucial in shaping regional investment outcomes. Subnational, anti-center, popular mobilization raised the stakes and tilted the political discourse of the regional state against the center; regional elites were shaped by regionalist sentiments, but also actively mobilized such regionalist sentiments to craft regional winning coalitions, as in West Bengal and Tamil Nadu. In Gujarat, the absence of a strong regionalist culture and the tradition of integrationist mobilization allowed its officials to monitor and lobby the center for licensed investment without fear of popular reprisal, while in West Bengal and in Tamil Nadu, ruling parties were shaped by but also activated regional "publics." Such strategies reduced the regional elite's flexibility in bargaining for investment with ruling parties at the center, but allowed them to claim the rewards of regionalist mobilization from their local populace. Such a dynamic characterized West Bengal and Tamil Nadu (during crucial regimes). The immediate neighboring context in the three regions—western India, southern India, and eastern India—offered varying incentives for industrial development. In western India, the presence of Bombay close to the newly formed Gujarat state and the particular nature of the intra-regional linkages pressured the state's elite to evolve competitive policies, while in eastern India, Bengal could not benefit from its historical legacies. In southern India, the presence of Bangalore near Tamil Nadu's border and the instability of industrial conditions in neighboring Kerala did benefit Tamil Nadu, although the government did not use these advantages as well as was potentially possible. These factors, together, provided the political and social basis for the formation and then the sustenance of subnational developmental states within India.

In a federal democracy such as India, regional political actors must win reelection within their regions; this shapes their developmental motivations and incentives in powerful ways. Social coalitions and subnational mobilization potential and structural features of the regional economy are equally important, although political parties and the party-state activate or make invisible the underlying social forces in the policy regime. These factors in combination shape the pursuit of industrial policy by subnational developmental states. This chapter has fleshed out a deeper regional political-economy argument that gives historical and sociological perspective to our understanding of more surface-level factors such as the vertical strategies of the regional incumbents and local state institutions, elaborated in Chapters 4 and 5. While a comparative mapping of the regional elites' strategies both toward the center and within their respective regions is important, as it is political elites who act, their actions can make sense only if we analyze the deeper political incentives and socioeconomic constraints affecting them within the region. The analysis of these deeper variables was the purpose of this chapter.

7 | Weapons of the Strong
Business Responses in the Regions

THIS CHAPTER ASSESSES the relative impact of various regional state institutions on businesses' decisions to locate their manufacturing plants in one regional state or another. In the Indian context, previous studies of business came to the following conclusions.[1] First, certain large-scale business families (such as the Birlas, Ambanis, or Thapars) did not let the licensing system deter them but were able to ensure licenses through developing close relationships with the central bureaucracy and the party in power (Hazari 1967; Kochanek 1974). Second, these relations did not enhance the long-term growth and productive potential of the economy, but instead strengthened particularistic privileges that accrued as a result of the monopoly power that licenses provided. These linkages between certain big houses were informal, behind closed doors, and "particularistic" (Kochanek 1974; Herring 1999). Third, general public opinion in India has been antibusiness; this goes back to the nationalist movement and its picture of business as exploitative. Nationalist fervor cast industrialists as rapacious exploiters who were always suspect (Weiner 1962, 97–129; Erdman 1967, 16–21). Nehru played his own part in building this image when he criticized the "profit motive." However, these generalizations have rarely been confronted with actual interviews of a large number of business leaders, as will be presented in this chapter.[2]

This analysis will address two specific questions: First, were decisions by businesspersons to locate in a particular regional state influenced by provincial variables, as opposed to the regulatory constraints framed by the central government? Answers to this question will enable me to confirm whether my analysis of joint and combined interaction presented in Chapter 3 is corroborated by the experiences of businesspeople. In what exact way did the divided structure of regulatory rules affect the decisions of investors?

Second, moving the analysis to the regional level, I analyze how the various types of investors responded to the differences in state-level institutional capacities and industrial policies documented in Chapter 5. How did regulations at the state level affect entry, regulatory, and exit barriers faced by investors? Were there systematic regional differences in the way investors experienced the entry, exit, and regulatory barriers? Various authors have bemoaned the critical obstacles to private investment imposed by the license-*raj*, but are these "bad" effects mitigated by the differences between formal law and actual practice in different regional states?

At the very least, any viable state theory must be able to tell us how the specific mechanisms affect (a) the *rate* of return and (b) the *risk* of return for investors. These are the bedrock factors that must be addressed in any taxonomy of state capacity. There are two basic areas where state-level regulatory institutions (in addition to national-level constraints) could create critical obstacles to private investment. These aspects involve transactions between business and government at the provincial level:

(i) The start-up of a new business (Entry)
(ii) The everyday regulation of business; for example, the implementation of environmental regulations

In analyzing the state-level and the national-level aspects of regulation, this chapter provides a *ground-level micro-foundational analysis of the business-people's perspective* about the strategic and institutional differences outlined in Chapters 3 and 5.[3] This helps to identify, in the order of importance, the parameters used by industrialists to determine the state to locate their project in. This kind of research illuminates what the real investors believe they need and what their experiences are at the local level, rather than assuming that investors optimize a textbook firm's utility function. Such a detailed ethnographic analysis of actual investors is quite rare, yet valuable in providing a sense of how regulation affects businesspeople.

The analysis of investors' perceptions is based on a detailed and open-ended questionnaire that gathered data on the perceived "responsiveness" of state policies, institutions, and the policy process across the three states. I asked investors about their experiences with the licensing and institutional framework in each of the regional states.[4] Thus, this chapter pays attention to Putnam's fourth criterion, "responsiveness," to determine which of the components of the institutional capacity outlined in Chapter 5 are more important to investors (Putnam 1993, 64–65).

The data are drawn from semi-structured interviews of eighty-three businesspeople. Interviews were conducted with a total of seventy-eight businesspeople across the three states, plus five who had not yet invested in any of the three states.[5] The sample was stratified by three criteria: those who had invested in more than one state (either two or three states within my sample), the size of the firm, and those who were located in any of the industrial estates of the states. Most of those located in industrial estates were small-scale investors, and many of those who had invested in more than one regional state were either medium- or large-scale industrialists. Thus my sample consists of large-scale investors (who are usually large family-owned firms and who usually invest in more than one state), small-scale investors, industrial-estate users, and finally some managers of the joint sector in the three states. This stratification enables me to assess whether the statewide variation coheres across different policy domains: Large-Scale Private Sector, Joint Sector, and Industrial Estates. Additional interviews were conducted with members and leaders of industry associations and estate-based associations and with joint-sector managers.[6] I also spoke with researchers from the Indian Institute of Management in Calcutta and Ahmedabad. This survey schedule had two aims: a more general assessment of issues of strategic capacity and institutional performance, and more focused questions about specific policy effects. The analysis of specific policy effects becomes most apparent when I analyze the industrial estate program across the states in considerable detail.

This chapter is organized as follows. The first section reviews my respondents' responses to the system of licensing. I argued in Chapter 3 that the structure of the licensing system was federally segmented in providing "choice points" to all states to affect the location of licenses. In this first section, I address whether the business leaders, the direct consumers of the licensing system, experience it as divided. Remaining sections are not organized state-wise as the other chapters of the book are. Rather, I take up certain salient themes that affect investment patterns, such as entry barriers, regulatory costs, credibility, and corruption, and assess the responses of businesspersons to these issues in the three states. In each section, the discussion of businesspersons' responses is comparative across the three states. Thus, I present the themes that concerned actual investors rather than what neoclassical theory says constitutes the "material interests" of investors. This provides a fine-grained sense of what businesspeople actually want, how state regulation affects their decisions, and what they actually do rather than what they should do. This discussion acquires significance as most business risk analyses are based on the opinion of experts rather than information provided by investors themselves (Borner, Brunetti, and Weder 1995).

Business Responses to Licensing

Before 1991, licensing was a major constraint. It proved to be a significant barrier to entry and was also an important regulatory cost to investors. The large firms had to first apply for the license to the central government; the whole process could take anywhere from one to three years. I asked all large-scale industrialists (N = 38/83) how the licensing procedures affected their decision to invest or their locational choices.[7] Was it a major cost or impediment to them? Further, having posed the research problem to them, I asked whether *they* could explain the puzzle of the wide variation across states despite the constraint of the licensing framework and explicit regional dispersal policies.

About 82 percent of them said that getting a national license was important, but merely the first step in enabling their projects. About 18 percent said that before 1991 licensing was everything; it made you or broke you. Puzzled by the fact that licensing did not seem to be as important in the calculations of most investors, I asked them to explain why not. Some of their answers illustrate the segmented and porous character of the license-*raj* and the federally coordinate structure of regulation, even for the licensed sectors. One large-scale industrialist said, "Getting a license was necessary but not sufficient in those days."[8] Another industrialist said, on assurance of anonymity,

> We soon learnt how to work the system to our advantage. Most of us were from big companies and could afford to pursue the licensing applications. We hired "consultants" who did the job for us. The actual costs were high by international standards but it was worth it, as the license gave us almost total monopoly power over the market. The real issue, then, was getting the clearances from the state governments—getting the land, the power connection, and other clearances that were in the state's hands. Those things took time and careful planning. For those things we had to work with them [state governments] on a regular basis and the attitudes of the state bureaucracy really affected us.[9]

Another source said, "Yes, the license was important, but more so if it was a very competitive sector and your competitor could sit tight on the license and thus pre-empt capacity. That was a real problem with the license system, but it was a fraction of the actual licenses that went through."[10] Another investor said, "The political interference in the licensing system only came for very big projects like the Maruti unit for Haryana. For all other projects the licenses were an important first step, but only one of the first steps."[11] Still another said, "The license was like a passport; you needed it to get in but it did not assure that you would have a good trip. I know of many cases that had the license but their projects failed for different sets of reasons."[12] A medium-scale investor said enviously, "Look at Ambani, did he let any licensing system stop him? The big companies knew how to get past it. They write it down to their entertainment costs and that's it. Do they do the running around themselves? No."[13]

One investor who had had very wide experience with the licensing machinery said,

> Licenses? It was a hurdle. But it was as if we had ten hurdles to cross, and the license amounted to only two; the other eight had still to be solved. The license was a hurdle depending upon the competition. There was a lot of competition for some sectors. For example, the GoI may decide to grant only

five licenses. If there were twenty applicants, they would all lobby to get the license. How a state-level minister or bureaucrat lobbied for you at the central government mattered a lot. License was important because, once you got the license, the market was assured. However, starting production after getting a license was not automatic or easy. The other hurdles were in the states: land, approval for electricity, raw materials, pollution controls, and labor regulations. So today [after liberalization] we have the same problem. We still need land; we still have to work with state governments. Thus the attitudes of the state government matter a lot. They mattered a lot then, they matter a lot now. Then [pre-1991] no one talked about then but they did make a difference.[14]

Regional states could and did make the process of licensing faster and easier by intervening on the investor's behalf. A state government official from Gujarat confirmed this:

A lot of private entrepreneurs came to us and told us that it was difficult to get licenses; it was then we got the idea of applying for licenses ourselves. In the early 1980s the SIA [Secretariat of Industrial Approvals] passed a new ruling which said that SIDCs could apply for licenses and would be preferred over the private sector. We did some independent research with some private parties and applied for licenses which some of them were willing to take up. After receiving the license, we simply converted the project into a joint sector and invited the relevant private party as a partner. Slowly we did and could transfer the full ownership to them. Sometimes we continued with the joint-sector setup. But this enabled us to bypass the strictness of the licensing regulations.[15]

I asked the industrialists if the state government had applied on their behalf. A few industrialists had had similar experiences. One investor said that after he was denied a license, he then went to the industry secretary of his state to request help. The investor and his industry secretary combined their technical knowledge to reapply successfully. The investor formed a joint-sector firm with the GIIC. West Bengal Electronic Corporation (WEBEL) too applied for licenses on behalf of private investors in the late 1980s.

Many other investors said that the state government's help was also useful in different ways. "I had applied for a license and I found out through informal channels that it was being considered in the licensing committee meeting. There were other projects for different locations also being considered. I spoke with the Industry Commissioner of my state who sent his officials to Delhi immediately. Having being forewarned, they made a forceful presentation in the licensing committee meeting and my project was accepted over others."[16] It is clear from these examples that the regional states did play crucial roles in redirecting the output of the national-level licensing system. The specific anecdotes confirm the overwhelming evidence that 82 percent of the investors considered the state-level help or absence within the licensing process to be crucial.

The specific state-level comparisons provide interesting and telling regional contrasts. The reactions of the businesspeople differed across the three states: where one state was eager to attract investment, another was indifferent, and a third was perceived as dangerously corrupt. This clearly affected whether investors sought assistance. One question in my survey asked: "What was your experience with the licensing administration of the state you invested in? Did they play any role in the speed or efficiency with which your license was acquired?" A businessman who had given Gujarat as his preferred location said,

> I was surprised to receive a letter from the Government of Gujarat soon after I had applied for a license. They welcomed me to Gujarat and asked me to visit the state to see possible locations. I was pleasantly surprised. I knew that the central government sent one copy of my applications to them, but I certainly did not expect such a fast reply.[17]

Another said,

> I had not even thought about the possible location, but was flabbergasted on receiving a letter from the Gujarat government soon after my Letter of Intent was converted to a license inviting me to Gujarat. I went to see what they had to offer and they took me to an Industrial estate near Ahmedabad and showed me various possible locations. They were willing to hand the land over to me in a matter of days. Many officers met me who assured me that they will coordinate things and told me about the various finance schemes they had. Their approach was very professional and coordinated. I was very impressed."[18]

A CEO of a unit, who was a nonresident Indian from East Africa, said in an interview,

> I had attended a meeting of iNDEXTb and was interested in exploring the possibility of setting up a unit in Gujarat. I decided to visit Gujarat. I arrived on Sunday and there was an official to meet me at the airport. He escorted me everywhere and showed me various locations, talked about the possible financial structure and I met many other officers. The professional actions and coordination of all the industry people was credible.[19]

Before 1991, almost no other state government wooed the private entrepreneurs as Gujarat (and perhaps Maharashtra) did. When I asked the entrepreneurs in West Bengal about their experiences with the licensing administration, they looked blankly at me and said, "What licensing help?" Many industrialists confirmed that the procedure in Delhi was cumbersome, that they had to learn to deal with it themselves, and that they did not have any help from the state government. One of them said, "I didn't even think that I could go to them for help. What would be the use?"[20]

I asked whether they thought that the licensing structure discriminated against them if their location was for West Bengal or eastern India. Eighty-five percent of them said that they did not feel any discrimination against West Bengal applications. However, one industrialist said that the discrimination operated in a positive way: in the 1980s, all Uttar Pradesh applications were being accepted as N. D. Tewari (a politician from Uttar Pradesh) was the industry minister. Another entrepreneur felt that there was discrimination against West Bengal, but according to him it was because the central government and the ministry of industry did not have enough Bengali officers: "Unlike other regions, all Bengalis prefer to stay in Calcutta and do not like central postings. This means, however, that large percent of people looking at the applications are non-Bengalis. If some implicit discrimination operates, it does through that route."[21] One large-scale industrialist located in West Bengal, who explicitly requested anonymity, said that the "West Bengal government has exaggerated the discrimination argument." He further added that "West Bengal had faced a very bad press after late 1960s. Even after things had improved as they did after 1978 or so, the press continued to highlight only bad stories about Bengal. That did discourage investors from coming here but it was not through licensing."[22] Another said, "Birlas [a large-scale family-owned company] in the 1970s were being discriminated against, but not because of West Bengal but [because of] their relations with Indira Gandhi."[23] The majority of interviewees (85 percent) agreed that while some discrimination operated in the location of the central public-sector units, the license system was too elaborate and detailed for systematic interference to take place.

Tamil Nadu's industrialists suggested that in certain projects such as Southern Petrochemical Corporation Ltd. (SPIC) and some public-sector ventures, the Tamil Nadu government took a lot of initiative in pursuing the central government, although they did not pursue the private sector in the same way. R. Venkataraman, industry minister of Tamil Nadu in the 1960s, was very powerful both when he was Tamil Nadu's industry minister and later when he became the advisor to the National Planning Commission. He did ensure that many projects came Tamil Nadu's way, but his influence operated more through the public-sector allocations in New Delhi.[24] None of the Tamil Nadu–located entrepreneurs said that they had received help during the licensing process. Many prominent industrialists said, in effect, that "In Tamil Nadu we don't go the government to ask for help. It's a cultural thing. Some people call it entrepreneurial inwardness. But in my experience, the government in Tamil Nadu is very corrupt and we have made it a point not to interact with it much."[25]

These conclusions and examples tell us a surprising fact: the national licensing system was by no means autonomous, but instead operated through the shared and nested actions of both the central government and regional states. The assessment by businesspersons confirms that acquiring a license was a necessary but not a sufficient condition for the setting up of a business.

State-Level Entry Costs

In addition to designing ways to mitigate the effects of the license-quota-*raj*, some states tried to influence the preferences of the entrepreneurs directly so that they would apply for a license to be located in that state. The states' efforts included direct-investment promotion measures. Did this have any effect on any investor? My interviews with the entrepreneurs revealed that during the licensing regime very few states pursued the private industrialists directly; but those that did reaped the advantages of increased investment flow. Gujarat did pursue competitive strategies to attract entrepreneurs, especially those from Bombay and Calcutta. This was confirmed by an industrialist who spoke about the meeting held in Calcutta in the early 1980s: "There was a meeting of the GoG advertised in the Calcutta newspaper and I was just curious and so I went. I had a few small units in West Bengal and had no wish to consider going to Gujarat. They had some industry officers who made some presentations; I was much impressed. I actually went on a trip to Gujarat as a result of that meeting and ended up setting up a small unit there."[26]

Many industrialists in Bombay city did know about the regular meetings held by the Gujarat government throughout the 1970s and 1980s. They seemed to be more regular in Bombay than in Calcutta. One medium-scale industrialist who had units in Vapi, the industrial estate bordering Maharashtra, told me that the Bombay meetings organized by the Gujarat government had all the relevant officers from the Land, Power, and Pollution Control Departments. "They even gave clearances there and then. And allowed us to fill applications for finances. That drastically shortened the time it took to reach the zero date of a project."[27]

It is clear that some of these measures eased the entry time and costs of prospective industrialists at the state level. Barriers to entry are a crucial factor affecting the amount of investment as well as the competitiveness of an economy. Organizations such as the iNDEXTb and Udyog Mitra formed with that explicit purpose did ease the process of entry for new investors. In my questionnaire I asked a set of questions that attempted to compare similar organizations in the three states. I asked: "How do you rate iNDEXTb/Udyog Mitra/WBIDC/the Industry Department, Tamil Nadu as an organization?[28] Is it effective? Is it powerful vis-à-vis other agencies?" This was an important evaluative measure, as none of the state organizations had statutory powers to give clearances; they facilitated and monitored projects but did not have any enforcement instruments. The power and influence of organizations such as iNDEXTb was informal, and their effectiveness was a function of bringing together various organizations that usually acted separately. The majority of those who had invested in Gujarat knew of iNDEXTb and had gone through it at one point or another. Only very big industrialists such as the Ambani group, Essar, and Larsen and Tourbo (L&T) asserted that they did not need to go through iNDEXTb since they had a direct line through the chief minister! iNDEXTb got "good" or "excellent" ratings in my survey from about 95 percent of the respondents; this high rating was partly a reflection of the fact that no comparable organization existed in any of the other states. Udyog Mitra of Maharashtra was also rated highly.

In West Bengal and Tamil Nadu, by contrast, the industrialists complained about the lack of coordinated information or advice about where and how to invest. One industrialist in Tamil Nadu said, "No centralized information existed about what clearances were needed to start a project. I had to go myself from door to door, from one agency or department to another and collate all that information myself. Now for example, Guidance does most of that job and is extremely useful."[29] In West Bengal one industrialist told me, "The current organization, Shilpa Bandhu is not perfect and does act slowly, but it is a radical improvement. Before 1994 there was no such organization."[30]

I asked the respondents what about the iNDEXTb they liked or needed the most. Many of them said that collated information at one place was the greatest advantage.[31] Most industrialists said that iNDEXTb was a "reliable organization." They knew that they could go iNDEXTb to ask whether this or that clearance was needed and how to get it. In addition, many medium-scale entrepreneurs said that the iNDEXTb also came to them with projects. Regarding one such project, one industrialist said, "They had done a lot of industrial research and also told us about the financial tie-ups available. That was useful."[32]

Another entrepreneur, who had interacted closely with the industrial bureaucracies of both Gujarat and Tamil Nadu, said, "The single-window clearance worked very well in Gujarat even before the idea was known as a 'single-window' idea. The Gujarat Bhavan in Bombay had officers from every department. I could finalize the whole project sitting in Bombay.[33] In Madras we could not do that."[34]

One entrepreneur outlined the recent decline in the effectiveness of iNDEXTb. In his detailed analysis he pointed to the earlier usefulness of the body. However, he said, "It has become, in recent years, as slow and bureaucratic as the other organizations. Moreover, it really does not have the power to give clearances. If one other agency such as the power department refuses to give clearance then it can't do much. Earlier, it used to be very dynamic and forceful. It used to bring together entrepreneurs and address their needs in a coordinated fashion. Now it runs after big projects."[35]

One of the other entry-related constraints at the state level was land acquisition. In this respect, state-level experiences varied widely. In Gujarat, getting the land was relatively easy, in contrast to West Bengal. Most entrepreneurs who had set up units in Gujarat said that land acquisition could take a long time, especially if the land had a lot of claimants, but that the state government agencies supported them. They did, however, say that the land and revenue administrations of the industry departments were corrupt (see "Micro-Regulatory Costs at the State Level" in this chapter for a detailed analysis of corruption). One industrialist said, "The GoG came up with various innovative ways of ensuring that land could be procured easily for industrial purposes. They declared an area a 'Notified Area,' which meant that the Government law would supersede the Panchyat law, making it easier for private parties to sell land. Also if the government took land themselves and gave it to entrepreneurs on a lease system they could bypass the cumbersome process of transferring land."[36] In south Gujarat, Gujarat bought land from indigenous communities ("tribals") in the 1960s at what would be considered throwaway prices and made industrial estates out of them. In contrast, in West Bengal the population density, the pressure on land for agricultural purposes, and the ideological disposition against alienation of land meant that procurement of land remained one of the most serious problems for industry location. Most industrialists in West Bengal saw the issue of acquisition of land to be a serious bottleneck in the setting up of industry. One said, "The government showed no inclination to help us procure land. Even if we got a green signal from the party bosses, the local party units always acted to create obstacles at the village level. The slow acquisition of land was a serious issue, before 1992. Even now it is a serious issue although the government is a little careful about speeding up the process."[37] Another large-scale industrialist told me, "The government was unable to implement even their own laws, for example the WBIDC act, which allowed them to procure land for industrial uses in certain areas. The local party cadres prevented it from happening."[38]

To summarize, there is no doubt that the license-*raj* imposed crucial *regulatory* costs on business transactions in India; the private sector would have benefited from simplicity, transparency, and consistency of enforcement. However, the adverse costs of the license-*raj* were mitigated in some states such as Gujarat, where established effective institutional substitutes reduced the costs of *formal rules* on entry.

Incentives versus Infrastructure: Corporate Responses

One central issue in determining investment flow is the relative role of incentives versus that of infrastructure. A general point that emerged from my interviews was that the condition of the infrastructure of the state and of the relevant industrial estates formed a major criterion for location choice. Many entrepreneurs admitted that they had made their locational choices on the basis of initial incentives alone but would not do so in hindsight. One industrialist commented,

> Infrastructure is important because it has an important impact on the long-term viability of the project and its profits. Getting some incentives might seem very attractive at the start of the project, but is not as important in the long run. I had to close down one unit in an industrial estate, which was extremely poor in terms of its infrastructure. I have had to rethink my position on the question of tax and other concessions. Roads, power, and water are much more important.[39]

More recently, a nationwide survey conducted by *Business Today,* a business magazine, found that "for investors, the most important quality of a state is its physical infrastructure—a complete package of land availability and cost, water supply, road and railway networks and communication systems—with 88 percent of the respondents rating the parameter as important."[40] This was confirmed by the second *Business Today* survey in 1998, which found that 81 percent of the respondents regarded physical infrastructure to be a crucial determinant in locational choice. "Power availability" (61 percent) and the "cost and quality of power" (51 percent) were identified as other key factors.[41] My interviews with the *large-scale owners* confirm this result: most of them agreed that infrastructure is more important than initial incentives.

There was a large difference in the preferences of small-scale and large-scale investors on the question of incentives versus infrastructure. Most small-scale industrialists (about 90 percent in all regional states) echoed what one small-scale owner told me:

> Only big units can afford to ignore incentives. For small units, incentives make a lot of difference. At the start of a project, before profits can really kick in, sales tax deferral or interest free loans make all the difference. Moreover, many small-scale entrepreneurs live through a production cycle with credit. They take credit to buy raw materials and try to produce goods. If the government gave me no credit on concessional terms and other sales and power concessions, I would have become bankrupt.[42]

The *Business Today* surveys address large companies since their sample is drawn from the Big 500 Indian companies. Moreover, the actual interviews in the *BT* survey show that second in importance to physical infrastructure, the various incentives, subsidies, and tax breaks play an important role in influencing the decisions even of large businesses to locate in a particular area. One official of the Tamil Nadu government, who had been trained as an economist, explained:

As an economist I admit that some of these fiscal sops actually introduce micro-level distortions into the market. These should be temporary and with their withdrawal the economy should come back to its competitive equilibrium. Competition should not be based on tax concessions and the like, but should be about fundamentals of the economy. However, while in the business of providing these incentives and faced with heavy demand for them, I look at the whole problem of incentives another way. Industry needs better infrastructure. There are a lot of inefficiencies in the provision of infrastructure. Since we can't provide high-class infrastructure, industry has to be compensated for the state's inefficiencies. So these fiscal concessions are in the nature of compensation. This is the only economic logic I can offer, because it does create distortions at the firm, state, and the national level. If everything was equal, ceteris paribus, the states and I won't give these concessions. I predict that there will be a race between states in the first phase of liberalization. But after that, the states will re-group themselves. I think that they should get together and rethink the concession strategy.[43]

The second survey of large investors revealed that there had been a recent reassessment of the role of incentives. The *BT* poll of 1998 reported a declining emphasis on monetary incentives: "Sure, sops are still considered important, but CEOs are increasingly placing greater value on the quality of local administration, the law and order situation, and policy implementation, indicating a clear shift in emphasis from the state government's role as a subsidy-provider to a facilitator of investment."[44]

Industrial Estates: Comparative Responses

This dilemma between incentives and infrastructure led me to an in-depth analysis of industrial estates where the various state governments attempted to combine the provision of specialized infrastructure with incentives, mostly to small-scale investors. The analysis in Chapter 5 showed that *specialized and not general infrastructure* is crucial for increased flow of investments.[45] And industrial estates in Gujarat are far superior to those in West Bengal and Tamil Nadu in terms of both numbers and the quality of infrastructure within them. In this chapter, I assess how investors—the users of these facilities—compare the three states' provision of these services. The responses of the users of these industrial infrastructures in the three regional states enable us to comparatively evaluate the states' infrastructural facilities, a crucial precondition for investment. These interviews provide a window into the views of the small-scale industrialists, as the majority of the units (around 96 percent)[46] in these estates are small-scale units.[47] There is a very wide variation in the performance of the industrial estate program across regional states. The following comparative analysis is based on direct and participant observation of five industrial estates in three states[48] and interviews with government officials in charge of running the program, officials at the sites, and owners of the units located at the industrial estates.[49] Table 5.8 showed that industrial estates in Gujarat are larger in number and have a much higher number of industrial units within them. What were the responses of the entrepreneurs who used these estates? I interviewed a total of 44 (18 Gujarat + 17 West Bengal + 9 Tamil Nadu) small-scale industrialists, 40 of whom had units in the industrial estates. For Gujarat, in addition to my own survey, I draw upon an independent survey done by Gujarat Industrial and Technical Consultancy Organization Ltd. (GITCO) 1996 of industrial estates.[50] For West Bengal an early evaluation study (1975) conducted by the government of West Bengal offers comparative data.

I asked three kinds of questions about industrial estates: first, a general assessment of the overall planning of the estates and the role played by GIDC and parallel organizations; second, a specific assessment about the infrastructural facilities such as roads, water, and power facilities provided; and third, questions relating to the specific interaction with the industrial estate officials (GIDC, WBIDC, and SIPCOT) and industrialists' satisfaction with them.

There was a wide variation in general assessment across the three states. Around 90 percent of the respondents in Gujarat estates expressed satisfaction with the overall manner in which the GIDC planned its estates and provided facilities. They found the location of the estates to be good in terms of the connection with local markets and raw materials. In West Bengal, by contrast, I found a very high degree of dissatisfaction with the general location and planning of estates. Only 25 percent of those interviewed were satisfied, with others saying that everything took too long, the provision of electricity was always a problem, and the functioning of estates was non-efficient. In Tamil Nadu, I found general satisfaction high, at around 80 percent.

However, on the question of specific infrastructural facilities, I found that most respondents from all three regional states expressed somewhat comparable dissatisfaction. Roads were a main concern for the investors, closely followed by the quality of power supply. Only 40 percent of the respondents were satisfied by the state of roads within the industrial estates in Gujarat.[51] In West Bengal, only 10 percent expressed satisfaction at the state of the roads. In Tamil Nadu, again, 45 percent of the people expressed satisfaction at the state of the roads and their maintenance. The power supply was a major area of concern. In GIDC estates, 45 percent expressed satisfaction; in Tamil Nadu, 15 percent expressed satisfaction; and in West Bengal, 20 percent were happy with the extent and quality of power supply. In West Bengal most respondents tried to distinguish between recent changes, when the power supply had become better, and the situation ten years before, when "many industries closed and had to pack their bags because of inadequate power supply.[52] However, a longtime resident of Kalyani said, "It's sad, but now there is adequate power; yet due to the fact that demand of power is very low, the State Electricity Board is forced to do 'load-shedding' as it used to before. But things are better now; they were pitiable then."[53]

Water supply was another infrastructural facility important to most users. In Gujarat, adequate water supply was found in the estates in south and central Gujarat, some of which I visited: 80 percent of the interviewees were happy with supply of water. However, most complained that in the 1990s, water supply had become constrained, causing many problems for especially water-intensive chemical industries. In Tamil Nadu, water was a very serious problem: 70 percent of the respondents said that was a major area of concern for them, as the SIPCOT facilities in this regard were not very good. In West Bengal water supply was relatively good, with 60 percent of the respondents expressing satisfaction.

Sewage or effluent disposal came up as a major concern of many units in the Gujarat estates. Most of the entrepreneurs were extremely critical of the government's recent attempt to push all units to establish their own effluent disposal plants. They said that their firms were too small to be able to afford effluent disposal plants, and the GIDC should share the burden.[54]

A third set of questions enabled me to get a comparative sense of the efficiency with which the estate government offices delivered various services. The units located in the industrial estates were eligible for many incentives, such as "backward area" incentives, sales tax concessions, power subsidy, and so on. How efficient was the states' disbursal of incentives? A consistent variation was evident across the three states. The system of disbursal of incentives was relatively efficient in the Gujarat estates according to 85 percent of persons interviewed. However, the administrative structure that disbursed the incentives was quite corrupt. Many entrepreneurs complained of widespread corruption permeating the administration that supervised the location of sheds, the acquisition of the electricity connections, and the effective disbursement of fiscal incentives.[55]

Extremely poor disbursement of incentives characterized West Bengal. Most investors suggested that the promised incentives were not given, and the process was extremely slow and cumbersome: 75 percent of the owners of units gave a rating of "extremely poor" to West Bengal's system of disbursal of incentives. One small-scale investor noted, "I was supposed to get some interest-free loan for the purpose of paying my sales tax. The loan was so late that it became meaningless." Most people stated that corruption was negligible, however. In Tamil Nadu incentives dispersal was riddled with corruption, while the actual disbursal was also very arbitrary and ad hoc. Thus a majority of the interviews gave the rating of "Poor" to the Tamil Nadu's estate administration.

Institutional Credibility

As stressed in Chapter 5, credibility of institutions is extremely important in *predicting investment patterns*. Since investment flows depend upon how investors assess the potential profitability of a project, institutional credibility can matter more than efficiency or transaction costs (Borner, Brunetti, and Weder 1995). Credibility refers to a general assessment of the institutional system rather than to specific details. Hence, I assess the credibility of each of the regional states in my survey. The interviews reveal a surprising result: Noncredible policy shifts, uncertainties in the policy environment, non-credible promises, and inconsistent behavior on the part of state officials matter more to business leaders than corruption or the costs of dealing with cumbersome regulations per se. The *Business Today* analysis of state-level differences in 1996 found that inconsistency in the economic philosophy of the state—changes in the policy framework under which a decision to invest was made—could force a reconsideration of an investment's viability (*Business Today,* June 7–21, 1996, 85).

One entrepreneur said to me, "If one actually studied the changes in the political level in Gujarat, one would find that only one CM has lasted his full five year term. Formal political instability has been high in Gujarat. Despite this, the policy environment favoring industry has been extremely consistent and predictable. That's what I like about Gujarat: its solidity and predictability. In Gujarat, I don't even bother to read the newspapers to figure out if any political changes are going to affect my business."[56] Similarly, the *Business Today* poll reported:

> Consistency is the hallmark of this western Indian State, where the 1994 shift from a Congress (I) administration to a BJP government hasn't stopped the State from trawling for investment. Its physical infrastructure and government support are the two qualities that corporate India admires the most. And the State leads its competitors on four government-related parameters —government support, policy implementation, government flexibility on policy and political stability—and two labor related factors: cost of labor and labor relations. As a result, 51 percent of respondents are toying with the idea of investing here.[57]

Businesspeople don't like sudden policy shifts or uncertain policy signals from the government.

In order to assess the relative credibility of the three regional state governments regarding industry, I asked about policy stability.[58] "As an entrepreneur, do you regularly have to cope with unexpected changes in laws or policies which could seriously affect your business? Do you expect the government to stick to announced policies (a new tax, a new infrastructure project, or a budget change)? Are policies implemented in consistent ways? Or are regulations so complicated and contradictory that it is difficult to follow them?" Essentially a game-theoretic concept, credibility requires the investors to analyze whether the government consistently follows what it has announced or is expected to renege on its commitments.[59] As the interview quoted above reveals, *political* stability may or may not be relevant. In certain situations it may enhance credibility, but in other situations it may detract from it. However, *policy* stability remains essential.

Respondents' answers reveal an interesting pattern: almost 95 percent of the respondents said that policies in Gujarat were predictable and they expected the government to stick to announced policies. In West Bengal, although the credibility of the government has increased in the last few years, it was still relatively low. However, this varied a lot by whether the investors had ever invested in the state. Thus, complete outsiders to the state had a very low assessment of West Bengal's credibility, while those who had some experience and information about the government had greater confidence in the government.[60] However, credibility of the Left Front government before 1994 was very low.[61] In Tamil Nadu, credibility varied by regimes. The AIADMK government of M. G. Ramachandran, the chief minister of Tamil Nadu from 1977 to 1984, had a very low credibility vis-à-vis industry, while the DMK and Congress regimes were perceived more positively.

When I inquired more deeply into the reasons for these patterns, certain interesting aspects of the perceived policy environment of the states became apparent. Most businesspeople don't pay attention to policy statements by leaders, however liberal and supportive for business. However, they do pay attention if those policy statements are accompanied by institutional changes and are consistently revealed. I asked some entrepreneurs from West Bengal about policy shifts there: "Soon after being elected in 1977 Jyoti Basu started pro-investment policies but not much investment flowed in. How did the businessmen respond to his efforts then? How do you know when a policy has credibility?" One entrepreneur replied, "We knew then that he didn't have support from his party. Moreover, his statements were inconsistent—he spoke with different voices in different places. Today, he does not do that. So we know the difference."[62]

Micro-Regulatory Costs at the State Level

I asked all the industrialists whether government-related state-level business environments matter. The overwhelming answer was yes. How do they matter? A large-scale industrialist based in Tamil Nadu who had manufacturing units only in the state of Tamil Nadu said to me in an interview, "If I had to go outside the South, I would have chosen Gujarat." I asked him why. He answered, "Both Gujarat and Maharashtra are visionary states although I get a gut feeling about Gujarat that I don't get about Maharashtra or any other state. The government there is extremely oriented towards industry and that feeling is permeated in and through all of the government agencies."[63]

Investors perceive the effects of institutional strengths and weaknesses through the everyday regulatory output of the state agencies. In this everyday interaction corruption was a serious issue. The Transparency International Corruption Index ranks India as sixty-sixth, with a score of 2.9 where 0 is the most corrupt. Moreover, corruption is perceived by most people to harm the interests of investors. But what do investors themselves say about corruption? The *Business Today* survey (1998) in its "objective" analysis of states ranks Gujarat as ninth in terms of its Corruption Index, and Maharashtra and Tamil Nadu are ranked fifteenth, while West Bengal is ranked second.[64] Kerala occupies first rank in terms of *BT*'s objective assessment as least corrupt. This assessment of the extent of corruption agrees with my interview results about corruption in the three states I analyzed.

This presented me with a paradox. The state government that scores high on most pro-investment parameters has one of the highest scores on corruption, while the states that attract very low investment have very good ratings in terms of corruption. Similarly, an early *Business India* study noted the paradoxical relationship between corruption and investment: "[I]f Gujarat is flooded with investments it is *partly due to a corrupt but well-organized regime*. Industrialists know that in Gujarat everything has a price. Land, water and power concessions, not to mention environmental clearances are hassle free if one has the right political connections. Similarly files move fast and lengthy duplicate procedures are simply non-existent if one knows which palms to grease."[65] This sounds like a discretionary system most investors might want to avoid. However, Gujarat has continued to receive one of the highest amounts of investment from 1970 onward. Is corruption, then, meaningless as an indicator?

Other evidence suggests that corruption does matter. Many investors from Tamil Nadu argued that corruption was extremely high and this had influenced their decision not to invest in Tamil Nadu.[66] Other illustrative evidence from Bihar and Uttar Pradesh suggests that these states are perceived to be so corrupt that investors are extremely wary of investing there. I attempted in my interviews to go a little deeper into this paradox. How does corruption matter? What kind of corrupt practices are more likely to be harmful for investment activity?

Almost every industrialist I talked to in Gujarat told me that the extent of corruption was very high in Gujarat. While none were willing to give me numbers, almost all, quoted on assurance of anonymity, indicated that the range of corruption was around 5 percent to 8 percent of the total project. For example if my loan was for 10 lakh Rs. I could expect to pay Rs. 50,000 to Rs. 80,000 as bribes to bureaucrats responsible for clearing my loan.

Puzzled by this, I quizzed a few entrepreneurs about whether the extent of corrupt practices mattered in their decision to invest. The overwhelming answer was No! One of them said, "Corruption is part of the game. You learn to deal with it. Don't quote me on this, but I just jot it down to 'entertainment expense' in my accounts and go on." Another said, "Almost every state agency is corrupt and so what can you do? It does not bother me any more. In fact it smoothes the process of getting clearances." I reported the fact that investors found the Gujarat bureaucracy to be extremely corrupt to a senior official of an SIDC. He said, "You know something; there are two kinds of bureaucrats. One who takes a bribe and does your work and another who takes your bribe and does *not* do the work. There is *no* third type. Now tell me, what kind do you want?" (emphasis added).[67]

An entrepreneur told another version of the same story: "In my experience in many states within India, I have met three kinds of bureaucrats: one who is honest but ties you up in all the procedural delay of regulations. Another type is one who will charge a bribe money up-front and do your work speedily. And a third, who takes your money but does not do your work. I, as a businessman, prefer the second category." Another entrepreneur told me smilingly, "Corruption in Gujarat is transparent, predictable and consistent. It is very clear right from the start that a bribe is expected. Even the terms are laid out, and everybody knows what or how much is expected for that kind of work. It is almost general knowledge. But, and this is important; I know that if I pay the bribe, I will get my work done. There is certain accountability about the system."[68]

I was fascinated to hear from a manager of an extremely reputable company in West Bengal, "I wish there was more corruption in West Bengal. Then things might move and I would know that I could do something to speed things up. Currently, nothing moves; the government officers are usually honest and morally superior, but they refuse to help you."[69] As reported earlier, West Bengal is regarded by most people to have very little corruption.

A study by *Business India* revealed this same paradox, concluding, "But it is imperative to maintain a certain amount of honesty within the corrupt regime. In Gujarat once the fee has been paid to the power-that-be in the state capital, you can rest assured that the local factory inspector will not harass you further. And if for some reason, the project is not sanctioned, the fee is returned."[70] The same article notes a statement by an entrepreneur: "We don't mind corruption so long as it delivers the goods. In the case of the AIADMK government, the irritant is that it fails to honor its commitment for which we have already paid the fee."[71]

One investor from Tamil Nadu who had also invested in Gujarat said,

Bribes can be a hurdle or a facilitator. It depends upon how they work and are used by the bureaucrats who have to manage them. In Gujarat the system of corruption is *professional.* In Tamil Nadu the attitudes are very different. They make us wait and keep demanding [more] money. I have had to wait to get my NoC [No Objection certificate] from the Pollution Control Board for 6 months. The attitude is if you don't pay, I won't pass your request or project. In Gujarat, the attitudes are: I am helping you and want to help you so that you can start this project, you too please "help" me. We are in this project together.[72]

Various investors from Tamil Nadu concurred with one interviewee who said, "Corruption in Tamil Nadu is very high. It is sometimes around 10 percent to 12 percent of the project cost. That high amount really makes it difficult. Moreover, I have to shell out money at every level. There is petty lower-level corruption as well as at the higher level. From the bottom to the top, every bureaucrat is corrupt."[73] Another investor from Tamil Nadu said, "Corruption was high," and was at times "routinized and predictable and hence useful," but at other times, it "became so high as to be intolerable."[74] Both officials and investors admitted that in Tamil Nadu officials were required to give a share of the bribe to the politicians, making the total amount unsustainable for investors.

These various anecdotes build up to a systematic picture that suggests that it is not simply corruption that matters, *not even its intensity,* but the *nature of corruption.* Thus the relationship between corruption and investment flow is nonlinear. Up to a certain high but manageable point, corruption of a certain type does not impede investment and may even facilitate because it "greases the system." However, beyond a certain point corruption starts to have a negative effect on investments, and uncertainty about outcomes, even with low levels of corruption, is important.

A study on political credibility and economic growth that relied on "listening to entrepreneurs" as a research strategy similarly concluded:

Corruption and political credibility are not necessarily linked. Many, even most forms of corruption were judged by entrepreneurs as not nearly as harmful as a lack of credibility. The reason for this lies in the degree of uncertainty produced by each. While most forms of corruption are rather predictable and act more as transaction costs, lack of credibility creates a destructive climate of uncertainty that suppresses most private-sector activity. (Borner, Brunetti, and Weder 1995, 59)

All my interviews lead to the conclusion that it is not mere red tape and bureaucratic procedures that matter for investment flows, but the overall institutional and political context in which they are placed. Moreover, in heavily regulated systems such as India, bribes may provide institutional and noninstitutional substitutes to facilitate investment, an activity discouraged by formal rules. Thus, it makes sense to pay attention to "empirical assessments" of how regulations actually affect investors rather than a priori injunctions about whether we expect less corruption and less transaction costs. What is extremely relevant is that we begin to make distinctions between *types* of corruption rather than between corruption and no corruption. Different *types* of corruption have very different economic effects.[75]

Conclusion

My data show us convincingly that the impact of government regulation on business decisions and rent-seeking activities is complex, despite the systematic articulation of the argument that governmental regulation, of necessity, engenders rent-seeking and imposes deadweight losses on the economy. In my opinion, the argument that controls encourage the private sector to lobby the government, thus dissipating valuable resources, conflates two stages of the interaction between government and businesspeople: the first, the question of clientistic, particularistic relations with the business sector; and the second, which need not necessarily follow the first, the creation of monopoly rents and dissipation of resources through rent-seeking. In India, particularistic relations *did* exist between some businesspeople and the national bureaucracy. However, at the state level—in some states and in some periods—these same modes of clientistic interaction facilitated complementarities between high-growth outcomes and state actions and encouraged competition rather than · monopolistic rent-seeking. This chapter, which outlines the states' variations in business responses despite the existence of regulation in all contexts, provides some corroboration for this complex variation. It is clear that certain mechanisms and informal institutions emerged in some areas to provide substitutes for formal competitive practices, and thus facilitated investment flows even in the clientistic environment of India.

In conclusion, let me address an issue that came up in all my interviews but one, which I did not analyze in detail until now. When I expressed my bafflement at the fact that investors seem to choose to invest in the seemingly unstable and highly corrupt environment of Gujarat, one investor told me, "It depends upon what your aims are. Are you looking to make quick profits or engage in long-term production so that you can compete with your competitors and establish your reputation in the market?"[76] Intermediate mechanisms that affect investment patterns can be specified more precisely. High private investment is possible only if investors invest. When do they find it profitable to invest? Despite the presumption in the literature that businesspeople might prefer efficient political institutions that facilitate their business transactions, it is not very clear what the goals of investors are and whether others also benefit. Investors might be looking for diverse sets of benefits: (1) Returns to investment: high versus low. However, this can be measured in different ways, as profits or as protected market share. (2) The risk horizon of their investment: short-run versus long-term risk. The latter is especially relevant in certain developing-country contexts, where there might be high short-run risk but low long-term risk. These calculations might also depend upon whether the investor is risk-averse or risk-neutral or risk-loving. (3) The cost of transactions. These costs are usually measured in terms of the money lost, but transactions also affect time, which can be as precious. In the New Institutional Economics (NIE) framework both financial and time costs are affected by institutions. In heavily regulated countries such institutions may be nonmarket ones.[77] Thus, the issue of what the investors want is a contested one and cannot be settled a priori.

This chapter accomplishes two things. It empirically assesses the impact of regional level regulation on private firms, differentiating between national- and state-level regulation in India. This strengthens the analysis presented in Chapters 3 to 4, where I argued that the central state in India was divided and that diverse state-level variations served to mitigate the effects of the central licensing system. The stories narrated by investors who invested in these subnational states spoke of the power of some of these formal and informal institutional substitutes. Second, some of the surprising results that emerged from interviews with investors tell us that we need to focus attention on industrialists and investors in building our theories about governmental regulation, corruption, and institutional effects. The comparative analysis of business responses across the three states provides a sense of variation of institutional differences from the perspective of actual investors.

PART IV

India in Comparative Perspective

8 | Comparative Extensions

Whether developmental states succeed or fail depends not on their possession of a coherent state capacity but on a combined and unintended outcome of central capacities and regional responses. This is the main finding of this book. This dynamic between central and regional elites at the heart of developmental trajectories leads me to challenge prevailing unilateral conceptions of states and top-down theories of economic development. To see how this perspective might invigorate studies of other regions, the role of theoretically informed comparative analysis, this chapter looks to other large nation-states with substantial subnational variation and different systems of center-periphery dynamics. Can we find similar actions by regional elites in other strong and centralized contexts? The Indian case raises important comparative questions for other units of analysis and for regional variation in the developmental trajectory of states. I tease out the implications of the analysis of India for an analysis of China, Brazil, the former Soviet Union (FSU), and post-Soviet Russia, four large nation-states. Do the modifications suggested in this book pose new and different questions about these diverse cases? I also explore the implications of my argument for both democratic and authoritarian Brazil as well as authoritarian Soviet Union and democratic Russia.

These countries vary in terms of developmental outcomes and regime types and also in their extent of decentralization (with authoritarian Brazil, Russia, and pre-1990s India being more centralized than contemporary Brazil, contemporary India, or China). Thus, these cases differ significantly from India in terms of historical legacies, regime types, levels of development, and types of political institutions. This chapter explores different paths of a common policy domain (industrial and fiscal policy) in very different countries that lead to similar outcomes (developmental failures).[1] Yet, given these obvious differences, it is the similarities between these cases that beg explanation: Regional elites matter in shaping economic policy in each of these countries *despite* macro-differences.[2] In each of these countries, regional elites interact with central rulers and national rules of the game in expected ways and significantly influence national policy while doing so. Moreover, the sources of how and why regional elites matter lie in a combination of subnational incentives and vertical interactions.

By comparing the Indian case with a similar substantive theme in Brazil, China, and Russia, I demonstrate that the Indian case is not unique—regional actors shape national frameworks despite formal centralism in other important cases. This analysis fortifies a conclusion integral to the interactive approach developed in this book: Regional elites matter in strong states (the FSU and China), intermediate states (India and Brazil), and weak states (contemporary Russia) in the manner in which they respond to central incentives and regional pressures.[3] Extending the arguments to other cases yields counterintuitive insights not found in the case-specific literature on each of these countries. This preliminary comparative analysis suggests that it may be possible to find similar subnational interventions and central-local competition in diverse contexts. In the future, disaggregation of one of the key concepts of political science— the state—and its conceptualization as a multilevel "polyarchy"[4] must be on the agenda of both scholars and policy makers.

To document the types and sources of regional variation in any one of these countries poses formidable challenges. Much writing on these countries focuses on the national level, neglecting subnational processes and variations. New and different questions need to be asked to address the issues raised in this study: Do regional elites pursue circumvention or confrontation toward the centralized state? What discursive form does regional autonomy take? In addition, empirical demands posed by the theoretical framework elaborated in this book require different kinds of empirical data and evidence than previously gathered. The information in this chapter is generated from extensive reading of the secondary material; this means that important empirical gaps remain that can be plugged only with independent primary work. For example, it is difficult to observe subnational strategies of circumvention without doing primary fieldwork. I am also unable to measure subnational institutional variation across these states. The analysis in this chapter is a rough estimate of the range of regional responses to central policy frameworks in different types of systems. No claims of comprehensive analysis can be made; yet, I find that the conclusions of my analytical framework are surprisingly robust when extended to these diverse nation-states.

The first section outlines the empirical expectations generated by the theoretical framework developed in Chapter 2 and elaborated for India. An analysis of authoritarian Brazil (1964–85), the former Soviet Union, and China follows. A small section speculates about the role of regime type in shaping developmental outputs. Deploying the hypothesis generated in this section, I analyze democratic Brazil and contemporary Russia in the next section. The analysis of each of the five cases (authoritarian Brazil, FSU, China, democratic Brazil, and contemporary Russia) pays attention to the extent and nature of regional variation as well as the nature of central-local relations. Table 8.1

Table 8.1. Basic Characteristics of Large States

	India	FSU (1988 figures)	Brazil	China	Russia (post-1991)
Area as % of World Land Area	2.2%	14.9%	5.7%	6.4%	11.4%
Population as % of World Population (1999)	16.6%	5.6%	2.8%	20.9%	2.4%
GDP per capita in 1999 (constant 1995 US$)	450.2	3,747.3	4,478.7	768.7	2,210

Source: Europa Yearbook, various years; the Soviet Union figures for population are taken from Table 1 in Richard E. Feinberg, John Echeverri-Gent, and F. Muller, eds., *Economic Reform in Three Giants* (New Brunswick, N.J.: Transaction Books, 1990), p. 5.

summarizes the basic characteristics of these states. The conclusion summarizes the comparative implications of the analysis.

A Comparative Theory of Developmental Failure and Success

Failed states can teach us as much about what causes economic development as developmental success can. In this book I am concerned about a type of developmental failure in which there is a divergence between initial goals, initial state autonomy, and ultimate developmental consequences. Each of these countries (India, Brazil, China, and the FSU) started with strong and competent states, but their state capacities withered over time; developmental potential was not realized. The question of how this divergence occurs in India was analyzed in the rest of the book.

The analysis of India leads me to parse out three important analytical mechanisms in understanding developmental states: (1) incentives generated by the micro-institutions within the national state, (2) regional strategies to those rules, and (3) provincial institutional capacities. Most crucially, an interactive framework is stressed. The regional strategies are the product of tradeoffs that regional politicians make between regional support and central rewards or sanctions. I argue that regional elites in many countries evolve their responses to the central state by balancing regional political (electoral or career) incentives and the possibility of central rewards and sanctions. Can we find similar mechanisms and processes in the other countries? How may we extend the conclusions generated from the analysis of India to other cases? The theoretical framework outlined in Chapter 2 and the analysis of India yields the following four propositions; they will be analyzed in different contexts later in the chapter.

Strong or centralized states may aim at uniformity, but they rarely achieve it. The very process of state-led development *invites* diverse socially and regionally based elites to reorder and reregulate central policies. All regional elites—in both centralized and noncentralized systems—seek to reregulate central policies to serve regional ends and goals; in doing so they may contradict and go beyond the intentions of central rulers. Thus, irrespective of regime type, state regulation creates powerful incentives for subnational leaders to pursue local interests, formulate regional agendas, and reregulate central policies. Moreover, despite common national frameworks, regional and local elites do differ in their strategies toward the center and in their abilities to translate central policies. Thus, subnational variation in economic outputs, such as investment patterns and industrial growth, are found even in strong or overly centralized states. Moreover, subnational institutional differences affect the pursuit of economic policy in both centralized and decentralized states, which implies that subnational institutional variation and political choices of regional elites must be analyzed in any study of central policies or developmental outcomes; an analysis of state capacity cannot be exhausted at the central level. This leads to the first two of the four propositions:

PROPOSITION I:

In most states, regional rulers are crucial intermediate actors who play important roles in agenda-setting, policy formulation, and policy implementation. Therefore, the success and failure of national economic policies, and thereby national developmental outcomes, depends upon regional actors and institutions in most states.

The second proposition follows as a natural corollary:

PROPOSITION II:

Regional and subnational *variation* in policies, strategies, and state structures matters even in centralized or strong states and across regime types (democratic vs. authoritarian systems).

How is this regional or local variation within a strong or supposed centralized state to be explained? I posit that regional elites face *similar* tradeoffs between regional developmental agendas and central constraints in many nation-states. Despite this common impetus, variation in typical strategies that regional elites in these different systems pursue does exist. This variation is a product of the specific structure of the central state (whether it has open or closed choice points) and regional compulsions. Any application of this theory must analyze incentives created by central institutions and regional politics.

Both central rules of the game and regional political economy shape political choices made by crucial intermediate elites—local and subnational actors. Subnational variation is enhanced if regional elites have strong political or economic incentives to redirect central policies toward regional agendas. The representation and expression of regional responses take different forms in different countries, given the structure of incentives generated by the rules of the game and the nature of local/regional political competition.

The sources of regional variation lie with the nature of central institutions and national elites' strategies, subnational politics and mobilization within the regions, and subnational institutional capacity, which is usually independent of central state capacity. Thus, my analysis outlines three important mechanisms—incentives generated by the micro-institutions within the national state, regional strategies to those centrally determined rules, and provincial institutional capacities—in understanding subnational variation. This is summarized as follows:

PROPOSITION III:

Subnational variation in policy implementation is a function of:

1. central policy or rules of the game (conceptualized both as constraints and opportunities),
2. local elites' preferences,
3. career incentives of subnational officials (electoral or bureaucratic), and
4. subnational institutional capacity.

Some differences across regime transitions are also suggested by this proposition. During bureaucratic authoritarian periods, regional imperatives to reorient central policies for regional developmental goals will have strongly integrationist impulses as regional politicians attempt to make the most of the national expansion of the state and public sector. In such contexts, regional elites serve regional agendas through circumvention strategies that bypass directive central rules and enhance central regulations, when possible. In such cases, regional variation would be a simple and direct product of subnational institutional capacities with greater harmonization in central-local political relations. Vertical collaboration, bargaining, and strategies of circumvention would characterize most central-region relations. In such contexts, horizontal provincial capacities would determine regional variation in economic outcomes.

In a democratic regime, local political choices will become diverse and central-local relations will become more divergent, with some states pursuing bargaining while others adopt aggressive postures. Thus, *strategies of confrontation* might supplement or even replace *strategies of circumvention* deployed during nondemocratic regimes. In both systems, however, regional state structures and responses will emerge as salient: During the bureaucratic period more subnational provinces will adopt circumvention and mitigation strategies to counteract the strong state, while in the democratic regime, regional responses will adopt various types of confrontation and bargaining strategies. That is, during the bureaucratic authoritarian period, regional elites adopt "weapons of the weak" that are consequential; during the democratic period, regional electoral incentives drive their vertical strategies, which might be termed as "weapons of the strong."

The interactive model urges attention not only at the subnational level but also at the national rulers' incentives and strategies. National elites have their own compulsions, which might facilitate regional divergence or undermine it. In large as well as territorially complex states, concern about political stability and control tends to dominate economic policy.[5] Technical prescriptions (e.g., location of industrial firms), state autonomy for the purpose of insulation from societal pressures (or local or regional pressures), ideological control, and international pressures, while of importance in these decisions, usually remain subordinate to concerns about the stability or survival of the regime in power. Put another way, all national leaders in large and territorially divided countries need to make economic policy and political (democratic or nondemocratic) stability convergent.[6] In such contexts, policy choices about the "correct" economic policies are tied to their implications for regional dispersal, location choices, and the need to allow regional mediation of centrally determined policies. Thus, subnational states and regional elites acquire crucial prominence in large and territorially complex states irrespective of regime type or the institutional form (unitary vs. federal). The necessity of negotiating the contradiction between a centralist economic policy and political continuity in large and territorially divided countries leads central politicians committed to central state autonomy to acquiesce in its divided structure. In such states:

PROPOSITION IV:

National elites may acquiesce to regional claims, enabling greater access to regional actors at the national level. Thus, in large and multilevel countries, policies of territorial accommodation, and therefore the number of choice (veto or access) points within the state, would be greater.

This proposition implies that most large countries have divided policy processes and possibly segmented states. In such countries, it is important to look at the internal architecture of the state to analyze the access points within such states. Regional actors are able to access the state to the extent to which such choice or access points are present.

Applying the Theory to Other Cases

The regimes in many developing nations in the first half of the twentieth century (1920s–50s) designed similar state-led developmental strategies and policy responses to a common set of economic problems. Political responses, however, differed: India followed a democratic route, while China and the former Soviet Union attempted their modernization program under the auspices of the Communist Party, and Brazil made the transition to what has been termed a "bureaucratic-authoritarian" modernizing regime in 1964. The behavior of regional elites in such diverse settings allows us to undertake a "most-different system design," wherein the purpose is to identify similar mechanisms and processes in diverse contexts (Tarrow 1999): the actions and motivation of subnational actors and the pattern of central-local relations. The choice of cases allows me to analyze three different types of states: a strong state (Brazil in the bureaucratic authoritarian period, China, and the FSU); an intermediate state (India and contemporary Brazil); and a weak state (Russia).[7]

The Former Soviet Union

The former Soviet Union by all accounts was one of the most centralized countries in the world (Watts 1999).[8] Despite this centralist legacy, regional elites and provincial governments wrested regional autonomy soon after the breakup of the Soviet Union (Solnick 1996b; Stoner-Weiss 1997; Treisman 2001). Contemporary scholarship tends to overdraw the contrast between the two regimes to argue that center-periphery relations under the Soviet regime were dominated by the center. Stoner-Weiss (2000) echoes the conventional position: "Central dominance over the periphery [in the former Soviet Union] was ensured by a multi-layered and overlapping system of institutional subordination. The four institutional cornerstones of the center's control over the periphery were: the Communist party, the unitary system of soviets, the vertical organization of ministries and the planning mechanisms of the economy" (107). In this view, the recent regional activism is seen to be a natural product of the disintegration of the Soviet state and the corresponding weakness of the current Russian state.

This assessment of Soviet political economy raises a question not addressed within the theoretical assumptions of a centralist top-down model of the Soviet system: How did various republics (analogous to provinces in other federal systems) respond to vertical centralization in the FSU? Did their responses make a difference in shaping policy making or implementation? The contrast between the former Soviet Union and contemporary Russia is overdrawn. In the former Soviet Union, regional elites wrested autonomy from the center in many policy domains; democratization makes such regional autonomy more visible and partisan. The current confrontational pattern of central-regional relations is endogenously produced in response to the institutionalization of regional democratic competition and the specific rules of the game (asymmetric treaties) set by the center. In the former Soviet Union, central-local interactions were as consequential although less overtly visible and less partisan. As Bahry's (1987) study of the budgetary process in the Soviet Union reveals: "Instead of waiting for policy to trickle down from on high, leaders in the periphery [in the FSU] look for ways to influence national policies. Their role is far more complex than one of obedient lieutenants carrying out directives from Moscow: confronted with demands from above and from below, they are activists out to protect local interests in the face of a limited budget" (2).

Regionalist claims over central policy persisted in the former Soviet Union since the onset of the command economy in the late 1940s. Regional equity and location policy was incorporated in the First Five-Year Plan on the insistence of regional and central officials in the 1920s (Bahry 1987, 100). Regional competition became much more overt under Khrushchev's regime (1958–64) (Hough and Fainsod 1979, 223). Under Khrushchev, republican leaders were given more prominent representation in the cabinet, and more funds and programs were reallocated to the republics. In the language of the concepts developed in this study, "choice points" increased within the central state after 1953, similar to choice points within the Indian licensing system. Also, Leonid Brezhnev's regime (1964–82) did little to discourage regionalism. Moses argues that during Brezhnev's regime, provinces gained "increasing political authority to assert their particular interests in central policy making" (Moses 1985, 184).

In response, regional attempts to reregulate economic policy were significantly enhanced. Bahry notes: "[R]epublic politicians are players in an elaborate bargaining process between center and periphery. They lobby constantly for more support from higher-ups and they sometimes manage to win. . . . And regional politicians rarely get all they request. Yet regional lobbying definitely pays" (1987, 63–64). Regional leaders sometimes "redirect central appropriations and re-work Moscow's directives to serve local ends" (71). Many regional leaders complained to central authorities, lobbied extensively for more funds, drafted proposals for the development of their regions, and even challenged the appropriation process as favoring other regions (102–5). Similarly, Jerry Hough (1969, ch. 12) outlined the role played by local party organizations and local administration in the early Soviet years. He suggested that center-periphery conflicts were widespread and significant.[9] Moreover, local officials are not mere "stern enforcers of central priorities" but "incorrigible representatives of localism" (256). Nove pointed out that the "nominally total power of the central organs is not as absolute as it might seem. . . . Local organs and local management do in fact have room to maneuver, a range of decisions to take within necessarily broad (and sometimes contradictory) guidelines from Moscow" (1981, 4). Breslauer's systematic empirical analysis of "demand articulation" by provincial party first secretaries shows that these republic party officials pursue a number of demands, including (a) "traditional discrete demands" for specific projects or funds, (b) "regional policy" demands that require changes in central policy, (c) "national policy" demands that refer to the whole gamut of center-state relations, and (d) devolution of authority demands, which make claims about increasing the political status of regional organizations. Breslauer notes that the content of the demands is "not predetermined . . . by central directives; they all allowed for choice at the local levels" (1986, 650-52).[10]

An analysis of the strategies adopted by the regional elites during the Soviet regime shows the predominance of what I have called "circumvention strategies." One such strategy was to adopt a larger budget than was specified by the Supreme Soviet (Bahry 1987, 66); another was to "sneak in a new local investment project by underestimating costs or dividing the project into smaller components . . . once started it offers substantial leverage in appealing for added funds, to ensure that initial investment would not go to waste" (71-72). Labeling projects differently—for example, as reconstruction or repair work, where central monitoring is less extensive—is another such strategy of circumvention. Bahry calls these examples of "defacto power" (1987, 69). Manipulation of information by local elites—farmers, enterprise managers, and party secretaries—was an extremely powerful circumvention strategy and its use widespread in the former Soviet Union.[11] For example, Moscow planners attempted to encourage mechanical harvesting by paying a premium for mechanically harvested cotton in the central Asian republics of Uzbekistan, Kyrgyzstan, Turkmenistan, Azerbaijan, and Tadzhikistan. Local farmers simply started claiming handpicked cotton as mechanically harvested (Gleason 1990, 71). Such conscious strategies of misinformation extended to the state-controlled public funds, where monitoring was much better (and thus misinformation more surprising). In 1998, Soviet economists complained in frustration, "[T]here is no information as to what and how much the republics contribute to the all-union fund and what and how much they receive from it."[12]

Regional politicians also protect regional interests through explicit lobbying by "appealing directly to the central government and the party apparat" (Bahry 1987, 75). Regional leaders take their complaints to the individual ministries and to Gosplan (the council of ministers), as well as to the party congresses and the legislature. At the twenty-sixth congress in 1981, Kazakhstan's party boss (D. A. Kunaev), the Russian (RSFSR) premier (M. S. Solomentsev), and Georgia's first secretary (E. A. Shevardnadze) all requested various regional projects with great intensity. Such regional requests dominated the various congresses. Republic party leaders also asked for more power to conduct economic policy making within their regional boundaries (Bahry 1987, 6). Gleason's study of center-periphery relations between the Soviet regime and the central Asian republics notes the power of *obstruction* deployed by local elites—the party secretaries:

> [L]ocal leaders [in central Asia] may have been more successful in promoting their own agenda than we—or Moscow leaders—have given them credit for. . . . Sharf R. Rashidov was Uzbek party secretary from 1959 until his death in 1983. He is now widely regarded in the Soviet press as a willing accomplice in the Brezhnevite policies of stagnation, but perhaps "accomplice" is too mild a word . . . local elites felt that a delay of industrialization would keep Russians out while ensuring that indigenous birthrates would remain high and guarantee the indigenous domination of the area (Gleason 1990, 86).[13]

These strategies of circumvention, misinformation, and obstruction were aimed at fulfilling regional developmental agendas, and also created variation across republics and other subnational units. Republics adopted different strategies toward the central government. Breslauer's research notes that one of the most puzzling results of his analysis of first-secretary level of demands from the center is "the huge variation among these provincial party secretaries in the degree of demandingness and impatience they express in print" (1984, 3). For example, Siberian secretaries (West Siberia, East Siberia, and the far eastern region), confronted with more difficult regional problems—heavy competition for funds, supplies, and favor in dealing with the energy situation—also show a higher level of "impatience and demandingness" than other secretaries; "three of the four most demanding and impatient secretaries in our total sample are from this group" (Breslauer 1984, 16). Bogomyakov, the secretary of West Siberia during the post-Stalin period, expressed a very high score of protest against the center (41.4), compared with Ignatov, the secretary of Voronezh, whose score is a mere 3.3 (Breslauer 1984, 16).

Regional differences in ownership patterns and political-economy relations are also evident. By 1989, Estonia, with less than one percent of the USSR's population, had encouraged the largest number of joint ventures (except for Russia). In Latvia and Armenia, the share of cooperatives in total republic employment was more than double the rate of 3.4 percent for the USSR as a whole (Bahry 1991, 225). Nizhnii Novgorod's (an oblast in central European Russia) regional economy was dominated by twenty or so large factories producing military equipment in strong alliance with the regional government. In Yaroslavl (an oblast in northern Russia), for example, contrasts in regional political economy are also evident, despite industry's strong presence in the economy, the local communist party was linked to the local agricultural lobby. This conflict between the industrial and agrarian lobbies created serious conflict between these two sectors in Yaroslavl, while business–local government relations in Nizhnii Novgorod made for a more cooperative relationship (Stoner-Weiss 1997, ch. 6).

Thus, despite formal centralism, regional leaders are not passive implementers or acquiescent agents, but actively utilize the room to maneuver and reregulate national policies for regional ends, in the process modifying the "rational economic" agenda of national policy makers. These regional responses were facilitated by the solidification of informal networks (many of them corrupt networks) of local party leaders, economic leaders of industrial enterprise, and state officials at the local level (Vaksberg 1991; Remnick 1993, ch. 12).

The nested interactive model developed in this book suggests an additional insight: The discursive structure of such regionalist claims and the route of their expression are likely to be different under an authoritarian regime such as the former Soviet Union than in a democracy. Regional rulers' incentives are tied to their upwardly directed careers rather than to election and reelection chances in the regions; this dynamic drives greater invocation of pro-center *language* to make even anti-center claims. Thus, the claims to the center were framed in favor of such "national" and central goals as defense, nationality policy, regional equity, and economic development of the nation (Bahry 1987). Regional leaders took great pains to show that their proposals are consistent with and enhance central goals (77). Further, the form of regional interaction with the center is nonpartisan and takes place through *administrative* or intra-party channels rather than the *partisan* and *public* routes deployed in democratic systems such as India and contemporary Russia.

Another interesting pattern emerges: There is much greater *clustering* of regional appeals in the FSU than in contemporary Russia or in democratic India. A regional leader's "inclination to lobby" is similar across different regions (Bahry 1987, 85). In India (and democratic Russia), in contrast, regional political competition drives much greater variation in political strategies adopted by different regional states; some pursue confrontational strategies that eschew lobbying explicitly (West Bengal), while others (Gujarat and Maharastra) lobby the center in a integrationist manner. Multiple and contradictory regional strategies coexist in democracies.

Evidence from the former Soviet Union, thus, confirms two interlinked arguments stressed in this book. First, in the FSU, regional elites from republics use the room to maneuver within the centralized budgetary process to redirect central funds and projects toward the regions. Their actions modify significant aspects of the national policy—especially the national budget. Second, under the centralized character of the planning machinery, strategies of circumvention are more widely prevalent than strategies of confrontation. Moreover, strategies of confrontation are also couched within the discursive frame of "integration" and "national" goals rather than ideals of regional autonomy or regional goals. These arguments suggest first that regional elites pursue self-interested strategies even in centralized states where the logic of the system might preclude such strategies, and second that such strategies are a rational response to the trade-off between regional pressures and incentives generated by central rules of the game. Regional strategies under authoritarian regimes are not as overtly confrontational and visible as after democratization, but they do reregulate, modify, and transform central policies. China, another territorially diverse country, undergoing significant yet gradual economic reforms since 1978, might be important to analyze to assess these conclusions.

The Chinese Case

While studies of regional variation in India are relatively rare, studies of local autonomy in China, especially for the post-Mao period, have proliferated.[14] It is argued that the Deng reforms (started in 1978), by undertaking an explicit process of fiscal decentralization, created incentives for local government and enterprise officers to engage in innovative and entrepreneurial activities. A longer historical perspective shows, however, that regional and local variation in China was endogenously produced both during the pre-reform era and after Deng's reforms. Local state variation has marked a number of regime types in twentieth-century China (Remick 2002). China has been a monarchy, a constitutional republic, an authoritarian capitalist state, a centrally planned communist state, and finally an authoritarian market-socialist state; all of these were strong states, yet regional responses modified and went beyond central policy in most of these systems (Remick 2002).[15]

Remick's study (2002) of two localities during the Nanjing Decade (1927–37), when China was ruled by the KMT (Kuomintang), a weak central government, shows variable regional patterns of tax administration and diverse state practices vis-à-vis society. Even more interesting, the relations of the localities with the central government differed. Guangdong province's (in south China) administrative capacity was more effective than that in Hebei province (north China). In Guangdong "the provincial government established new powers to train and appoint county finance heads, resurveyed the land to compile new land tax registers, and established a new bureaucracy reaching down to the township to collect a newly organized and farther-reaching land tax" (14). The local tax and public finance bureaucracy was constituted differently in the two regions, with Guangdong's administration made up of lineage groups while the Hebei government relied on merchant groups to collect taxes (14). In addition, the vertical strategies of the local leaders differed substantially. Zhang Xueliang, a warlord of Hebei, "had close relations with the KMT government and observed central policy on fiscal issues" (12), while the warlord of Guangdong followed a much more independent and confrontational posture, even to the extent of establishing a rival KMT central government in 1931.

Did the inauguration of the People's Republic of China (PRC) in 1949 and the institution of a centralized party state modeled on the Soviet Union erase and homogenize these regional variations? The evidence suggests otherwise. Regional and local variation continued to persist and reshape central policy even during centralization episodes in the Mao era.[16] David Granick (1990) argues that *local* property rights originated as early as 1957 in China and were fairly stable from the 1970s.[17] While the founding of the PRC in 1949 achieved a level of centralization congruous with the Leninist principles of "democratic centralism," both Mao Zedong's specific vision of socialism and the political exigencies of internal power struggles in China after the revolution (on which more below) meant that the nature and structure of the economic policy regime differed from the Soviet system precisely in the extent of "administrative decentralization" (Fischer and Gelb 1990; Riskin 1987; Hao and Zhimin 1994). Mao's "third road" relied on neither Soviet-style planning nor the market, but tried to "substitute locally initiated mass economic activity for the detailed blueprints worked out by professional planners and gave greater economic and political authority to local and regional units" (Riskin 1987, 137).[18]

Despite the goal of "integration of the center and periphery" during the Mao years, pressures to decentralize both functions and authority to lower-level units became strong (Shue 1988). In the late 1950s, the Chinese government transferred power from the central ministries to the regions and especially to the provinces (55). Shirk argues that decentralization initiatives were started in 1957 by Mao to consolidate his power base in the face of internal party struggles (Shirk 1993, 158). Thus, the provinces became a countervailing force to the opposition Mao faced in the central bureaucracy. The current "playing to the coastal provinces" policy has its roots in the administrative decentralization of 1957–58 (155–62). As Mao said to the enlarged meeting of the Chinese Communist Party (CCP) politburo in 1956: "Our territory is so vast, our population is so large and conditions so complex, that it is far better to have the initiatives come from both the center and the local authorities than from one source alone.... We must not follow the example of the Soviet Union in concentrating everything in the hands of the central authorities, shackling the local authorities and denying them the right of independent action" (cited in Hao and Zhimin 1994, 26).

As documented by Susan Shirk in her comparison of the Soviet Union and China, "Beginning in 1951 ... the Chinese system became a multi-tiered, regionally based system in which much of the responsibility for planning and coordination devolved to the local governments" (1993, 29).[19] George Rosen (1992) notes that in China the degree of centralization was far less than in the Soviet Union. "At the height of centralization fewer than 600 goods were centrally allocated and 10,000 enterprises were under central control. These figures were much below the equivalent Russian figures" (35–36). Moreover, the CCP is organized more territorially than the CPSU (Communist Party of the Soviet Union), which was organized along functional and ministerial lines.[20] A more accurate picture of Mao's China would be a cyclical one. Mao's China constantly oscillated between centralization and decentralization, facilitated by elite dissension over policy goals (Ahn 1976; Winckler 1976; Chung 2000). Moreover, consistent with Proposition IV, the central rulers accommodated regional interests in national policy.

This analysis of regional responses during previous authoritarian regimes in China shows that scholars have placed disproportionate attention on the enhancement of local power during the Deng era (1977–97). Divergent regional responses during earlier "authoritarian" regimes—the republican period and the Mao regime—highlight a crucial point emphasized by the interactive model developed in this book: Under *all* regimes, regional actors respond to national policy shaped as much by central rules as by local conditions and local preferences.

Regional reregulation attempts of the economic reform measures were certainly accelerated by the fiscal reform undertaken by Deng Xiaoping in 1978. The new fiscal compact allowed local governments to keep the fiscal residue from the local revenues; de-collectivization reassigned property rights both in the rural countryside and in the townships (Wong 1992; Oi 1999, 17–57). Simultaneously, the shift in fiscal resources was accompanied by a transfer of spending responsibilities displacing state-society conflicts at the subnational levels. These twin processes unleashed an intense "local investment hunger" and fiscal incentives on the part of the local governments—both town and country—in China to promote local economic growth to raise revenue and create employment (Shirk 1993, 1994; Huang 1996; Yang 1997; Whiting 2001). Local governments—township and village enterprises (or TVEs)— embody the most growth-oriented sectors of the post-reform Chinese economy. Rural industrial output grew at the rate of nearly 25 percent in real terms since 1978 (Whiting 2001, 2); a large share of this growth was accounted for by the local enterprises empowered by the new fiscal contract system.

Important intra-regional variations in this economic dynamism have also been noted. Overall, coastal regions have exhibited higher growth rates and have attracted a larger share of FDI than the interior provinces. Yang (1997) notes that central policy toward the coastal regions played a not-insignificant part in this pattern.

The next question is: How are we to understand these regional responses to a strong Chinese state? Two diametrically opposite views prevail on the impact of economic reforms on subnational autonomy in China. The majority of scholars argue that economic reforms increased local autonomy over fiscal and economic policy. Among those who agree with this view, there are different views concerning the mechanisms that led to this transition to a more decentralized system. Jean Oi (1999) theorized this confluence of local household and state interests as "local state corporatism," arguing that it represented a fusion of state officials' and local managers' property rights over increased income. Most scholars agree that the encouragement of organizational hybrids facilitated local control over the economy (Nee, Stark, and Selden 1989). Other scholars understood this process as the creation of private property and marketization, whose dynamic lay in the embedding of a "market-preserving federalism" that gave lower units power against the center (Montinola, Qian, and Weingast 1995). Victor Nee (1989) showed that local officials —cadre-entrepreneurs—have similar incentives as private businesspeople.[21] Walder (1994) called this process a shift from hierarchical authority to "bilateral contracting."

A different and in some ways opposing view is taken by a smaller number of scholars who argue that despite fiscal and economic decentralization, the center uses other mechanisms, for example, the nomenclature system (Wong 1991) and personnel policy more generally (Huang 1996), to keep control over the reform program. Susan Shirk similarly concluded that even under Deng's reforms devolution of power to local governments ran little risk of "loss of central control" because the center never lost the power to appoint local officials (1993, 150). Thus, Huang (1996) argues that economic decentralization coexists with political centralization in China. Jean Oi (1999) countered this view of the "center in control" by arguing that central controls become operative only when there is a obvious case of confrontation with higher-level officials; the local officials ensure that their strategies of local development remain below the radar screen of the higher officials.

Both of these competing arguments view central-local relations as a zero-sum game, where the gains in economic or political power for one actor (say, local governments) mean the loss of power for the other actor (center). The perspective elaborated in this book alerts us against taking such a necessarily conflicting view of the strategies adopted by different players. Rather, in my framework, local strategies and responses must be understood through a multilevel model that views local responses as a *combined* product of incentives created by central policies (or central rules of the game) and local preferences. In contrast, the zero-sum view of central-local relations views the policy process as a tug-of-war between a centralized, conservative state and a reformist-minded and resurgent set of local governments. This fixation on center-local *dichotomy* obscures intriguing and crosscutting linkages underlining the reform process.

In contrast to this conflicting picture, a strategic interactive perspective suggests that local actors adopt their strategies toward the central regime by balancing local interests and their own career or electoral incentives against incentives arising out of central rules of the game and rewards. This approach suggests that regional rulers are not intrinsically reform-minded (the assumption in the first set of arguments) or passive followers (the assumption in the second set of claims), but adopt strategies toward reform, given the internal balance of power and choice points within the central state and their own (regional) political incentives. Conceptualizing both actors as strategic, that is, adopting choices in response to other actors' strategies, allows us to make sense of the enormous variation in local responses, the divide between coastal and interior local state capacities, and cycles in central responses to local initiative. Terms such as *center* and *local* are simply too gross to capture the enormous variation within them and the linkages across them.

This variation across time and across localities can, however, be better grasped if we think of their relationship through a multilevel interactive model. In such a model, subnational units during the post-Mao reform period cannot be interpreted as a strengthened local level facing and undermining the uniform center (Montinola, Qian, and Weingast 1995); and the center cannot be seen as a hierarchical party state disciplining the localities successfully (Shirk 1993; Huang 1996). Local elites make trade-offs between pursuing pro-center and anti-center strategies; these calculations are shaped by the extent of endogenously produced local compulsions and central rules of the game. Thus, some localities—for example, the coastal cities—may pursue developmentalist agendas, while other local governments may adopt more passive strategies appealing for central largesse.[22] Simultaneously, the reformist faction in Beijing may attempt to get support for their policies by building vertical alliances with reform-minded provincial elites and thereby seek to defeat the conservative wings within the central government.[23] Such alliances, in turn, are facilitated when divisions (choice points) within the central party state are more pervasive and endemic (for example, between 1980 and 1989) rather than muted (as after 1989 Tianamen, when internal opposition had been removed).

Regional Responses in Authoritarian Brazil (1964–85)[24]

Brazil, in contrast to the FSU and China, was not centrally planned. Its economy, similar to India, is a private-sector economy dominated by the state. In both countries, the state organized and controlled investment, launched new industries, and regulated the private sector through diverse policy instruments.[25] The governments in India and Brazil charted a "grand vision"[26] that relied on an expansive state role in the economy through a public sector–led import-substitution strategy, commonly understood as state capitalist (Baer,

Newfarmer, and Trebat 1976; Rudolph and Rudolph 1987). The Brazilian "Economic Miracle" of the 1960s and 1970s is attributed to the heavy-handed central state. Even after the transition to a fragile democracy in the early 1980s, the Brazilian state continued to occupy a preeminent role. In both countries, the state capacity to affect the developmental well-being of its citizens declined over time (Fishlow 1973; Frankel 1978; Bardhan 1984; Rudolph and Rudolph 1987; Weyland 1998).[27] The Brazilian economy grew at the average rate of 7.1 percent from 1940 until 1980, transforming the economy into an urbanized and industrialized economy; in the process it was confronted with serious economic and political problems in the 1980s and 1990s (Weyland 1998). How can we understand this developmental failure in countries with grand developmental ambitions such as India and Brazil?

The military regime that came to power in 1964 charted a radically new course for Brazil (Stepan 1973; Hagopian 1996). State intervention expanded, "sharpening the tools of regulation and distribution and extending the state's control over the foreign and private sectors" (Hagopian 1996, 76). As in India, the public sector expanded; 108 federal state enterprises were added between 1967 and 1973; by 1983, there were 683 public-sector companies in Brazil. This period in Brazilian history is seen as a centralist bureaucratic-authoritarian period when regionalist forces were weak.[28] The approach adopted in this book cautions against such a unitary, top-down, and zero-sum view of center and the regions. In contrast, the key question is not *if* the provinces are strong or weak, but rather *how* do regional actors respond to state expansion, centralization, and modernization?

The regional elites in Minas Gerais, a southeastern state close to São Paulo, positioned themselves favorably to take advantage of the dirigiste national development.[29] The regional state expanded its role in the regional economy "in a manner strikingly similar to that of the national state" (Hagopian 1996, 81). Minas Gerais thus represents the *bureaucratic-liberal* model found in India in the western state of Gujarat.

A number of indicators underscore the state-led path of development that the provincial leadership in Minas Gerais followed. The political leadership designed a number of state agencies between 1960 and 1977 that represented almost one-fifth of all non-entrepreneurial public spending and provided key services to industrialists and consumers alike (Hagopian 1996, 82–83). In India, the western state of Gujarat provided infrastructure services to industries, attracting numerous investors from the neighboring state of Maharashtra. As Montero (2001a) shows,

> Those industries that did leave São Paulo required developed infrastructure and qualified labor. These conditions might well have favored a comparatively more industrialized Rio de Janeiro over Minas Gerais, but it was Minas that seemed to take more advantage of the situation. Despite a rela-

tively weaker industrial base, Minas's political leadership during the 1960s and 1970s built an array of public agencies that quickly developed a solid record of success in economic planning. (54–55)

The findings of this book also suggest new questions that might be raised about central-local relations during the military regime in Brazil. Scholars stress the role played by the region's "traditional elites" (Hagopian 1996), "political technocracy," and horizontal interagency cooperation (Montero 2001b); I argue that vertical interactions play an equally important role. Thus, "vertical" strategies toward the constraints and opportunities presented by the central military government may be *more* consequential than previously thought.

The vertical linkage of the state of Minas Gerais to the central regime confirms that in large countries, integrationist and bargaining strategies may facilitate regional development. Montero (2001b) notes that the traditional oligarchy of the state "built strategic alliances with national state-builders such as Getulio Vargas during the 1930s and the 1940s and former governor of the state, Juscelino Kubitschek, in the 1950s, linking the *mineiro* elites' fate with the national development policies" (67). In 1947, Kubitschek initiated a "recuperation plan" that defined areas to be the developed by the state (Montero 2001a). This plan relied on heavy public investments in traditional public-goods industries such as the electricity sector, which are also crucial for industrial development. In 1952, a regional electricity company (Electrical Centers of Minas Gerais, CEMIG) was formed, acting as the development agency of the state government. This congruence with the national developmental pattern continued when the military came to power in 1964: "Mineiro political leaders supported them [the military regime] in exchange for the placement of public firms in the state" (Montero 2001b, 67). Simultaneously, the state pursued independent industrial development measures by setting up agencies, expending resources, and coordinating across agencies (Hagopian 1996; Montero 2001b). These state agencies pursued capital goods development and "public investment in infrastructure, fiscal incentives, subsidized finance, and logistic support helping to attract an array of multinational firms to Minas, most notably the Italian automaker, Fiat" (Montero 2001b, 68). Increased foreign and domestic investment resulted; Minas industrial growth rates far outpaced Brazil miracle rates (Montero 2001b).

One important question is the influence of fiscal centralization on the regional state. After 1964, the military initiated a program of fiscal centralization. The 1966 tax reform package had as its goal the enhancement of federal revenues. Elites in Minas Gerais adopted circumvention and nibbling strategies in the face of this fiscal centralization from above. Despite restrictions placed on state government spending by the fiscal centralization initiative of 1966, Minas Gerais's state spending continued unabated. Minas Gerais supplemented its tax base with external funds. In the 1970s, the state regularly borrowed at least 10 percent of its total revenue. As Hagopian demonstrates, "Imaginative negotiations with foreign development banks produced matching federal grants. Overall, states continued to lobby against the fiscal centralization reversing many of its provisions; in 1980 they were successful in requesting the federal government to enhance state revenues" (1996, 144). Thus, provinces in Brazil, similar to regional states in India, deployed their room to maneuver for regional developmental agendas despite extensive fiscal centralization and de jure federal control over industrial policy.

Moreover, the lack of electoral incentives at the subnational levels in this period meant that these integrationist and circumvention strategies were more common than confrontational strategies. Similar pro-center strategies enhanced industrial development in the northeast during the military rule. In the state of Maranhão (located in northeast Brazil), Jose Sarney (the then state governor who later became first civilian president, 1985–90) took advantage of the central government's resources to build local infrastructure.[30] Bahia's Antoni Carlos Magalhaes (state governor) also used the central government's financial resources to modernize Bahia's infrastructure and industrial growth (Ames 2001).[31] In the democratic period (1985 onward), much greater conflict and confrontation between center and states became apparent as subnational elites responded to both electoral incentives in the regions and the necessity of central transfers. I elaborate the regional responses in the democratic period later in this chapter.

The Impact of Size and Territorial Differentiation on Central Rulers

The interaction perspective developed in this book urges attention to national institutions, national rulers, and their strategic calculations as much as to local political conditions that shape the political choices of regional elites. In addition, Proposition IV, outlined in the beginning of the chapter, suggests that national rulers in large-sized states would have different compulsions than those in small-sized states. Stability is a more important goal than efficiency, and national elites might acquiesce or accept formal or informal mediations from regional interests to formal representations of power and the bureaucratic state.

During the military regime (1964–85), the Brazilian military initiated a fiscal reform in 1967, which allowed the state governments to administer new taxes, thus increasing their fiscal power. This reform benefited the northern and northeastern states disproportionately, where the military found conservative support for its antidemocratic policies. This also served to counter the power of the southern and southeastern states, where much of the opposition to authoritarianism lay (Montero 2000). Bahia's relationship to the military government illustrates the two-way relationship between the northern states and the central government. Within Bahia, Antoni Carlos Magalhaes (known as ACM) developed a strong patronage machine but also modernized Bahia's economy. He constructed a developmentalist technocratic image (Ames 2001, 131). He was aided in his effort by the military government, which "lavished government spending and favorable industrial policies on Bahia" (Ames 2001, 135). In the democratic period, national elites, notably presidents, have similarly needed to build alliances with key regional states. President Sarney (president from 1985 to 1990) in 1988 increased nontax federal transfers to the states and municipalities 23 percent above their 1980 level in an effort to solicit the support of governors, federal deputies, and mayors (Montero 2000).

Similarly, in the Soviet Union, most national leaders were overly concerned with political stability, making alliances with regional leaders and allowing greater regional mediation of central policies to achieve this goal. Brezhnev (Soviet Union leader from 1964 to 1982), for example, gave priority to stability and was extremely sensitive to social unrest arising from any of the regions. Gleason in his study of cotton federal politics notes that Brezhnev encouraged a policy of

> stagnation for the central Asian republics because he felt that he could delay unrest and protest by "delaying development, mechanization and migration" for 10, perhaps 15 years . . . the republican first secretaries [from the republics] may well have been encouraging Brezhnev in this direction. Clearly, the general secretary was willing to guarantee job security to regional leaders who themselves could maintain political stability. Four of the first secretaries of central Asia and Kazakhstan of 1961 were still in power in 1982. (1990, 85)

In large and territorially diverse nation-states, stability and internal accommodation of regional interests take precedence over efficiency and economic rationality in economic policy.

Comparing China with Democratic India and Democratic Brazil: Does Democracy Matter?

Subnational variation across diverse nation-states shows that choices by regional elites matter. Subnational variation in political strategies and institutional capacities is a combined product of central control and local discretion. This raises a question: What difference does the regime type—democracy versus authoritarian—make? How do macro-regime differences enter into this analysis of micro-institutions and strategies adopted by regional elites?

Until now, this chapter has argued against the common presumption in studies of subnational and local variation that it is democracy that produces regional variation by itself.[32] Thus, even in centralized or authoritarian states—the military regime of Brazil, Mao's China, and the former Soviet Union—regional elites respond to the central state in diverse ways, circumventing and transforming the goals and instruments of central policy. In this section, I argue that while regional rulers reregulate central policies in all systems, the *form and specific pattern* of that reregulation does differ across regime types. Democracy affects the specific *incentives* of local and central rulers differently, shaping the vertical behavior of subnational elites accordingly. Regional elites must get elected and reelected in the regional arenas; this means that they must balance their locally induced electoral potential with the possibility of central transfers or punishment. Thus, local or provincial elites faced with the electoral imperative (in democracies) pursue their vertical strategies differently than those faced with bureaucratic career incentives (in non-democracies).

How does the separation of regional and national incentives affect intergovernmental interactions in the pursuit of economic policy? Democratic incentives at the regional level affect the pattern and the discursive structure of vertical interactions. In nondemocratic systems, bargaining, circumvention, and convergence (bandwagoning) across subnational units are more pronounced than confrontational and exit strategies on the part of subnational elites. As important, vertical conflict is expressed within a discursive frame of integration and compliance rather than aggression and noncompliance.

First, regional democratic competition shapes the *discursive* structure within which central-local relations are negotiated. Subnational democratic competition makes reelection incentives of regional elites more imperative, making confrontational and aggressive postures much more likely in democratic systems than in an authoritarian regime, where local incentives are upwardly directed. These *conflictual* discursive strategies, in turn, may produce greater central-local conflict. Simultaneously, democratic central rulers may pursue either cooptation or appeasement strategies (rather than coercion) to ensure compliance from the regions. Chapter 4 documented some of the confrontational strategies pursued by some regions in India, where in the state of West Bengal, a subnationalist mobilizational strategy makes an anti-center rhetoric an essential part of its political strategy.

In authoritarian regimes, by contrast, regional rulers frame confrontation within an integrationist discursive framework. In Mao's China, local elites evaded and challenged central policy, but did so without open opposition (Shue 1988, 141). As one county cadre official told Shue: "The plans [we made at the county for each of the communes to follow] departed from reality not by an enormous amount, but by little" (142). Shue calls this "defensive strategy." She also notes the presence of a more aggressive strategy during this period, in which local interests enhanced their own power within the system (143–45), but in comparison with democratic India, the extent of discursive *compliance* with the center was higher in China. Chung's study of decollectivization of agriculture in the early 1980s—in a way very similar to my study—outlines different types of strategies pursued by different local states in China—innovation, bandwagoning, and resistance—but also notes that while some are innovators (e.g., Anhui), most local elites are "risk averse" and pursue bandwagoning, that is, they follow the center's lead in an opportunistic vein. Thus, the Chinese system, as a result of its nondemocratic and upwardly oriented incentives, shaped regional strategies and especially the frames with which regional elites balance their locally induced interests. Similarly, Hough shows that in the former Soviet Union, local party officials complain to, challenge, and lobby Moscow in a particular way: by insisting that their actions fulfill central priorities (1969, 256–63). Thus, in democratic systems, regional rulers frame their bargaining within a *conflictual and autonomy-oriented* discursive structure, while in nondemocratic systems, confrontational actions are framed within a rhetoric of *compliance and integration*.

Second, in nondemocratic countries, regional/local politicians' bureaucratic and career incentives will privilege the pursuit of bargaining and lobbying strategies (collaborative or defensive) toward the center; in democratic countries, regional elections will make regional politicians' incentives locally directed. In such contexts, subnational politicians will be more likely to adopt aggressive or confrontational postures toward the center.

The framework developed in this study, thus, has the power to explain both *similarities* in regional responses to central policy across widely varying cases and *differences* between defensive and aggressive strategies of regional rulers in different regime types. In *both* cases, far from serving as robotic agents of the central authority, regional actors modify both the designs and the capacity of central agencies. I analyze regional responses under democratic regimes in Brazil and contemporary Russia below.

Democratic Brazil

Starting in the early 1980s and more definitely after 1985, Brazil became a democracy. During this democratic transition, institutions governing federal relations were radically transformed. Decentralization of political authority coproduced democratization, in the process shaping the structure of democratic institutions that emerged in the 1980s. A number of scholars have noted that contemporary Brazilian federalism creates incentives for legislators to privilege state-based issues while neglecting national issues (Samuels 2000, 2). State governors enjoy disproportionate power in this system, both financial and political, through their control over pork-barrel funds and the power to hire and fire legislators from their state. Presidents in the 1990s and in the 2000s must negotiate with state governors to pass their legislative agendas; governors deploy this power to bargain for their state and ensure their political and economic survival. These changes in federalism have enhanced the power of regional actors, creating the possibility of central-regional conflicts over economic policy. It is well recognized that Brazil's developmental failure and crisis cannot be understood without understanding the regional roots of economic policy implementation. How does democratization affect center-periphery relations? My theory predicts that with the democratic transition, regional reregulation attempts should become more diverse and divergent, and central-regional conflict should increase. Is that borne out in Brazil?

In contrast to the congruent relationship between Minas Gerais and the federal government in the 1970s and the early 1980s, more recently the governor of Minas Gerais refused to accede to the Plano Real initiated by President Cardoso. In January 1999, Itamar Franco, the newly inaugurated governor of Brazil's second-most-populous state, Minas Gerais, announced a unilateral ninety-day moratorium on repayment of his state's estimated $13.5 billion debt to the federal government, precipitating a financial crisis. This forced the central government to cover the debts in order to prevent the perception of a generalized default. The *New York Times* concluded, "Brazil's economic crisis pits president against governors."[33] How can we explain this transformation in federal-state relations in Brazil?

Most commentators attribute the current intergovernmental conflict to provincial governors' increased fiscal power and their ability to control public consumption and the fiscal purse granted by the 1988 constitution. Thus subnational fiscal deficits are attributed to the "soft-budget" constraints of Brazil's federal system that enable subnational politicians to transfer fiscal deficits to the central government. The subnational governments expend while the center pays for that expenditure; in such circumstances the provincial governments' incentives are to be fiscally irresponsible.

Most crucially for the present argument, this increased central-regional conflict began with democratization in the 1980s, when subnational political arenas became democratic before democracy was achieved at the federal level.[34] During the transitional period, a crucial governor's election in 1982 "produced a group of nationally prominent subnational elites" (Montero 2000, 63). In 1984, a movement at the municipal and state levels crystallized to expand the size of the state and the state's control of taxing powers over goods and ultimately services (known as the ICMS, for tax on the circulation of goods and services). The governors and opposition municipal and federal representatives organized other like-minded groups and politicians at the subnational level, solidifying collective action against the center (Montero 2000,

65). Thus, the governor's political incentives became tied to local elections and party competition, engendering the proliferation of central-regional conflict embodied in the default by Itamar Franco, the governor of Minas Gerais, in 1999. Thus, the separation of regional electoral logic from that of federal democratic transition enhanced center-regional conflict.

This analysis of subnational responses in Brazil under two different regime types generates the following conclusions. First, subnational responses to national policies shape regional developmental patterns even during authoritarian regimes. Thus, even strong or centralized states generate diverse regional responses, creating persistent regional variation in policies, institutions, and strategic choices. Some of these subnational policy regimes may be developmental, while others may be clientistic or populist, shaped as much by local politics as by central rules of the game. The trajectory of Minas Gerais during the military regime in Brazil (and of Gujarat and West Bengal in India) highlights this variation. Second, the creation of local political incentives, which usually follows democratization, leads to an enhancement of political conflict between the center and the regions, as regional politicians follow the compulsions of regional logics. Thus democracy might create political incentives for subnational politicians to pursue both confrontational and lobbying tactics toward the center and to do it in a partisan and public way.

Contemporary Democratic Russia

As the democratization process unfolded in contemporary Russia, regional challenges to the federal government simultaneously proliferated.[35] Soon after the break-up of the Soviet federation, regional republics in Russia declared themselves to be sovereign states, adopting constitutions, flags, and even national anthems. Many refused to remit taxes to the central state, challenging the basic fiscal capacity of the state. The fiscal crisis seemed to choke the Russian state; the finance minister, Boris Fyodorov, appropriately called it "financial asphyxiation."[36] Most threatened protest, strikes, and confiscation of federal property. Many republics imposed trade restrictions against other republics, and threats of tax withholding continued until 1998. Monetary fragmentation from 1994 to 1998 challenged one of the basic symbols of national sovereignty, the use of national currency (Woodruff 1999). Demands for autonomy spread rapidly; regional elites have wrested, created, and exploited almost every opportunity to take control over their regional agendas. Andrews and Stoner-Weiss (1995) noted, in a survey conducted as early as 1993, that regional governments enjoy greater support from their constituents than did the national government, and they found a pervasive regionalist sentiment amongst the Russian population.[37] In addition to challenges to central authority, many regions established bilateral and asymmetric agreements, with the federal government augmenting regionalist claims and the contagion effect (Solnick 1996b; Stoner-Weiss 2000). How are we to understand this spurt of regional activism across Russia's periphery in the 1990s?

In my argument, the Russian federal system in combination with the consolidation of local democratic competition in the regions creates powerful incentives for subnational leaders to pursue regionally specific agendas, but to do so in confrontational ways. Thus, politics of integration and bargaining gives way to the rhetoric of confrontation and discourse of noncompliance.[38] This suggests that regional elites' economic strategies in this changed scenario are a product of opportunities presented by a weak state and incentives generated by local democratic competition. However, confrontation is only one type of political strategy, represented by some regions; many other regions in Russia are much more pro-center. It is also expected that we may find varying levels of local democratic support driving a wide range of vertical strategies across Russian regions.

These expectations generated from my theoretical model are confirmed for the Russian experience. Most notably, Treisman's account of regional strategies vis-à-vis the question of compliance with the national federation is consistent with my expectations derived out of an analysis of India. Treisman is concerned with a different problem than the question of developmental success or failure; he is concerned with the question, Why did post-Soviet Russia not fall apart? Yet his arguments bear some relation to this study. He argues that the center's fiscal policy of "selective fiscal appeasement" prevented explicit protests or secessionism from the Russian federation. Central rulers directed budget transfers and tax breaks toward protest-prone regions, in effect buying electoral support for central rulers (2001, 3–4). Treisman's theoretical framework (of interaction between central rulers' strategies and provincial elites' choices), derived from a game-theoretic framework similar to mine, leads him to model the regional elites as strategic actors. He notes that in contemporary Russia, "confrontation appeared to be the order of the day . . . regional leaders employed a repertoire of obstructive measures. Some declared their provinces autonomous, sovereign, or even independent, refused to remit tax, claimed natural resources, sued federal institutions in court, withheld grain supplies, or refused to send conscripts to serve in the army" (120). Thus, in contrast to most accounts of center-periphery relations, he does not portray regional targets of the center's fiscal appeasement as passive recipients. Treisman models the regional elites as choosing between "supporting or opposing President Yeltsin."[39] In my framework, these political strategies of subnational elites will be driven by the nature of subnational political support for either of these strategies. Treisman's account is consistent with my expectation: "In brief, the strategies of regional leaders in dealing with the central government at moments of crisis seem to have been fundamentally shaped by their perception of the institutional context of center-region politics and their own place and interests within it. Elections appeared to have found an important place within it" (128). Andrews and Stoner-Weiss's survey results (1995, 404) also confirm that by being anti-center, regional elites in post-Soviet Russia were representing the views of the majority of their local constituents. Thus, as argued in the rest of this book for India, regional elites' strategies in post-Soviet Russia are a product of the trade-off between central rewards and subnational levels of political support. Confrontation and divergence across republics mark intergovernmental relations in democratic Russia.

Conclusion

Brazilian leaders in the 1960s spoke of "grand" visions, India's prime minister outlined a powerful plan of national development in 1947, and Chinese leaders spoke of carving out "Chinese socialism" in 1949. Each saw the enhancement of central state capacity to be crucial for their developmental ambitions. They deployed the state—in all cases the central state—to implement coherent developmental goals. Yet, in each case, central capacity proved incapable of fulfilling their developmental ambitions; each of them confronted failures of varying types. Even more significantly, centralization of *formal* authority was common in these cases.

This book generally, and this chapter more specifically, has argued that these widespread state failures cannot be understood unless we disaggregate our understanding of state capacity to incorporate subnational levels. I urge attention not only to central state capacity but also to how regional elites modify, circumvent, and implement policies initiated at the center. Regional choices and strategies matter. We need to incorporate territory within our understanding of developmental states, modifying our nation-centric and top-down notions of state capacity with a multilevel concept of polyarchy. Such a concept urges analytical attention to the subnational level and to central-local interactions not only in federal systems but also in centralized systems. The comparative analysis undertaken in this chapter poses *different* questions to the cases and yields some counterintuitive conclusions about the cases analyzed.

First, this comparative analysis challenges the commonly held view that regional elites do not matter in strong states or under authoritarian regimes; we need to understand the exact pattern of central-local interaction in such systems rather than assume it away. State regulation in territorially complex systems (or heterogeneous polities) invites reregulation by regional elites irrespective of regime type. Such an analysis of multilevel interactions in centralized or strong-state contexts is also necessary for understanding the persistence of regional patterns *after* democratic consolidation. This structured nested comparison allows understanding of both the *common* logic of regional responses and inter-level (between central and subnational) interactions across nation-states and the *differences* created by cross-national variations in regime type.

In *all* states, especially ones with a strong-state intervention tradition, regional actors attempt to modify, and succeed in modifying, central policy in ways that enhance regional developmental agendas. Regional variation and subnational differences continue to persist despite strong or centralized states. Competition between central and local governments is much more pervasive than predicted by alternative theories of development or state building. Even more, regime type does not affect these patterns; in both democratic and nondemocratic states regional elites act in widely varying ways that reflect both clientistic and developmental behavior.

Second, such regional reregulation attempts are shaped partially by the structure of central rules of the game and most crucially by incentives generated by the local or subnational politics. Thus, the pattern of regional responses to central policy (vertical strategies) is shaped by the extent of regional democracy and the career incentives (whether they are electoral or bureaucratic) prevalent in the system. Therefore, in China and the former Soviet Union, the career compulsions of regional party officials compel strategies of circumvention and bandwagoning by regional elites. By contrast, in democratic India and Brazil and in contemporary democratic Russia, regional elites pursue both developmentalist and confrontational strategies with an eye toward regional elections and regional public opinion.

The regime type affects the precise nature of *local incentives,* shaping the extent of partisan conflict between the center and the regions. Thus in democracies, *partisan* interaction between vertical and regional politicians and within the regions is more pervasive and coexists with an *administrative* and intergovernmental logic between the center and the regions.

The institutional form of the country—federal versus unitary—does not affect the *existence* of regional strategies but does affect the possibility of their success and the consequences for subnational developmental prospects. In a unitary country, regional activism, more often than not, instigates counter-centralization responses. In a federal country, regional strategies and regional variation are more consequential and effective.

Internal heterogeneity emerges as crucially important not only for analyzing regional responses but for assessing the variation in the responses of central rulers—both nondemocratic and democratic rulers. In heterogeneous multilevel countries, all national rulers are compelled to respond to regional claims irrespective of regime type or of institutional form; thus, intergovernmental conflict is much higher in such large countries as China, Russia, India, and Brazil. In more homogeneous countries, the compulsions of national leaders lie much less with political stability and territorial equities, precluding compromise and policies of appeasement by the central rulers.[40]

Scholars of the state, or of economic development, have too often neglected to examine the regional roots of policies and outputs originating at the center; regional actions and central-local interaction matter in a wide variety of cases. Even more crucially, the comparative theory outlined in this book is able to account for some of these similarities (the role of regional elites in all systems), as well as some of the differences (partisan and confrontational nature of regional strategies in democratic systems), by focusing on a parsimonious set of variables across nation-states. These variables are: central rules of the games and central strategies, subnational preferences and strategies to central frameworks, and subnational institutional capacities. Subnational political incentives—electoral or career—drive subnational political strategies toward the center, while central rulers' compulsions are to maintain the state and ensure a minimal winning coalition. It is the *interaction* of these various elements that affects developmental successes or failures. This comparative analysis succeeds in explaining national variance through an analysis of local variance and multilevel interactions.

9 | Conclusion
Regional Landscapes and Economic Development in Dirigiste States

Even centralized or strong states engender different kinds of new institutions at the regional level, resulting in new and diverse patterns of market governance. Diversity of institutions and trajectories, not uniformity or hierarchy, can be found within a nation-state. This is the main finding of this study. This finding challenges the expectations of both supporters and opponents of state-centric theories, who share the assumption that states are exhausted at the national or central level. In the alternative framework developed in this book, states are conceptualized as polycentric hierarchies encompassing vertical and horizontal interactions within their boundaries. Scholars in the statist tradition may be surprised by the bottom-up responses of regional states, which suggest that state capacity is not national or unitary. Subnational institutions modify the agendas of strong or failed states in significant ways. Neoliberal theorists, with their emphasis on price-mediated markets, may also be surprised by the persistence of consequential developmental states at different levels within a country. In many countries developmental states exist at local levels, shaping both the local and the national policy process in powerful ways. Synergistic public-private organizational innovations at the subnational levels challenge the dichotomous assumptions of neoliberal and statist accounts alike. The evidence presented in this study instead shows that policies at the central level unleash diverse regional responses encompassing strategic choices about economic principles as well as new institutions. These divergent trajectories within a centralized state are persistent and self-reinforcing.

Counterintuitively, I argue that central states' control over economic outputs (investment or transfers, for example) creates a strong impetus on the part of societal and regional actors to reregulate central policies.[1] Central rulers create institutional veto and access points, a situation that gives regional political entrepreneurs opportunities to circumvent and reshape investment policies. Regional or local motivations also enhance such aspirations. In democratic states such as India, local democratic control and popular pressures in the region fuel regional investment hunger. In nondemocratic countries such as China and the former Soviet Union, control over the fiscal residue and local officials' career incentives create strong incentives in favor of regional activism. These incentives drive regional politicians and officials to circumvent constraints and seize opportunities to reorder central policies. Thus, in territorially divided states, the conduct of economic policy is a political process in which central rulers and regional incumbents bargain over the output and rules of the game, but also create new institutions and new markets.[2] Regional elites' political choices are driven by both potential benefits from integration with the center and the necessity of designing winning coalitions in the regions. This political compulsion may necessitate anti-center or pro-center mobilization strategies. This interactive dynamic results in a diverse array of market-governance patterns, despite formal centralism or national state autonomy. Diverse institutions and regional responses drive divergent, rather than convergent, investment flows within a nation-state.

Chapters 1 and 2 cast this argument in a systematic form by proposing a new framework for analyzing the politics of developmental failure in strong states. The framework consists of a two-level model with a focus on vertical interactions between diverse regional elites and central rules, horizontal regional investment policies that translate and modify central guidelines but also create new institutions to reregulate investment, and business responses. First, politicians adopt vertical strategies toward constraints imposed by the central rules of the game by either bargaining or opposing the central state. These strategies toward the center are driven by regional compulsions and the degree to which provincial incumbents are integrated into the central bureaucratic and political apparatus. Strategic interaction characterizes relationships between central and regional incumbents. Second, these regional elites adopt different configurations of public and private sectors in the regional economy and create new institutions to compensate for credibility, coordination, and information dilemmas created by a strong centralist state. Variations in the creation and effectiveness of these institutions explain the patterns of regional investments across different local arenas. States at lower levels of the system are stimulated to correct for central state failures and crucial market failures. Third, business actors do not behave as pure functional actors but respond to these spatially specific central and regional variations, reinforcing subnational and central-local patterns.

By shifting the focus from central states to interaction between levels of government and to subnational processes, this study goes beyond existing and recent work on developmental states and comparative political economy. The literature on the developmental state takes a top-down approach that robs lower levels of government of their autonomy and their capacity to have an independent or even intervening impact on economic development. The framework outlined above introduces an analysis of vertical interaction between local rulers and the central state officials within conventional top-down models in comparative political economy. These arguments urge us to rethink the dominant nation-centric frameworks in comparative politics in the same way as debates in international relations challenged the realist assumptions of international relations theory.[3] The analysis theorizes the interactions among individuals, institutions, and the larger multilevel polity explicitly. In doing so, spatial considerations are united with a neo-institutional framework that pays attention to the political institution of federalism and contributes to state theory.

Substantial regional variation in the Indian case and in other countries cannot be adequately explained by top-down approaches. The shortcomings of the top-down approach can perhaps be obviated by the recent literature on federalism, which does focus on the regional level. However, the public finance literature concerned with the developmental effects of federalism and found most notably in the theory of "market-preserving federalism" is clearly apolitical. It conflates economic development with the interests of subnational political leaders, although their interests cannot be easily equated with economic development. On the contrary, in my framework, regional political leaders are seen as operating on two levels, in which they not only fashion their relations with central governments, but also must build popular support among their local constituencies.[4] In contrast to the apolitical public finance approach, my approach demonstrates that regional politics shapes the strategies that regional leaders take in dealing with central governments. These political incentives are likely to create persistent diverse strategies within nation-states, an outcome not well explained by the public finance approach.

These conclusions are derived through comparison of regions within India, analysis of subnational economic data not analyzed until now, and detailed ethnographic fieldwork. Most of the existing literature, while focusing on developmental states, lacks the perspectives of those who make policy decisions and whose choices actually affect economic outputs. This study relied on interviews with two relevant sets of actors—businesspersons and bureaucratic officials—so as to uncover the process through which actual decisions were made. This methodology combined detailed interviews with bureaucrats and businesspersons with historical and macroeconomic data. Through these methods, I built a comparative measuring framework to evaluate micro-institutions across regional states and provided a phenomenological account of what capitalists need from the state. This allowed me to approach the developmental state from *below*—through the eyes of regional actors and businesspersons—and in a *comparative frame*.

In this chapter, I revisit the distinct patterns of subnational developmentalism found in India. I go on to analyze the relationship between the national political context and subnational innovations. The next section speculates about the implications of this analysis for institutional and policy change under way in India and much of the developing world in recent years. I conclude by exploring the larger theoretical implications of this analysis for state theory, theories of development, territorial politics, and the subnational comparative method.

Lessons from Subnational Pathways in India

Multiple subnational trajectories of development within a centralized state are counterintuitive. This discovery of different developmental pathways within a centralist state in just one country provides a strong basis for expecting that a diverse array of varying patterns of governance have unfolded across other nations and other strong states.[5] From the Indian case we can distinguish two plausible patterns of state intervention in the economy: a "bureaucratic-statist" model and a "partisan" model. In one case (Gujarat), bureaucrats and technocrats led the way, infiltrating the dirigiste central bureaucracy, circumventing its rules for institutional creation and innovation, and evolving a developmentalist agenda. While political support from politicians was facilitative, the bureaucrats succeeded by removing key economic functions from the purview of political decision making, and thereby public scrutiny, and by "tying their own hands" through institutionalized linkages with key private actors.

The second dominant pattern (in both West Bengal and Tamil Nadu) was led by politicians who crafted a more public and partisan path of political pressure on the dirigiste state. A higher degree of political mobilization in favor of a public sector–led agenda and protection of established social groups characterized this political strategy. In contrast, the productive sectors of the regional economy were disenfranchised and excluded. While political innovation of diverse rhetorical and mobilization strategies as well as institutional innovation made this pattern electorally successful, its impact on developmental outcomes was weak and ineffective. A subnationalist and mobilized society supported this political strategy, allowing the reproduction of an economically irrational, but politically rational, developmental trajectory.

In line with the second generation of research on the developmental state,[6] all the varying patterns of market governance rely on the state, but in one case, micro-institutions of the state were better able to solve crucial *market and state failures* pervasive in many contexts: coordination, uncertainty, and informational dilemmas. This suggests that attention should be directed not to macro-allocation institutions (state versus markets) but to micro "causal mechanisms." Both states *and* markets generate pervasive and endemic dilemmas; three of these are crucial for development and confront markets and states alike: failures of *coordination,* when decentralized actions of investors cannot be coordinated; problems of uncertainty and credibility, when policies are not *consistent* and state actions are *non-credible;* and problems of access to *information*. These problems are magnified in multilevel polities, where co-ordination across levels is difficult to achieve, where regional governments implement many central policies *after* they have been announced, and where both central actors and regional actors have incentives to manipulate control over information. Subnational developmental states will exist so long as regional elites and institutions are able to compensate for the central-level failures of coordination and credibility and circumvent information control by the center by devising their own informational flows. In addition, subnational states, to be effective, will have to bypass many vetoes and constraints imposed by the central state.

State fundamentalism is as misleading as market fundamentalism in understanding the political economy of development. In addition, the current theories of development fail to attend to vertical patterns of interaction, which may differ substantially within nation-states and across countries. This book has shown that in India, while all provinces are subject to national rules, some utilize choice points internal to the regulatory regime to bargain effectively with the central state, aiming for integration, while others use strategies of confrontation. Still others adopt a mixed strategy that is "opportunistic," meaning that these regional leaders disobey and adopt confrontation whenever regional compulsions support such a policy, but comply when possible. In addition, innovative hybrid organizational forms can create complementarities between public and private sectors in some states. New institutions at the subnational level may compensate for the credibility deficit of the central state by creating institutional innovation, increasing coordination with investors, and providing information to investors directly. This set of differentiated political variables helps to account for systematic regional divergence in investment flows despite a centralist state.

In the western state of Gujarat, regional incumbents attempting to devise competitive strategies with the neighboring Maharashtra began to implement innovative *circumvention* strategies in the late 1960s. They began attracting private-sector investors from Bombay, Calcutta, and East Africa in a bid to compete with Maharashtra. The pervasive power of the license-*raj* could not be fully bypassed; thus the bureaucrats in Gujarat devised ways to mitigate the adverse rules of the game originating at the center. They monitored the outputs of the central bureaucracy and exploited its multiple choice points to redirect the flow of investments toward Gujarat. In the process, institutional innovations—the joint sector, promotional organizations such as the iNDEXTb—and effective coordination resulted. All these changes at the subnational level created and sustained a "liberal bureaucratic" system, which was led by state agencies but which harnessed many private-sector mechanisms in the service of rapid industrial development. These institutional changes and innovations were sustained by a politics that relied not on subnationalist mobilization but on vertical integration with the national system. The hegemony of the Congress Party with a strong and differentiated class basis in the 1960s and 1970s led to extensive political support for this pro-industry strategy. Strong linkages between commercial farmers and industrialists dispersed labor-intensive industrialization in the early years and generated political support for successive governments. The absence of a strongly redistributive force (a social democratic party like the CPI(M), for example) prevented any credible challenge to this pro-capital developmental trajectory from emerging. Further, Gujarat lacked any strong regional movements; thus a pro-center strategy followed by its bureaucratic elites was rewarded, rather than punished, by the regional population.

In West Bengal, the regional elites stressed a purist partisan strategy that excluded hybrid and private-sector elements; this was much more convergent with the national-level stress on the public sector as the "commanding heights of the Indian economy." In pursuit of this strategy, and lacking any regional competitor in eastern India, West Bengal rulers neglected to infiltrate the central state system, evolving a *partisan confrontation* route in pursuit of development. This strategy toward the central political elites and its constraining effects led them to neglect the task of institutional innovation. However, political innovation in the strategy of rhetoric and a public strategy of confrontation ensured continued electoral success. Political and cultural institutions did emerge to carry out this strategy. A strong regionalist sentiment in West Bengal, a radical anti-systemic mobilization tradition, and a cultural heritage of Bengali subnationalism rewarded the anti-center political strategy; the ruling party in West Bengal continued to win elections despite industrial decline.

In Tamil Nadu, the immediate context was more competitive than in eastern India; its neighbor, Karnataka, was relatively well developed. This led to a strong impetus for industrial development. During the 1950s and 1960s, the regional Congress Party politicians followed a partisan strategy, seeking to utilize their political capital at the center in favor of a public sector–led developmental pattern. This strategy served Tamil Nadu well during the 1950s and 1960s. However, with the decline of the Congress Party in the regional state in the late 1960s and the rise of regional parties with strongly anti-center rhetoric and a pro-cultural focus, their investment policy turned inward and fell into disuse. Institutions at the regional level were neglected, and the effectiveness of institutions declined. Political support for an anti-center strategy made this strategy sustainable. In the 1980s, declining anti-center sentiment led the regional rulers to become opportunistic, making alliances and bargains with the central government whenever they could. This contributed to definite gains in Tamil Nadu's industrial development, but the state's investment prospects remained somewhat inconsistent. Subnational institutions were relatively more effective than in West Bengal, ensuring greater coordination with local investors, compensation of the credibility deficit, and better information flows. However, the institutional effectiveness was also circumscribed by inconsistencies and reliance on a partisan tradition, which meant that the bureaucracy in Tamil Nadu was dependent upon the central influence of its politicians. Thus, investment levels in Tamil Nadu oscillated over time.

National Political Institutions and Regional Strategies

In an analysis of economic policy, preference variation and divergence are usually assumed to be exogenous. This assumption allows scholars to engage in comparative institutional analysis more successfully, as the effect of institutions can be analyzed independently of the preferences about economic goals (Alston, Eggertsson, and North 1996). This study has shown, in contrast, that although provincial officials place income and material objectives high on their regional agenda, some do so less than others. Moreover, regional investment preferences diverge sharply from those of the central government in some provinces, but in some other regional states they may converge with those of the central government. This raises a key question: Why do investment preferences converge in some circumstances and not in others?

As this study has shown, political institutions—such as license-*raj*, joint decision structure, and federalism—produce preference divergence. Political institutions shape preferences by manipulating the incentive structures of agents. In India during the license-*raj* period, the immense fiscal power of the central state, the control over allocation of investment, and the bureaucratic structure oriented the incentive structure of provincial rulers in such a way that all states needed to adopt vertical strategies toward the central state. The presence of a segmented central state is consistent with the pursuit of diverse vertical strategies by regional rulers. The Indian central-local system was, and continues to be, an octopus-like structure.[7] The states have to deal with the center, either to bargain within it (Gujarat), to confront it in public or political ways (West Bengal), or to engage in opportunistic behavior (Tamil Nadu). The Indian central state shapes the action and behavior of regional officials as they make trade-offs between pursuing positive (bargaining) or negative (partisan confrontation) strategies. Analogously, the spatial separation of political incentives necessitated by federal democratic institutions—between national and regional arenas—modified the expected rational incentive in favor of seeking political support in the relevant region.[8]

This book has emphasized that subnational variation is engendered by the structure of national institutions and political compulsions of national elites, who even in centralized systems do not use their power to impose national uniformity across subnational units. The internal architecture of national institutions may create porous access and choice points, which allow regional states and societal actors to subvert the system from within. These spaces within the state suit the regional agendas of regional incumbents but may also be necessitated by political compulsions of the national elite, who must balance national stability with the pursuit of "rational" economic policies. In large-sized territorially divided systems (for example, India, China, Brazil, and Russia), national elites create (or accept) such regional heterogeneity to ensure that the nation-state stays together. Central state autonomy, a prerequisite for economically rational policies, is subverted not only by subnational politicians but also by national rulers. Regional strategies are partially in response to the structure of rules embodied in the central institutions and in the structure of local incentives. These insights are generated by the multilevel interactive model that analyzes both national institutions and regional strategies as endogenously produced. Regional innovation and policy autonomy do not take place in a vacuum, but are responses to the national context and the spaces of opportunities within the central state system. In this book, the national political context is not exogenous to the analysis, but interaction between national and regional policy is theorized explicitly. Future research should focus on comparative expectations: Under what conditions do national elites tolerate or even promote regional diversity across subnational arenas? And, similarly: Under what contexts do subnational elites find it rational to sustain preference divergence with central preferences?

Neoliberalism, Institutional Change, and Regional Activism

What happens when macro-institutions (policy regimes or federal institutions) change? Starting tentatively in 1985, but more decisively in 1991, India's central government changed the policy regime governing industry, reducing the veto points enjoyed by the erstwhile central state. Institutional changes in the rules of the game governing industry accompanied policy changes.

The framework developed in this book makes sense of these institutional and policy changes. The 1991 policy change can be treated as an exogenous change in central institutions, transforming the incentives and constraints faced by regional rulers. The analysis presented in Chapters 3 through 5 shows that political conflicts created by the erstwhile divided institutions were an impetus for the sudden autonomy exhibited by the regional states after 1991. This allows us to determine the sources of the resurgence of policy initiatives by the various states as well as the pressures to reorganize fiscal relations between the center and the regional states observed recently by scholars (Venkatesan 1994; Sinha 1996; Observer Research Foundation 1996; Jenkins 1999; Paul 2000; Rudolph and Rudolph 2001). The increased role of regional states in the post-1991 period is not a sudden phenomenon. Its roots lie in the nature of the erstwhile segmented state documented in Chapter 3, and the accelerating role of the regional incumbents in circumventing and managing their industrial development policies throughout the 1970s and the 1980s. With the institutional vacuum created by changes at the central level, the regional institutional differences have become more visible. Even more, this situation gives regional incumbents opportunities to reregulate the new central policies the same way they attempted to reregulate licensing policies in the 1970s.

Two distinct aspects of this changing process deserve note. First, as incentives and constraints created by the central state changed, trade-offs between vertical and horizontal strategies also changed, leading to greater harmonization in central-local strategies. Many states followed pro-liberalization policies after 1991. The removal of central constraints has reduced the need for circumvention strategies or confrontation strategies that were necessary during the license-*raj*, but has not removed the need for vertical maneuvering completely. Regional states directed some of those energies to foreign investors and international organizations rather than the central state after 1991.

Second, the regional reregulation strategies in this changed scenario draw from provincial strategies followed during the license-*raj* era. Gujarat follows a more bureaucratic route that relied on intrastate lobbying and monitoring after 1991, while Tamil Nadu and West Bengal pursue a partisan route that attempts to deploy their political influence at the center for greater economic rewards. Most notably, West Bengal's political elites continue to deploy an anti-center rhetoric despite a decline in the credibility of that strategy.

Even more startling, the continuing east-west divide within India can be understood in light of the framework outlined in this book. Western states— Gujarat and Maharashtra—attract a larger share of private investment than the states of Bihar, Orissa, and West Bengal, despite the latter states' pro-liberalization policies in the 1990s (Sinha 1996; Saez 1999; Montek Singh Ahluwalia 2000). In fact, this book shows that regional variation after 1991 stems in large part from patterns of regional intervention in the economy that prevailed in the license-*raj* period. Thus, path-dependence in regional institutions continues to create different regional levels of investment. This framework explains both the unexpected regional variation in investment flows during the dirigiste regime (1955–90) and the apparently dramatic yet expected regional activism once the central constraints changed (post-1991).

These empirical results about institutional change in India's policy regime have important implications. Analyses of the liberalization phase should attend to the path-dependence of regional industrial orders in India. The logic underlying a divided and segmented leviathan affects the nature and process of post-1991 decentralization. The year 1991 seems like a radical turning point in central-local economic relations only if one views India's policy framework to be originating at the center. Regional constraints and strategies in interaction with the central rules used to, and continue to, shape the pattern of economic policy in India, augmenting the preexisting segmented character of the Indian state.

This two-step argument about the changing dynamics of competition and the continuity in guided state interventions is better able to explain both the remarkable change of policies and ideas at the state level and the continued variation in investment patterns. Analogous dramatic changes in fiscal and political structures in the 1990s can be readily understood in the context of the arguments developed in this study.

This analysis of the regional basis of institutional and policy changes in India has implications for a larger debate about globalization and the supposed resilience of nation-states to resist convergence. Two competing views can be found on the question of whether globalization leads to greater convergence, reducing nation-centric variations, or whether nation-states continue to shape their own development strategies (Berger and Dore 1996). One view argues that internalization and globalization reduce the room to maneuver that nation-states might have enjoyed until then. Others argue that states continue to retain policy autonomy (Wade 1996) in some domains (trade versus finance, for example) and that, more crucially, the *terms* on which globalization is implemented are shaped by domestic politics (Garrett 1998).

Subnational variations within domestic economies, it is argued, facilitate globalization, leading to "glocalization" (Doner and Hershberg 1999). First, localities, communities, firms, and regions adjust to global changes in different ways; this challenges the notion of a coherent national response to global pressures. Neoliberalism does not lead to the triumph of free or laissez-faire markets but to locally and nationally diverse institutional patterns that are spatially embedded. The spatial embeddedness of the national state and the national economy leads to different patterns of market governance; both analytical categories of divergence and convergence are misplaced. Second, while nation-states might be undermined from both above and below, states and hybrid public-private institutional forms at different levels within a nation-state continue to mediate the transition toward global integration. Intermediate forms of coordination—different types of states (hierarchies), networks, joint-sector associations, self-governing institutions, and polyarchies[9]—have proliferated. Each of these forms continues to be shaped by its specific spatial contexts and local linkages and attempts to reregulate national or international rules of the game. I turn now to the implications of this study for larger theoretical debates and to some issues of future research.

Toward a Comparative Theory of Developmental Failure and Success

State Theory, Development Theory, and Subnational Variations

Most recent work on the developmental state focuses on the role of the state either to argue for its importance or to suggest that states' solutions generate their own problems. This study, by contrast, *disaggregates* the state spatially and relationally, showing how variation within a state and interaction across governmental levels may affect investment flows and contribute to national "developmental failure."

Analysis of these infranational variations in state capacity and policy outcomes is a neglected topic in political science and state theory. State theorists concerned with state formation as well as state effects focus disproportionately on the central level of analysis. State formation is seen to arise as a result of standardization and centralization (Tilly 1975; 1990; Downing 1992; Ertman 1997).[10] The Weberian tradition's influence on state theory means that centralization and the creation of uniformity out of local particularistic order is seen to be necessary to the process of state-building.[11] State autonomy is seen to be a key defining feature of modern states, implying that isolation from societal- and territorial-based groups is an intrinsic part of state formation. This perspective on state formation conceptualizes state formation as a top-down process that ignores how subnational authority gets embedded within a state.

Linked to this problem is a lack of attention to territorial dimensions of state formation. Most studies of state formation attend to the extraterritorial dimension more intensively than to the intraterritorial dimension; the state is seen to be primarily facing the external international system.[12] Migdal's (2001) state-in-society approach, while grappling with a statist anti-societal bias, is trapped by this separation of extraterritorial and infraterritorial dimensions of state formation and state effects. Migdal's characterization of the "state image" as encompassing two boundaries—territorial and social—is a valuable gain in the literature, but fails to recognize that both extra-relations and infra-relations are territorial. Territorial boundaries reorganize social boundaries within the nation-state as much as reorder the international state system.[13]

The lack of sensitivity to how variations in the "infrastate" affect the central state is pervasive in studies of state action and state effects among both economists and political scientists. Most studies of the "Bringing the State Back In" movement focused on the central state and its effects, thereby ignoring varying capacities of local states and their implications for our notions of the central state (Evans, Rueschemeyer, and Skocpol 1985). Institutional economists invariably focus on the "national structure of property rights or other market institutions" (Alston, Eggertsson, and North 1996).

Some of these blind spots in state theory and development have been addressed in this book. Concerned with developmental outcomes, I have argued that development is shaped by the manner in which institutions create incentives that affect the micro-decisions of economic actors. The impact of central policies is mediated by local institutions that are often responsible for translating central government policies into action and have substantial autonomy from the central government in terms of both conversion of policy into action and policy-making capacity. Ironically, while much of the recent literature on the developmental state emphasizes the importance of state institutions, by neglecting local institutions its conceptualization of how institutions affect economic decision making is drastically inadequate.

I proposed an alternative framework that incorporates an attention to levels of analysis in understanding developmental states. The framework consists of two—vertical and horizontal—models, linked to each other in a two-level interaction. The dual focus—on regional elites' strategic choices toward the central rules and horizontal institutional variation—shapes the nature of national-level regulation and regional investment flows. This linkage of different spatial arenas in understanding national-level regulation is important for challenging comparative political-economy debates that rely exclusively on national governance models.[14]

This stress on the central-local dimensions of development also presents a more challenging insight for scholars of subnational variation and local government. In countries with some degree of multitiered authority (or territorially heterogeneous systems), increasing or fine-tuning central or even local "state capacity," while important, may not be enough. The type and extent of conflict and competition *within* the system will also affect the output of nation-states. Hence, the developmental state needs a theory of multitiered decision making within a nation-state and the developmental state literature needs to be combined with the literature on federalism and multitiered systems. This study reminds us that spatial concerns or central-local dynamics have a bearing on national and subnational developmental patterns. The state is not exhausted by the actions of its central rulers, but is a complex aggregation or disaggregation (as the case may be) of lower-level states and local elites. The provincial states are poised between regional society and the larger state system. Depending upon their strategic capacity, they can either evolve as an independent developmental state, subtly wresting power away from the central state, or be a dependent state. Unless we understand the full and multilevel complexity of the regional actors' relationship to the nation-state and the external world, we cannot understand how the nation-state system is constituted —how it is both made and remade. This relational argument can recast the debates within nation-centric comparative political economy as well as urge attention to central-local relations by those scholars who are interested in the subnational processes and outcomes. Subnational reregulation attempts, as outlined by Snyder for Mexico, Locke for Italy, and Herrigel for Germany,[15] may be engendered by policy imperatives of the central rulers and thus require a multilevel framework that is able to theorize *linkages across levels*. Thus, local variation has a vertical intergovernmental dimension not yet analyzed explicitly by scholars attentive to subnational variations.[16]

It is important to tease out two other implications of the multilevel framework developed in this book. First, in contrast to most studies' implicit positive bias toward local government and therefore decentralization, the arguments fleshed out in this study point toward a counterintuitive insight. Developmental states on India's (and other countries') periphery are born and bred through a struggle with a dominant center; this interaction involves both competition and collaboration. The central policy framework and national rulers' political strategies provide both opportunities and constraints. The zero-sum picture found in many studies that celebrate the power of local governments and decentralization (or of central state capacity) is unwarranted. Dirigiste central regulation did not diminish the power of subnational states; rather an interactive dynamic is revealed, where some subnational governments deployed the opportunities and constraints provided by the central state to *enhance* regional regulation and local state capacity.

Second, it is important to modify the "systemic" nature of both neoliberal and developmental state theories. Both neoliberal and developmental state theorists focus on macro-allocation mechanisms (states or markets) that operate at the systemic level. In contrast, this book urges a microanalysis of such macro-phenomena as investment rates, economic policy, or state strength. The focus of attention should be on how state agencies *and* markets solve endemic micro-dilemmas of *coordination, information, and credibility* rather than blunt notions of state strength. Simultaneously, investment rates are the result of micro-decisions of individual investors whose perspectives must be explicitly incorporated in an analysis of development and state theory. Successful subnational states are of different types and embody different mixes of public and private principles. Cross-national and systematic comparisons may fail to illuminate the crucial meso-institutional and micro-political variables that make a difference. These findings resonate with similar evidence of mixed organizational forms in China's provinces and in Eastern Europe and with notions of synergy developed by Peter Evans in his recent work.[17]

Subnational Comparative Method

This argument has important lessons for the methodology of traditional cross-national work.[18] Questions of state intervention may be best studied by examination at the subnational, rather than the nation-state, level. Comparative cross-national studies of economic performance are marred by too few cases chasing too many variables. In understanding the effects of institutions and institutional change, a comparative statics exercise, which holds one variable constant while changing others, may be the most fruitful. A comparative statics exercise assumes the ceteris paribus clause or a most-similar research design. In much of cross-national work, that is difficult to achieve. However, infranational institutional analysis allows us to fine-tune the variables found in cross-national work: the ceteris paribus clause can be more confidently relied upon. The study of different regions within a nation-state allows us to evolve more finely tuned analytical categories to study developmental "stateness"—categories that control for nationwide variables and emphasize subnational micro-institutional variables. New units of analysis and a multi-level framework must be the focus of analytical attention in comparative political economy. Insights about subnational variation in the pursuit of economic policy in Brazil, Mexico, Russia, and China strengthen the point I make here that we may find developmental states at different levels. Tendler (1997) finds that strong public sectors at the provincial level, despite the weak national state, continue to shape the developmental fortunes of their constituents at the local level in Brazil. Stoner-Weiss's analysis (1997) of democratic performance in Russia challenges nation-centric theories of democratic transitions. Richard Snyder (1999) documents subnational variation in reregulation after liberalization of the coffee sector in Mexico, challenging the assumption of uniform effects of neoliberalism.

Territorial Complexity and Internal Heterogeneity

Political economy is rooted in territory.[19] This book brings together two divorced debates in comparative politics: the theory of the developmental state and the theory of federalism. It extends the argument developed through an analysis of India in order to understand regional variation and the logic of developmental politics in three large federal and quasi-federal states—Brazil, Russia, and China. These comparative extensions alert us to pay attention not only to national-level state capacity, but to how the local and national levels are *aggregated* to pursue developmental policies.

All of the countries analyzed in this book are large and territorially divided systems; such states confront special developmental challenges. One intriguing area for future research concerns how territorial and cultural heterogeneity affects central-local interactions and *national* policies. I have proposed that internal diversity affects the compulsions faced by national rulers, making the policies of accommodation much more likely in such states. The Indian case shows that dirigiste state autonomy in a large system can trigger varying vertical and horizontal strategies at the subnational level. In response, national rulers are compelled to accommodate and respond to such regional claims. The internal architecture of the state, even in a highly bureaucratized system such as India (and most other dirigiste countries), is likely to become divided, enhancing choice points within its structure.

The size of the country may also interact with internal heterogeneity. Defining size more precisely and outlining which aspect of size—area, population, or market—is crucial. India and China are both giants with large populations and large markets as well as large areas. Russia and Brazil are large countries in terms of area and the size of the markets.[20]

Although the distinction between large and small size is important, examples from some important small states—Italy—suggest that size by itself may not predict how reregulation works (Putnam 1993; Locke 1995).[21] Historical legacies of territorial differentiation—cultural, economic, or political—as well as the form of the political institution—unitary versus federal—may be more important than size in shaping the extent of subnational responses and the level of vertical interactions.

In unitary systems, for example, top-down actions would have greater power to disrupt local initiatives and regional agendas. Analysis of central-local relations in Britain—for example, between London and West Midlands and the Northeast—shows that initiatives of these regions depended on central support (or disruption) and coordination at the intra-regional level (Anderson 1992, ch. 4). As an illustration, between 1934 and 1965, a regional organization formed in northeast areas in 1934—the Regional Development Organization (RDO)—was able to propose crucial regional demands to Whitehall in a coordinated manner. But the government's Hailsham initiative in 1963 encouraged local authorities to submit infrastructure and other projects directly to a newly formed interdepartmental group. This top-down initiative rendered ineffective the RDO's powerful but voluntary organization of regional groups, officials, and business interests (Anderson 1992). Thus, while regional/subnational actors seek to modify and reregulate central policies in unitary states, such reregulation attempts are more tenuous than in federal systems.

This study argues that the developmental project in India was and continues to be constrained by the pattern of mediation between the center and the regions and the need to marshal political support for economic stabilization and development from its sprawling periphery. Paradoxically, a center-led capitalist development led to the expansion of regionalism in that it enhanced both the powers of the center and those of the regional states. The number of regions vertically interacting with the state increased as the state's productive, regulatory, and distributive roles were enhanced. At the same time, regional politics and subnationalist mobilization in the regions made the pursuit of diverse strategies toward the center more compelling. Interestingly, by leading and supporting a negotiated transition away from a dirigiste regime during the recent era of liberalization, the regional political elites have secured prominent positions in the post-dirigiste state and political system.

Large countries with internal regional units the size of nations, as in India, are appropriate contexts in which to ask questions about variable infranational relations and their consequences for growth patterns. Studies of India and of developmental states, while de facto focusing on "national" politics, never modify their claims. Regional differences and the politico-economic conflicts arising out of those divisions may crucially shape the nature and the output of the national political economy itself. Regional logics influence not only identity formation but economies-in-formation. Knowledge of activities of the constituent parts can say something to the understanding of the whole. Unraveling the riddle of the regional developmental states can enlighten us not only about the political economy of industrialization, but about the nature of the state in general. It is time to reorient the "nation-state" frame of reference of comparative studies toward a regional political economy of governance.

Appendix

A Game Theory Model of Economic Policy in a Centralized Federation

HERE, I DEVELOP a simple game model of economic policy in a parliamentary federalism. The model captures the evolving nature of strategic interaction between a dominant center and two regional states, when the central government needs the states to implement central policy and regional incumbents seek reelection. Despite the central government's ability to impose punishment on states, it emerges that regional states pursue different strategies toward the central government. This counterintuitive result arises from the fact that regional states may have divergent interests—preferences—from those of the central government. Their divergent preferences are themselves the product of regional political-economy and reelection pressures. This model allows me to explicate the strategic structure of the federal game in India and its consequences for the extent of conflict and collaboration in federal states.

The Structure of the Game

This chapter models the relationship between a central government and two regional states in a federal setting in the domain of economic policy. The key assumption is that the central government has the power to approve or reject the application for a license to set up a manufacturing plant in either one of the regional states. Private entrepreneurs apply to the central government for the license for a specific province (treated as exogenous to the game itself) and then the central government, CG, decides either to accept (Decision A) or to reject (Decision R) the application for State A. The rules of regulation are such that interaction by regional states—who want the project to be set up in each of their respective states—can change the decision. Thus, rules allow the central government to change its decisions. Given this, the regional states decide either to lobby (L) or to confront (C) the central government. The decision to lobby is a commonsensical one. The decision to confront alludes to the fact that rather than quietly persuading the central government to grant the license to its regional state (lobbying) the states make it a political issue, both in the national press and in the regional (the relevant state's region) political arena.[1]

The order of moves is as follows:

1. After the central government, CG, receives the application for the relevant regional State I, it decides to accept or reject the application for a license.
2. If it accepts, then the regional leader from State II chooses between lobbying, L, or confronting the CG's action, C.
3. If the CG chooses to reject the application, then both states (I and II) decide to lobby or confront, which here is modeled sequentially.[2]
4. First, State I decides to lobby (L) or confront (C).
5. Finally, State II decides to lobby or confront.

Since the regional leaders need to get elected, they derive utility from local political support, which is necessary for them to stay in office. Local political support is seen to depend upon two types of factors. First, an assumption is made that constituents support a leader who is able to put forward anti-center policies or positions. This assumption is external to this game but is plausible, as in most heterogeneous societies there is some political support that might accrue to regional leaders for their anti-center posture. In the Indian case, strong regionalist movements in Tamil Nadu, Punjab, Kashmir, the Northeast, and Assam have all relied upon anti-center mobilizational tactics and strategies.[3] Most importantly, the regional state derives some taxes from the project, once established. In case the project is not established, there is a net negative flow of taxes (includes the subsidy or grant that the central government will give to the regional state if it supports the central government). Hence, the utility of the leader of State I deciding to lobby or confront can be written in the form of two different equations:

$$U_s(C) = \mu - T(s) \qquad \text{(Equation 1)}$$

where μ is the regional leader's political support from his/her constituents when he/she confronts. I assume that for all i (regional states' leaders), $\mu > 0$. $T(s)$ is the tax that accrues to the state as a result of the license and is negative in this case. The plausible assumption is the that state leader does lose net tax (tax–subsidy) benefit. If she chooses L, she will get the taxes but lose the local political support from anti-center constituents. In this equation, k is the rate at which she loses political support from her constituents; it is assumed to be between 0 and 1. This gets at the idea that lobbying involves the loss of political support but at a slower rate. Thus, lobbying does not transform the variable of political support μ into "hate." The value of k will emerge out of the state politics and from the game between the state leader and its members. If k is 1, μ becomes negative.

Thus the utility of the regional state to lobby becomes:

$$U_s(L) = T(s) - k\mu \qquad \text{(Equation 2)}$$

The CG needs to balance three things. First, given the structure of parliamentary federal democracy, the CG needs the support of regional leaders to form its government at the center. Parliamentary majorities at the central level are constructed by adding the seats gained by a relevant party in all the regional states. This is the crucial feature of this model. The CG has to decide whether to accept or reject the application for license. If it accepts it will gain the political support from the relevant state; I characterize it as the CG's support function: $C(\alpha)$. The second element of the central government's utility function is the tax that accrues to the central government from the project $\{T(c)\}$.[4] The third element is the utility it gains from rejecting a license $U(r)$. The sources of this utility can be twofold: If the central state is a predatory state, then by rejecting the license the central government opens the possibility of receiving some bribe money from the regional states. Second, if the state is a developmental one, then the ability to reject licenses allows it to retain the authority to regulate the economy toward some national goal. This power enables it to give directive guidance to the economy to impose certain production targets on firms and regional states.[5] Thus, the CG derives some independent utility from the power of rejection. Thus,

$$U_{cg}(A) = T(c) + C(\alpha) \qquad \text{(Equation 3)}$$

The utility out of rejection is $U(R)$; no tax accrues to the center and hence $T(c)$ is 0 and the center loses the support of the regional states. In fact it might encourage the confrontation of the states and hence is negative $[-C(\alpha)]$. I assume this to be equivalent to μ, the political support factor, which states get if they oppose the center.

$$U_{cg}(R) = U(R) - C(\alpha) \qquad \text{(Equation 4)}$$

Analysis of the Equilibrium Solutions

In order to derive the equilibrium the following conditions must be true: For the states, from equations (1) and (2):

$$U_s(C) > U_s(L)$$

IF

$$k > [2T(s)/\mu]-1$$

That is, the states will confront if k is greater than twice the net tax divided by the regional political support factor, and then subtracted by 1.

For the center, from equations (3) and (4)

$$U_{cg}(R) < T(c) + 2C(\alpha) \qquad \text{(Equation 5)}$$

That is, the CG will always accept if (Equation 5) is true.

For the sake of comparing various situations and generating various hypotheses, let's analyze various situations assuming that the values of k and U(r) hold. The various possible equilibriums can be summarized as follows:

	$U_s(C) > U(L)$	$U_s(C) < U(L)$
$U_{cg}(R) > T(c) + C(\alpha)$	(R; C; C)	(R; L; L)
$U_{cg}(R) < T(c) + C(\alpha)$	(A; C)	(A; L)

When the regional political support factor is higher than the tax lost, the regional states will find it conducive to confront and the CG will reject the application. This seems to suggest that a strategy of confrontation by both states, given a utility of rejection to the center, leads to an increase in regional conflict. This situation can be characterized as one of "polarized conflict" in a federal setting. If the two states have different μ's (when for example, the party in power in one state is the same as the central party and the other state is ruled by an opposition party),[6] the situation becomes one of "fragmented" federal relations.

However, the interesting conclusion that emerges is that if μ is high enough, then even if both the regional states belong to the central ruling party, the regional leaders will follow a strategy of confrontation. This leads us to speculate about the conditions under which μ can be high or, alternatively, the institutional conditions that encourage various regional states to pre-commit to confront or to lobby. In provinces with a high premium over subnationalist mobilization—West Bengal and Tamil Nadu in the 1940s and 1950s—μ is likely to be very high. The institutionalization of a strategy in a credible way may be further facilitated by the formation of new institutions. Governmental agencies formed with the sole purpose of lobbying will predispose the state elites to lobby in the future. One example of lobbying agencies is the state embassies formed in New Delhi. Equally interestingly, the formation of regional conclaves (conference of opposition-ruled states) that are expected to raise the issue of center-state relations gives the strategy of confrontation much greater bite both to the regional states and to the central government in New Delhi. These, in effect, pre-commit the states to playing one of the options.

Conclusion

The analysis offered here helps in specifying the conditions under which regional incumbents rebel against the policies and decisions of the center. This model enables us to specify more carefully the conditions under which *collaboration or conflict* between the center and the states results. This analysis models the political incentives of actors in a democratic federal setting; federalism is approached as a political relationship rather than an administrative and functional division of power. The electoral incentives of both the regional government and the central government are modeled explicitly, and their interaction generates counterintuitive insights. Some states, those with a high μ—the propensity for subnationalist mobilization—will pursue anti-center political strategy even at the cost of development and investment flows (a high $T(x)$). This game also suggests that multiple strategies with widely divergent political consequences may emerge, even in a centralized state. Thus, despite the theoretical expectation that a highly regulated and centralized system will tend to encourage *convergence* in regional political strategies, regional *divergence* is the result.

Notes

1. The Puzzle of Developmental Failure and Success

1. Most scholars recognize that India's failures cannot be easily attributed to the predatory nature of its state; India is thus a developmental state that failed to realize its potential.

2. The word *state* has multiple usages in this book. The following conventions are followed: "state" with small "s" refers to the general concept of the state. Indian provinces are also called states, and are referred to as provinces or regional states. The federal government is usually referred to as the "central government." "Central state" or "Center" or "Union government" are used in the India-specific literature.

3. Herring 1999.

4. This term is attributed to the late Professor Raj Krishna, who used the term to refer to the unchanging aggregate growth rate of the Indian economy at 3.5 percent per annum from 1960 to 1985. Also see Lal 1988.

5. Harriss 1987.

6. See Anne Krueger's comparison of India and Korea; she notes, "If one takes 1955 as an initial date for some degree of normalcy after the Korean war, the contrast between India and Korea is stark. . . . The Government of India was announcing its development plan and had already set in place much of the basic policy framework that was to govern; its objectives were long-term and its strategy was set. . . . The Government of Korea, by contrast, was engaged in short-termism and economic policy, such as it was, was chaotic: the rate of inflation was the highest in the world; there were multiple exchange rates; gross domestic savings as a percent of the GDP were at most 5 percent in Korea contrasted with India's 11–12 percent . . . most observers were far more optimistic with respect to Indian developmental prospects than they were with respect to Korean. Development economists around the world avidly followed the Indian planning efforts. . . . Korea, by contrast, was regarded as so much of a 'basket case' that the US congress decided in 1956 to remove Korea's eligibility for development assistance" (Krueger 1998, 180–181). Also see Datta-Chaudhuri 1990 and Westphal 1990; both note the low expectations of Korea in the 1940s and 1950s.

7. Also see Wade 1985.

8. Bardhan quoted in Rodrik 1997, 434.

9. Krueger 1974.

10. *Economist*, "Survey of India," May 4, 1991; a later survey of 1995 also reported, "Economic reforms have helped, but India's [central] government is still frustrating its people's ambitions" (*Economist*, "Survey of India," Jan. 21, 1995).

11. Aziz Hanifa, "Bureaucracy Is a Major Threat to India's Economic Ambitions," *India Abroad*, Dec. 14, 2001, p. 38.

12. Sumit Ganguly and T. Srinivasan, "Open Up to Competition: India Can Go One Better than China," *Times of India*, Aug. 15, 2001, p. 12.

13. The *Economist* 2001 further warned that without further reform "the new Hindu rate of growth could subside to the old" (p. 4).

14. Das 2001 and Bhagwati 1993.

15. Bhagwati, one of the earliest critics of the policy framework in India, writes, "[T]he framework of her economic policies (as defined by the iron fist of controls over the private sector, the spreading stain of controls of inefficient public enterprises and an inward-looking trade and investment strategy) has produced, not merely the dismal economic performance, but also the added sense of senseless adherence to policies that have long been seen by others to have little rationale" (1993, 17–18). Also see Bhagwati and Desai 1970; Bhagwati 1998; Dreze and Sen 1997; Isher Ahluwalia 1985; Bardhan 1984.

16. Rudolph and Rudolph noted the paradoxical nature of the Indian state most starkly: "India is a political and economic paradox; a rich-poor nation with a weak-strong state . . . the paradox of a state that has, over the four decades since independence, alternated between autonomous and reflexive relations with the society in which it is embedded" (1987, 1).

17. It would be necessary to evaluate economic and geographical factors, demographic conditions, and the agriculture-led versus industry-led sources of growth in an analysis of growth rates.

18. Both neoclassical (Solow 1956) and structural models (Taylor 1983) emphasize investment capital as causing rapid economic growth. The more recent endogenous growth models emphasize human capital in addition to physical capital.

19. A detailed analysis of a few cases has distinct advantages over correlational analysis across all Indian states. Conventional literature has convincingly demonstrated regional divergence in India, but any analysis of the political processes and mechanisms through which these differences are reproduced through time is lacking. Such a process-oriented analysis can yield disproportionate results at the current level of knowledge. Second, a deeper analysis of few cases allows the gathering of data on comparable political and institutional variables related to investment policy. See Chapter 2 for case selection.

20. This success story has been accompanied by environmental degradation and economic inequalities; Gujarat's development represents a classic "liberal capitalism" model rather than a "social democratic" or "corporatist" model of capitalism (see Katzenstein 1985 for different types of capitalism). Despite the presence of these endemic problems, it is worthwhile to compare Gujarat's industrial policies with those of other regional states; no state in India combines equality with economic growth in full measure.

21. As early as 1962 and then again in 1968, Myron Weiner suggested that state-level variation in industrial development must be analyzed in a comparative frame (1962; 1968a). Yet, till this work, a comparative analysis of industrial policy of regional states had not been done. One exception is Rosen 1987, who analyzes the three southern states' (Tamil Nadu, Andhra Pradesh, and Karnataka) industrial policy in one chapter. Heller's (1999) discussion of Kerala as a "democratic developmental state" also resonates with my discussion of subnational developmental states.

22. Maddison's projections show that aggregate GDP in India (in 1990 international dollars) will be $3,776 billion in 2015. China's GDP will be $9,406 billion, United States', $9,338 billion, and Japan's, $3,337 billion (Maddison 1998, 97).

23. Chapter 3 elaborates this argument.

24. Arnold (1988, 524) makes a similar point about regulatory policy.

25. Each of these three mechanisms has been well elaborated on in the literature. For a selective sample, see Fernandez and Rodrik 1998; Krehbiel 1991; and North 1993.

26. Tsebelis 1990. Also, see the two-level framework in international relations theory

outlined in Evans, Jacobson, and Putnam 1993. This framework has not yet been deployed to understand intergovernmental relations in federal and/or large countries.

27. Subnational analysis in India has been widely used. Studies that use a subnational method are: antipoverty policies (West Bengal, Karnataka, and Uttar Pradesh), Kohli 1987; employment and poverty policies (West Bengal and Maharashtra), Echeverri-Gent 1993; party development, Kohli 1990; democratic protest (Gujarat and Orissa), Mitra 1992; class and caste relations, Frankel and Rao 1989; land reform, Herring 1983; the political economy of the sugar industry, Baru 1990; and labor relations in West Bengal, Karnataka, and Rajasthan, Chatterji 1980. Jenkins 2004 combines a comparative (of two states) with a thematic approach. Important single-state studies on industrial development patterns are Mallick 1993 on West Bengal, and Heller 1999 on Kerala. Also see Inoue's (1992) chapter on Karnataka's industrial development. This book, in addition, insists that a comparative subnational framework can yield important insights about not only subnational processes but also the nature of the developmental state in India.

28. The book focuses on industrial policy, but I differentiate between different types of policy instruments that affect industry in terms of whether they allow regional units autonomy from the center. Licensing policy is a policy instrument under the control of the central government; industrial estates are the policy domain of regional states. In federal systems such differentiation of functions allows for evaluation of both horizontal variation and vertical interactions. Further, in terms of case selection, the comparison of noncontiguous subnational units in this study allows for confidence in the independence of the subnational cases.

29. Examples of such organizations include Gujarat (or West Bengal) Industrial Development Corporation (GIDC); Gujarat Industrial Investment Corporation (GIIC); and Gujarat State Financial Corporation (GSFC).

30. Usually, I sent a questionnaire before a visit and used that to structure questions, but the personalized technique yielded far greater dividends.

31. Information on what is called "physical capital" (distinct from human capital) in economic theory gives us information on the total usable capital stock in an economy. Evidence on capital stock and capital formation is the best indicator of the rate of investment. However, statewide estimates of total (public and private, large-scale and small-scale) capital formation do not exist. The most comprehensive proxy is what is called "productive capital" for the factory sector (that is, those factories that employ 10 workers or more), which can serve as an important indicator for "physical capital." Productive capital, simply put, is the total and depreciated value of capital. It consists of all fixed assets—new, used, constructed or deployed, etc.—owned by the factory, as well as working capital (inventories, all materials, etc.) and all cash deposits in hand and in the bank.

2. A Theory of Polycentric Hierarchy

1. While the history of the concept of a developmental state may lie with the German economist Friedrich List, its recent reincarnation was implicit in the writings of the post–World War II development economists. The idea of a "Big Push," a classic statist idea, can originally be found in Rosenstein-Rodan 1943 and Young 1928. The concept owes its current usage to Chalmers Johnson who, in addition to socialist and free-market systems, posited a third category, the capitalist "developmental state." Johnson 1982 used this conceptual innovation to offer a revisionist account of Japan's rise to power. The concept has survived the public-choice onslaught because of its empirical robustness in understanding the East Asian cases (Amsden 1989 for South Korea; Johnson 1982 for Japan; Wade 1990 for

Taiwan; and Woo-Cumings 1999). The World Bank for the first time in 1993 (World Bank 1993) recognized that the state did play a role in sustaining high growth; subsequently its 1997 World Development report was devoted to analyzing the role of *The State in the Changing World* (World Bank 1997).

2. A comparative chapter (Chapter 8) combines subnational analysis with cross-national analysis in analyzing Brazil, China, the former Soviet Union, and Russia.

3. There is some research on the effects of small size but relatively little work on the consequences of large size for political economy. For analysis of small size and political economy, see Katzenstein 1985. Dahl and Tufte explicitly consider how size affects political outcomes (1973). For an economic approach to size, see Robinson 1960, Perkins and Syrquin 1989, and Jalan 1981. On India, see Lewis 1995 and Feinberg, Echeverri-Gent, and Muller 1990.

4. This framework, I contend, is relevant for understanding the politics of development in any large state irrespective of the federal form, and also important for small states with some regional differentiation. See Richard J. Samuels 1983 for attention to regional variables in Japan. Thus, this analysis becomes important for supposedly centralized countries such as the former Soviet Union, China, Indonesia, and even Japan. It is equally relevant for large democratic countries: Canada, Brazil, Mexico, and Russia.

5. Krueger (1974) and Lal (1988, 1994), among others, argue that the Indian government's restrictions on the private sector resulted in an abundance of rent-seeking activities centered on the appropriation of monopoly rents arising from trading in governmental licenses and other scarce public interventions. See Buchanan, Tollison, and Tullock 1980; Bhagwati 1982; Srinivasan 1985; Findlay 1990; and Toye 1987 for a review of debates on rent-seeking.

6. Bardhan's arguments unite insights from Olson 1982 and Krueger 1974 with those from the neo-Marxist class-analytic tradition to argue that the problem with India's industrial growth has been the decline of public investment, which is the result of constraints imposed on the state by dominant proprietary classes. See Ronald Herring 1986, which makes this point. Analogously, Alavi 1982 presents his notion of the *overdeveloped state*. According to Alavi, the peculiar class structure of third-world societies allowed a state apparatus with roots in the colonial period to play a considerably more dominant role than in the "classical transitions of Europe." The balance of power among the three dominant propertied classes—the metropolitan bourgeoisie, the indigenous bourgeoisie, and the landed classes—permitted the civilian and military bureaucracies to perform a relatively independent mediating role. Also see a very good review article that characterizes Bardhan's arguments in a similar way: Sridharan 1993. He characterizes Bardhan's approach as a "fusion of a modified Marxism with neoclassical political economy" (1993, 28).

7. Bardhan does acknowledge that India's size and the existence of high-growth regions within India should be considered in cross-national comparisons (1984, 7–8) but he goes on to conduct his analysis at the national level.

8. For a recent attempt to pose this paradox see Nayar 1996. Herring 1999 also notes that contradictory conceptions of the Indian state coexist in the literature. Other more nuanced interpretations of India's political economy can be found in Kapur 1994; Sridharan 1996; Nayar 1989, 1990, 1996, 2001, 2003; and Pingle 1999. Yet, all books adopt a national-level framework.

9. For example, in the early years the Indian state exhibited state autonomy, similar to South Korea: firms were disciplined to produce export targets. The Indian government in the late 1950s and early 1960s insisted that part of the profits of firms be used for enhancing exports. Even more similarly, some firms were told that "to begin with, their import quotas will be cut, but the cuts will be restored if they achieve a specified target for exports" (Place, Siddons, and Gough 1962, xliii–xliv).

10. See Stiglitz 1989, Musgrave 1997, and Lin and Nugent 1995 for important works in this approach.

11. The neo-institutionalist approach to the state differs from each of these three approaches on this issue; I deploy some of its insights in undertaking a comparative analysis later in the chapter.

12. See Niskanen 1971, Levi 1988, Krueger 1974, and Colander 1984 for public-choice critiques. Herring's conceptualization of the Indian state as a form of "embedded particularism" (1999) and Bardhan's analysis (1984) resonate with these larger general debates.

13. Scholars who have analyzed the role of subnational states as local developmental states for other countries are: Herrigel 1996 for Germany; Locke 1995 for Italy; Snyder 2000 for Mexico; Tendler 1997 and Montero 2002 for Brazil; Oi 1999, Tsai 2002, Shue 1988, Robinson and White 1998, Ming Hsia and Ming Xia 2000, and Remick 2002 for China; Montero 2002 for Spain; and Stoner-Weiss 1997 for Russia.

14. A few exceptions are Tarrow 1977; Tarrow, Katzenstein, and Graziano 1978; Hollingsworth and Boyer 1997; Anderson 1992; and Richard J. Samuels 1983.

15. The classic treatment by Tiebout 1956 deals with the problem of attaining social welfare gains in a spatial context where citizen mobility is possible. The literature on fiscal federalism is vast. See McKinnon and Nechyba 1997 for a good thematic summary.

16. This is also known as "voting with one's feet," to capture the idea that populations sort themselves out into local jurisdictions according to their tastes in local public goods and their abilities to pay.

17. Market-preserving federalism encompasses five sets of conditions: (1) There is a hierarchy of governments where a delimited scope of authority exists. (2) The subnational governments have primary authority over the economy within their jurisdictions. (3) National government has the authority to police the common market. (4) All governments face a hard budget constraint. (5) The allocation of authority has an institutionalized degree of durability (Montinola, Qian, and Weingast 1995, 55). Also see Weingast 1995.

18. William Riker (1964; 1975) was one of the first theorists to point out that the economic theory of federalism is one of administrative decentralization, and fails to account for the political incentives of governmental actors at the two levels.

19. This game-theoretic model can be found in the Appendix.

20. The territorial spread of incentives refers to the fact that politicians located at different levels of the system have different political incentives linked to the boundaries within which they have to get elected. A similar phenomenon can be found in other multilevel countries. In Brazil, deputies (members of the national legislature) do not aim to build careers within the chamber of deputies, but seek to further their careers at the state or municipal (subnational) levels (David Samuels 2003).

21. I use the term *polyarchy* in this book to mean a combination of "hierarchy" and "polycentric in the domain of political economy." I use it to argue that the dichotomy between markets or price-based systems and hierarchy (the state) may be inadequate. Thus, a polyarchy is a distinctive hierarchy, one where the lower levels of the system have overlapping authority with the higher levels of decision making. The most widespread use of the term is by Robert Dahl (1971), who created the term to refer to a democracy. Sah and Stiglitz (1986; 1988) use the term *polyarchy* to refer to a decentralized organization. They contrast polyarchies with hierarchies. Milner's (1997) use of the term *polyarchy* to understand the domestic politics of states in international relations is more compatible with the approach adopted here. I, in contrast to Milner, infuse the term with the territorial structure of domestic politics to refer to relations between the central state and its subnational units. The idea of the state as a polyarchy is also similar to the notion of polycentric government initially outlined by Ostrom, Tiebout, and Warren (1961) and developed in three volumes edited by McGinnis (1999; 2000; 2001).

22. Tsebelis's work on nested games (1990; 1999) focuses exclusively on political games where the interlinked logic of parliamentary versus electoral arenas is explored. He, however, suggests that "the interaction between economics and politics can also be conceptualized as several different games played by the same actors" (1999, 5). Treisman (2001) employs a two-level framework to understand political stability in Russia that incorporates political-economy considerations.

23. Treisman (2001) is one exception. He employs a game theory model to understand democratic stability in Russia.

24. I elaborate this argument in Chapter 8 of this book with evidence from Brazil, China, the FSU, and Russia.

25. Given the central bureaucratic institutions' autonomy from the political masters, I visualize it as a game between regional elites and central rules of the game. I do analyze how the central rules of the game are politically sustained by central political elites in Chapter 3. The second game is played between the regional elites and their constituents, mediated by regional party competition.

26. These propositions emerge from the game theory analysis that models a dominant center and two provinces. See Appendix for an elaboration.

27. Weimer 1995 and Goodin 1996.

28. For a sampling, see Barro 1991 and Edwards and Tabellini 1991. These two articles focus on the relationship between political stability and economic growth. More recently, there have been increasing attempts to focus on the impact of institutional frameworks on economic developments beyond mere political stability. For such studies, see Scully 1988; Doeringer and Streeten 1990; Knack and Keefer 1995; also see Clague et al. 1995; Lin and Nugent 1995. On India, see Olson 1995 and Bardhan 1995a.

29. The notion of credible commitment has developed in the context of monetary policy. It is argued that two main solutions exist for the time inconsistency problem. One is the reputation equilibrium in which the future reputation of the agent acts as a constraining element. The other solution is "rules" or institutions. See the literature on rules vs. discretion, Barro and Gordon 1983 and Kydland and Prescott 1977.

30. Susanne Lohmann, "Optimal Commitment in Monetary Policy: Credibility versus Flexibility" (1992), points out that credibility might imply a trade-off with flexibility. The policy consistency, a sine qua non for credible commitments, might have negative implications for the state's ability to change its policies, a characteristic of flexibility.

31. Shepsle 1996, 230.

32. In Chapter 3 I show how the licensing system worked in India.

33. In economics, informational issues come into play when one party has an incentive to spread misinformation, as in the market for used cars (Akerlof 1970) or in labor contracts (Spence 1976). In political science, the role of information has been studied. See Calvert 1985 and 1986 and Krehbiel 1991. I am concerned in this book with how informational asymmetry of rulers located at different levels affects economic policy making and implementation.

34. The problematic of information in a state-dominated context is seen to rise from incentives of self-interested bureaucrats who desire to regulate ensuing rents from information control.

35. In centralized systems where regional officials can place blame with a higher-level state agent, the provincial state agent may have as much incentive to spread misinformation to his/her constituents whether they are investors or voters. Yet, I argue, this incentive depends upon the nature of the regional political economy and regional politics. In Chapter 6 I show that incentives for the dissemination of misinformation become greater if subnationalist public opinion in the region rewards anti-center behavior.

36. In China, in contrast, local governments would be the appropriate political unit for comparison.

37. It is plausible to define "initial" as around 1947, when independence from British colonialism was achieved.

38. Bagchi 1972; Bharadwaj 1982.

39. Bagchi 1972; Chattopadhya and Raza 1975; Sharma 1946.

40. The positive relationship of urbanization to economic growth has been a consistent theme in the economic-growth literature. The term *agglomeration economies* is used to describe the risk-spreading opportunities of denser markets and informational benefits that accrue to a firm located in close proximity to a large number of its customers, suppliers, and competitors (Shukla 1996). Thus, certain types of activities, principally manufacturing, are more productively undertaken in an urban environment as a result of considerations of absolute size and concentration.

41. The counterfactual expectation is well expressed by Markovits's analysis of the advantages of Calcutta as the dominant city in the country in the colonial period: "In the ongoing contest for supremacy between the two metropolitan cities of India, Calcutta's advantages were many. It was the seat of the colonial government till 1911, a not unimportant consideration since, . . . the government of India played a big role in allocating resources between regions especially through the way it gave concessions to railway companies, and was particularly susceptible to pressures from Calcutta's business community. Calcutta had the largest concentration of European population and European capital in India . . . and it drained Indian entrepreneurial talent and capital from as far afield as Marwar. It had easy communications with a vast hinterland extending from eastern United province to Assam, which produced most of the two major export crops grown in India, tea and jute . . . ; and it had access to an abundant supply of labor attracted from this hinterland and even from as far as Madras Presidency. It was close to the major energy source used in the 'modern' sector of the Indian economy, coal, which Bombay had to import from far afield. On the other hand Bombay's area of labor recruitment was largely limited to Maharashtra and its indigenous entrepreneurial class came exclusively from Gujarat" (1996, 31).

42. The population of the three states in 2001 [latest census] was: 50.5 million in Gujarat, 80.2 million in West Bengal, and 62.1 million in Tamil Nadu.

43. Banerjee and Ghosh 1988.

44. Also see Tomlinson (1981), who reaches a similar conclusion.

45. Goswami challenges the widely prevalent view that European managing agencies dominated East India until 1947 due to proximity with British colonialism, while indigenous owners were curtailed and constrained. In contrast, he shows that while that scenario might have held true for the pre–World War I period, from the 1920s onward Indian entrepreneurs entered into and dominated many diverse sectors in West Bengal. He notes, "[T]he period 1935–40 represents a sort of structural break in the growth of Marwari entrepreneurship [in West Bengal]: while they carried on unabated in the more traditional sectors of modern industry, they had conspicuously entered the relatively technologically advanced sectors as well" (1985, 243).

3. Disaggregating the Central State

1. The specific Mahalanobis model adopted, a "supply-side model," formed the basis of the Nehruvian developmental strategy (Sukhamoy Chakravarty 1987). While the strategy was primarily formulated by P. C. Mahalanobis and Nehru, it is important to note that in the 1950s and 1960s the Planning Commission organized extensive consultations with foreign

development economists such as P. Rosentein-Rodan, Arnold Harberger, Richard Eckaus, Alan Manne, James Mirrlees, Ian Little, Brian Reddaway, Oskar Lange, Ragner Frisch, Richard Goodwin, and Jan Tinbergen (Mohan 1992, 92).

2. Rosenstein-Rodan 1943.

3. The Mahalanobis model maintained, "If industrialization has to be rapid enough, the country must aim at developing basic industries and industries which make machines to make the machines needed for further development" (Government of India, Second Five-Year Plan 1956). Basic industries were defined as industries such as iron and steel, nonferrous metals, machine building, coal, and heavy chemicals.

4. Institutionally, the central state acquired immense power to carry out its policies. In 1950, the Planning Commission was instituted. This agency's legal status was advisory, but it became "an executive body of enormous power, an alter ego of the cabinet, showing a persistent and increasing concern with administrative matters outside its province, and supporting its pretensions by equipping itself with an excessively large bureaucratic apparatus" (A. H. Hanson 1968, 45–46).

5. In contrast, Canada and Botswana, for example, used specific licensing instruments. Botswana after 1984 formulated an industrial development policy that used licensing instruments. In this case, financial assistance is subject to the enterprise obtaining a manufacturing license, which is given by the Ministry of Commerce and Industry after consideration of "profitable market opportunities" (Kapilinsky 1993, 154). Another country that has used licensing is Canada, which created a national licensing system in 1919 to regulate the airline industry. The licensing system was strengthened in 1937–38 with the creation of a federal crown corporation, Trans-Canada Airline (TCA), as a chosen instrument for the attainment of national air policy (Schultz and Alexandroff 1985, 37–40).

6. *Productive capital* refers to total fixed capital (land, buildings, plant and machinery, and other fixed assets) plus working capital (raw materials, stocks of finished and semi-finished products, and cash in hand) and may be taken to mean total capital in the large-scale sector.

7. West Bengal's total productive capital in 1960 at current prices was Rs. 4 billion, while that of Gujarat was Rs. 1 billion (computed from Annual Survey of India Old Series, 1965). In 1965, West Bengal ranked first, with Rs. 12 billion of productive capital.

8. Computed from Government of India 1956, xv–xx.

9. The central Industry Ministry granted Letters of Intent after an investor submitted an investment application to that ministry.

10. There have been few systematic studies of the regional pattern of licenses. One study that analyzes the licensing pattern but limits the analysis until 1967 is Banerjee and Ghosh 1988. Another is Biswas and Margit 2002. We do not have complete time-series data from 1952 (when the licensing rules came into effect) onward. The data from 1956 to 1966 and then from 1970 to 1994 are available.

11. The data are drawn from the Annual Survey of India (ASI), *Summary Results for the Factory Sector,* Central Statistical Organization (CSO), Government of India, various years. The scope of the ASI covers the registered factory sector in India, which is defined as those factories that use power and employ ten or more workers on any day, and those that do not use power and employ twenty or more workers on any day and that are required to be registered under sections 2 m (i) and 2 m (ii), respectively, of the "Indian Factories Act," 1948. The primary unit of data collection is the factory. The office responsible for data collection is the Chief Inspectors of Factories. The factory sector is commonly known as the "organized manufacturing sector" and covers all manufacturing and processing establishments classified as factories and registered under the Indian Factories Act, 1948.

12. It must be noted that for a complete analysis, data on the number of applications is

needed. Yet, these data on the number of licenses granted to different regional states tell us a significant story about regional divergence.

13. Sukhamoy Chakravarty 1994, 143. It is difficult to find a scholarly analysis of this argument, but this view is widespread among scholars and in journalistic writings.

14. A retired industry secretary of Gujarat admitted in an interview that state government officials used the argument of central discrimination for strategic purposes in order to exert pressure on the central government. Interview, Aug. 1997, Madras. Also see Gujarat Chamber of Commerce and Industry 1988.

15. The centrally directed regulatory regime led to a "federal moral hazard problem" as every state had private information about its ability to manage its industrial program, which it wanted to hide. Given the overall power of direction in central hands, the state could easily argue that industrial management power was *totally* in central hands. This problem was complicated in a democratic setting as the central discrimination argument was made by politicians with an eye toward state assembly elections.

16. *Times of India* (Ahmedabad edition), June 4, 2001, p. 3.

17. The total central public-sector investment in West Bengal between 1955 and 1966 was of the order of 143.25 crores; Bombay, 9.50 crores; Madras, 72.0 crores; and Bihar, 8.40 crores (Commerce, Various Years). Between 1955 and 1960, West Bengal received a number of projects, totaling the highest amount of central investment in comparison to other states.

18. Some of West Bengal's share comes from the industries that were nationalized in West Bengal. West Bengal has a larger than normal share of such industries, and hence it is true that there is some overestimation in the share of West Bengal, but it does not bias the overall trend.

19. Article 356 of the Indian Constitution allows the suspension of the elected state government and the imposition of central authority in the relevant state. This provision must be approved by the parliament within the year and can be renewed a limited number of times, but given a majority in the parliament, President's Rule can be passed without too much trouble.

20. The seventh schedule (Article 246) of the Constitution consists of three lists outlining the subjects for which each of the levels of government has the principal responsibility. They are: the Union List (List I), which includes such topics as national security, foreign affairs, interstate trade, commerce, and banking; the State List (List II), which has 66 entries, such as public order, police, communications, and industries subject to the provision of entries 7 and 52 of List I; and the Concurrent List, which includes shared subjects.

21. The central ministry dealing with industry has undergone many changes of its name. It was earlier called the Ministry of Industrial Development and Company Affairs, later Ministry of Industry, and currently Ministry of Commerce and Industry.

22. In order to deal with the licensing and MRTP aspects in a coordinated manner a Licensing cum MRTP Committee was formed on November 1, 1973 (Government of India 1974).

23. Ministry of Industry, Annual Report, Various Years.

24. One government official said, "At that time, there was a lot of hostility against business people; there was a feeling that profit motive was illegitimate." Interview, Nov. 1998.

25. Interview with a high Ministry of Industry official, Nov. 1998.

26. Interview with a former central government member of the Full Licensing Committee, New Delhi, Nov. 1999. I confirmed this information by interviewing a number of Ministry of Industry officials and regional government officers.

27. Interview, Ahmedabad, May 1997.

28. Eighty-two percent of large-scale businesspeople interviewed confirmed this fact.

29. See Chapter 4, where I present evidence on the strategic choices of regional states within the licensing system.

30. Biswas and Margit's (2002) analysis of licenses (based on Rongli Biswas's thesis) also attempts to evaluate the role of states in the allocation of licenses. In their study Biswas and Margit find that "lobbying power matters" in the licenses granted to regional states. They conceptualize this "lobbying power" in terms of the representation of regional states in the cabinet and regress that against the allocation of licenses (2002, 719). This study is sophisticated and makes a significant advance in measuring the political variables that affected the licensing process. However, it lacks a theoretical explanation for the exact mechanisms that underlay the license-*raj*. The cabinet was not the body deciding the location of licenses; thus, while Biswas and Margit's econometric analysis is on the right track, they are unable to conceptualize the micro-institutions of the central regulatory framework. This lacuna leads them to omit a crucial variable in their analysis: the role of the regional states in infiltrating the licensing system from within. Thus, in my argument, it's important to combine a micro-foundational analysis of the licensing system with an analysis of the regional pattern of licenses.

31. Reframed in another way, if it is the Indian state that contributed to the slow growth equilibrium in India, how did the regulatory state emerge? To my knowledge, the only other Indian scholar who has addressed a similar question is P. N. Dhar. In a review of Bardhan's argument he asked, "How and why did the low-level slow growth equilibrium came about?" (Dhar 1987, 3).

32. The Congress in 1920 was linguistically structured with twenty-one Provincial Congress Committees (PCCs). The PCCs coincided with linguistic boundaries and not administrative (British) divisions. The linguistic principle meant that linguistic areas such as Gujarat, which were not provinces, also had their Provincial Congress Committees. See David Hardiman for an analysis vis-à-vis the Gujarat PCC: "Before 1921 the nationalist movement in Gujarat lacked formal unity, being merely an alliance of the Gujarat Sabha, the Home Rule League and various other small political associations. In December 1920, Gandhi reorganized the Indian National Congress into what he hoped would be *a form of parallel government*, with a hierarchy of provincial, district, taluqa and village Congress committees in imitation of the administrative structure of the British" (1981, 114; emphasis added). As a consequence, a new Gujarat Provincial Congress Committee (GPCC) was formed. It's not an accident that the Congress became a mass organization at the same time that it was reorganized into linguistic units. For studies of the Congress Party, see Kochanek 1968 and Weiner 1967.

33. Nehru 1964, 4:14.

34. Rosen's analysis (1966) confirms a strong two-way interaction in the realm of the location of industrial projects.

35. Interview with retired IAS official who said "All these policy changes happened in the 1960s and 1970s on account of political pressures from the state rather than a policy initiative of the central ministries." Interview, Dec. 1997.

36. See the compilation of Nehru's fortnightly letters to the chief ministers (Nehru 1987, 5 vols.).

37. While the scholarly literature has focused on the right-versus-left debates, it is important to note that the struggle over economic policy was as much between centralizing and decentralization tendencies within the Congress Party. See Frankel 1978 about the Left-vs.-Right debates in the Nehruvian period.

38. I thank Richard Bensel for a discussion on this point.

39. I draw from Rudolph and Rudolph 1987; Frankel 1978; Hart 1976; Manor 1994; Choudhury and Mansur 1994; Kaviraj 1986; and Brass 1982, 1994.

40. Vote-banks are social groups that may vote as a bloc for one political party.

41. In 1967 she lost many state assembly elections, and many Congress PCCs came to challenge her autonomy between 1966 and 1971.

42. According to Article 356 of the Indian Constitution, the central government can suspend a regional state's assembly and establish direct "President's Rule."

43. Lele 1994.

44. Gujarat symbolized this political realignment most starkly, with the evolution of the KHAM strategy (Wood 1984b) by the Congress (I) party.

45. This is in contrast to the dominant interpretation of Congress as a catch-all umbrella party that accommodated all strata and all classes. Chhibber and Petrocik's evidence (1990) confirms my argument.

46. In a parliamentary system, the party allots tickets to candidates, and only those candidates that have been allotted these tickets can run for elections on the party platform. In each electoral constituency only one candidate can stand per party, but many candidates "hope" for a party ticket. The allocation of party tickets is extremely crucial in parliamentary systems, ensuring the control of the party over individual candidates and thereby enabling majorities in the parliament (Lok Sabha).

47. See Editorial, "Keeping the Party in Tow," *Times of India* (Ahmedabad edition), Jan. 10, 1981, p. 10.

48. "Centre for Higher Price for Farm Produce: Antulay," *Times of India* (Ahmedabad edition), Jan. 8, 1981, p. 1.

49. Also see Editorial, "Welcome Signs," *Times of India* (Ahmedabad edition), Jan. 1, 1981, p. 10.

50. These industries related to "security, strategic, social purposes, hazardous chemicals, overriding environmental reasons and items of elitist consumption" (Government of India 1991, Appendix).

51. Some of the industries are alcohol, sugar, tobacco, industrial explosives, hazardous chemicals (Government of India, 2001, 27). Consumer electronics has been de-licensed. In 1998 coal and petroleum were de-licensed (Government of India, Handbook of Industrial Policy, 2001).

52. These include World Bank loans, subnational structural adjustment programs, and Asian Development Bank loans.

53. This term is used by Echeverri-Gent 2002.

54. Mamata Bannerjee and Mursuli Maran have been especially active.

55. *India Abroad*, Dec. 1999.

56. Interview, Tamil Nadu government official, Chennai, Aug. 1997.

57. An AP government official admitted that intervention at the "highest level" was made to ensure the loan. This intervention was through the central government but also directly through the World Bank. Interview, July 30, 2001. Also see http://www.worldbank.org.in for details on the structural adjustment loan to Andhra Pradesh.

58. The United States offers an example of a system where the reverse is true: that is, the legislature (Senate) acts as an arena for the expression of regional interests, and hence intergovernmental politics is less important (Simeon 1972, 8).

4. Regional Strategies toward the Dirigiste State

1. The third strategy translates as political opportunism. Opportunism refers to the motto: Disobey whenever it suits your interest and comply whenever you gain from complying.

2. These three strategies—bureaucratic liberalism, partisan confrontation, and popu-

list protection—are also followed by other subnational states within India. Maharashtra follows the bargaining strategy, while Kerala follows the partisan strategy. In addition, most provincial states follow what I call "passive dependence" strategy, one that depends upon the center for transfers and licenses but does not actively engage with the opportunities or constraints provided by its rules of the game. States that follow this passive dependent strategy are Bihar, Uttar Pradesh, Madhya Pradesh, Rajasthan, and Andhra Pradesh.

3. Government of Gujarat 1970.

4. Interview with N. Vittal, Dec. 1997. Vittal was a Gujarat cadre IAS official who occupied crucial posts in the Ministry of Industry and the Joint sector in Gujarat in the 1970s.

5. A senior Gujarat government official used this term in an interview. Interview, Madras, Sept. 1997.

6. Interviews with retired IAS officials suggest that Tamil Nadu did not practice infiltration. Interviews suggest that this strategy started in the late 1960s in Gujarat and picked up momentum in the 1970s. Gujarat institutionalized it in the 1970s, while West Bengal stopped following it or did so inconsistently after the 1960s.

7. Each state has offices, or "embassies," located in New Delhi for the purpose of creating liaisons with the central government; this intermediation was necessitated by a strong centralized government. Gujarat in 1968 established a Gujarat Industrial Investment Corporation (GIIC) office in New Delhi, apart from the Gujarat Bhavan.

8. Gujarat had to engage in "industrial espionage" to obtain information about licenses to other states and those unallocated licenses that had not been granted location.

9. This information proved to be extremely valuable as preemption of licensed capacities was a common practice used by investors to prevent their competitors from getting a market share.

10. See Chapter 7.

11. Interview with Government of Gujarat (GoG) official, New Delhi, Feb. 1997. I corroborated this by interviewing businesspeople, who admitted that at times they had not decided, or even thought too much about, where to invest. The Gujarat government had contacted them, and had given them information regarding possible locations within Gujarat. Hence they had decided to invest in Gujarat.

12. In New Delhi governmental circles, social dinners, parties, and cocktail meetings provided the loosening lubricant that allowed officials to glean these useful pieces of information. Interviews revealed that Gujarat gathered these data about the list of applications in systematic ways.

13. Interview, April 1997. No such monitoring devices were present in West Bengal or in Tamil Nadu.

14. GoG officials remained in constant touch with the central departments to obtain regular information about central priorities and other states' activities.

15. Interview, high-level government official of Gujarat, Sept. 1997. These facts were confirmed by other interviews of GoG officials. Also, my interviews with some erstwhile members of the licensing committee at the central level confirmed that Gujarat's representatives were generally well prepared in the Licensing Committee meetings.

16. Interview, retired Industry secretary, Government of Gujarat, Chennai, Sept. 1997.

17. Interview, GIIC official, New Delhi, Dec. 1997. The GIIC official mentioned three projects: a tire project, a carbon black project, and a transceiver project, which were procured by GIIC for various private partners.

18. The short form for "Industrial Extension Bureau," the first and last letters are usually written in lowercase to denote that the ego of this agency was low (i) and it was not bureaucratic (b).

19. Maharashtra too established a similar agency in 1978: Udyog Mitra. Other states followed this strategy but, in most cases, much later. Gujarat and Maharashtra seem to be pioneers in establishing this agency. Analogous agencies in other states are Tamil Nadu: Guidance Bureau, established in 1992; West Bengal: Shilpa Bandhu, restructured in 1994.

20. I discuss these corporations and their institutional differences in Chapter 5.

21. I did systematic research in Gujarat, Tamil Nadu, and West Bengal and also have some reliable evidence about Maharashtra, Bihar, and Kerala.

22. Since 1991, with the scope of licensing reduced, a more general strategy of attraction of investors has been practiced by almost all states.

23. Interview, Shikha Mukherjee, Calcutta, Summer 1996 and Sept. 1997.

24. Interview, GIIC official in New Delhi, Dec. 1997.

25. I spent many days observing the functioning of all three regional "embassies" in New Delhi.

26. The committee comprised extremely high-level ministers and politicians of the Left Front government: Dr. Ashok Mitra (chairman), Shri Somnath Chatterjee (member of parliament), and Shri R. N. Sengupta (home secretary, GoWB). In 1997, when I did my research, some of the recommendations of the Reforms Committee were being instituted, but nothing had been done from 1983 to 1994.

27. In 1969 the erstwhile Congress Party split into two groups: Congress (O) and Congress (I). Congress (I) was associated with Mrs. Indira Gandhi and took on the mantle of the Congree Party successfully.

28. Chakravarty 1974, 140.

29. Ibid., 145.

30. Her government tried to establish a link between the 1967–69 United Front experience in West Bengal and the Left Front rule (1977 onward) in an effort to discredit the Left Front by association. However, scholarship across partisan lines confirms that since 1977, CPI(M) has been a reformist party, and the Left Front has turned its back on many of the radical promises of the United Front stage.

31. Its remarkable success in the pursuance of a partisan confrontation strategy contributed in no small measure to the consistent victories of the Left Front in all legislative assembly elections.

32. Jyoti Basu 1981, 1982. The purpose of the letters and their publication is outlined in the foreword: "It may not be out of place to reiterate that the need for overhauling the Centre-State relations as they obtain now, is of paramount importance to strengthen democratic-federal structure of the country. . . . Following the installation of the new central government in Delhi . . . we have taken up with the central government some of our pressing problems and have placed our legitimate demands in this regard. This book is an attempt to acquaint the people with some of the issues covered in the correspondence mostly with the Prime Minister" (1981, foreword).

33. The Assam agitation led to a refugee flow into West Bengal.

34. Jyoti Basu 1981, 45–46, Letter of July 16, 1980.

35. Ibid., 64, Letter of March 12, 1980.

36. Basu, the CM, is forthright about the need to shape public opinion on the subject of center-state relations. His foreword to *CM's Letters to the Central Government* (1982) says, "The letters throw more light on the present state of Centre-State relations and bring to focus our persistent efforts to impress upon the Center the need for taking effective measures in certain spheres of public welfare where the State government has little or no administrative power to act on its own. . . . These letters, I believe, will further help the people to understand our attitudes and approaches to the various issues. Such an understanding is necessary in the interest of sound public opinion."

37. Government of West Bengal 1982.

38. One such conference organized by the CPI(M) took place on Jan. 13–15, 1984, in Calcutta. See the address by Jyoti Basu to this conference (Basu 1984).

39. The term "populist protection" is used by Swamy (1996). Subramanian (1999) also uses similar concepts.

40. From 1955 to 1968, 12 central public-sector units were set up in Tamil Nadu. These included: the Integral Coach Factory (Perambur, Madras), 1955; Neyveli Lignite Corporation, 1956; Hindustan Teleprinters Ltd. (Madras), 1960; Hindustan Photo Films, 1960; Bharat Heavy Electricals (Tiruchirapalli), 1960. After 1968, a public-sector unit was not established until 1977.

41. Industry minister in Tamil Nadu in the 1950s and 1960s; later planning commission member and the president of India.

42. Interview, Madras, Aug. 1997.

43. Government of Tamil Nadu (1971).

44. Special Correspondent, *Hindu*, June 2, 1967, p. 16, col. 3.

45. It is interesting that the use of the term "Marwari" in Tamil Nadu does not refer to an ethnicity but to any "northern commercial and business interest." In the context of Tamil Nadu's economic culture, it is an umbrella term for all traders and industrialists from the north, including Gujarat and Bombay.

46. Interviews with investors across three states.

47. The change of name to All-India Anna DMK reflected this move toward integration.

48. In the assembly elections of 1982, 1984, and 1987 there was an electoral alliance between the Congress and the AIADMK.

49. "Special Feature on Tamil Nadu," *Hindu*, June 21, 1984, p. 29.

50. Interview, Madras, Sept. 1997.

51. I present these strategies as three successful models; other states within India also pursued some of these strategies. For example, Kerala pursued a confrontational strategy, while Maharashtra pursued a bureaucratic liberalism strategy. The question arises whether these strategies exhaust the actions of all states within India. They do not. One other strategy can be found: passive dependence. Bihar and Madhya Pradesh have pursued a passive strategy toward the center. In this book I do not analyze in depth this other strategy; its existence confirms my argument that the combined structure of central rules and politics at the state level engendered a plethora of divergent strategies within India's political economy.

52. In Hirschmanian language, "Bureaucratic Liberalism" represents a form of "economic voice," although the Hirschman framework of Exit, Voice, and Loyalty does not precisely incorporate this hybrid category.

53. A modified Hirschmanian framework might characterize this as "political voice."

54. Interview, Madras, Aug. 1997.

55. During the license-*raj*, Gujarat bureaucracy was distinctive in targeting the central licensing administration, licensed (domestic) private-sector investors, and Gujarati capital from West Bengal, Maharashtra, East Africa, and United Kingdom. In the 1980s and especially after 1991, it the bureaucracy became much more indiscriminate, targeting non-Gujarati as well as Gujarati investors from all over India as well as from Europe, Africa, and United States. However, the skills and institutions employed before 1991 proved to be extremely transportable to the post-1991 context; no other state had this advantage, allowing Gujarat to take an "institutional" head start.

56. A state agency complaining about the delay at the central level in a confidential memo to the Ministry of Industrial Development, GoI. Internal Memo, *IEM [Industrial Entrepreneur Memorandum] Progress Report*, Jan. 13, 1995, Personal Collection.

57. Jyoti Basu (the chief minister of West Bengal from 1977 to 2000) initiated policy

reform at the subnational level in the mid-1980s. Around 1985, Basu announced that the industrial orientation of the state must change and its working culture be modified. At that time, many projects with the private sector were initiated (*India Today,* July 15, 1985). Attempts to involve a private-sector partner in the Haldia petrochemical project were first started in 1985. In 1990, at a time when the national government of V. P. Singh was moving against big business (1989–90), Basu defended big business houses such as Reliance. His office compared his policy initiatives to promote joint ventures with private capital with Gorbachev's perestroika reforms (*Indian Express,* July 8, 1990). At that time this reform effort went nowhere as Basu was unable or unwilling to convince other members of his government. Also see Sinha 2004b, where I elaborate on post-1991 strategies adopted by Gujarat and West Bengal.

58. The joint sector refers to combined management of industrial firms by both private and state-level public sectors. The state government holds around 26 percent of the equity in the joint sector and around 11 percent in the assisted sector.

59. Government of West Bengal 1994, 5–6.

60. Ibid.

61. Shilpa Bandhu means "a Friend of Industry." Government of West Bengal, *Memorandum on the Reconstitution of SilpaBandhu,* Oct. 6, 1994.

62. Scott (1976) uses the concept of a moral economy.

63. Basu 1997, xiv.

64. Interview, *Business World,* June 22, 1997, p. 94. Also, see *Business Standard,* "Centre Blamed for Bengal's Poor Image Abroad," Oct. 20, 1995. This theme, that it is the "bourgeoisie press" and the "Center" that has "falsely" created the impression that West Bengal is not interested in attracting industry, was repeatedly stressed by Somnath Chatterjee in different interviews.

65. *Business Standard,* Oct. 20, 1995.

66. See *Business Standard,* "Bengal Seeks Central Funding for Haldia Industrial Park," Oct. 14, 1995; *Business Standard,* "West Bengal Plea to Centre on Incentives," Oct. 13, 1995.

67. "Centre to Blame: Says Industry Minister," *Telegraph,* Aug. 1996, p. 7.

68. Mursoli Maran, a member of the DMK (a regional party ruling Tamil Nadu) was the minister of industry in the central cabinet in Deve Gowda's government in 1996 and in I. K. Gujral's government in 1997, and continued to be the minister of commerce and industry in the BJP-led coalition government formed in 1999.

69. Confidential interview, Chennai, Sept. 1997. This information was confirmed by a journalist based in Chennai.

70. U.S.A. offers an example of a system where the reverse is true: that is, the legislature (Senate) acts as an arena for the expression of regional interests, and hence intergovernmental politics is less important (Simeon 1972, 8).

5. The Subnational State as a Developmental Actor

1. A popular joke in West Bengal.

2. The need to focus on local institutions can be found in some public administration studies, but their insights have not been integrated into state theory: see especially Lipsky 1980 and Pressman and Wildavsky 1984.

3. Interview, Ahmedabad (Gujarat), May 17, 1997.

4. The idea of complementarity is similar to the concepts of co-production and synergy outlined by Elinor Ostrom 1999, and by Peter Evans 1996.

5. This chapter relies on a comparative methodological strategy. I interviewed all the top officials of the Industry Ministry in all the three states. I also interviewed officials of all industry-related organizations established by state governments across the three states. Similarly placed medium-level and lower-level officials across the three states were also interviewed. These interviews revealed information about both formal decision-making structures and informal processes inside these organizations. Retired IAS officials from all three states provided an invaluable source of historical information. The organizations included the ministerial industry department (the apex department that coordinates all other industry-related organizations in each state), state industrial development corporations (called SIDCs), state industrial investment corporations (SIICs), infrastructure organizations, and state financial corporations. Each of these had parallel organizations dealing with the small-scale sector in each state. I also interviewed officials of these specialized organizations. I combined these interviews with participant observation, visiting many of these organizations many times and observing their operations. I procured policy-related materials that were made available to private investors or that were matters of internal debate. Annual reports of the state organizations also provided a wealth of information. This research strategy provided *comparable* sources of information across the three states. In addition, interviews with businesspersons were useful in assessing how these institutions affected actual investors.

6. Interview with H. R. Patnakar (industry secretary, Government of Gujarat, in the 1960s), Ahmedabad, April 1997. V. Eswaran (chief secretary of Gujarat in 1960) also suggested this (Interview, New Delhi, Oct. 1997).

7. Interview with H. R. Patnakar, April 1997.

8. Simultaneously, the leadership sought to enhance food grain production. To this end, they considered a fertilizer factory necessary. The importance of a fertilizer unit in the leadership's economic thinking is evident from the fact that barely fourteen days after the formation of the state, on May 14, 1960, the Government of Gujarat created a Fertilizer Committee, made up of high-level officials, such as the GoG chief secretary and the GoG secretary of industry, among others. See Government of Gujarat 1960.

9. See Drèze and Sen 2002 for the notion of "market-enhancing" state intervention.

10. Dr. Jivraj N. Mehta (the first CM of Gujarat) outlined his perspective on the public vs. private sector thus: "There seems to be on and off an unhappy controversy about private and public sectors in industry, as if they are in opposition to each other. . . . If we look at the nature and development of several industries in the country, it would seem that the public sector came into existence largely because the private sector had not been able, for various reasons, . . . to take up certain undertakings and which the government took up because of their importance to the state as a whole" (speech delivered June 15, 1961; Mehta 1961, 402). See Erdman 1973 for specific comments about Jivraj Mehta that confirm that he took a pragmatic view toward the public and the private sector.

11. Interviews with retired Gujarat cadre officials who had worked closely with these chief ministers. Interviews were held in April–May 1997 in Ahmedabad, and in December 1997 in New Delhi.

12. The number of public-sector units is insufficient information; we also need data on the amount of investment. However, it does give a sense of state-level priorities. Kerala (till 1994) had the highest number of state-level public enterprises, as a matter of explicit policy, even if it meant spreading the investment thinly across them.

13. Interview, May 12, 1997.

14. Different ownership forms can be found in India's regions: the central public sector, which is financed by the central budget and regulated by the central ministries; the state public sector, which is set up by the state governments from their own budgets; and the joint sector, which combines state government equity with private-sector support. In addition,

there are the cooperative sector (the sugar cooperatives in Maharashtra and the milk cooperatives in Gujarat are examples) and the assisted sector, in which the state equity is about 11 percent. The joint sector combines public and private sectors, with the government investing 26 percent equity and the rest held by the private firms and shareholders.

15. In a speech titled "Solid Base for [a] Bright Future," in Government of Gujarat 1970.

16. Cover story, "India's Biggest Wealth Creators," *Business Today*, Feb. 17, 2002.

17. Interview, GoG official, May 17, 1997. Also see Erdman (1973, 35), who cites a director's statement to the effect that Gujarat actively pursued the matter in Delhi for some time.

18. Interview with a director of Gujarat State Fertilizer Corporation, Baroda (Gujarat), May 16, 1997. Also see Erdman 1973, 35.

19. Fixed-capital formation in the public sector at 1970–71 prices grew at an annual rate of 11.3 percent in the period 1950–51 to 1965–66, but its growth rate declined to 5.5 percent from 1966–67 to 1981–82 (Bardhan 1984, 23).

20. Government of West Bengal 1978.

21. "Industrial Policy of the Left Front," trans. from *Ganashakti,* Jan. 7, 1978, p. 1, col. 1. Also see *Ganashakti,* Jan. 1, 3, 5, 1978.

22. Government of West Bengal 1978, 3–5.

23. Ibid.

24. Government of West Bengal 1985; 1986.

25. Government of West Bengal 1986, 66.

26. The Tamil Nadu Industrial Investment Corporation Ltd., established in 1949 under the Companies Act as Madras Industrial Investment Corporation, also functions as an SFC.

27. Supply side vs. demand side corresponds to the neoclassical and Keynesian policy instruments. While the supply-side argument directs itself to changing the incentives for labor or capital to locate in certain areas, a demand-side emphasis directs itself to raising the consumption and income levels so that more of the goods are demanded.

28. See George and Gulati 1985 for the argument that regional states do not have any role in matters relating to industry in India.

29. Gujarat instituted a working group, Industry, Power, and Mining, in the late 1960s, which came out with a report, "The Perspective Plan of Gujarat, 1974-1984," in 1972. Government of Gujarat 1972. Similarly, Tamil Nadu designed a 20-year "Perspective Plan" in the 1960s.

30. This section relies on a detailed examination of provincial policy documents not analyzed before by any scholar. Documents include policy statements and brochures from the 1960s to the 1980s, budgets of state governments, five-year-plan documents of states, incentive policies of states, party documents, party newspapers (CPI(M) mostly), and regional editions of national newspapers (such as the Ahmedabad edition of the *Times of India*).

31. A tax levied on goods traveling across the state's borders.

32. Government of Gujarat 1972.

33. Commerce 1975, 55.

34. Ibid., 73.

35. A few exceptions are Kerala and Uttar Pradesh. Kerala formed the Kerala State Export Trade Development Council in the early 1980s, and Uttar Pradesh formed the Uttar Pradesh State Export Corporation Ltd. in the mid-1980s (Commerce 1985).

36. The acronym iNDEXTb is written with a lowercase "i" and "b" to denote that its "ego" and bureaucratic red tape are minimized.

37. Interview, Industry Department Commissioner; Interview, G. Jha, director of iNDEXTb, Gandhinagar, April 29, 1997.

38. The term means "Industry's Friend."

39. Interview, Mr. Kamble, Maharashtra State Financial Corporation (MSFC), and also a member of Udyog Mitra, March 9, 1997.

40. Each of these programs was a regional-level program. In this section, I focus on only one: the investor promotion service. Pages 143–145 discuss the industrial estate program. The entrepreneurship development program (EDP) and the joint-sector program receive less emphasis in this book. Also, I did primary field research for the investor promotion service, industrial estate program, and the joint sector, but my information about EDP is drawn from secondary sources.

41. Maharashtra Industrial Development Corporation Act, 1960; Gujarat Industrial Development Act, 1962; Memorandum and Articles of Association of WBIDC, 1967.

42. Interviews with state government officials in Bombay and Ahmedabad, March and April 1997.

43. Interview, Calcutta, Oct. 15, 1997.

44. N. Vittal, the IAS official of the Gujarat cadre, has served in the Home Department of the state and as the managing director of Narmada Valley Fertilizer Company, an SLPE in Gujarat; he was also the director of the Geological and Mining Department for four years in Gujarat and the managing director of Gujarat Mineral Development Corporation (GMDC). In addition, he served as the development commissioner of the Kandla Free Trade Zone, Gujarat.

45. The procedures were not clear or simple in any of the states, but in some states discretion was used in implementing them. This, in effect, compensated for the problem of their complicated nature. More important, the investors perceived more of a problem with *not knowing* what the detailed procedures were than with the procedures themselves.

46. Interviews with the incentive departments of GIIC, GIDC, and iNDEXTb. I also personally reviewed all the information provided to investors and corroborated it with investors.

47. This raises the interesting issue of the role of corruption in economic development. I discuss it in detail in Chapter 7.

48. Interview with Gujarat-based investor, Ahmedabad, April 27, 1997.

49. Interview, Ahmedabad, May 20, 1997.

50. Interview, GoG official, Gandhinagar, May 21, 1997.

51. Interview, Gujarat government official, Gandhinagar, April 19, 1997.

52. Interview, WBIDC official, Calcutta, Oct. 20, 1997. Also independent verification of packages made available to investors.

53. Interview of a West Bengal–based investor, Kalyani (West Bengal), Oct. 29, 1997.

54. Interview of a small-scale investor, Kalyani (West Bengal), Nov. 1997.

55. Interview of a government official, Kalyani (West Bengal), Nov. 1997.

56. Interview of a West Bengal government official, who admitted this on assurance of anonymity.

57. Interviews with Tamil Nadu–based investors, Aug.–Sept. 1997.

58. Interview with official, Chennai, Aug. 25, 1997. This official, who had been with the industrial bureaucracy for a long time, admitted that the output of his own office varied a lot by the amount of pressure from the upper-level official.

59. Interview, Chennai, Aug. 27, 1997.

60. Interview, Chennai, Aug. 27, 1997.

61. See Chapter 7 for different forms of corruption in the three states.

62. Interview, March 17, 1997.

63. Interview, Calcutta, Nov. 21, 1997.

64. The first industrial estate was started in 1952 after Bombay State appointed a special officer in 1947 to recommend areas where industrial estates could be established. In 1952 the Poona Municipal Corporation developed an industrial estate at Hadaspur; this was followed by the establishment of an industrial estate at Rajkot, the Gujarat part of Bombay. After these early initiatives the Government of India launched a national program. In 1955, the Small-Scale Industries Board launched the industrial estate program. In the Second Five-Year Plan, the entire cost of estates was advanced as a loan from the central government; however, the program took off only in the Third Five-Year Plan (1969-74), when the regional states took independent initiative in financing the program. Since then the institutional management of estates is the responsibility of the states in which they reside, thus encouraging differentiation.

65. Government of India 1982, ii.

66. Government of India 1980, 14.

67. An internal memo from the Department of Industry, Government of Gujarat, shows a minute and detailed attention to licenses granted for Gujarat, the export-oriented units, DGTD registrations, and their "implementation status." The implementation status was measured in terms of eight parameters, each of which was categorized under three implementation categories: Arranged, Awaiting, and Not applied [for]. The eight parameters are: Land, Electricity, Finance, Environment Clearance, Land/Finance/Power tied up, Construction, Procurement of Machinery, and Production (interview with Mr. R. J. Shah, GoG official, June 15, 1997). R. J. Shah, the director of the Investment Promotion Cell, reported in an interview how the attempt to ensure the flow of investment in the 1970s led the Department of Industry to evolve a systematic system of monitoring the licenses from the stage of allotment to actual production. Despite my best efforts to determine the method followed by West Bengal and Tamil Nadu to monitor licenses, I did not find any "investment promotion cell" or any method to monitor the various stages of the licenses there. The above information is drawn from many interviews conducted at the Delhi office of iNDEXTb, Feb. 1997, and interviews of officials in the industry departments of the three states.

68. The library of iNDEXTb is a large room filled with hundreds of reports about feasible projects and sectoral information gathered by iNDEXTb and other consultancy organizations.

69. It must be noted that Jay Narayan Vyas was a pioneer in realizing that iNDEXTb could perform such data-gathering tasks. He tried to give to other state agencies what they did not have: information!

70. In the post-reform period, after 1991, information generation and distribution has become common across many more regional states.

71. Interview to Ramesh Menon, *India Today*, Sept. 30, 1994, p. 108.

72. iNDEXTb 1996.

73. Interview with various current and retired officials of iNDEXTb, May–June 1997.

74. The mere presence of the private sector may not be enough, especially if business-people are the cronies of the government in power. However, these specific individuals were well regarded in Gujarat and seen to be men of independent thought. Moreover, organizations such as the joint sector in Gujarat gave actual decision-making power, not mere formal roles, to these businesspeople. In some cases, such as GSFC and GNFC, they could override the decisions of the political rulers for the sake of "efficiency." This is confirmed in interviews with managers of the various joint-sector units in Baroda. Erdman 1973 confirms this about GSFC.

75. The inspector-*raj* refers to regional inspectors who visit factories on a regular basis to implement various regulations. This inspector-*raj* has existed since the early 1960s. The first part of this chapter provided evidence in support of this argument.

76. Kennedy (2004) analyzes the framing of liberalization policies in Andhra Pradesh.

77. In 2003 Andhra Pradesh won an award, instituted by the Computer Society of India, designating it as the "Best e-Governed State." Nine governance parameters, including a reduction in paperwork, overall service to customers, and the use of Indian language interface, were used to evaluate sixty entries (*India Network Economic News* 15, no. 37 [March 7, 2003]).

78. During the license-*raj*, Gujarat bureaucracy was distinctive in targeting the central licensing administration, licensed (domestic) private-sector investors, and Gujarati capital from West Bengal, Maharashtra, East Africa, and United Kingdom. In the 1980s and especially after 1991, it has become much more indiscriminate, targeting non-Gujarati as well as Gujarati investors from all over India as well as from Europe, Africa, and the United States. However, the skills and institutions employed before 1991 proved to be extremely transportable to the post-1991 context; no other state had this advantage, allowing Gujarat to take an "institutional" head start.

79. This information is drawn from interviews conducted in July 2001.

80. "Is Maharashtra Losing Out?" *Business India,* March 25–April 7, 1996, p. 62.

81. Ibid.

82. Interviews were conducted with about forty-five large-scale and small-scale investors located in Bengal.

83. Ibid.

84. Interview, Chennai, Sept. 17, 1997.

85. Interview with Guidance official, Sept. 25, 1997.

86. *Hindu,* Feb. 12, 1994.

87. This information is drawn from observation of the functioning of this organization and from analysis of its various documents.

6. Divided Loyalties

1. Gujarat's model of development was one that stressed capital-intensive industrial sectors common in the first and second industrial revolutions—engineering, textile machinery, chemicals, and pharmaceuticals; as a result its impact on the ecological base of the region has been extremely deleterious. The regional state's "entrepreneurship" made sure that national or state-level regulation regarding pollution were flouted; as a result, Gujarat is one of the most polluted places in the country. Thus, Gujarat's model of development is similar to the evolution of capitalism in late industrializers (Russia, Germany, and Japan), who in their haste to catch up neglected equity and environmental considerations. In the 1990s, Gujarat High Court's activism spurred some action on the environmental front. In the mid-1990s the High Court ordered the cleaning up of many sites and the setting up of the Gujarat Ecology Commission; the state government, however, continues to flout environment regulations under pressure to be a competitive location for investment.

2. Gujarat also faced internal problems at that time. Gujarat in 1960 was "an economically non-viable State burdened with a tremendous backlog of political fragmentation and under-developed infrastructure . . . " (Nagindas Sanghvi 1996, 151). Wood (1984a) also analyzes the impact of divergent traditions left by British and princely states on Gujarat's development in the 1950s to 1960s.

3. Muslims were incorporated into the political coalition through a patronage system.

Some tribals (indigenous communities) and small peasants were incorporated as agricultural and industrial laborers in the agrarian and industrial economy of south Gujarat.

4. Patidars used to be known as Kanbis in west and north Gujarat. A middle-caste group, it is the second-largest caste group and dominated the Congress Party since the nationalist movement (1930–1940s).

5. An acronym to refer to the electoral and political alliance of four caste groups—Kshatriyas, Harijans, Adivasis, and Muslims—that dominated Gujarat's politics from about 1975 to the 1980s.

6. Brahmins, Vanias, and Rajputs, constituting 12 percent, are the upper-caste groups; Patidars, also known as Kanbis, form 12 percent of the population and are the largest single caste group. Kolis, a large caste cluster, also known as Kshatriyas in central and north Gujarat, constitute around 24 percent of Gujarat's population. Scheduled castes, or ex-untouchables, are about 7 percent, while scheduled tribes (indigenous communities) are 14 percent of the population of the state; Muslims form 8 percent of the population. Gujarat is also home of Parsis settled in Gujarat since the eighth century, who constitute less than 1 percent of the population, but have migrated to Bombay in large numbers since the nineteenth century.

7. The traders and merchants in Gujarat are mostly Banias, the farmers that moved into industry are Patidars, and the small-scale industrialists were some Patidars, Kolis, tribals, and "other backward castes" like Kshatriyas.

8. This transition contradicts the argument of some (Bagchi 1976; Banerjee and Ghosh 1988) who maintain that it is difficult for traders to develop into industrialists. Bagchi further suggests that if they do become industrialists they retain short-run and trader traits. The transformation of traders into industrialists in Gujarat contradicts this argument. In Gujarat, shopkeepers, moneylenders, and rice, grain, and timber merchants became small-scale industrialists after 1960 (Streefkerk 1985, 128).

9. This link differentiates Gujarat from West Bengal and Tamil Nadu. Within Tamil Nadu, in Coimbatore district similar linkage between agricultural surplus and agro-industry can be found (Harriss-White 1996). More recently (1980s and 1990s), similar links between the rural and industrial classes are evident in Andhra Pradesh, Tamil Nadu, and Punjab.

10. Industrialization in Gujarat is relatively more regionally dispersed than in Maharashtra or West Bengal (Kundu and Raza 1982). With the exception of Kutch, south, central, and west Gujarat have experienced widespread industrialization. There are two main industrial belts: one that runs north to south from central-north to south Gujarat along the national railway line to Bombay and a second that extends from central Gujarat to the west coast, along Rajkot, Morbi, Bhavnagar, and Jamnagar.

11. "Backward castes" refers to a social category of castes that have been socially and economically discriminated against; the constitution of India and subsequent policy debates make a distinction between "forward," "backward," and "other backward" castes.

12. Lava Patidars is a subcaste within the Patidar caste group.

13. The incidence of chronic unemployment is low, 0.62 percent for men and 0.30 for women in rural Gujarat and 4.7 percent (men) and 0.50 (women) for urban Gujarat. Gujarat has not seen a decline in the level of employment in recent decades; in fact, the workforce participation rates showed a marginal increase between 1981 and 1991 while the all-India participation rates declined (Hirway 2002, 17). As for poverty, Gujarat's situation is better than the all-India figures. The incidence of poverty in Gujarat has declined considerably, from 46.35 percent in 1972–1973 to 22.18 percent in 1993–1994 in rural areas and from 41.21 percent in 1972–1973 to 27.7 percent in urban areas. Hirway and Terhal reluctantly conclude: "economic growth has helped in poverty reduction" (2002, 48).

14. It was only after the early twentieth century that the name "Patidar" came to des-

ignate a collection of caste groups who were mostly lower and medium castes. Earlier they were known as "Kunbis and Bhabhas," which are pejorative terms indicating the rural and backward character of the caste (Bhatt 1970).

15. The farming of these oil crops is extremely lucrative. More than 45 percent of the gross cropped area of the state is under cash crops as against the all-India average of 24 percent (Hirway 1995).

16. Gujarat has always had abundant external trading links, but their socioeconomic nature and direction has changed over time. In the nineteenth century Gujarati immigration was to South and East Africa and usually of trading communities such as Banias. In the twentieth century, Patels have immigrated to the U.K. and the U.S.A.

17. This was confirmed in my interviews with many Patel businesspeople.

18. For details of the social reform movement within the Patidar community see Bhatt (1970), who documents the way in which reform of the Patidars proceeded in conjunction with the development of "caste unity" and the formation of Patidars as a caste.

19. Although during the 1960s and 1970s many Patidars moved to urban centers, they continued to retain their links to their villages and employed their economic and physical resources to urbanize the villages in the areas under their dominance (Nagindas Sanghvi 1996, 68).

20. Coastal Andhra Pradesh in the 1980s has also witnessed a similar phenomenon. See Upadhya (1988a; 1988b) for an analysis of farmer-capitalists in coastal Andhra.

21. There, too, the strength of the rich peasantry engaged in the production of commercial cash crops (especially peanuts) played a role in extending industrialization to the region.

22. This argument is elaborated in Sinha (2004b).

23. See Baru (2000) for his urging the analysis of newly emerging regional bourgeoisie in India; his examples are drawn from Andhra Pradesh's political economy.

24. See Breman (1974, 1985, 1990, 1993, 1996, 2003) for a careful and detailed documentation of exploitative conditions of the informal sector workers in south and central Gujarat. Also see Ghanshyam Shah, Rutten, and Streefkerk (2002); Hirway, Kashyap, and Shah (2002); and Shinoda (2002) for fine-grained and updated documentation of the situation of all subaltern classes—workers, women, untouchables, and indigenous communities—in Gujarat, especially for the period after liberalization (1991).

25. This point is about *relative* deprivation compared to such progressive states as West Bengal; poverty and deprivation of lower and working classes in Gujarat cannot be denied.

26. In 1910, the conferences organized by the Patidar Yuvak Mandal passed a resolution resolving to "*integrate various segments and divisions of the patidar caste*. Other resolutions emphasized the need to educate Patidar children, requesting the government to make education compulsory" (Bhatt 1970, 307; emphasis in original). Interestingly, while many of these institutions began as caste associations, they soon began to involve non-Patidars—even scheduled castes and tribals—within them. Bhatt asserts that this gave these organizations "a secular character without antagonizing the caste leaders" (Bhatt 1970, 313–14). See Bhatt (1970) for the details of the organizational work of the association Patidar Yuvak Mandal.

27. Also see Hardiman (1981) for a detailed analysis of the nationalist movement in south and central Gujarat.

28. Many scheduled castes in Gujarat have moved into small-scale industry. As an illustration, the Scheduled Castes Chamber of Commerce and Industry was started in 1993 in Ahmedabad (Shinoda 2002, xx).

29. Industrialization and migration of Adivasis have created class differentiation amongst the indigenous communities, which also hurts the process of mobilization of exploited classes.

30. This acquiescence or the lack of political mobilization within the weaker sections was also historically present in the Dalit community in Gujarat. In contrast to the more militant tradition of Dalit mobilization in Maharashtra under the leadership of Ambedkar, in Gujarat, Dalits failed to carry forward their struggles on the temple entry issue in the 1920s and 1930s due to the Gandhian views of non-confrontation and consensus building (Makrand Mehta 2002).

31. Also see Streefkerk (1985, 208–13).

32. Breman characterizes this phenomenon as "Caste-for-itself type of mobilization" (1985, 361).

33. Breman documents the influx of migrant workers and extensive "circulation" between industrial and agricultural workers (1985, chs. 7 and 8).

34. For example, migrant workers in the city of Surat engaged in riotous violence against the Muslims, diamond workers, in the city (Breman 1993b); this intra-class conflict makes difficult any collective protest to make capitalism more humane. Some nascent mobilization has begun amongst the Dalit workers in recent years, who have begun to organize worker unions under the banner of B. R. Ambedkar.

35. Also see Breman 1996, 243–54.

36. To this domination by Patel-Kanbi groups, Kshatriyas, who constitute about 40 percent of the state's population, did offer resistance and challenge. However, from 1960 to 1975 the Congress Party managed to "divide and rule," thus preventing the emergence of potential Patel-Kshatriya opposition against it. Factionalism within the Kshatriyas was used by the Congress Party, which "retained its position as a party in power by understanding the political underpinnings of the alignment of these numerical and dominant castes and tactfully forging more balanced combination of the two than its rival" (Sheth 1976a, 74). When the Kshatriya population shifted its support from the Congress party to the Swatantra party (in 1962), in 1967 "the Congress Party divided this group by floating a rival Kshatriya organization of the backward and poor Bariyas and thus reduced the shock of Kshatriya's departure as a support base of the Congress party" (Sheth 1976a, 74–76).

37. The anti-reservation agitation in 1980 and 1985 was in the form of a zero-sum game between the "forward" and "backward" castes (categories in public policy) vis-à-vis patronage resources such as seats in medical colleges and jobs in the state bureaucracy, and did not extend to industrial concessions.

38. The chairman of the SIDCs regularly gave checks to various chief ministers. Interview, director, GIDC, and manager, GIIC. Photographs of such "presents" from various SIDCs have appeared in the newspaper regularly. See *Times of India*, 1980–1985 (Ahmedabad Edition).

39. It is notable that electoral and public debates, especially but not only during municipal (local) elections, did raise issues affecting industry and growth. Such developmental issues came up much more in the 1980s, by which time Gujarat's industrial achievements had become a matter of pride for the state's leadership. Many politicians and the Chief Minister spoke about issues such as energy management for industry, loans for industry, infrastructure, entrepreneurial and technical training for indigenous peoples, coastal shipping for export, and location of central projects in the state during and around election campaigns. In 1981, during a joint election meeting with Indira Gandhi, the PM and the CM (elections for the city municipal corporation were held in February 1981), issues relating to industrial projects in Gujarat came up directly. M. Solanki (the chief minister) expressed confidence that "Other demands of the State like a third fertilizer plant and an atomic power station would be met [by the Center]." Later in the meeting, the managing director of GNFC (Gujarat Narmada Fertilizer Corporation, a premier joint-sector company of the Govern-

ment of Gujarat) told reporters that the GNFC would be ready to take up the construction of the third fertilizer plant (Staff Correspondent, "Opposition Criticized for Malicious Propaganda," *Times of India*, Jan. 23, 1981, p. 3, Ahmedabad edition). For newspaper reports that show that industrial issues were raised during elections and public debates, see "CM Lists Steps to Develop Coastal Shipping," *Times of India*, Jan. 9, 1981, p. 3, Ahmedabad edition; "GSFC Loans for 31 Units," *Times of India*, Feb. 14, 1981, Ahmedabad edition; "Clearance for Petro-Chem Unit Soon," *Times of India*, Feb. 28, 1981, pp. 1, 4, Ahmedabad edition; "Industrialists from Dubai Coming," *Times of India*, Jan. 25, 1981, p. 3, Ahmedabad edition; "I. Gandhi Arrives Today," *Times of India*, Jan. 21, 1981, p. 4, Ahmedabad edition; "Incentives for Pioneer Units," *Times of India*, Feb. 18, 1981, p. 7, Ahmedabad edition.

40. The mid-1970s was a period of confused realignment in Gujarat's politics wherein Patels were increasingly becoming alienated from Congress (I) but were unsure of a viable alternative. Simultaneously, the alternative KHAM strategy was being evolved slowly. It was after 1980 that political patterns congealed into a new pattern. However, industrial policy came to occupy an autonomous place by the 1970s and was relatively insulated by these realignments.

41. In the 1960s, the Congress Party brought together the Patidars and Kshatriyas into their political coalition; however, the realignment of the Gujarat party system toward a more divided pattern and the evolution of the KHAM strategy by the Congress Party led to the exit of the Patels and dominant castes to the Congress (O), then the Janata Party, and finally to the BJP in the 1990s.

42. There was widespread violence in Gujarat from January to March 1981.

43. Comparatively, in Tamil Nadu, an extensive populist policy agenda of both regional parties could not be sustained without the tax revenues and other fiscal support from the industrial sector. Washbrook (1990, 261) notes that Dravidian parties faced serious problems owing to the drying up of resources for redistribution. Subramanian (1999) shows how different governments after 1967 had to roll back their populist initiatives on account of fiscal pressures. In Gujarat, the populist initiatives were financed by the industrial sector and dividends from the State Industry Corporations, which were run efficiently and produced regular profits.

44. This was in contrast to West Bengal and Tamil Nadu, states reconstituted from a dominant presidency tradition. Tamil Nadu did incorporate a part of the Travancore princely state (southern Kerala) but it was a small area. Most of Tamil Nadu was the erstwhile Madras Presidency.

45. The princely states of Baroda, Kutch, Junagadh, Nawabnagar, and Bhavnagar were of substantial sizes, and the other princely states were tiny but numerous. It was a bargaining nightmare to incorporate units of such diverse sizes into the Indian Union and integrate them with Gujarat. Patel and V. P. Menon had to decide whether to treat them equally or to offer asymmetric deals.

46. One of the first newspapers in Bombay, *Mumbai Samachar,* first published in 1822, was written in Gujarati.

47. Kaviraj (1992) presents a novel argument about the relationship between the so-called "regional" and "national" identities during colonial India. He suggests that the Indian nationalist project "succeeded" because it was able to organize and create the regional identities as a subset of national identities. Based on the horizontal and vertical relationships between a bilingual cultural and political elite, the Congress party could transcend an anticolonial movement into a "nationalist" one. Thus, the Indian nation at the eve of independence was distinguished by the existence of regional subnations as subcircles of the Indian identity. It is possible to argue that in 1960 this process was incomplete in Gujarat.

48. Even those who wanted a separate state of Gujarat did not want to lose Bombay city.

49. The loss of Bombay city had to be weighed against the gain arising out of Ahmedabad's elevation as a capital city; the supporters of the separate Gujarat movement were Ahmedabad businesspeople and land speculators who stood to profit if Ahmedabad gained capital status. However, it must be noted that the relevant proposal on the table against which the Maha-Gujarat movement gained strength was one in which Greater Bombay was to include not only mainland Gujarat, Saurashtra, and Kutch, but also Vidharbha. This would have meant Maharashtrian and Maratha dominance and the diminution of the mainland Gujaratis. Support for the unilingual idea in Gujarat in 1960 was accompanied by regret at having lost Bombay city.

50. Interviews, Ahmedabad, April 1997.

51. The erstwhile industry secretary laughed at the irony. Interview, April 1997.

52. Interview with a Gujarat investor, till then settled in Bombay, who recalled how he had decided to move his new investments to Gujarat in the early 1970s after the onset of Shiv Sena's mobilization against outsiders. Interview, April 16, 1997.

53. Katzenstein (1979).

54. Interview, H. R. Patankar, May 1997. Similarly, the chief secretary of Gujarat in 1997, S. K. Shelat, said, "Early 1960s were quiet but the real boost to GIDC [Gujarat Industrial Development Corporation] came in 1968 with the rise of Shiv Sena. We kept setting up industrial estates in Vapi, Halol, Umaragoan etc. in an effort to attract Bombay based industrialists" (Interview, Ahmedabad, May 1997).

55. Interview with officials of the Department of Industry, Government of Gujarat, May 1997.

56. Interview, retired Gujarat cadre official (IAS), May 1997. My research findings on competitive efforts by the Gujarat government are confirmed by similar suggestions by earlier researchers: "[Gujarat] attracted many industrialists from West Bengal and Maharashtra to establish industries in Gujarat" (Sheth 1976a, 81).

57. Interview, managing director of GIDC, April 1997.

58. See Bagchi 1982, Bannerjee and Ghosh 1988, Markovits 1996, and Kohli 1990 for this argument.

59. Bhadralok, neither a single class nor caste, literally, "a respectable person" or "gentleman" (sometimes called just borolok or "big people," or baboos, a derogatory term), refers to a cross section of elites unique to the Bengali-speaking area. Most often drawn from the three highest castes (Brahmans, Kayasthas, and Vaidyas), they are well-educated men and women, proud of their language and cultural leadership in the regional cultural life. They are usually engaged in white-collar professions of various types such as banking, courts, schools, colleges, and clerical service. See Broomfield (1968, 1–41) for a detailed historical analysis of "Bhadralok" as a social, cultural, and political elite.

60. This goes against the conventional understanding of West Bengal being dominated by "class questions." See Chatterjee (1997) and Mukherjee (1985) for post-1967 accounts that outline the Bhadralok character of Left politics in the state; Weiner (1963) and Franda (1968) uncover the middle-caste structure of politics in West Bengal for the pre-1967 phase.

61. The following account draws upon Chatterjee (1997), Franda (1968), and Weiner (1967).

62. See David Kopf (1969) for an account of the Bengal renaissance.

63. Bengali subnationalism, thus, has deep cultural, intellectual, and political roots in the state.

64. Also see Atul Kohli (1990, 391) for the "elitism" of the Bhadralok in the twentieth century and post-independence period.

65. Kayasthas in Gujarat are considered the backward castes. One notable aspect of the caste system in India is that the relative power of castes/jatis varies across states, as is evident from the radically different position of Kayasthas in the caste hierarchy in West Bengal.

66. Also see Nossiter (1988, 115–20) and Franda (1973, 14, 184–91).

67. For example, the Patels in Gujarat represent a "kulak"—rich peasant—interest. Their incorporation into the Congress Party meant that the Congress Party would ensure their political and material interests.

68. One strand of nationalism in Bengal took a terrorist form against the British state. The terrorist movement in Bengal acquired deep roots and a presence in almost every village in the 1930s and 1940s.

69. My argument reformulates the argument presented by Banerjee and Ghosh (1988) and Markovits (1996) significantly. They argue that the ethnic character of the business class was far removed from the linguistic character of the region. Maharashtra too has had a nonorganic business class, but the social and political links between the nonregional business class and the politico-economic elite are more important than the mere existence of a regionally organic business class.

70. Interview, economic advisor of the BCCI, Sept. 1997. Also see BCCI (1971, 1973, 1975).

71. See Bannerjee and Ghosh (1988) for the argument that the nonorganic non-Bengali business community in Bengal—the Marwaris—were alien to the region and did not invest in its economic potential.

72. The central government initiated liberalization policies in July 1991, while the state government introduced key policy changes in September 1994.

73. Although many business leaders acknowledged in confidential interviews that the CPI(M) in power is better than the CPI(M) out of power.

74. The following account is drawn from Choudhury (1985).

75. Translated from *Ganashakti*, July 2, 1977. Also see *Ganashakti*, 1978.

76. Chatterjee notes, "Since the efforts of the left parties have been confined largely to the question of the choice of appropriate representatives and not as much to the task of conscious organization to overthrow existing relations of power" (1997, 86).

77. Despite the anti-industry rhetoric of the West Bengal Communists in the 1960s, in 1979, out of the 50 largest transnational companies in the world, 23 existed in India, out of which 19 existed in West Bengal.

78. This argument can be found in Sinha (2004b).

79. Kundu and Raza 1982 and Bharadwaj 1982.

80. Calculated from Government of West Bengal (1997).

81. Rural industrialization in states like Gujarat, Tamil Nadu, Andhra Pradesh, Punjab, and Haryana makes for a different political-economy logic.

82. One important distinction is between West Bengal's wing of the CPI(M) and the positions of the central national party. While West Bengal party delegates have always been the dominant faction in the national CPI(M) party, there has been a conflict of interest between the two. This phenomenon deserves further research.

83. Interviews with businesspeople based in West Bengal, Sept.–Nov. 1997.

84. *India Today*, March 31, 1987, p. 43, cited in Nossiter 1988, 195.

85. Thirty percent of CPI(M)'s membership came from West Bengal in 1987. After the parliamentary elections of 1999, in 2000 CPI(M) lost its "national party" status as it did not have a significant presence in four states, the criterion for national recognition. More recently, the Election Commission redefined its criteria to include a party's presence in the national parliament, by virtue of which the CPI(M) regained its national party status. See

Hindu, Dec. 3, 2003. But increasingly, CPI(M) wins its support only in two or three regional states, and its presence in other states has been declining.

86. See Swaminathan (1994).

87. The analysis in this chapter focuses on developments from 1967 to 1991.

88. I draw the term from Swamy (1996). Swamy's use of the term is different from mine in that I use it to denote Tamil Nadu's strategy toward the center while he deploys it in the context of the regional politics. Subramanian characterizes the Dravidian parties moving between "paternalist populism and assertive populism" (1999, chs. 4–6); thus, most scholars of Tamil Nadu agree that its parties follow populist strategies.

89. In the nineteenth century, the racial theory that overlapped with the Brahman and non-Brahman social division became predominant. A number of Indian and European scholars posited the idea that non-Brahmans belonged to the Dravidian "race" and were the original residents of the region, and the Brahmans were the Aryan invaders from the north. Linguistically they posed a contrast between Sanskrit, the language of the priestly Brahman caste, and Tamil, the language of the southern non-Brahmans. In religious terms, they challenged the Sanskritic "Aryan religion" and the caste system by which the non-Brahmans had been kept in an inferior position (Irschick 1969, xiv).

90. M. Gopala Ramachandran (MGR), the chief minister of Tamil Nadu from 1977 to 1987, broadened the normal political understanding of people to include poor women; in doing so he broadened the scope of populist politics and ensured repeated electoral success for the AIADMK.

91. Barnett analyzes the transformation of the non-Brahman movement into the Tamil movement.

92. These various incarnations were the result of progressive splits within the party. The South Indian Liberal Federation (Justice Party), formed in 1916, changed its name to DK in 1944; in 1949 there was a formal split led by Annadurai, who formed the DMK; in 1972 MGR split from the DMK to form the ADMK; its name was later changed to AIADMK.

93. This ideological distinctiveness of the Justice Party and the DK was most notable from 1917 to 1944.

94. The social divisions in what was then called Madras were tripartite: Brahmans, non-Brahmans (constituted by a diverse set of subcastes/jatis), and the untouchables. Historically, there was an absence of Kshatriya and Vaishya castes in the Madras presidency. It is notable that the DMK and AIADMK attempted to represent the backward non-Brahmans against the forward, elite non-Brahman castes.

95. Barnett's careful historical study documents how different versions of the Dravidian movement articulated these different ideological spaces in response to the changing leadership, electoral constraints, and intra-party politics. Swamy suggests this too (1996, 155). Subramanian shows how this transition aided a reconciliation with Tamil Brahmans (1999, 137–38).

96. One slogan made poplar by DMK was "The North Prospers, while the South Decays," cited in Subramanian (1999, 143).

97. Interestingly, it could not implement its policy of Tamil medium instruction in schools, as students concerned more with job prospects than with their "Tamilness" protested. Despite passing a law on this in 1970, the government had to withdraw it in the face of protest from students (Subramanian 1999, 224). In addition, populist policies were also implemented. The price of rice was reduced to one rupee a measure in Madras and Coimbatore, cheap public housing was provided to around ten thousand families in Madras, and concessions to small farmers were given. In addition, a ministry of backward classes, the first

in India, was created in 1971, backward quota was increased, and SC converts to Christianity and Muslims were made eligible for SC quotas.

98. *India Today*, Nov. 15, 1984, cited in Widlund 2000.

99. Many scholars have studied the role of cinema in Tamil Nadu's politics: Pandian 1992, 1993, 1996; Dickey 1993a, 1993b; Hardgrave 1971, 1973; Hardgrave and Niedhart 1975; Forrester 1976; Price 1989, and Sivathamby 1981. Yet, writing on the possible implications of a political culture of films and cultural nationalism for industrial development is rarer.

100. *India Today*, July 31, 1987.

101. Interviews with businesspersons in Chennai. Also see Chapter 6 for details of responses by businesspersons.

102. While laborers did find Kerala to be a haven, over time, the decline in employment opportunities led many of them to seek employment elsewhere.

103. The Dewan (prime minister), Sir M. Visveswarayaya of Mysore, the princely state that became Karnataka, took pioneering initiatives to develop Mysore industrially between 1912 and 1918 (Inoue 1992, 116–17).

104. Interview, SIPCOT official, Sept 1997. Interview, manager of Ashok Leyland, Sept. 1997; also see SIPCOT, *On the Industrial Horizon: Your Guiding Star*, n.d.

105. Interview with state government official, Madras, Sept. 1997.

106. Oommen 1979.

7. Weapons of the Strong

1. Studies of business in India (especially in comparison to studies on labor) are very few and dated. See Erdman 1971, 1973, 1976; Nayar 1971; and Kochanek 1974. Two studies that focus on the pre-independence period are Markovits 1985 and Gordon 1978.

2. Two exceptions are Erdman (1971), who analyzes the Baroda elite, and Kochanek (1974), who focuses on national-level business associations.

3. The majority of businesspeople are men, but it might be worthwhile to explore the perspective of businesswomen in subsequent research.

4. I specifically asked questions about the pre-liberalization period.

5. I interviewed thirty businesspeople in Gujarat, twenty-nine in West Bengal, and about nineteen in Tamil Nadu.

6. I have promised to keep the identities of the interviewees confidential. Many of the opinions expressed were at variance with some of the positions in public and in the journalistic press, and many interviewees requested anonymity. Most of the interviews were with CEOs, managing directors, and vice-presidents.

7. Most of those surveyed had units in more than one state although not always all the three states of my sample.

8. Interview, Delhi, Nov. 1997.

9. Interview, Calcutta, Oct. 1997.

10. Interview with an investor, April 1997.

11. Interview, Ahmedabad, May 1997.

12. Interview with an investor, Sept. 1997.

13. Interview with an investor, May 1997.

14. Interview, Madras, Sept. 1997. This investor had invested in Gujarat and Tamil Nadu.

15. Interview with retired industry secretary, Madras, Sept. 1997.

16. Interview, May 1997.

17. Interview with a large-scale investor who had invested in Kerala, Tamil Nadu, and Gujarat; Chennai, Sept. 1997.

18. Interview, April 1997.

19. Around 1978, a nonresident Indian (NRI) cell had been formed within iNDEXTb, which looked after the attraction of investment from NRIs. The NRIs were treated very well as the industrial bureaucracy hoped that huge amounts of foreign investment would flow in.

20. Interview, Sept. 1997.

21. Ibid.

22. This person admitted to me that if the press had asked him that question he would have given a very different answer, as he did support Jyoti Basu and his policy of encouraging the private sector. But he said that to be honest, he had to admit that there is not much discrimination during the license-*raj*.

23. Interview with an investor, Oct. 1997.

24. This was confirmed through many discussions with the industry associations and journalists.

25. Interview, Aug. 1997.

26. It is interesting to note that he was a small-scale investor; small-scale investors usually don't invest outside their home states. His decision to invest in Gujarat in western India is even more remarkable.

27. Interview with an investor, May 1997.

28. Before 1991, only Gujarat and Maharashtra had a specialized organization that handled new investors; in West Bengal new investors were handled by WBIDC, and in Tamil Nadu, by the Industry Department. In 1992 Tamil Nadu set up an organization called Guidance, and West Bengal in 1994 refurbished Shilpa Bandhu as a wing of WBIDC to serve similar functions.

29. Interview, Sept. 1997.

30. Interview with an investor, June 1997.

31. The iNDEXTb regularly brought out brochures that listed all the clearances that investors needed at both the central and the state level.

32. Interview with an investor, Sept. 1997.

33. A slight exaggeration perhaps but indicative of Gujarat's good repute and success with investors.

34. That situation has changed in recent times. In 1997 Tamil Nadu was one of the few states to pass a single-window law, but through 2003, no other state had done so.

35. Interview with an investor, May 1997.

36. Interview, Ahmedabad, May 1997.

37. Interview with an investor, Oct. 1997.

38. Interview with an investor, Oct. 1997.

39. Interview with an investor, Oct. 1997.

40. Cover story, "The Best States to Invest In: A BT-Gallup-MBA Survey," *Business Today*, June 7–21, 1996, p. 82.

41. Parasarthy, "Best States to Invest In: A BT-Gallup-MBA Survey," *Business Today*, Dec. 22–Jan. 6, 1998, p. 94.

42. Interview with a small-scale investor, Oct. 1997.

43. Interview with a Tamil Nadu government official, Aug. 1997.

44. Parasarthy, "Best States to Invest in: A BT-Gallup-MBA Survey," *Business Today*, Dec. 22–Jan. 6, 1998, p. 88.

45. See Chapter 5.

46. This figure is an approximate figure drawn from GITCO (1996, 7).

47. Some estates, such as Ankleshwar and Panoli (Gujarat), are not limited to small

units, but also contain medium and larger-scale enterprises. Moreover, after liberalization (1991), many large-scale companies set up units in industrial estates.

48. Naroda (Ahmedabad) and Anand in Gujarat; Kalyani and Diamond Harbor Industrial area (Calcutta) in West Bengal; and Guindy (Chennai) in Tamil Nadu.

49. In addition, I also consulted the annual reports of the state agencies that pertain to the industrial estates (GIDC, WBIDC, and TIDCO) and committee reports on industrial estates.

50. I discovered this survey much later in my field research, so it serves as a good check for my own survey results.

51. Here, it must be noted that the respondents did not have a comparative sense, as they had not visited industrial estates in other states. I, in contrast, visited industrial estates across the states within a space of six months. I did find comparative statewide maintenance differences. Gujarat's internal roads were better than roads in Calcutta's estates. In Tamil Nadu, the roads were in quite good shape. In Maharashtra the roads within industrial estates were in good shape.

52. Interview, Oct. 1997.

53. Interview, Oct. 1997.

54. A recent High Court judgment ordered many industrial estates to close down until effluent disposal plants could be established. This led GIDC to change its earlier liberal policy toward pollution control. In some recently established estates, GIDC is thinking of establishing collective effluent management plants for the whole estate. Interview, May 1997.

55. I discuss the nature of corruption in the next section, "Micro-Regulatory Costs at the State Level," in greater detail.

56. Interview with a CEO of a large-scale firm.

57. Cover story, "The Best States to Invest In: A BT-Gallup-MBA Survey," *Business Today,* June 7–21, 1996, p. 98.

58. Some of these questions are modified from Borner, Brunetti, and Weder 1995.

59. The notion of credibility originated in the literature on monetary policy.

60. This tells us that the costs of information collection have a direct impact on the extent of credibility.

61. In 1994 the Left Front government came out with a new industrial policy and many other institutional changes.

62. Interview, Calcutta, Oct. 1997.

63. I asked him what his locational choices were based on. He said, "Of course, I do all the careful analysis about labor cost, raw materials, infrastructure but after a point, I go for a gut feeling about the future trajectory of a state."

64. The *Business Today* survey arrived at a measure of "Objective Rankings" in contrast to "Perception Rankings."

65. Cover feature, "The Ten Best States for Business," *Business India,* June 6–14, 1994, pp. 57–58.

66. Interviews, Chennai, Aug.–Sept. 1997.

67. Interviews with entrepreneurs based in Gujarat, April–May 1997.

68. Interviews with investors, Gujarat, May 1997.

69. Interview with a manager of a large-scale company, Calcutta, Oct. 1997.

70. Cover feature, "The Ten Best States for Business," *Business India,* June 6–14, 1994, p. 58.

71. Ibid.

72. Interview with an investor, May 1997 (emphasis added).

73. Interview with an investor based in Tamil Nadu, Oct. 1997.

74. Interview, Madras, Sept. 1997.

75. I don't address here the question of what creates or sustains the "professional" or "accountable" types of corruption across these states within India, a subject that deserves further research.

76. Interview with an investor, Gujarat, April 1997.

77. See Baron 1996, one of the few textbooks to pay attention to the nonmarket "environment" of business, rather than fixating on market environment as do the traditional economic textbooks.

8. Comparative Extensions

1. This research strategy's strength lies in "identifying causal mechanisms that repeat themselves across broad ranges of variation and concatenate differently with other mechanisms and environmental factors" (Tarrow 1999, 10).

2. I focus on economic and industrial policy in each of the nation-states.

3. The conclusions of this analysis could also be applied to small but territorially complex states such as Italy and Spain. For attention to subnational variables see Locke 1995 for Italy, Herrigel 1996 for Germany, and Montero 2001b for Spain. Few scholars have also explored the role of territorial variables in unitary and relatively homogeneous states. See Richard J. Samuels 1983 for Japan, Anderson 1992 for the United Kingdom and Germany, and Gourevitch 1980 for France. Also see Tarrow, Katzenstein, and Graziano 1978.

4. In Chapter 2, I put forward this concept, "polyarchy," combining "polycentric" and "hierarchy," to denote a multilevel state.

5. See Bensel 2000 for an analysis of the United States in the nineteenth century that pays attention to the political economy of uneven regional development. Also, see Bensel 1984.

6. In conventional analysis, recognition of the compulsion of political stability and regime continuity is seen to be limited to authoritarian elites, while democracies are presumed to be bedeviled by problems of legitimacy. However, in large and territorially divided states (irrespective of regime type), imperatives of stability, arising from challenges from the periphery, are tied to questions of legitimacy and extract a direct response from national rulers.

7. Scholars are divided over characterizing Brazil and India as either strong or weak. The Brazilian state has been considered to have been a strong state in the late nineteenth century (Topik 1988) and a weak (Weyland 1998), or alternatively an intermediate, state in the 1980s and 1990s (Evans 1995). Similarly, scholars on India are as divided. Some suggest that India is a strongly interventionist state (Bhagwati and Desai 1970; Isher Ahluwalia 1985; Krueger 2000) or an overdeveloped state (Alavi 1982); others see it as a soft state (Myrdal 1968) or as a failed developmental state (Herring 1999). Rudolph and Rudolph explicitly note the contradictory nature of the Indian state (1987).

8. The Soviet Union comprised fifteen Union republics, more than a hundred oblasti and regions, and forty thousand local governments. The degree of centralization and state power was enormously greater in the FSU than in any comparable period in post-independence Indian history. For a comparative analysis of linguistic and ethnic conflict in India and FSU, see Brass 1991, ch. 8.

9. Also see Taubman 1973 for an analysis of Soviet cities.

10. Also see Breslauer 1984.

11. This is similar to the "ratchet effect," a term coined by Berliner (1952) in his analy-

sis of management behavior in Soviet firms. Under central planning, managers are given strong incentives to overfill the plan, and each additional percent of overfilling would be rewarded by additional bonuses. Despite this strong incentive, managers failed to take this opportunity, as they were afraid that the next year's plan would be ratcheted up if they used all their capacity. This amounted to managers' hiding true productivity, leading, in addition, to misinformation. While outlined here in the context of Soviet planning, a similar dynamic may be found in many dirigiste societies, where agents' interests diverge from those of the principal.

12. Cited in Gleason 1990, 77.

13. In many Central Asian republics, the local leaders' interest lay in preventing industrialization, as they feared that premature industrialization would, by producing in-migration of skilled Russians from outside, overwhelm the local population (Zimmer 1986, cited in Gleason 1990, 86).

14. See, for a selective sample, Oi 1999; Shirk 1993, 1994; Baum and Shevchenko 1999; Wong 1991, 1992; Perry 1994; Hao and Zhimin 1994; Whiting 2001; Remick 2002; and Yang 1991, 1996, 1997.

15. Also see Tsai (2002), who also addresses the paradox of local variation in developmental patterns. Importantly, similar to Remick (2002), she also makes a path-dependent argument about how Mao-era legacies have influenced the present-day orientation of local governments toward the private sector (and in turn, informal finance).

16. See Oi 1999, 95. Also see Riskin 1987; Hao and Zhimin 1994; and Huang 1994.

17. Granick's analysis points toward extensive local autonomy during the Mao period itself. Other scholars argue that while Mao's period saw greater decentralization than in the Soviet Union, local autonomy was circumscribed by hierarchical controls, most notably of appointment and recruitment, exercised by the Chinese Communist party state (Shirk 1993, 150).

18. Also see Rosen 1992, 35–36.

19. Also see Schurmann 1966 and Shue 1988.

20. Many scholars have noted this contrast. See Oi 1999, 96.

21. Victor Nee's (1992) position on the sources of changes in the Chinese economy has changed over time. In his 1992 piece he saw the emergence of hybrid forms more akin to the local state corporatism outlined by Oi.

22. These differences may themselves be explained in terms of the local elites' perceptions of their own careers and reputations. See Shue (1988, 56), whose arguments about the persistence of "nested" vertical interaction between the center and the localities resonate with the arguments in this book.

23. See Fewsmith 1994 for an account of debates and divisions among the elite on the question of economic reform from 1978 to 1989.

24. This section relies on a number of excellent studies on Brazil; a few are Evans 1979, 1995; Schneider 1991; Hagopian 1996; Samuels 2000; and Montero 2001a, 2001b. Personal conversations with Fran Hagopian, Scott Mainwaring, and Francisco Zapata also were extremely useful.

25. The one difference between the two political economies is the role of foreign firms. Brazil incorporated foreign firms extensively, while India was hostile to foreign and multinational firms. In the 1970s and 1980s, many MNCs left India (Encarnation 1989), while in Brazil the 1960s saw alliances between local, national, and foreign firms (Evans 1979).

26. A term used in Brazil to describe the ambitions of the state vis-à-vis the economy. The state-led strategy of industrialization began with Kubitschek's Plano De Metas in 1956, but the military regime (1964–85) marks the full consolidation of that trajectory. It was at this time that "grande" was used to describe the government's developmental strategy. In

India, Nehru in a similar way talked of rebuilding the Indian economy and making the public sector the "commanding heights" of the Indian economy.

27. Weyland's description of Brazil as Gulliver is strikingly similar to Bardhan's description of the Indian state. Weyland says: "Starting out as a powerful Leviathan in the 1940s, Brazil's developmental state ended up as an obese, uncoordinated Gulliver, unable to turn its weight into strength and tied down by innumerable bonds to narrow interest groups and clientelist networks" (1998, 53). In Brazil the decline in state capacity is seen to occur in the late 1970s, while in India it began in the late 1960s.

28. See Love 1971 for a fascinating historical study of ebbs and flows of the fortunes of provinces in Brazil that focuses on southern states (São Paulo, Minas Gerais, and Rio Grande do Sul), especially Rio Grande do Sul.

29. See Hagopian 1996, ch. 4 and conclusion.

30. Sarney was elected the state governor in 1965. He made a conscious attempt to attract infrastructure programs from the federal government, linking the development of the state to capitalist agriculture and succeeding in redirecting federal largesse to what was till then an undeveloped province. His program transformed Maranhão's economic and social landscape (Ames 2001, 123-25).

31. Antoni Carlos Magalhaes (ACM) was made Bahia's governor in 1970 by the military. In his gubernatorial term of 1978-82 he used his links with the military president, Figueiredo, to attract key industrial projects and federal transfers. These included a petrochemical complex and federal grants amounting to 25 percent of the state total receipts (Ames 2001, 131).

32. Putnam (1993), Kohli (1987), and Mitra (1992), by focusing on democracies, assume that linkage. Remick 2002 also makes this point.

33. *New York Times*, Jan. 25, 1999.

34. Many scholars on Brazilian democratization have noted that the sequence of elections in the early transition period affected the subsequent power of subnational provinces. Samuels and Abrucio, drawing from Linz and Stepan's comparative arguments (1992), argue that "because Brazil had subnational elections prior to national elections during its transition, the political elite's electoral energies focused on state politics and the conquest of state offices, to the detriment of national parties" (Samuels and Abrucio 2000, 54). Montero (2000) makes a similar point. The sequencing of elections in post-Soviet Russia confirms this hypothesis: Yeltsin conducted subnational elections in 1992-93 before presidential elections.

35. Contemporary Russia is a large and multilayered federation. It is divided into 89 subunits. Among these, 21 are republics, named after one or more non-Russian ethnicity; 49 oblasts are provinces, and 6 krais are territories. In addition, there are two federal cities, Moscow and St. Petersburg; 10 autonomous okrugs; and one autonomous oblast. These autonomous okrugs and oblasts are like republics, based on titular nationalities.

36. Cited in Treisman 2001, 2.

37. They define regionalist sentiment as the "belief that regions should have more (than the center) control over their own destinies" (Andrews and Stoner-Weiss 1995).

38. Solnick (2000) in a similar way notes that Russian regions' flirtations with secession by units within the Russian federation were brief, and republics sought to "elevate their status within the federation" rather than exit from it. This suggests that the discourse of confrontational threats is a strategy of rhetoric. It also suggests that the target for such a strategy of one-upmanship might be the regional constituents or regional public opinion rather than the center; with the separation of political arenas (subnational and national), such Janus-faced behavior on the part of regional elites will be enhanced.

39. I would characterize them in a more general way: as pro-center and anti-center.

40. I thank one anonymous reviewer for comments on this point.

9. Conclusion

1. Most recently, Richard Snyder has stressed the reregulation of neoliberal policies unleashed by subnational actors in Mexico (2001a). However, I differ with him in identifying the source for such reregulation. His argument stresses that neoliberalism vacates policy space at the national level, enabling subnational elites to reregulate policy arenas that until then were occupied by the central state. I argue, in contrast, that state regulation itself invites diverse subnational and societal actors to reregulate central polices, inserting their agendas into central policy frameworks. Snyder argues, "In cases of robust federalism, where local governments are weakly constrained by the center, the dynamics of re-regulation may vary widely at the subnational level. Brazil exemplifies robust federalism. By contrast, in more centralized federal systems, such as Argentina, India, and China, regulation processes may vary to a lesser degree across subnational units" (2001a, 208). My analysis of subnational reregulation processes in India, a centralized system, shows that that expectation is misplaced. In my framework, centralized systems may invite *greater* reregulation than decentralized systems, as regional elites' interests conflict more directly with national plans.

2. This generalization holds irrespective of regime type and the extent of centralization in a polity.

3. The challenge to the realist assumptions of international relations theories began in the 1970s, largely conducted in the pages of *International Organization*. The classic texts include Katzenstein 1978 (see introduction and conclusion); Gourevitch 1978, 1986; and Allison and Zelikow 1999.

4. This is modeled as a two-level game; the model can be found in the Appendix of the book.

5. This result resonates with the literature on varieties of capitalism. See Hollingsworth and Boyer 1997; Hall and Soskice 2001; and Kitschelt et al. 1999. Ostrom's concept of "co-production" is a similar idea; see McGinnis 1999, 2000, 2001.

6. In contrast to the first-generation scholarship that stressed what Evans has called the "Great Divide" in political economy, the second generation focuses more on synergistic linkages between states and markets. See the special issue of *World Development* titled "Government Action, Social Capital and Development: Creating Synergy Across the Public-Private Divide" (June 1996) for a number of articles on this theme. See also De Janvry, Sadoulet, and Thorbecke 1995; Dutt, Kim, and Singh 1994.

7. Vivienne Shue, in a similar way, characterizes post-Maoist China as a web (1988, 131).

8. A rational economic incentive would imply that regional elites would prefer to get more economic resources from the center and thus pursue pro-center strategies.

9. The European Union, it might be argued, is a polyarchy, or polycentric hierarchy, as are India, China, Russia, and Brazil.

10. Skowronek's pathbreaking study of state formation in the United States defines the organizational characteristics of states as "(1) the concentration of authority at the national center of government; (2) the penetration of institutional controls from the governmental center throughout the territory; (3) the centralization of authority within the national government; and (4) the specialization of institutional tasks and individual roles within the government" (1982, 20).

11. The other Weberian characteristic of state formation is bureaucratization arising out of rationalization of authority.

12. See Spruyt 1994 for an important study in this genre; his purpose is to ask "How did the sovereign state emerge? How has its rise affected international relations?" (1). Studies of war making and state making also focus on international dimensions of statehood (Tilly

1990). For an exception that looks at how war affects local communities, see Kenneth Gregory Lawson, "War in the Grassroots: The Great War and the Nationalization of Civic Life" (Ph.D. dissertation, University of Washington, 2000).

13. See also Migdal, Kohli, and Shue 1994 for an elaboration of the state-in-society approach.

14. The classic study in this genre is Shonfield 1965, but it has spawned a vast literature. A few important contributions are Katzenstein 1985, Zysman 1983, and Hall 1986.

15. Snyder 1999, Locke 1995, and Herrigel 1996.

16. One exception is Treisman 2001.

17. Nee and Stark with Selden 1989; and Evans 1996.

18. Similar methodological modifications are implicitly suggested by a body of research in comparative politics. See Kohli 1987, Mitra 1992, Locke 1995, Herrigel 1996, and Stoner-Weiss 1997. There is not enough explicit methodological discussion on the "cross-national bias" in comparative politics. A few exceptions are Linz and de Miguel 1966, Fredrickson 1997, and Snyder 2001b.

19. Following Tarrow, I make a distinction between politics *about* territory and "politics about other issues that are fought out *across* territory" (1978, 1; emphasis in original). Till now, I was concerned with the latter, but in this section I explore how territory or size affects political economy.

20. In 1999 China's population was 20.9 percent of the world population, while India's population was 16.6 percent. China's area is 6.4 percent of total world area, while India's is 2.2 percent. Russia, the largest country in the world, has 11.6 percent of total world area, while Brazil's area is 5.7 percent of total world area. Market size may be observed by the PPP (purchasing power parity) gross national income rather than gross national income. PPP figures for 2000 are India—$2,432 billion, $2,390 per capita; Russia—$1,168 billion, $8,030 per capita; Brazil—$1,245 billion, $7,320 per capita (World Bank 2001).

21. Richard J. Samuels also looks at the operation of a regional policy in Japan (1983).

Appendix

1. Such actions have been witnessed at various times in India. After every decision to locate any project in a province, some regional leaders raised the issue of center-state discrimination. West Bengal has done this repeatedly. Other states that have confronted the center are Tamil Nadu, Punjab, Assam, and Kerala.

2. One can make the two regional states move simultaneously, a more plausible behavioral assumption, but for the sake of simplicity, they are seen to move sequentially.

3. Daniel Treisman (1996) similarly models the federal situation in Russia. For a more complete game, this needs to be modeled as a game between the regional leader and the constituents of that region. That will reveal the conditions under which regionalist sentiments arise from within the regional states.

4. In the Indian system each project generates taxes with two components, one that accrues to the regional states and another that accrues to the central government.

5. See Amsden 1989.

6. In India, this situation has existed since 1967 and more strongly since 1977, as many states are ruled by opposition party governments.

Works Cited

Newspapers and Magazines Consulted

Business India, 1991–99
Business Line, 1995–2004
Business Standard, 1995–99
Business Today, 1995–2004
Economic Times, 1990–98
Economist, 1990–2002
India Abroad
Ganashakti, 1977–79, 1994–99
Hindu (Madras edition), 1996–99
Times of India
Times of India (Ahmedabad edition), 1981–89
Times of India (Delhi edition), 1996–2004
The Statesman, 1997–2004

Primary Documents, Official Publications, and Government Documents

Annual Survey of India. 1965. Old Series. *Summary Results of the Factory Sector.* New Delhi: Central Statistical Organization, Government of India.
Annual Survey of Industries. Various Years. *Summary Results of the Factory Sector, New Series.* New Delhi: Central Statistical Organization, Government of India.
Bakshi, P. M., ed. 1996. *The Constitution of India.* New Delhi: Universal Law Publishing Co. Ltd.
Basu, Jyoti. 1981. *Chief Minister's Letters to the Central Government.* Vol. 1. Calcutta: Government of West Bengal.
———. 1982. *Chief Minister's Letters to the Central Government: Other Important Letters.* Vol. 2. Calcutta: Government of West Bengal.
———. 1984. *Address by Basu: Conference of Political Parties and Chief Ministers in Calcutta.* Calcutta: Government of West Bengal.
———. 1997. *People's Power in Practice: 20 Years of Left Front in West Bengal.* Calcutta: National Book Agency Private Ltd.
Bureau of Public Enterprises. 1960–89. *Annual Report on the Working of the Industrial and Commercial Undertakings of the Central Government or Public Enterprise Survey.* New Delhi: Government of India.

Commerce. 1973–74. *Commerce Yearbook of the Public Sector.* Bombay: Commerce.
——. 1975. *Commerce Yearbook of the Public Sector.* Bombay: Commerce.
——. 1976. *Commerce Yearbook of the Public Sector.* Bombay: Commerce.
——. 1986. *Commerce Yearbook of the Public Sector.* Bombay: Commerce.
Government of Andhra Pradesh. 1999. *Vision 2020: Industrial Policy of Andhra Pradesh.* Hyderabad: Government of Andhra Pradesh.
Government of Gujarat. 1960. *Fertilizer Project for Gujarat.* Ahmedabad: Gujarat Fertilizer Production Committee, Government of Gujarat.
——. 1970. *Gujarat: Ten Eventful Years.* Ahmedabad: Government of Gujarat.
——. 1972. *The Perspective Plan of Gujarat, 1974–1984.* Baroda (Gujarat): Government Press.
——. 1989. *Overseas Indian Business and Technology Exposition at New York, USA: Tour Report of the Gujarat Team.* Ahmedabad: Government of Gujarat.
——. 1994. *Report of the Gujarat State Finance Commission.* Ahmedabad: State Finance Commission, Government of Gujarat.
——. 1995. *Gujarat 2000 A.D. and Beyond.* Gandhinagar: Government of Gujarat.
Government of India. 1949. *First Census of Manufactures, Statistics by Industries and Provinces 1946.* Vol. 1. New Delhi: Government of India Press.
——. 1950. *White Paper on Indian States.* New Delhi: Government of India.
——. 1953. *First Five-Year Plan.* New Delhi: Planning Commission.
——. 1956a. *Second Five-Year Plan.* New Delhi: Planning Commission.
——. 1956b. *Industrial Policy Resolution.* Delhi: Government of India Press.
——. 1956c. *Census of Manufactures, 1956.* Delhi: Government of India Press.
——. 1969. *"Industrial Licensing Policy Inquiry Committee Report (ILPIC)."* New Delhi: Department of Industrial Development.
——. 1974. *Annual Report, 1973–1974.* New Delhi: Ministry of Industrial Development.
——. 1974–90. *Data on Letters of Intents.* Unpublished: Ministry of Industry.
——. 1980. *"Report on Industrial Dispersal, National Committee on the Development of Backward Areas."* New Delhi: Planning Commission.
——. 1982. *"Evaluation Report on Concessional Finance and Other Incentives in Industrially Backward Areas."* New Delhi: Planning Commission.
——. 1991. *Statement on Industrial Policy, 1991.* New Delhi: Government of India.
——. 1996–97. *Economic Survey.* New Delhi: Ministry of Finance.
——. 1997. *SIA Newsletter.* New Delhi: Government of India.
——. 2001. *Handbook of Industrial Policy.* New Delhi: Government of India.
——. Various Years. *Quarterly Bulletin of Industrial Statistics.* New Delhi: Government of India.
Government of Tamil Nadu. 1971. *"Report of the Centre-State Relations Inquiry Committee (Rajamannar Report)."* Madras: Government of Tamil Nadu.
——. 1989. *Incentives.* Madras: Government of Tamil Nadu.
Government of West Bengal. 1971. *The West Bengal Incentive Scheme, 1971.* Alipore (West Bengal): Government of West Bengal Press.
——. 1975a. *"Evaluation Report on Industrial Estates in West Bengal."* Calcutta: Planning Department.
——. 1975b. *Annual Review.* Calcutta: Government of West Bengal Press.
——. 1977. *Guidelines for Cottage and Small-Scale Industries.* Calcutta: Directorate, Cottage and Small Scale Industries Department.

——. 1978. *Industrial Policy.* Alipore: Government of West Bengal Press.

——. 1982. *Reply to the Questionnaire to the Commission on Centre-State Relations.* Calcutta: Department of Information and Cultural Affairs.

——. 1983. *"Report of the Administrative Reforms Committee."* Calcutta: Home Department.

——. 1984. *West Bengal's Incentives and Opportunities for New Industries in West Bengal, 1984.* Alipore (West Bengal): Government of West Bengal Press.

——. 1994a. *Policy Statement on Industrial Development.* Calcutta: Government of West Bengal.

——. 1994b. *Memorandum on the Reconstitution of Silpa Bandhu,* Oct. 6, 1994.

——. Various Years. *A Review of Industry in West Bengal.* Calcutta: Government of West Bengal.

Government of West Bengal, Industry Department. 1989. *Review of Industrial Scene in West Bengal.* Calcutta: Government of West Bengal.

Government of West Bengal, Information and Cultural Affairs Department. 1978. *Industrial Policy for West Bengal.* Calcutta: Government of West Bengal.

——. 1985. *Left Front Government after Eight Years.* Calcutta: Government of West Bengal.

——. 1986. *Left Front Government's Nine Years.* Calcutta: Government of West Bengal.

——. 1989. *Review of Industrial Scene in West Bengal.* Calcutta: Government of West Bengal.

Guidance, Government of Tamil Nadu. 1994. *Incentives of Tamil Nadu.* Madras: Government of Tamil Nadu.

Gujarat Chamber of Commerce and Industry. 1988. *Memorandum to Shri Rajiv Gandhi Regarding the Establishment of Central Industrial Projects in Gujarat.* Ahmedabad: Gujarat Chamber of Commerce and Industry.

Gujarat Industrial and Technical Consultancy Organization Limited (GITCO). 1996. *Economic Survey of GIDC Estates.* Ahmedabad: Gujarat Industrial and Technical Consultancy Organization Limited. (Prepared for Gujarat Industrial Development Corporation).

Gujarat Industrial Development Corporation (GIDC). 1972. *Annual Report.* Ahmedabad: GIDC.

Gujarat Legislative Assembly. 1962. *Gujarat Industrial Development Act. 1962.* Ahmedabad: Gujarat Industrial Development Corporation.

Hazari, R. K. 1967. *"Industrial Planning and Licensing Policy."* Planning Commission, New Delhi.

iNDEXTb. 1977. *Gujarat's New Package of Financial Incentives, 1977-1982.* Ahmedabad: iNDEXTb, Government of Gujarat.

——. 1982. *Gujarat Presents a Winning Combination: Attractive Incentives + A Congenial Industrial Environment 1982-1987.* Ahmedabad: iNDEXTb, Government of Gujarat.

——. 1986. *Gujarat Like Nowhere Else in India, 1986-1991.* Ahmedabad: iNDEXTb, Government of Gujarat.

——. 1989. *Business and Technology Exposition at New York, USA: Tour Report of the Gujarat Team.* Ahmedabad: iNDEXTb, Government of Gujarat.

——. 1996. *Agenda Items: 67th meeting of the Governing Body of the Industrial Extension Bureau.* Ahmedabad: iNDEXTb, Government of Gujarat.

Indian Institute of Foreign Trade (IIFT). 1987. *Report of the Workshop on "Role of States in Export Promotion."* New Delhi: Indian Institute of Foreign Trade.

Indian Investment Center. 1972. *West Bengal: Potential for Industrial Investment.* New Delhi: Indian Investment Center (Government of India).

Maharashtra Legislative Assembly. 1960. *Maharashtra Industrial Development Corporation Act, 1960.* Bombay: Maharashtra Industrial Development Corporation.

PHD Chamber of Commerce and Industry (PHDCCI). 1985a. *State-Level Incentives.* New Delhi: PHDCCI.

———. 1985b. *Incentives to Industry: An Inter-State Comparison.* New Delhi: PHDCCI.

Ramakrishna Report. 1978. *Report of the Study Group on Industrial Regulations and Procedures.* New Delhi: Department of Industrial Development, Ministry of Industry, Government of India.

Registrar General and Census Commissioner of India. 1981. *Census of India.* New Delhi: Registrar General.

———. 1991. *Census of India.* New Delhi: Registrar General.

Registrar of Newspapers for India. *Press in India, 1965.* Part I: 9th Annual Report, Ministry of Information and Broadcasting, Government of India, 1965.

State Promotional Corporation of Tamil Nadu (SIPCOT). n.d. *On the Industrial Horizon: Our Guiding Star.* Madras: SIPCOT.

West Bengal Legislative Assembly. 1967. *Memorandum and Articles of Association of WBIDC, 1967.* Calcutta: West Bengal Industrial Development Corporation.

Secondary Sources

Ahluwalia, Isher J. 1985. *Industrial Growth in India: Stagnation Since the Mid 1960s.* Delhi: Oxford University Press.

———. 1991. *Productivity and Growth in Indian Manufacturing.* Oxford: Oxford University Press.

Ahluwalia, Montek Singh. 2000. "The Economic Performance of the States in the Post-Reforms Period." *Economic and Political Weekly* 35, no. 19: 1637–48.

Ahn, Byung-joon. 1976. *Chinese Politics and the Cultural Revolution: Dynamics of Policy Process.* Seattle: University of Washington Press.

Akerlof, George A. 1970. "The Market for 'Lemons': Quality Uncertainty and the Market Mechanism." *Quarterly Journal of Economics* 84, no. 3: 488–500.

Alavi, Hamza. 1982. "State and Class under Peripheral Capitalism." In Hamza Alavi and T. Shanin, eds., *Introduction to the Sociology of Developing Societies.* London: Macmillan.

Allison, Graham, and Philip Zelikow. 1999. *Essence of Decision: Exploring the Cuban Missile Crisis.* 2nd ed. New York: Longman.

Alston, Lee J., Thrain Eggertsson, and Douglass North, eds. 1996. *Empirical Studies in Institutional Change.* Cambridge: Cambridge University Press.

Ames, Barry. 2001. *The Deadlock of Democracy in Brazil.* Ann Arbor: University of Michigan Press.

Amsden, Alice. 1989. *Asia's Next Giant: South Korea and Late Industrialization.* New York: Oxford University Press.

Anderson, J. J. 1992. *The Territorial Imperative: Pluralism, Corporatism and Economic Crisis.* Cambridge: Cambridge University Press.

Andrews, Josephine, and Kathryn Stoner-Weiss. 1995. "Regionalism and Reform in Provincial Russia." *Post-Soviet Russia* 11, no. 4: 384–406.

Aoki, Masahiko. 1988. *Information, Incentives, and Bargaining in the Japanese Economy.* Cambridge and New York: Cambridge University Press.

Appleby, Paul. 1953. *Public Administration in India, Report of a Survey.* New Delhi: Government of India.

Arnold, R. Douglas. 1988. "Legislators, Bureaucrats and Locational Decisions." In Mathew McCubbins and Terry Sullivan, eds., *Congress: Structure and Policy.* Cambridge, Mass.: Cambridge University Press.

Arrow, Kenneth J. 1998. "The Place of Institutions in the Economy: A Theoretical Perspective." In Y. Hayami and M. Aoki, eds., *The Institutional Foundations of East Asian Economic Development.* New York: Macmillan Press.

Baer, Werner, Richard Newfarmer, and Thomas Trebat. 1976. "On State Capitalism in Brazil: Some New Issues and Questions." *Inter-American Economic Affairs* 30 (Winter): 69–96.

Bagchi, Amiya K. 1972. *Private Investment in India 1900–1939.* Cambridge: Cambridge University Press.

———. 1976. "Reflections on the Pattern of Regional Growth in India." *Bengal Past and Present* 95, no. 1: 247–89.

Bagchi, Amiya K., and Nirmala Banerjee, eds. 1981. *Change and Choice in Indian Industry.* Calcutta: K. P. Bagchi and Co.

Bahry, Donna. 1987. *Outside Moscow: Power, Politics and Budgetary Policy in the Soviet Republics.* New York: Columbia University Press.

———. 1991. "The Union Republics and Contradictions in Gorbachev's Economic Reform." *Soviet Economy* 7: 215–55.

Banerjee, Debdas, and Anjan Ghosh. 1988. "Indian Planning and Regional Disparity in Growth." In Amiya Bagchi, ed., *Economy, Society and Polity: Essays in the Political Economy of Indian Planning.* Calcutta: Oxford University Press.

Bardhan, Pranab. 1984. *The Political Economy of Development in India.* Oxford: Blackwell.

———. 1992. "A Political-Economy Perspective on Development." In Bimal Jalan, ed., *The Indian Economy: Problems and Prospects.* New Delhi: Penguin Books.

———. 1995a. "The Nature of Institutional Impediments to Economic Development." IRIS Conference Paper. College Park: IRIS Center, University of Maryland.

———. 1995b. "The Contributions of Endogenous Growth Theory to the Analysis of Development Problems: An Assessment." In J. Behrman and T. N. Srinivasan, eds., *Handbook of Development Economics.* Vol. 3. Amsterdam, N.Y.: Elsevier Science.

Barnett, Marguerite Ross. 1976. *The Politics of Cultural Nationalism in South India.* Princeton, N.J.: Princeton University Press.

Baron, David. 1996. *Business and Its Environment.* 2nd ed. Upper Saddle River, N.J.: Prentice Hall.

Barro, Robert. 1991. "Economic Growth in a Cross-section of Countries." *Quarterly Journal of Economics* 106: 407–43.

Barro, Robert, and David Gordon. 1983. "Rules, Discretion and Reputation in a Model of Monetary Policy." *Journal of Monetary Economics* 12: 101–22.

Baru, Sanjaya. 1990. *The Political Economy of Indian Sugar: State Intervention and Structural Change.* Delhi and New York: Oxford University Press.

———. 2000. "Economic Policy and the Development of Capitalism in India: The Role of Regional Capitalists and Political Parties." In Francine R. Frankel, ed., *Transforming India: Social and Political Dynamics of Democracy.* New Delhi and New York: Oxford University Press.

Basu, Kaushik. 1992. "Markets, Laws and Governments." In Bimal Jalan, ed., *The Indian Economy: Problems and Prospects.* New Delhi: Penguin.

Bates, Robert. 1988. "Social Dilemmas and Rational Individuals: An Assessment of the New Institutionalism." In John Harriss, Janet Hunter, and Colin Lewis, eds., *The New Institutional Economics and Third World Development.* London: Routledge.

Baum, Richard, and Alexei Shevchenko. 1999. "The State of the State." In Merle Goldman and Roderick Macfaruhar, eds., *The Paradox of China's Post-Mao Reforms.* Cambridge, Mass.: Harvard University Press.

BCCI (Bengal Chamber of Commerce and Industry). 1971. *West Bengal: An Analytical Study.* Calcutta: Oxford University Press.

———. 1973. *Supplement to West Bengal: An Analytical Study.* Calcutta: Oxford University Press.

———. 1975. *Bengal: The Travail Continues.* New Delhi: Oxford and IBH Co.

———. 1982. *Eastern India: An Analytical Study.* New Delhi: Oxford and IBH Co.

Bensel, Richard. 1984. *Sectionalism and American Political Development: 1880–1980.* Madison: University of Wisconsin Press.

———. 2000. *The Political Economy of American Industrialization, 1877–1900.* Cambridge: Cambridge University Press.

Berger, Suzanne, and Ronald Dore, eds. 1996. *National Diversity and Global Capitalism.* Ithaca, N.Y.: Cornell University Press.

Berliner, Joseph. 1952. "The Informal Organization of the Soviet Firm." *Quarterly Journal of Economics* 66: 342–65.

Bhagwati, Jagdish. 1982. "Directly Unproductive Profit-Seeking (DUP) Activities." *Journal of Political Economy* 90, no. 5 (Oct.): 988–1002.

———. 1993. *India in Transition: Freeing the Economy.* Oxford: Clarendon.

———. 1998. *A Stream of Windows: Unsettling Reflections on Trade, Immigration, and Democracy.* Cambridge, Mass.: MIT Press.

———. 2000. *The Wind of the Hundred Days: How Washington Mismanaged Globalization.* Cambridge, Mass.: MIT Press.

Bhagwati, Jagdish, and Padma Desai. 1970. *India: Planning for Industrialization: Industrialization and Trade Policies since 1951.* London: Oxford University Press.

Bhagwati, J., and T. N. Srinivasan. 1975. *Foreign Trade Regimes and Economic Development: India.* New York: Columbia University Press.

———. 1984. "Indian Development Strategy: Some Comments." *Economic and Political Weekly,* Nov. 24, 1984, pp. 2006–2008.

Bharadwaj, Krishna. 1982. "Regional Differentiation in India: A Note." *Economic and Political Weekly* 17, nos. 14–16: 605–14.

Bharathan, K. 1985. *Development through Industrialization: An Analysis and Case-Study of Backward Area Development.* Madras: Madras Institute of Development Studies.

Bharti, R. K. 1978. *Industrial Estates in Developing Economies.* New Delhi: National.

Bhatt, Anil. 1970. "Caste and Political Mobilization in a Gujarat District." In Rajni Kothari, ed., *Caste and Politics in India.* New Delhi: Orient Longman Ltd.

Bhattacharya, Dwaipayan. 1999. "Politics of Middleness: The Changing Character of the Communist Party of India (Marxist) in Rural West Bengal (1977–1990)." In

Ben Rogaly, Barbara Harriss-White, and Sugata Bose, eds., *Sonar Bangla? Agricultural Growth and Agrarian Change in West Bengal and Bangladesh.* New Delhi: Sage.

Bhattacharya, N. C. 1967. "Leadership in the Communist Party of India." In Iqbal Narain, ed., *State Politics in India.* Meerut: Meenakshi Prakashan.

Biswas, Rongli, and Sugata Margit. 2002. "Political Lobbying and Fiscal Federalism: Case of Industrial Licenses and Letters of Intent." *Economic and Political Weekly* 27, no. 8: 716–25.

Borner, Silvio, Aymo Brunetti, and Beatrice Weder. 1995. *Political Credibility and Economic Development.* New York: St. Martin's Press.

Bramall, Chris. 2000. *Sources of Chinese Economic Growth, 1978–1996.* Oxford: Oxford University Press.

Brass, Paul. 1982. "Pluralism, Regionalism and Decentralizing Tendencies in Contemporary Indian Politics." In A. Jeyaratnam Wilson and D. Dalton, eds., *The States of South Asia: Problems of National Integration: Essays in Honor of W. H. Moriss-Jones.* London: C. Hurst and Co.

———. 1991. *Ethnicity and Nationalism: Theory and Comparison.* New Delhi, Newbury, and London: Sage.

———. 1994. *The Politics of India since Independence.* 2nd Indian ed. New Delhi: Cambridge University Press.

Breman, Jan. 1974. *Patronage and Exploitation: Changing Agrarian Relations in South Gujarat, India.* Berkeley: University of California Press.

———. 1985. *Of Peasants, Migrants and Paupers: Rural Labour Circulation and Capitalist Production in West India.* Delhi: Oxford University Press.

———. 1990. "Even Dogs Are Better Off: The On-going Battle between Capital and Labor in the Cane Fields of Gujarat." Occasional Papers and Reprints, Indian Council of Social Science Research, 1990.

———. 1993a. *Beyond Patronage and Exploitation: Changing Agrarian Relations in South Gujarat.* Delhi: Oxford University Press.

———. 1993b. "The Anti-Muslim Pogrom in Surat." *Economic and Political Weekly* 28, no. 16: 737–41.

———. 1994. *Wage Hunters and Gatherers: Search for Work in the Urban and Rural Economy of South Gujarat.* Delhi: Oxford University Press.

———. 1996. *Footloose Labour: Working in India's Informal Economy.* Cambridge: Cambridge University Press.

———. 2003. *The Labouring Poor in India: Patterns of Exploitation, Subordination and Exclusion.* New Delhi: Oxford University Press.

Breman, Jan, and Arvind Das. 2000. *Down and Out: Labouring under Global Capitalism.* New Delhi: Oxford University Press.

Breslauer, George. 1984. "Is There a Generation Gap in the Soviet Political Establishment? Demand Articulation by RSFSR Provincial Party Secretaries." *Soviet Studies* 36, no. 1: 1–25.

———. 1986. "Provincial Party Leaders' Demand Articulation and the Nature of Center-Periphery Relations in the USSR." *Slavic Review* 45, no. 4: 650–72.

Broomfield, J. H. 1968. *Elite Conflict in a Plural Society: Twentieth-Century Bengal.* Berkeley: University of California Press.

Buchanan, J. M., R. D. Tollison, and G. Tullock, eds. 1980. *Towards a Theory of the Rent-Seeking Society.* Austin: Texas A and M University Press.

Bueno de Mesquita, Bruce, and Hilton L. Root. 2000. *Governing for Prosperity*. New Haven, Conn.: Yale University Press.

Bueno de Mesquita, Bruce, and David Lalman. 1992. *War and Reason: Domestic and International Imperatives*. New Haven, Conn., and London: Yale University Press.

Butler, David, Ashok Lahiri, and Prannoy Roy. 1995. *India Decides: Elections 1952–1995*. New Delhi: Books and Things.

Byres, T. J., ed. 1994. *The State and Development Planning in India*. SOAS Studies On South Asia. Delhi: Oxford University Press.

Calvert, Randall L. 1985. "The Value of Biased Information: A Rational Choice Model of Political Advice." *Journal of Politics* 47: 530–55.

———. 1986. *Models of Imperfect Information in Politics*. Chur, Switzerland: Harwood Academic Publishers.

Campos, Jose Edgardo, and Hilton L. Root. 1996. *The Key to the Asian Miracle: Making Shared Growth Credible*. Washington, D.C.: Brookings Institution.

Chakravarty, Saroj. 1974. *With Dr. B. C. Roy and Other Chief Ministers (A Record up to 1962)*. Calcutta: Benson's.

———. 1978. *With West Bengal Chief Ministers: Memoirs 1962–1977*. New Delhi: Orient Longman.

Chakravarty, Sukhamoy. 1987. *Development Planning: The Indian Experience*. New Delhi: Oxford University Press.

———. 1994. "Problems of Plan Implementation." In Terence J. Byres, ed., *The State and Development Planning in India*. Delhi: Oxford University Press.

Chanda, Asok. 1965. *Federalism in India: A Study of Union-State Relations*. London: George Allen and Unwin Ltd.

Chatterjee, Partha. 1994. "Development Planning and the Indian State." In Terence J. Byres, ed., *The State and Development Planning in India*. Delhi: Oxford University Press.

———. 1997. *The Present History of West Bengal: Essays in Political Criticism*. Delhi: Oxford University Press.

Chatterji, Rakhahari. 1980. *Union, Politics and the State: A Study of Indian Labour Politics*. New Delhi: South Asian Publishers Pvt. Ltd.

Chattopadhya, B., and M. Raza. 1975. "Regional Development: Analytical Framework and Indicators." *Indian Journal of Regional Science* 7: 25–39.

Chaudhuri, Nirmal C. B. R. 1976. "West Bengal: The Vortex of Ideological Politics." In Iqbal Narain, ed., *State Politics in India*. Meerut: Meenakshi Prakashan.

Chhibber, Pradeep K., and John R. Petrocik. 1990. "Social Cleavages, Elections and the Indian Party System." In Richard Sisson and Ramashray Roy, eds., *Diversity and Dominance in Indian Politics*. Vol. 1: *Changing Bases of Congress Support*. New Delhi: Sage.

Chibber, Vivek. 2003. *Locked in Place: State-Building and Capitalist Industrialization in India, 1940–1970*. Princeton, N.J.: Princeton University Press.

Choudhury, Nanda K., and Salim Mansur, eds. 1994. *The Indira-Rajiv Years: The Indian Economy and Polity, 1966–1991*. Toronto: University of Toronto, Centre for South Asian Studies.

Choudhury, Profulla Roy. 1985. *Left Experiment in West Bengal*. New Delhi: Patriot Publishers.

Chung, Jae Ho. 1995. "Studies of Central-Provincial Relations in the PRC: A Midterm Appraisal." *China Quarterly* 142: 492–500.

——. 2000. *Central Control and Local Discretion in China: Leadership and Implementation during Post-Mao Decollectivization.* Oxford: Oxford University Press.

Clague, C., Philip Keefer, Stephen Knack, and Mancur Olson. 1995. "Contract-Intensive Money: Contract Enforcement, Property Rights and Economic Performance." IRIS Working Paper, No. 151. College Park: IRIS Center, University of Maryland.

CMIE (Centre for Monitoring the Indian Economy). 1978. *Shape of Things to Come.* Bombay: CMIE.

——. 1988. *Basic Statistics Relating to the Indian Economy.* Bombay: CMIE.

——. 1989. *Basic Statistics Relating to the Indian Economy.* Bombay: CMIE.

——. 1991. *Shape of Things to Come.* Bombay: CMIE.

——. 1997. *Profiles of States.* Bombay: CMIE.

——. Various Years. *Shape of Things to Come.* Bombay: CMIE.

Colander, David, ed., 1984. *Neoclassical Political Economy: The Analysis of Rent-Seeking and DUP Activities.* Cambridge, Mass.: Ballinger.

Collier, David. 1979. *The New Authoritarianism in Latin America.* Princeton, N.J.: Princeton University Press.

Crook, Richard C., and James Manor. 1998. *Democracy and Decentralization in South Asia and West Africa.* Cambridge: Cambridge University Press.

Dahl, Robert. 1971. *Polyarchy: Participation and Opposition.* New Haven, Conn., and London: Yale University Press.

Dahl, Robert A., and Edward R. Tufte. 1973. *Size and Democracy.* Stanford, Calif.: Stanford University Press.

Das, Gurcharan. 2001. *India Unbound: A Personal Account of a Social and Economic Evolution, from Independence to the Global Information Age.* New York: Alfred Knopf.

Dasgupta, Srimanto. n.d. "Industrialization in West Bengal: A Regional Perspective. State Planning Board." Unpublished manuscript.

Datta-Chaudhuri, Mrinal. 1990. "Market Failures and Government Failure." *Journal of Economic Perspectives* 4, no. 3: 25–40.

De Janvry, Alain, Elizabeth Sadoulet, and Erik Thorbecke, eds. 1995. *State, Market, and Civil Organizations: New Theories, New Practices, and Their Implications for Rural Development.* London: Macmillan.

Desai, I. P. 1981. "Anti-Reservation Agitation and Structure of Gujarat Society." *Economic and Political Weekly* 16, no. 18: 819–23.

Desai, K. D. 1965. "Socio-Economic Infrastructure of Gujarat Politics." In Iqbal Narain, ed., *State Politics in India.* Meerut: Meenakshi Prakashan.

Desai, Meghnad. 1995. "Economic Reform: Stalled by Politics?" In Philip Oldenburg, ed., *India Briefing: Staying the Course.* Boulder, Colo.: Westview Press.

Dhar, P. N. 1987. "The Political Economy of Development in India." *Indian Economic Review* 22, no. 1: 1–18.

Dickey, Sara. 1993a. "The Politics of Adulation: Cinema and the Production of Politicians in South India." *Journal of Asian Studies* 52, no. 2: 340–72.

——. 1993b. *Cinema and the Urban Poor in South India.* Cambridge: Cambridge University Press.

Doeringer, Peter B., and Paul Streeten. 1990. "How Economic Institutions Affect Economic Performance in Industrialized Countries: Lessons for Development." *World Development* 18: 1249–53.

Doner, Richard, and Eric Hershberg. 1999. "Flexible Production and Political Decentralization in the Developing World: Elective Affinities in the Pursuit of Competitiveness." *Studies in Comparative International Development* 34, no. 3: 45–82.

Downing, Brian M. 1992. *The Military Revolution and Political Change: Origins of Democracy and Autocracy in Early Modern Europe.* Princeton, N.J.: Princeton University Press.

Drèze, Jean, and Amartya Sen. 1997. *India: Economic Development and Social Opportunity.* New Delhi: Oxford University Press.

———. 2002. *India, Development and Participation.* New Delhi: Oxford University Press.

Dua, B. D. 1979. *Presidential Rule in India 1950–1974: A Study in Crisis Politics.* New Delhi: S. Chand and Co.

Dunlavy, Colleen A. 1994. *Politics and Industrialization: Early Railroads in the United States and Prussia.* Princeton, N.J.: Princeton University Press.

Dutt, Amitaya Krishna, Kwan S. Kim, and Ajit Singh, eds. 1994. *The States, Markets, and Development: Beyond the Neoclassical Dichotomy.* London: Edward Elgar.

Echeverri-Gent, John. 1993. *The State and the Poor: Public Policy and Political Development in India and United States.* Indian ed. New Delhi: Vistaar (Sage).

———. 2002. "India's Decentered Polity." In Alyssa Ayres and Philip Oldenburg, eds., *India Briefing, 2002.* Armonk, N.Y.: M. E. Sharpe.

Eckstein, Harry. 1971. "The Evaluation of Political Performance: Problems and Dimensions." *Sage Professional Papers in Comparative Politics* 2, serial no. 1–17, vol. 2, pp. 1–84.

Economist. 1991. "India: The Caged Tiger (A Survey of India)." May 4, pp. 1–18.

———. 1995. "The Tiger Steps Out (A Survey of India)." Jan. 21, pp. 1–30.

———. 2001. "India's Economic Reform, Ten Years On (A Survey of India)." June 2, pp. 1–22.

Edwards, Sebastian, and Guido Tabellini. 1991. "Political Stability, Political Weakness and Inflation: An Empirical Analysis." NBER Working Paper No. 3721.

Eisinger, Peter K. 1988. *The Rise of the Entrepreneurial State: State and Local Economic Development Policy in the US.* Madison: University of Wisconsin Press.

Elster, Jon. 1984. *Ulysses and the Sirens.* Rev. ed. Cambridge: Cambridge University Press.

Encarnation, Dennis J. 1989. *Dislodging Multinationals: India's Strategy in Comparative Perspective.* Ithaca, N.Y.: Cornell University Press.

Erdman, Howard L. 1967. *The Swatantra Party and Indian Conservatism.* Cambridge: Cambridge University Press.

———. 1971. *Political Attitudes of Indian Industry: A Case Study of the Baroda Business Elite.* London: Athlone Press.

———. 1973. *Politics and Economic Development in India: The Gujarat State Fertilizer Company as a Joint Sector Enterprise.* Delhi: D. K. Publishing House.

———. 1976. "The Industrialists." In Henry C. Hart, ed., *Indira Gandhi's India: A Political System Appraised.* Boulder, Colo.: Westview Press.

Ertman, Thomas. 1997. *Birth of the Leviathan: Building States and Regimes in Medieval and Early Modern Europe.* Cambridge: Cambridge University Press.

Evans, Peter. 1979. *Dependent Development: The Alliance of Multinational, State and Local Capital in Brazil.* Princeton, N.J.: Princeton University Press.

———. 1995. *Embedded Autonomy.* Princeton, N.J.: Princeton University Press.

———. 1996. "Government Action, Social Capital and Development: Reviewing the Evidence on Synergy." *World Development* 24, no. 6: 1119–32.

Evans, Peter B., Dietrich Rueschemeyer, and T. Skocpol, eds., 1985. *Bringing the State Back In.* New York: Cambridge University Press.

Evans, Peter, Harold K. Jacobson, and Robert Putnam, eds. 1993. *Double-Edged Diplomacy: International Bargaining and Domestic Politics.* Berkeley: University of California Press.

Fadia, Babulal. 1984. *State Politics in India.* Vol. 1. New Delhi: Radiant Publishers.

Feinberg, Richard, E. J. Echeverri-Gent, and F. Muller, eds. 1990. *Economic Reform in Three Giants.* New Brunswick, N.J.: Transaction Books.

Fernandez, R., and Dani Rodrik. 1998. "Resistance to Reform: Status Quo Bias in the Presence of Individual-Specific Uncertainty." In Federico Sturzenegger and Mariano Tommasi, eds., *The Political Economy of Reform.* Cambridge, Mass.: MIT Press.

Fewsmith, Joseph. 1994. *Dilemmas of Reform in China: Political Conflict and Economic Debate.* Armonk, N.Y.: M. E. Sharpe.

Findlay, R. 1990. "The New Political Economy Applied to Developing Countries." *Economics and Politics* 2, no. 2: 193-221.

Fischer, Stanley, and Alan Gelb. 1990. *Issues in Socialist Economy Reform.* Washington, D.C.: World Bank.

Fishlow, Albert. 1973. "Some Reflections on Post-1964 Brazilian Economic Policy." In Alfred Stepan, ed., *Authoritarian Brazil.* New Haven, Conn., and London: Yale University Press.

Forrester, Duncan. 1976. "Factions and Filmstars: Tamil Nadu Politics since 1971." *Asian Survey* 16, no. 3: 43-61.

Franda, Marcus F. 1968. *West Bengal and the Federalizing Process in India.* Princeton, N.J.: Princeton University Press.

———. 1971. *Radical Politics in West Bengal.* Cambridge, Mass.: MIT Press.

———. 1973. "Radical Politics in West Bengal." In Paul Brass and Marcus Franda, eds., *Radical Politics in South Asia.* Cambridge, Mass.: MIT Press.

Frankel, Francine R. 1978. *India's Political Economy, 1947-1977: The Gradual Revolution.* Princeton, N.J.: Princeton University Press.

Frankel, Francine R., and M. S. A. Rao, eds. 1989. *Dominance and State Power in Modern India.* 2 vols. Delhi and New York: Oxford University Press.

Fredrickson, George M. 1997. *The Comparative Imagination: On the History of Racism, Nationalism, and Social Movements.* Berkeley: University of California Press.

Friedman, Edward. 1998. "Development, Revolution, Democracy, and Dictatorship: China Versus India?" In Theda Skocpol, ed., *Democracy, Revolution and History.* Ithaca, N.Y.: Cornell University Press.

Furubotn, Erik G., and Rudolf Richter. 2000. *Institutions and Economic Theory: The Contribution of the New Institutional Economics.* Ann Arbor: University of Michigan Press.

Garrett, Geoffrey. 1998. *Partisan Politics in the Global Economy.* Cambridge and New York: Cambridge University Press.

George, K. K., and I. S. Gulati. 1985. "Central Inroads in States Subjects: An Analysis of Economic Services." Kerala, India: Centre for Development Studies.

Ghosh, B., Sugata Margit, and C. Neogi. 1998. "Economic Growth and Regional Divergence in India, 1960-1995." *Economic and Political Weekly* 33, no. 26 (June 27-July 3): 1623-30.

Gleason, Gregory. 1990. "Marketization and Migration: The Politics of Cotton in Central Asia." *Journal of Soviet Nationalities* 1, no. 2: 66-98.

Goldthorpe, John H., ed., 1984. *Order and Conflict in Contemporary Capitalism*. Oxford: Oxford University Press.

Goodin, Robert E., ed. 1996. *The Theory of Institutional Design*. Cambridge: Cambridge University Press.

Gordon, A. D. D. 1978. *Businessmen and Politics: Rising Nationalism and a Modernizing Economy in Bombay, 1918–1933*. New Delhi: Manohar Publications.

Gorter, Pieter. 1996. *Small Industrialists, Big Ambitions: Economic and Political Networks on a Large Industrial Estate in West India*. Indian ed. Delhi: Oxford University Press.

Goswami, Omkar. 1982. "Collaboration and Conflict: European and Indian Capitalists and the Jute Economy of Bengal, 1991–1939." *Indian Economic and Social History Review* 19, no. 2: 141–79.

——. 1985. "Then Came the Marwaris: Some Aspects of the Changes in the Pattern of Industrial Control in Eastern India." *Indian Economic and Social History Review* 22, no. 3: 225–49.

——. 1990. "Calcutta's Economy, 1918–1970: The Fall from Grace." In Sukanta Chaudhuri, ed., *Calcutta: The Living City*. Calcutta: Oxford University Press.

——. 1994. "Sahibs, Babus and Banias: Changes in Industrial Control in Eastern India, 1918–50." In Rajat K. Ray, ed., *Entrepreneurship and Industry in India, 1800–1947*. Delhi: Oxford University Press.

Gourevitch, Peter. 1978. "The Second Image Reversed: The International Sources of Domestic Politics." *International Organization* 32, no. 4: 881–912.

——. 1980. *Paris and the Provinces: The Politics of Local Government Reform in France*. Berkeley: University of California Press.

——. 1986. *Politics in Hard Times: Comparative Responses to International Economic Crisis*. Ithaca, N.Y.: Cornell University Press.

Granick, David. 1990. *Chinese State Enterprises: A Regional Property Rights Analysis*. Chicago: University of Chicago Press.

Grief, Avnar, Paul Milgrom, and Barry Weingast. 1994. "Coordination, Commitment and Enforcement: The Case of the Merchant Guild." *Journal of Political Economy* 102, no. 4: 745–75.

Haggard, Stephen. 1990. *Pathways from the Periphery: The Politics of Growth in the Newly Industrializing Countries*. Ithaca, N.Y.: Cornell University Press.

Hagopian, Frances. 1996. *Traditional Politics and Regime Change in Brazil*. Cambridge: Cambridge University Press.

Hall, Peter A. 1986. *Governing the Economy*. New York: Oxford University Press.

Hall, Peter A., and David Soskice, eds. 2001. *Varieties of Capitalism: The Institutional Foundations of Comparative Advantage*. Oxford: Oxford University Press.

Hanifa, Aziz. 2001. "Bureaucracy Is a Major Threat to India's Economic Ambitions." *India Abroad*, Sec. Business News, cols. 1–3, p. 38.

Hanson, A. H. 1966. *The Process of Planning*. London: Oxford University Press.

——. 1968. "Power Shifts and Regional Balances." In Paul Streeten and Michael Lipton, eds., *The Crisis of Indian Planning: Economic Planning in the 1960s*. London: Oxford University Press.

Hanson, Philip. 1991. "Soviet Economic Reform: Perestroika or Catostroika?" *World Policy Journal* 8, no. 2: 289–318.

Hao, Jia, and Lin Zhimin, eds. 1994. *Changing Central-Local Relations in China: Reform and State Capacity*. Boulder, Colo.: Westview Press.

Hardgrave, Robert. 1971. "The Celluloid God: MGR and the Tamil Film." *South Asian Review* 4, no. 4: 307–14.

———. 1973. "Politics and Film in Tamil Nadu: The Stars, and the DMK." *Asian Survey* 13, no. 3: 307–14.

———. 1979. "When Stars Displace the Gods: The Folk Culture of Cinema in Tamil Nadu." In Robert Hardgrave, *Essays in the Political Sociology of South India*. New Delhi: Usha Publications.

Hardgrave, Robert, and Anthony Niedhart. 1975. "Films and Political Consciousness in Tamil Nadu." *Economic and Political Weekly,* Jan. 11, pp. 27–35.

Hardiman, David. 1981. *Peasant Nationalists of Gujarat: Kheda District 1917–1934.* New Delhi: Oxford University Press.

———. 1987. *The Coming of the Devi: Adivasi Assertion in Western India.* Delhi and New York: Oxford University Press.

Harriss, John. 1987. "The State in Retreat: Why Has India Experienced Such Half-Hearted Liberalization in the 1980s?" *IDS Bulletin* 18, no. 4: 29–36.

Harriss-White, Barbara. 1996. *A Political Economy of Agricultural Markets in South India: Masters of the Country Side.* New Delhi, Thousand Oaks, Calif., and London: Sage.

Hart, Henry C., ed. 1976. *Indira Gandhi's India: A Political System Reappraised.* Boulder, Colo.: Westview Press.

Hayek, F. A. 1945. "The Use of Knowledge in Society." *American Economic Review* 35: 519–30.

Hazari, R. K., assisted by A. N. Oza et al. 1966. *The Structure of the Corporate Private Sector: A Study of Concentration, Ownership and Control.* Bombay and New York: Asia Publication House.

Heller, Patrick. 1999. *The Labor of Development: Workers and the Transformation of Capitalism in Kerala, India.* Ithaca, N.Y.: Cornell University Press.

Herrigel, Gary. 1996. *Industrial Constructions: The Sources of German Industrial Power.* Cambridge: Cambridge University.

Herring, Ronald J. 1983. *Land to the Tiller: The Political Economy of Agrarian Reform in South Asia.* New Haven, Conn.: Yale University Press.

———. 1986. Review of Pranab Bardhan, *The Political Economy of Development in India* (Oxford: Basil Blackwell). *Journal of Asian Studies* 45, no. 4 (Jan.).

———. 1999. "Embedded Particularism: India's Failed Developmental State." In Meredith Woo-Cumings, ed., *The Developmental State.* Ithaca, N.Y.: Cornell University Press.

Herring, Ronald, and N. Chandra Mohan. 2001. "Economic Crisis, Momentary Autonomy and Policy Reform: Liberalization in India, 1991–1995." In Amita Shastri and A. J. Wilson, eds., *The Post-Colonial States of South Asia: Democracy, Development and Identity.* London: Curzon Press.

Hirway, Indira. 1995. "Selective Development and Widening Disparities in Gujarat." *Economic and Political Weekly* 30, nos. 41–42: 2603–18.

———. 2002. "Dynamics of Development in Gujarat: Some Issues." In Indira Hirway, S. P. Kashyap, and Amita Shah, eds., *Dynamics of Development in Gujarat.* Ahmedabad: Concept Publishing Company.

Hirway, Indira, S. P. Kashyap, and Amita Shah, eds. 2002. *Dynamics of Development in Gujarat.* Ahmedabad: Concept Publishing Company.

Hirway, Indira, and Piet Terhal. 2002. "The Contradictions of Growth." In Ghanshyam

Shah, Mario Rutten, and Hein Streefkerk, eds., *Development and Deprivation in Gujarat: In Honor of Jan Breman.* New Delhi: Sage.

Hollingsworth, J. Rogers, and R. Boyer, eds. 1997. *Contemporary Capitalism: The Embeddedness of Institutions.* Cambridge: Cambridge University Press.

Horn, Murray J. 1995. *The Political Economy of Public Administration: Institutional Choice in the Public Sector.* Cambridge and New York: Cambridge University Press.

Hough, Jerry. 1969. *The Soviet Prefects: The Local Party Organs in Industrial Decision-Making.* Cambridge, Mass.: Harvard University Press.

Hough, Jerry F., and Merle Fainsod. 1979. *How the Soviet Union Is Governed.* Cambridge, Mass.: Harvard University Press.

Hsia, Ming. *See* Xia, Ming

Huang, Yasheng. 1994. "Information, Bureaucracy, and Economic Reforms in China and the Soviet Union." *World Politics* 47, no. 1: 102–34.

———. 1996. *Inflation and Investment Controls in China: The Political Economy of Central-Local Relations during the Reform Era.* Cambridge: Cambridge University Press.

Inoue, Kyoko. 1992. *Industrial Development Policy of India.* Tokyo: Institute of Developing Economies.

Irschick, Eugene F. 1969. *Politics and Social Conflict in South India: The Non-Brahman Movement and Tamil Separatism, 1916–1929.* Berkeley: University of California.

Jalan, B., ed. 1981. *Problems and Policies in Small Economies.* New York: St. Martin's Press.

Jeffrey, Robin. 1994. "The Prime Minister and the Ruling Party." In James Manor, ed., *Nehru to the Nineties: The Changing Office of Prime Minister in India.* Vancouver: UBC Press.

Jenkins, Rob. 1999. *Democratic Politics and Economic Reform in India.* Cambridge: Cambridge University Press.

Jenkins, Rob, ed. 2004. *Regional Reflections: Comparing Politics across India's States.* Delhi: Oxford University Press.

Jha, Rajani R., and Bhavana Mishra. 1993. "Centre-State Relations, 1980–90: The Experience of West Bengal." *Indian Journal of Political Science* 54, no. 2: 209–37.

Johnson, Chalmers. 1982. *MITI and the Japanese Miracle: The Growth of Industrial Policy, 1925–1975.* Stanford, Calif.: Stanford University Press.

Joshi, Vijay, and I. M. D. Little. 1994. *India: Macroeconomics and Political Economy, 1964–1991.* Washington, D.C.: World Bank.

Kamat, A. R. 1980. "Politico-Economic Developments in Maharashtra: A Review of Post-Independence Period." *Economic and Political Weekly* 40: 1669–78.

Kapilinsky, Raphael. 1993. "Industrialization in Botswana: How Getting the Prices Right Helped the Wrong People." In James Manor and Christopher Colclough, eds., *States or Markets? Neoliberalism and the Development Policy Debate.* Paperback ed. Oxford: Clarendon.

Kapur, Devesh. 1994. "On Industrial Performance: Technology, Policies and Institutions in the Indian Petrochemical Industry." Ph.D. thesis, Princeton University.

Katzenstein, Mary Fainsod. 1979. *Ethnicity and Equality: The Shiv Sena Party and Preferential Policies in Bombay.* Ithaca, N.Y.: Cornell University Press.

Katzenstein, Peter, ed. 1978. *Between Power and Plenty: Foreign Economic Policies of Advanced Industrial States.* Ithaca, N.Y.: Cornell University Press.

——. 1984. *Corporatism and Change: Austria, Switzerland and Politics of Industry.* Ithaca, N.Y.: Cornell University Press.

——. 1985. *Small States in World Markets: Industrial Policy in Europe.* Ithaca, N.Y.: Cornell University Press.

Kaviraj, Sudipta. 1986. "Indira Gandhi and Indian Politics." *Economic and Political Weekly* 21, nos. 38 and 39: 1697–1708.

——. 1992. "The Imaginary Institution of India." In Ranajit Guha, ed., *Subaltern Studies: Writings on South Asian History and Society,* vol. 7. Delhi and New York: Oxford University Press.

Kennedy, Loraine. 2004. "The Political Determinants of Reform Packaging: Contrasting Responses to Economic Liberalization in Andhra Pradesh and Tamil Nadu." In Rob Jenkins, ed., *Regional Reflections: Comparing Politics across India's States.* New Delhi: Oxford University Press.

King, Gary, Robert Keohane, and Sidney Verba. 1994. *Designing Social Inquiry: Scientific Inference in Qualitative Research.* Princeton, N.J.: Princeton University Press.

Knack, Stephen, and Philip Keefer. 1995. "Institutions and Economic Performance: Cross-Country Tests Using Alternative Institutional Measures." *Economics and Politics* 3: 207–27.

Kitschelt, Herbert, Peter Lange, and Mark Stephens, eds. 1999. *Continuity and Change in Contemporary Capitalism.* Cambridge: Cambridge University Press.

Kochanek, Stanley A. 1968. *The Congress Party of India: The Dynamics of One-Party Democracy.* Princeton, N.J.: Princeton University Press.

——. 1974. *Business and Politics in India.* Berkeley: University of California Press.

——. 1976. "Mrs. Gandhi's Pyramid: The New Congress." In Henry C. Hart, ed., *Indira Gandhi's India: A Political System Reappraised.* Boulder, Colo.: Westview Press.

Kohli, Atul. 1984. "Communist Reformers in West Bengal: Origins, Features and Relations with New Delhi." In John R. Wood, ed., *State Politics in Contemporary India: Crisis or Continuity?* Boulder, Colo., and London: Westview Press.

——. 1987. *The State and Poverty in India.* Cambridge: Cambridge University Press.

——. 1990a. *Democracy and Discontent: India's Crisis of Governability.* New Delhi: Oxford University Press.

——. 1990b. "From Elite Activism to Democratic Consolidation: The Rise of Reform Communism in West Bengal." In Francine R. Frankel and M. S. A. Rao, eds., *Dominance and State Power in Modern India: Decline of a Social Order,* vol. 2. Oxford: Oxford University Press.

Kopf, David. 1969. *British Colonialism and the Bengal Renaissance: The Dynamics of Indian Modernization, 1773–1835.* Berkeley: University of California Press, 1969.

Kornai, Janos. 1980. *Economics of Shortage.* Amsterdam and New York: North-Holland.

Krasner, Stephen D. 1984. "Approaches to the State: Alternative Conceptions and Historical Dynamics." *Comparative Politics* 16: 223–46.

Krehbiel, Keith. 1991. *Information and Legislative Organization.* Ann Arbor: University of Michigan Press.

Kreps, David. 1990. "Corporate Culture and Economic Theory." In James Alt and Kenneth Shepsle, eds., *Perspectives on Positive Political Economy.* Cambridge: Cambridge University Press.

Krueger, Anne O. 1974. "The Political Economy of the Rent Seeking Society." *American Economic Review* 64: 291–303.

——. 1998. "Contrasts in Transition to Market-Oriented Economies: India and Korea." In Y. Hayami and M. Aoki, eds., *The Institutional Foundations of East Asian Economic Development.* New York: Macmillan Press.

——, ed. 2000. *Economic Policy Reform: The Second Stage.* Chicago and London: University of Chicago Press.

Kundu, Amitabh, and Moonis Raza. 1982. *Indian Economy, the Regional Dimension.* New Delhi: Centre for the Study of Regional Development, Jawaharlal Nehru University.

Kydland, Finn, and Edward Prescott. 1977. "Rules Rather than Discretion: The Inconsistency of Optimal Plans." *Journal of Political Economy* 85: 473–91.

Lal, Deepak. 1988. *Cultural Stability and Economic Stagnation: India, c. 1500 BC–AD 1980.* New York: Clarendon Press.

——. 1994. *Against Dirigisme: The Case for Unshackling Economic Markets.* San Francisco, Calif.: ICS Press.

Lele, Jayant. 1994. "A Welfare State in Crisis: Reflections on the Indira-Rajiv Era." In Nanda K. Choudhury and Salim Mansur, eds., *The Indira-Rajiv Years: The Indian Economy and Polity, 1966–1991.* Toronto: University of Toronto Press.

Levi, Margaret. 1988. *Of Rule and Revenue.* Berkeley: University of California Press.

Lewis, John. 1995. *India's Political Economy: Governance and Reform.* Delhi: Oxford University Press.

Lin, Justin Y., and Jeffrey Nugent. 1995. "Institutions and Economic Development." In J. Behrman and T. N. Srinivasan, eds., *Handbook of Development Economics,* vol. 3. Amsterdam: Elsevier Science B.V.

Linz, Juan, and Alfred Stepan. 1992. "Political Identities and Electoral Sequences: Spain, the Soviet Union and Yugoslavia." *Daedalus* 121 (1992): 123–39.

Linz, Juan, and Armando de Miguel. 1966. "Within-Nation Differences and Comparisons: The Eight Spains." In Richard L. Merritt and S. Rokkan, eds., *Comparing Nations: The Use of Quantitative Data in Cross-National Research.* New Haven, Conn.: Yale University Press.

Lipsky, Michael. 1980. *Street-Level Bureaucracy: Dilemmas of the Individual in Public Services.* New York: Russell Sage Foundation.

Locke, Richard. 1995. *Remaking the Italian Economy.* Ithaca, N.Y.: Cornell University Press.

Lohmann, Susanne. 1992. "Optimal Commitment in Monetary Policy: Credibility versus Flexibility." *American Economic Review* 82, no. 1: 273–86.

Love, Joseph L. 1971. *Rio Grande do Sul and Brazilian Regionalism, 1882–1930.* Stanford, Calif.: Stanford University Press.

Maddison, Angus. 1995. *Explaining the Economic Performance of Nations.* Aldershot, Hants: Edward Elgar.

——. 1998. *Chinese Economic Performance in the Long Run.* Paris: Development Centre of the Organization for Economic Cooperation and Development.

Mallick, Ross. 1993. *Development Policy of a Communist Government: West Bengal since 1977.* Cambridge: Cambridge University Press.

Mallison, Françoise. 1995. "Bombay as the Intellectual Capital of the Gujaratis." In Sujata Patel and Alice Thorner, eds., *Bombay: Mosaic of Modern Culture.* Bombay: Oxford University Press.

Manion, Melanie. 1991. "Policy Implementation in the PRC: Authoritative Decisions versus Individual Interests." *Journal of Asian Studies* 50, no. 2: 253–79.

Manor, James, ed. 1994. *Nehru to the Nineties: The Changing Office of Prime Minister in India.* Vancouver: UBC Press.

Marathe, Sharad M. 1989. *Regulation and Development: India's Policy Experience of Controls over Industry.* 2nd ed. New Delhi: Sage.

Markovits, Claude. 1985. *Indian Business and Nationalist Politics, 1931–1939.* Cambridge: Cambridge University Press.

———. 1995. "Bombay as a Business Centre in the Colonial Period." In Sujata Patel and Alice Thorner, eds., *Bombay: Mosaic of Modern Culture.* Bombay: Oxford University Press.

McAuley, Alastair. 1991. "The Economic Consequences of Soviet Disintegration." *Soviet Economy* 7, no. 3: 189–214.

McGinnis, Michael D., ed. 1999. *Polycentric Governance and Development: Readings from the Workshop in Political Theory and Policy Analysis.* Ann Arbor: University of Michigan Press.

———, ed. 2000. *Polycentric Games and Institutions: Readings from the Workshop in Political Theory and Policy Analysis.* Ann Arbor: University of Michigan Press.

———, ed. 2001. *Polycentricity and Local Public Economies: Readings from the Workshop in Political Theory and Policy Analysis.* Ann Arbor: University of Michigan Press.

McKinnon, Ronald, and Thomas Nechyba. 1997. "Competition in Federal Systems: The Role of Political and Financial Constraints." In John A. Ferejohn and Barry R. Weingast, eds., *The New Federalism: Can the States Be Trusted?* Stanford, Calif.: Hoover Institution Press, Stanford University.

Mehta, Jivraj N. 1961. "Peace in Industry with Class Collaboration." *Vital Speeches and Documents of the Day* 1, no. 15: 402–404.

Mehta, Makrand. 2002. "The Dalit Temple Entry Movements in Maharashtra and Gujarat, 1930–1948." In Takashi Shinoda, ed., *The Other Gujarat: Social Transformations among Weaker Sections.* Mumbai: Popular Prakashan.

MIDS (Madras Institute of Development Studies). 1988. *Tamil Nadu Economy: Performance and Issues.* New Delhi: Oxford and IBH Publishing Co.

Migdal, Joel S. 2001. *State in Society: Studying How States and Societies Transform and Constitute One Another.* Cambridge: Cambridge University Press.

Migdal, Joel S., Atul Kohli, and Vivienne Shue, eds. 1994. *State Power and Social Forces: Domination and Transformation in the Third World.* Cambridge and New York: Cambridge University Press.

Milgrom, Paul R., Douglass North, and Barry Weingast. 1990. "The Role of Institutions in the Revival of Trade: The Medieval Law Merchant, Private Judges, and the Champagne Fairs." *Economics and Politics* 1: 1–23.

Milner, Helen. 1997. *Interest, Institutions and Information: Domestic Politics and International Relations.* Princeton, N.J.: Princeton University Press.

Mitra, Subrata K. 1992. *Power, Protest and Participation: Local Elites and the Politics of Development in India.* London and New York: Routledge.

Mohan, Rakesh. 1992. "Industrial Policy and Controls." In Bimal Jalan, ed., *The Indian Economy: Problems and Prospects.* New Delhi: Penguin Books.

Montero, Alfred P. 2000. "Devolving Democracy? Political Decentralization and New Brazilian Federalism." In Peter R. Kingstone and Timothy J. Power, eds., *Demo-*

cratic Brazil: Actors, Institutions, and Processes. Pittsburgh: University of Pittsburgh Press.

———. 2001a. "Making and Remaking 'Good Government' in Brazil: Subnational Industrial Policy in Minas Gerais." *Latin American Politics and Society* 43 (Summer): 49–80.

———. 2001b. "Delegative Dilemmas and Horizontal Logics: Subnational Industrial Policy in Spain and Brazil." *Studies in Comparative International Development* 36, no. 3: 58–89.

———. 2002. *Shifting States in Global Markets: Subnational Industrial Policy in Contemporary Brazil and Spain.* University Park: Pennsylvania State University Press.

Montesquieu, Charles de Secondat baron de. 1989. *The Spirit of the Laws.* 1989 ed. Translated by Basia C. Miller, Harold Stone, and Anne M. Cohler. Cambridge: Cambridge University Press.

Montinola, Gabriella, Yingyi Qian, and Barry R. Weingast. 1995. "Federalism, Chinese Style: The Political Basis for Economic Success in China." *World Politics* 48, no. 1: 50–81.

Moojamdar, Ajit. 1994. "The Rise and Decline of Development Planning In India." In T. J. Byres, ed., *The State and Development Planning in India.* Delhi: Oxford University Press.

Mookherjee, Dilip. 1994. "Market Failures and Information." In Bhaskar Dutta, ed., *Welfare Economics.* Delhi: Oxford University Press.

Moser, Joel C. 1985. "Regionalism in Soviet Politics: Continuity as a Source of Change, 1953–1982." *Soviet Studies* 37, no. 2 (April): 184–211.

Mukherjee, Sanjeeb. 1985. "The Bourgeoisie and Politics in West Bengal." In Rakhahari Chatterji, ed., *Politics in West Bengal: Institutions, Processes and Problems.* Calcutta: World Press Private Limited.

Musgrave, Richard A. 1997. "Reconsidering the Fiscal Role of Government." *American Economic Review* 87, no. 2: 156–59.

Myrdal, Gunnar. 1968. *Asian Drama: An Inquiry into the Poverty of Nations.* New York: Twentieth Century Fund.

Nayar, Baldev Raj. 1971. "Business Attitudes toward Economic Planning in India." *Asian Survey* 11, no. 9 (Sept.): 850.

———. 1989. *India's Mixed Economy: The Role of Ideology and Interest in Its Development.* Bombay: Popular Prakashan.

———. 1990. *The Political Economy of India's Public Sector: Policy and Performance.* Bombay: Popular Prakashan.

———. 1992. "The Politics of Economic Restructuring in India: The Paradox of State Strength and Policy Weakness." *Journal of Commonwealth and Comparative Politics* 30, no. 2: 145–71.

———. 1996. *The State and Market in India's Shipping: Nationalism, Globalization and Marginalization.* New Delhi: Manohar.

———. 2001. *Globalization and Nationalism: The Changing Balance in India's Economic Policy, 1950–2000.* New Delhi, Thousand Oaks, Calif., and London: Sage.

———. 2003. "Globalization and India's National Autonomy." *Journal of Commonwealth and Comparative Politics* 41, no. 2 (July): 1–34.

Nayyar, Deepak, ed. 1994. *Industrial Growth and Stagnation: The Debate in India.* Bombay: Oxford University Press.

Nee, Victor. 1989. "A Theory of Market Transition: From Redistribution to Markets in State Socialism." *American Sociological Review* 54: 663–81.
———. 1992. "Organizational Dilemmas and Market Transition: Hybrid Forms, Property Rights and Mixed Economy in China." *Administrative Science Quarterly* 37: 1–27.
Nee, Victor, and David Stark, with Mark Selden, eds. 1989. *Remaking the Economic Institutions of Socialism: China and Eastern Europe.* Stanford, Calif.: Stanford University Press.
Nehru, Jawaharlal. 1964. *Jawaharlal Nehru's Speeches: September 1957–April 1963.* Vol. 4. New Delhi: Ministry of Information and Broadcasting, Government of India.
———. 1987. *Letters to Chief Ministers.* 5 vols. Delhi: Oxford University Press.
Niskanen, William A., Jr. 1971. *Bureaucracy and Representative Government.* Chicago: Aldine-Atherton.
North, Douglass C. 1981. *Structure and Change in Economic History.* New York: Norton.
———. 1993. "Institutions and Credible Commitment." *Journal of Institutional and Theoretical Economics* 149, no. 1: 11–23.
North, Douglass C., and Barry Weingast. 1989. "Constitutions and Credible Commitments: The Evolution of the Institutions in 17th Century England." *Journal of Economic History* 49: 803–32.
Nossiter, Tom J. 1988. *Marxist State Governments in India: Politics, Economics and Society.* London: Pinter.
Nove, Alec. 1981. "An Overview." In I. S. Koropeckyj and Gertrude Schroeder, eds., *Economics of Soviet Regions.* New York: Praeger.
Nozick, Robert. 1974. *Anarchy, State and Utopia.* New York: Basic Books.
Observer Research Foundation, ed. 1996. *Economic Reforms and the Role of States and the Future of Center-State Relations.* New Delhi: Observer Research Foundation.
Oi, Jean. 1999. *Rural China Takes Off: The Institutional Foundations of Economic Reform.* Berkeley: University of California Press.
Olson, Mancur. 1982. *The Rise and Decline of Nations: Economic Growth, Stagflation and Social Rigidities.* New Haven, Conn.: Yale University Press.
———. 1995. "A Collective Choice Perspective on the Indian Economy." IRIS Conference Paper. College Park: IRIS Center, University of Maryland.
Oommen, M. A. 1979. "Inter Shifting of Industries from Kerala." Unpublished M.Phil. thesis, Centre for Development Studies, Trivandrum.
Ostrom, Elinor. 1999. "Crossing the Great Divide: Coproduction, Synergy, and Development." In Michael D. McGinnis, ed., *Polycentric Governance and Development: Readings from the Workshop in Political Theory and Policy Analysis.* Ann Arbor: University of Michigan Press.
Ostrom, Vincent, Charles M. Tiebout, and Robert Warren. 1961. "The Organization of Government in Metropolitan Areas: A Theoretical Inquiry." *American Political Science Review* 55, no. 4: 831–42.
Pandian, M. S. S. 1992. *The Image Trap: M. G. Ramachandran in Film and Politics.* New Delhi: Sage.
———. 1993. "Jayalalitha: 'Desire' and Political Legitimation." *Seminar* 401 (Jan.): 31–34.

———. 1996. "Politics of Representation: Women in the Films of M. G. Ramachandran." In T. V. Sathyamurthy, *Region, Religion, Caste, Gender and Culture in Contemporary India*, vol. 3. Delhi: Oxford University Press.

Patel, Sujata. 1987. *The Making of Industrial Relations: The Ahmedabad Textile Industry 1918–1939*. New Delhi: Oxford University Press.

———. 2002. "Corporatist Patronage in the Ahmedabad Textile Industry." In Ghanshyam Shah, Mario Rutten, and Hein Streefkerk, eds., *Development and Deprivation in Gujarat: In Honor of Jan Breman*. New Delhi: Sage.

Patnaik, Prabhat. 1995. *Whatever Happened to Imperialism and Other Essays*. New Delhi: Tulika.

Paul, Samuel. 2000. "Do States Have an Enabling Environment for Industrial Growth? Some Evidence from Karnataka." *Economic and Political Weekly* 35, nos. 43–44: 3861–69.

Perkins, Dwight, and Moshe Syrquin. 1989. "Large Countries: The Influence of Size." In Hollis Chenery and T. N. Srinivasan, eds., *Handbook of Development Economics*, vol. 2. Amsterdam: North Holland.

Perry, Elizabeth J. 1994. "Trends in the Study of Chinese Politics: State-Society Relations." *China Quarterly*, no. 139 (Sept. 1994): 704–13.

Peterson, Paul E. 1981. *City Limits*. Chicago: University of Chicago Press.

Pingle, Vibha. 1999. *Rethinking the Developmental State: India's Industry in Comparative Perspective*. New York: St. Martin's Press.

Place, Siddons, and Gough Private Limited, 1962. *The Investor's India Yearbook*. Calcutta: Orient Longmans Ltd.

Pocock, David Francis. 1972. *Kanbi and Patidar: A Study of the Patidar Community of Gujarat*. Oxford: Clarendon Press.

Polanyi, Karl. 1957. *The Great Transformation*. Boston: Beacon Press.

Potter, David C. 1996. *India's Political Administrators: From ICS to IAS*. 2nd Indian ed. Delhi: Oxford University Press.

Pressman, Jeffrey L., and Aaron Wildavsky. 1984. *Implementation: How Great Expectations in Washington Are Dashed in Oakland*. Berkeley: University of California Press.

Price, Pamela G. 1989. "Kingly Models in Indian Political Behavior: Culture as a Medium of History." *Asian Survey* 29, no. 6: 559–72.

Przeworski, Adam. 1999. "On the Design of the State: A Principal-Agent Perspective." In L. Pereira and Peter Spink, eds., *Reforming the State: Managerial Public Administration in Latin America*. Boulder, Colo.: Lynne Rienner.

Przeworski, Adam, and Henry Teune. 1982. *The Logic of Comparative Social Inquiry*. Malabar, Fla.: Krieger.

Putnam, Robert D. 1988. "Diplomacy and Domestic Politics: The Logic of Two-level Games." *International Organization* 42 (Summer): 427–60.

Putnam, Robert D., with Robert Leonardi and Raffaella Y. Nanetti. 1993. *Making Democracy Work: Civic Traditions in Modern Italy*. Princeton, N.J.: Princeton University Press.

Raj, K. N. 1973. "The Politics and Economics of 'Intermediate Regimes.'" *Economic and Political Weekly* 8: 1189–98.

Rajadurai, S. V., and V. Geetha. 1996. "DMK Hegemony: The Cultural Limits to Political Consensus." In T. V. Sathyamurthy, *Region, Religion, Caste, Gender and Culture in Contemporary India*, vol. 3. Delhi: Oxford University Press.

Ray, Rajat K. 1979. *Industrialization in India: Growth and Conflict in the Private Corporate Sector, 1914-1947.* Delhi: Oxford University Press.

Remick, Elizabeth J. 2002. "The Significance of Variation in Local States: The Case of 20th Century China." *Comparative Politics* 34, no. 4: 399–418.

Remnick, David. 1993. *Lenin's Tomb: The Last Days of the Soviet Empire.* New York: Random House.

Reserve Bank of India. 2000. *Handbook of the Indian Economy.* New Delhi: Government of India.

Riker, William H. 1964. *Federalism: Origins, Operation and Significance.* Boston: Little, Brown and Co.

———. 1975. "Federalism." In Fred I. Greenstein and Nelson Polsby, eds., *Handbook of Political Science.* Reading, Mass.: Addison-Wesley.

———. 1985. *The Development of American Federalism.* Boston: Kluwer Academic Publishers.

Riskin, Carl. 1987. *China's Political Economy: The Quest for Development since 1949.* Oxford: Oxford University Press.

Robinson, E. A. G. 1960. *Economic Consequences of the Size of Nations.* New York: St. Martin's Press.

Robinson, Mark, and Gordon White, eds. 1998. *The Democratic Developmental State: Politics and Institutional Design.* New York: Oxford University Press, 1998.

Rodrik, Dani. 1997. "The 'Paradoxes' of the Successful State." *European Economic Review* 41: 411–42.

Romer, Paul. 1990. "Endogenous Technological Change." *Journal of Political Economy* 98: S71–S102.

Root, Hilton L. 1994. *The Fountain of Privilege: Political Foundations of Markets in Old Regime France and England.* Berkeley: University of California Press.

Rosen, George. 1966. *Democracy and Economic Change in India.* Berkeley: University of California Press.

———. 1987. *Industrial Change in India 1970-2000.* Riverdale, Md.: Riverdale Co.

———. 1992. *Contrasting Styles of Industrial Reform: China and India in the 1980s.* Chicago: University of Chicago Press.

Rosenstein-Rodan, P. 1943. "Problems of Industrialization of Eastern and Southeastern Europe." *Economic Journal* 53: 202–11.

Rudolph, Lloyd I., and Susanne H. Rudolph. 1987. *In Pursuit of Lakshmi: The Political Economy of the Indian State.* Chicago and London: University of Chicago Press.

———. 2001. "The Iconization of Chandrababu: Sharing Sovereignty in India's Federal Market Economy." *Economic and Political Weekly* 36, no. 18: 1541–60.

Rutten, Mario. 1995. *Farms and Factories: Social Profile of Large Farmers and Rural Industrialists in West India.* Delhi and New York: Oxford University Press.

Saez, Lawrence. 1999. "India's Economic Liberalization, Interjurisdictional Competition and Development." *Contemporary South Asia* 8, no. 3: 323–45.

———. 2002. *Federalism without a Center: The Impact of Political and Economic Reform on India's Federal System.* New Delhi: Sage.

Sah, Raj Kumar, and J. Stiglitz. 1986. "The Architecture of Economic Systems: Hierarchies and Polyarchies." *American Economic Review* 75, no. 4: 716–27.

———. 1988. "Committees, Hierarchies and Polyarchies." *Economic Journal* 98: 451–70.

Samuels, David. 2000. "Concurrent Elections, Discordant Results: Presidentialism, Federalism and Governance in Brazil." *Comparative Politics* 33, no. 1: 1–20.

———. 2003. *Ambition, Federalism, and Legislative Politics in Brazil.* Cambridge and New York: Cambridge University Press.

Samuels, David, and Fernando Abrucio. 2000. "Federalism and Democratic Transitions: The 'New' Politics of the Governors in Brazil." *Publius* 30, no. 2: 43–61.

Samuels, Richard J. 1983. *The Politics of Regional Policy in Japan: Localities Incorporated?* Princeton, N.J.: Princeton University Press.

Sanghvi, Nagindas. 1996. *Gujarat: A Political Analysis.* Surat: Centre for Social Studies.

Sanghvi, R. L. 1979. *Role of Industrial Estates in a Developing Economy.* Bombay: Multi-Tech.

Sankar, T. L., R. K. Mishra, and R. Nandagopal. 1994. "State Level Public Enterprises in India: An Overview." *Economic and Political Weekly* 29, no. 35: M-115–M-121.

Sarwate, D. n.d. "The Industrial Development of Maharashtra." Unpublished article.

Sathyamurthy, T. V. 1997. "Political Change in Tamil Nadu: Evolution or Involution?" *Review of Development and Change* 2, no. 1: 1–23.

Scharpf, Fritz. 1997. *Games Real Actors Play: Actor-Centered Institutionalism in Policy Research.* Boulder, Colo.: Westview Press.

Schmitter, Phillipe. 1997. "Introduction." In J. Rogers Hollingsworth and Robert Boyer, eds., *Contemporary Capitalism: The Embeddedness of Institutions.* Cambridge: Cambridge University Press.

Schneider, Ben Ross. 1991. *Politics within the State: Elite Bureaucrats and Industrial Policy in Authoritarian Brazil.* Pittsburgh: University of Pittsburgh Press.

Schroeder, G. 1990. "Nationalities and the Soviet Economy." In Lubomyr Hajda and Mark Beissinger, eds., *The Nationalities Factor in Soviet Politics and Society.* Boulder, Colo.: Westview Press.

———. 1991. "Perestroika in the Aftermath of 1990." *Soviet Economy* 7, no. 1: 3–13.

Schultz, Richard, and Alan Alexandroff. 1985. *Economic Regulation and the Federal System.* Toronto: University of Toronto Press.

Schurmann, Franz. 1966. *Ideology and Organization in Communist China.* Berkeley: University of California Press.

Scott, James C. 1976. *The Moral Economy of the Peasant: Rebellion and Subsistence in Southeast Asia.* New Haven, Conn.: Yale University Press.

Scully, Gerald W. 1988. "The Institutional Framework and Economic Development." *Journal of Political Economy* 96: 652–62.

Senghaas, Dieter. 1985. *The European Experience: A Historical Critique of Development Theory.* Leamington Spa, Warwickshire, and Dover, N.H.: Berg Publishers.

Shah, Ghanshyam. 1990. "Caste Sentiments, Class Formation, and Dominance in Gujarat." In Francine R. Frankel and M. S. A. Rao, eds., *Dominance and State Power in Modern India: Decline of a Social Order,* vol. 2. New York: Oxford University Press.

Shah, Ghanshyam, Mario Rutten, and Hein Streefkerk, eds. 2002. *Development and Deprivation in Gujarat: In Honor of Jan Breman.* New Delhi: Sage.

Shah, Manubhai. 1961. "Dynamic Phase of Industrial Economy." *Vital Speeches and Documents of the Day* 1, no. 12: 311–18.

Sharma, T. R. 1946. *Location of Industries in India.* Bombay: Hind Kitab Ltd.

Shepsle, Kenneth. 1996. "Political Deals in Institutional Settings." In Robert E. Goodin, ed., *The Theory of Institutional Design.* Cambridge: Cambridge University Press.

Sheth, Praveen N. 1976a. "Gujarat: The Case of Small Majority Politics." In Iqbal Narain, ed., *State Politics in India.* Meerut: Meenakshi Prakashan.

———. 1976b. *Patterns of Political Behavior in Gujarat.* Ahmedabad: Sahitya Mudranalaya.

Shinoda, Takashi. 2000. "Institutional Change and Entrepreneurial Development: The SSI Sector." *Economic and Political Weekly,* Aug. 26–Sept. 2, pp. 3205–16.

———. 2002. "Introduction." In Takashi Shinoda, ed., *The Other Gujarat: Social Transformations among Weaker Sections.* Mumbai: Popular Prakashan.

Shinoda, Takashi, ed. 2002. *The Other Gujarat: Social Transformations among Weaker Sections.* Mumbai: Popular Prakashan.

Shirk, Susan L. 1993. *The Political Logic of Economic Reform in China.* Berkeley: University of California Press.

———. 1994. *How China Opened Its Door: The Political Success of the PRC's Foreign Trade and Investment Reforms.* Washington, D.C.: Brookings Institution.

Shonfield, Andrew. 1965. *Modern Capitalism: The Changing Balance of Public and Private Power.* London and New York: Oxford University Press.

Shue, Vivienne. 1988. *The Reach of the State: Sketches of the Chinese Body Politic.* Stanford, Calif.: Stanford University Press.

Shukla, Sonal. 1995. "Gujarati Cultural Revivalism." In Sujata Patel and Alice Thorner, eds., *Bombay: Mosaic of Modern Culture.* Bombay: Oxford University Press.

Shukla, Vibhooti. 1996. *Urbanization and Economic Growth.* Delhi: Oxford University Press.

Simeon, R. 1972. *Federal-Provincial Diplomacy: The Making of Recent Policy in Canada.* Toronto: University of Toronto Press.

Sinha, Aseema. 1996. "Regional Shifts and Power Balances: Liberalization at the State Level in India." 25th Annual Conference on South Asia, University of Wisconsin–Madison.

———. 1999. "From State to Market—via the State Governments: Horizontal Competition after 1991 in India." Association of Asian Studies, Annual meeting, Boston, April 1999.

———. 2000. "Divided Leviathan: Comparing Subnational Developmental States in India." Doctoral dissertation, Cornell University.

———. 2004a. "The Changing Political Economy of Federalism in India: A Historical Institutionalist Approach." *India Review* 3, no. 1 (Jan.).

———. 2004b. "Ideas, Interests and Institutions in Policy Change: A Comparison of Gujarat and West Bengal." In Rob Jenkins, ed., *Regional Reflections: Comparing Politics across India's States.* Delhi: Oxford University Press.

Sivathamby, Karthigesu. 1981. *The Tamil Film as a Medium of Communication.* Madras: New Century Book House.

Skowronek, Stephen. 1982. *Building a New American State: The Expansion of National Administrative Capacities, 1877–1920.* Cambridge: Cambridge University Press.

Snider, Lewis. 1996. *Growth, Debt and Politics of Economic Adjustment and the Political Performance of Developing Countries.* Boulder, Colo.: Westview Press.

Snyder, Richard. 1999. "After Neoliberalism: The Politics of Re-Regulation in Mexico." *World Politics* 51: 173–204.

———. 2001a. *After Neoliberalism: Re-regulation in Mexico.* Cambridge: Cambridge University Press.

———. 2001b. "Scaling Down: The Subnational Comparative Method." *Studies in Comparative and International Development* 36, no. 1: 93–111.

Solnick, Steven L. 1996a. "The Breakdown of Hierarchies in the Soviet Union and China: A New Institutionalist Perspective." *World Politics* 48 (Jan.): 209–38.

———. 1996b. "The Political Economy of Russian Federalism: A Framework for Analysis." *Problems of Post-Communism* 43, no. 6: 13–26.

———. 2000. "Big Deals: Territorial Bargaining and the Fate of Post-Colonial and Post-Soviet States." Unpublished paper.

Solow, Robert M. 1956. "A Contribution to the Theory of Economic Growth." *Quarterly Journal of Economics* 70, no. 1: 65–94.

Spence, Michael. 1976. "Informational Aspects of Market Structure: An Introduction." *Quarterly Journal of Economics* 90, no. 4: 591–97.

Spruyt, Hendrik. 1994. *The Sovereign State and Its Competitors.* Princeton, N.J.: Princeton University Press.

Sridharan, E. 1993. "Economic Liberalization and India's Political Economy: Toward a Paradigm Synthesis." *Journal of Commonwealth and Comparative Politics* 31, no. 3 (Nov.): 1–31.

———. 1996. *The Political Economy of Industrial Promotion: Indian, Brazilian, and Korean Electronics in Comparative Perspective 1969-1994.* Westport, Conn.: Praeger.

Srinivasan, T. N. 1985. "Neoclassical Political Economy, the State and Economic Development." *Asian Development Review* 3, no. 2: 38–58.

Steinmo, Sven. 1993. *Taxation and Democracy: Swedish, British and American Approaches to Financing the Modern State.* New Haven, Conn.: Yale University Press.

Stepan, Alfred, ed. 1973. *Authoritarian Brazil.* New Haven, Conn., and London: Yale University Press.

Stevens, Jacqueline. 1999. *Reproducing the State.* Princeton, N.J.: Princeton University Press.

Stiglitz, Joseph E., ed. 1989. *The Economic Role of the State.* Oxford: Blackwell.

———. 2000. "The Contributions of the Economics of Information to Twentieth Century Economics." *Quarterly Journal of Economics* 115, no. 4: 1441–78.

Stone, Andrew, Brian Levy, and Ricardo Paredes. 1996. "Public Institutions and Private Transactions: A Comparative Analysis of the Legal and Regulatory Environment for Business Transactions in Brazil and Chile." In Lee J. Alston, Thrain Eggertsson, and Douglass North, eds., *Empirical Studies in Institutional Change.* Cambridge: Cambridge University Press.

Stoner-Weiss, Kathryn. 1997. *Local Heroes: The Political Economy of Russian Regional Governance.* Princeton, N.J.: Princeton University Press.

———. 2000. "The Russian Central State in Crisis: Center and Periphery in the Post-Soviet Era." In Zoltan Barany and Robert G. Moser, eds., *Russian Politics: Challenges of Democratization.* Cambridge: Cambridge University Press.

Streefkerk, Hein. 1979. "Small Entrepreneurs—Agents in Underdevelopment?" In S. Devadas Pillai and Chris Baks, eds., *Winners and Losers: Styles of Development and Change in an Indian Region.* Bombay: Popular Prakashan.

———. 1985. *Industrial Transition in Rural India: Artisans, Traders, and Tribals in South Gujarat.* Bombay: Popular Prakashan.

Subramanian, Narendra. 1999. *Ethnicity and Populist Mobilization: Political Parties, Citizens and Democracy in South India.* Delhi: Oxford University Press.

Swaminathan, Padmini. 1994. "Where Are the Entrepreneurs? What the Data Reveal for Tamil Nadu." *Economic and Political Weekly* 29, no. 22: M-64–M-74.

Swamy, Arun Ranga. 1996. "The Nation, the People and the Poor: Sandwich Tactics in Party Competition and Policy Formation, India, 1931–1996." Doctoral dissertation, University of California.

Tarrow, Sidney G. 1977. *Between Center and Periphery: Grassroots Politicians in Italy and France.* New Haven, Conn.: Yale University Press.

———. 1978. "Introduction." In Sidney Tarrow, Peter Katzenstein, and Luigi Graziano, eds., *Territorial Politics in Industrial Nations.* New York: Praeger.

———. 1999. "Expanding Paired Comparison: A Modest Proposal." *APSA-CP* 10, no. 2: 9–12.

Tarrow, Sidney, Peter Katzenstein, and Luigi Graziano, eds. 1978. *Territorial Politics in Industrial Nations.* New York: Praeger.

Taubman, William. 1973. *Governing Soviet Cities: Bureaucratic Politics and Urban Development in the USSR.* New York: Praeger.

Taylor, Lance. 1983. *Structuralist Macroeconomics.* New York: Basic Books.

Tedstrom, John. 1989. *Radio Liberty Report on the USSR* 1, no. 16: 1–8.

Tendler, Judith. 1997. *Good Government in the Tropics.* Baltimore: Johns Hopkins University Press.

Tiebout, Charles. 1956. "A Pure Theory of Local Expenditures." *Journal of Political Economy* 64: 416–24.

Tilly, Charles. 1975. *The Formation of National States in Western Europe.* Princeton, N.J.: Princeton University Press.

———. 1990. *Coercion, Capital, and European States, AD 990–1990.* Cambridge, Mass.: B. Blackwell.

Tomlinson, Brian R. 1981. "Colonial Firms and the Decline of Colonialism in Eastern India." *Modern Asian Studies* 15, no. 3: 455–86.

Topik, Steven. 1988. "The Economic Role of the State in Liberal Regimes: Brazil and Mexico Compared, 1988–1910." In Joseph L. Love and Nils Jacobsen, eds., *Guiding the Invisible Hand: Economic Liberalism and the State in Latin American History.* New York: Praeger.

Toye, John. 1987. "The New Political Economy Applied to Indian Development." In John Toye, ed., *Dilemmas of Development.* Oxford: Basil Blackwell.

Treisman, Daniel. 1996. "The Politics of Intergovernmental Transfers in Post-Soviet Russia." *British Journal of Political Science* 26, no. 3 (July): 299–335.

———. 2001. *After the Deluge: Regional Crises and Political Consolidation in Russia.* Ann Arbor: University of Michigan Press.

Tsai, Kellee. 2002. *Back-Alley Banking: Private Entrepreneurs in China.* Ithaca, N.Y.: Cornell University Press.

Tsebelis, George. 1990. *Nested Games: Rational Choice in Comparative Politics.* Berkeley: University of California Press.

———. 1999. "Veto Players and Law Production in Parliamentary Democracies: An Empirical Analysis." *American Political Science Review* 93, no. 3: 591–608.

Tyagarajan, Meenaskshi. 1989. "Industrial Perspectives in Tamil Nadu." *Economic and Political Weekly* 24, no. 46: 2539–40.

Upadhya, Carol Boyack. 1988a. "The Farmer-Capitalists of Coastal Andhra Pradesh—I." *Economic and Political Weekly* 23, no. 27: 1376–82.

———. 1988b. "The Farmer-Capitalists of Coastal Andhra Pradesh—II." *Economic and Political Weekly* 23, no. 28: 1433–42.

Vaksberg, Arkady. 1991. *The Soviet Mafia.* London: Weidenfeld and Nicolson.

Varshney, Ashutosh. 1995. *Democracy, Development and the Countryside: Urban-Rural Struggles in India.* Cambridge: Cambridge University Press.

Venkatesan, R. 1994. *Problems in the Implementation of Economic Reforms at the State Level.* New Delhi: National Council of Applied Economic Research, India.

Wade, Robert. 1985. "The Market for Public Office: Why the Indian State is Not Better at Development." *World Development* 13, no. 4: 467–97.

———. 1990. *Governing the Market: Economic Theory and the Role of Government in East Asia.* Princeton, N.J.: Princeton University Press.

———. 1996. "Globalization and Its Limits: Reports of the Death of the National Economy Are Greatly Exaggerated." In Suzanne Berger and Ronald Dore, eds., *National Diversity and Global Capitalism.* Ithaca, N.Y.: Cornell University Press.

Walder, Andrew. 1994. "Corporate Organization and Local Government Property Rights in China." In Vedat Milor, ed., *Changing Political Economies: Privatization in Post-Communist and Reforming States.* Boulder, Colo.: Westview Press.

Washbrook, David A. 1989. "Caste, Class, and Dominance in Modern Tamil Nadu: Non-Brahmanism, Dravidianism and Tamil Nationalism." In Francine R. Frankel and M. S. A. Rao, eds., *Dominance and State Power in Modern India: Decline of a Social Order,* vol. 1. Oxford: Oxford University Press.

Watts, Ronald L. 1999. *Comparing Federal Systems.* Montreal: McGill-Queen's University Press.

Weimer, David L., ed. 1995. *Institutional Design.* Boston: Kluwer Academic Publishers.

———, ed. 1997. *The Political Economy of Property Rights: Institutional Change and Credibility in the Reform of Centrally Planned Economies.* New York: Cambridge University Press.

Weiner, Myron. 1962. *The Politics of Scarcity: Public Pressure and Political Response in India.* Chicago: University of Chicago Press.

———. 1963. *Political Change in South Asia.* Calcutta: Firma K. L. Mukhopadhyay.

———. 1967. *Party Building in a New Nation: The Indian National Congress.* Chicago and London: University of Chicago Press.

———. 1968a. "Political Development in the Indian States." In Myron Weiner, ed., *State Politics in India.* Princeton, N.J.: Princeton University Press.

———, ed. 1968b. *State Politics in India.* Princeton, N.J.: Princeton University Press.

Weingast, Barry. 1995. "The Economic Role of Political Institutions: Market-Preserving Federalism and Economic Development." *Journal of Law, Economics and Organization* 2, no. 1: 1–31.

Weir, Margaret, and T. Skocpol. 1985. "State Structures and the Possibilities of Keynesian Responses to the Great Depression." In Peter B. Evans, Dietrich Rueschemeyer, and T. Skocpol, eds., *Bringing the State Back In.* Cambridge: Cambridge University Press.

Westphal, Larry E. 1990. "Industrial Policy in an Export-Propelled Economy: Lessons from South Korea Experience." *Journal of Economic Perspectives* 4, no. 3: 41–60.

Weyland, Kurt. 1998. "From Leviathan to Gulliver? The Decline of the Developmental State in Brazil." *Governance* 11, no. 1: 51–75.

Whiting, Susan. 2001. *Power and Wealth in Rural China.* Cambridge: Cambridge University Press.

Widlund, Ingrid. 2000. *Paths to Power and Patterns of Influence: The Dravidian Parties in South Indian Politics.* Stockholm: Elanders Gotab.

Winckler, Edwin. 1976. "Policy Oscillations in the People's Republic of China: A Reply." *China Quarterly* 68 (Dec.): 734–50.

Wong, Christine. 1991. "Central-Local Relations in an Era of Fiscal Decline: The Paradox of Fiscal Decentralization in Post-Mao China." *China Quarterly* 128 (Dec.): 691–715.

——. 1992. "Fiscal Reform and Local Industrialization: The Problematic Sequencing of Reform in Post-Mao China." *Modern China* 18, no. 2 (April): 197–227.

Woo, Jung-en. 1991. *Race to the Swift: State and Finance in Korean Industrialization.* New York: Columbia University Press.

Woo-Cumings, Meredith, ed. 1999. *The Developmental State.* Ithaca, N.Y.: Cornell University Press.

Wood, John R. 1975. "Extra-Parliamentary Opposition in India: An Analysis of Populist Agitations in Gujarat and Bihar." *Pacific Affairs* 48, no. 3: 313–34.

——. 1984a. "British versus Princely Legacies and the Political Integration of Gujarat." *Journal of Asian Studies* 44, no. 1: 65–99.

——. 1984b. "Congress Restored? The 'KHAM' Strategy and Congress(I) Recruitment in Gujarat." In John R. Wood, ed., *State Politics in Contemporary India: Crisis or Continuity?* Boulder, Colo., and London: Westview Press.

——. 1995. "On the Periphery but in the Thick of It: Some Recent Indian Political Crises Viewed from Gujarat." In Philip Oldenburg, ed., *India Briefing: Staying the Course.* New York: M. E. Sharpe.

Woodruff, David. 1999. *Money Unmade: Barter and the Fate of Russian Capitalism.* Ithaca, N.Y.: Cornell University Press.

World Bank. 1993. *The East Asian Miracle: Economic Growth and Public Policy.* Washington, D.C.: Oxford University Press.

——. 1997a. *India: Achievements and Challenges in Reducing Poverty.* World Bank Country Study. Washington, D.C.: World Bank.

——. 1997b. *The State in a Changing World.* New York: Oxford University Press, published for the World Bank.

——. 2004. *World Development Report 2004: Making Services Work for Poor People.* New York: Oxford University Press.

Xia, Ming. 2000. *The Dual Developmental State: Development Strategy and Institutional Arrangements for China's Transition.* Brookfield, Vt.: Ashgate.

Yang, Dali L. 1991. "China Adjusts to the World Economy: The Political Economy of China's Development Strategy." *Pacific Affairs* 64, no. 1: 42–64.

——. 1996. "Governing China's Transition to the Market: Institutional Incentives, Politicians' Choices, and Unintended Outcomes." *World Politics* 48: 424–52.

——. 1997. *Beyond Beijing: Liberalization and the Regions in China.* London: Routledge.

Young, Allyn. 1928. "Increasing Returns and Economic Progress." *Economic Journal* 38, no. 152 (December): 527–42.

Zhao, Suisheng. 1994. "China's Central-Local Relationship: A Historical Perspective." In Jia Hao and Lin Zhimin, eds., *Changing Central-Local Relations in China: Reform and State Capacity.* Boulder, Colo.: Westview Press.

Zwart, Frank de. 1994. *The Bureaucratic Merry-Go-Round: Manipulating the Transfer of Indian Civil Servants.* Amsterdam: Amsterdam University Press.

Zysman, J. 1983. *Governments, Markets and Growth: Financial Systems, and the Politics of Industrial Change.* Ithaca, N.Y.: Cornell University Press.

Index

ASEEMA SINHA is Assistant Professor of Political Science at the University of Wisconsin-Madison.

Milton Keynes UK
Ingram Content Group UK Ltd.
UKHW020741260524
443179UK00010B/626

9 780253 216816